SOCIETY FOR NEW TESTAMENT STUDIES
MONOGRAPH SERIES

GENERAL EDITOR
MATTHEW BLACK, D.D., F.B.A.

ASSOCIATE EDITOR
R. McL. WILSON

24
PAUL'S INTERCESSORY PRAYERS

PAUL'S INTERCESSORY PRAYERS

THE SIGNIFICANCE OF THE INTERCESSORY PRAYER PASSAGES IN THE LETTERS OF ST PAUL

GORDON P. WILES

Professor of Religion
Connecticut College, New London, Connecticut

CAMBRIDGE UNIVERSITY PRESS

Published by the Syndics of the Cambridge University Press
Bentley House, 200 Euston Road, London NW1 2DB
American Branch: 32 East 57th Street, New York, N.Y. 10022

© Cambridge University Press 1974

Library of Congress Catalogue Card Number: 73–79310

ISBN: 0 521 20274 4

First published 1974

Printed in Great Britain
at the University Printing House, Cambridge
(Brooke Crutchley, University Printer)

CONTENTS

v

PREFACE

My attention was first drawn to the intercessory prayers of the New Testament, particularly in the letters of Paul, by what seemed to be an acute 'crisis of piety' in the Christian church. Men can no longer pray. Even those for whom God remains a reality find prayer an unreality. It is within that context that the present study was begun.

The basis of this monograph is a doctoral dissertation presented to the Yale University faculty in 1965, 'The Function of Intercessory Prayer in Paul's Apostolic Ministry with Special Reference to the First Epistle to the Thessalonians.' The material from that study, in revised form, constitutes about a third of the present work, which has been extended to include all seven recognized Pauline epistles.

I am deeply indebted to many for guidance and encouragement at all stages of the research: to Professors Nils A. Dahl, Paul Schubert, Paul Meyer, Floyd V. Filson, and especially to my dissertation adviser, Professor Paul S. Minear. Professor C. F. D. Moule has been unfailingly helpful. My thanks are due also to colleagues at Connecticut College who have willingly assisted in matters of style and in preparing the manuscript for publication, Professor Robert W. Jordan, Mrs Glenis Mollegen, and Professor Garrett D. Green; and to various students who have assisted in the typing and preparation of numerous drafts.

Finally, I express my gratitude to my wife, who has suffered through the growth of this work, and to whom it is affectionately dedicated.

Connecticut College   G. P. W.
New London, Connecticut
December 1972

TEXTS AND ABBREVIATIONS

BIBLICAL TEXTS

Biblia Hebraica, ed. R. Kittel, P. Kahle *et al.*, 11th edn (Stuttgart, 1951).

Novum Testamentum Graece cum apparatu critico, ed. E. Nestle and K. Aland, 25th edn (Stuttgart, 1963).

The Greek New Testament, ed. K. Aland, M. Black, B. M. Metzger, and A. Wikgren (American Bible Society, British and Foreign Bible Society, etc., Stuttgart, 1966).

Septuaginta. Id est Vetus Testamentum graece iuxta LXX interpretes, 2 vols, ed. A. Ralfs, 7th edn (Stuttgart, 1962).

Septuaginta Vetus Testamentum Graecum, ed. A. Rahlfs *et al.*, vols I–XVI² completed (Göttingen, 1926–).

BIBLICAL TRANSLATIONS

The Holy Bible. Revised Standard Version.... (New York, 1953).

The New English Bible (Oxford and Cambridge, 1961, 1970).

The translation used throughout this work is the *Revised Standard Version*, unless otherwise indicated.

ABBREVIATIONS

ATR *Anglican Theological Review* (Evanston)

BGU *Aegyptische Urkunden aus den Koeniglichen Museen zu Berlin*... *Griechische Urkunden*, 8 vols (Berlin, 1895–1933)

BJRL *Bulletin of the John Rylands Library* (Manchester)

CGTC Cambridge Greek Testament Commentary

E.Tr. English Translation

EphTL *Ephemerides Theologicae Lovanienses* (Louvain)

HNTC Harper's New Testament Commentaries

HTR *Harvard Theological Review* (Cambridge, Mass.)

HzNT *Handbuch zum Neuen Testament* (Tübingen)

IB *Interpreter's Bible*, general ed. G. A. Buttrick (New York and Nashville, 1952–6)

ICC International Critical Commentary

IDB *Interpreter's Dictionary of the Bible*, ed. G. A. Buttrick (New York and Nashville, 1962)

JBL   *Journal of Biblical Literature* (Missoula, Mont.)
JBR   *Journal of Bible and Religion* (Missoula, Mont.)
JTS   *Journal of Theological Studies* (Oxford)
Jud.   *Judaica* (Zürich)
MNTC   Moffatt New Testament Commentary
NEB   New English Bible
NTD   Das Neue Testament Deutsch (Göttingen)
RGG   *Die Religion in Geschichte und Gegenwart Handwörterbuch für Theologie und Religionswissenschaft*, ed. K. Galling *et al.*, 3rd edn (Tübingen, 1957–65)
RSPT   *Revue des Sciences Philosophiques et Théologiques* (Paris)
RSR   *Revue des Sciences Religieuses* (Strasbourg)
RSV   Revised Standard Version
SBT   *Studies in Biblical Theology* (London)
Scot. Journ. Theol.   *Scottish Journal of Theology* (Edinburgh)
SNTSM   Society of New Testament Studies Monograph Series (Cambridge)
TLZ   *Theologische Literaturzeitung* (Leipzig)
TWNT   *Theologisches Wörterbuch zum Neuen Testament*, ed. G. Kittel, G. Friedrich *et al.*, vols I–VIII completed (Stuttgart, 1913–)
TZ   *Theologische Zeitschrift* (Basel)
ZNW   *Zeitschrift für die Neutestamentliche Wissenschaft* (Berlin)
ZThK   *Zeitschrift für Theologie und Kirche* (Tübingen)

prayer requires an awareness of the many-sided nature of his apostleship.[1] As we cannot here enter into a detailed investigation of this broader question, we must take for granted that he viewed his function and mission in many dimensions. Yet it may be helpful at the outset to identify some of the principal areas of his apostolic activity so as to place his intercessory function rightly among them.

Of course there will always be the danger of forcing an artificial set of rôles upon him. In fact, there are few signs that his mission was shaped or restricted by any preconceived blueprint of official functions.[2] Rather, he rings the changes continually between various phases of his ministry – spiritual, ecclesiastical, and personal – and between his responsibility to God and to his fellow believers. We find an unstudied and flexible overlapping of such different aspects of his ministry as the pastoral and the priestly; ecclesiastical responsibility and a more personal concern; a mood of affectionate anxiety and an official interest; a bond of love and a bond of authority. To remember this will aid us in seeing the intercessory side of his apostleship not so much as a separate function, but in organic relation with all the other phases.

It should be noted first that his dynamic ministry involved a triangular relationship between God (known in Christ and through the Holy Spirit), himself as commissioned apostle, and the churches for which he was responsible (whose members had been called by God for salvation in Christ). A primary aspect of this relationship was his never-to-be-forgotten commission to preach the gospel – to spread to the Gentiles the 'good news'

---

[1] For reference to the vast literature about ἀπόστολος and Paul as apostle, see K. H. Rengstorf, *TWNT*, I, 438–44; also E. M. Kredel, 'Der Apostelbegriff in der neueren Exegese,' *Zeitschrift für Katholische Theologie*, 78 (1956), 169–93; 257–305. See also H. Windisch, *Paulus und Christus: Ein biblisch-religionsgeschichtlicher Vergleich* (Leipzig, 1934); G. Sass, *Apostelamt und Kirche; eine theologisch-exegetische untersuchung des paulinischen apostelbegriffs* (München, 1939); A. J. Fridrichsen, *The Apostle and his Message*, E.Tr. (Uppsala, 1947); H. Frhr. von Campenhausen, 'Der urchristliche Apostelbegriff,' *Studia Theologica*, I (1947), 96–130; E. Käsemann, *Die Legitimität des Apostels: Eine Untersuchung zu II Korinther 10–13* (Darmstadt, 1956); J. Munck, *Paul and the Salvation of Mankind*, E.Tr. (London, 1959); G. Klein, *Die Zwölf Apostel* (Göttingen, 1961); W. Schmithals, *The Office of Apostle in the Early Church*, E.Tr. (Nashville, 1969).

[2] Schmithals, p. 21, n. 7.

2

CHAPTER I

INTRODUCTORY

PAUL'S COMPLEX MINISTRY AND ITS
INTERCESSORY ASPECTS

The inquiry that follows will be concerned with the communal worship and private prayers of the early Christian church. In particular we shall consider the intercessory prayer passages in Paul's epistles.[1] The question will be asked as to what these reveal about the apostle's intercessory ministry, and what he expected in the way of intercessions from the churches to whom he was writing. Were his frequent claims to be praying continually for his readers merely epistolary clichés, polite exaggerations to be expected in an ancient letter? Were his request for their prayers merely incidental afterthoughts, quite secondary to his main intent in writing?

Our investigations will be focused upon the practical minist of the apostle Paul as a central figure in the New Testame whose vibrant letters may be expected to reveal much about hidden springs of prayer behind his own apostolic life and the of the early Christian community. To extend our purview to intercessory prayers throughout the New Testament w broaden our understanding of the early church as a whole preclude the detailed attention needed to arrive at solidly conclusions. So we shall restrict ourselves to the praye Paul's epistles. What do these reveal about his own image apostleship, especially with regard to the purpose and st of his mission, and his relationship with the members churches? What part did these prayers of supplicati others actually play in his ministry and among those to he ministered?

To assess Paul's practice and teaching about inte

[1] We shall concentrate our attention on the generally recogniz epistles: Romans, I and II Corinthians, Galatians, Philippians, lonians, and Philemon. Occasional references to Ephesians, Colo II Thessalonians may be included for comparison; they will be square brackets to distinguish them. But to enter into the rich prayer material of the deutero-Pauline epistles would extend t this volume unduly.

I

of God's saving action in Christ. It was from the risen Christ himself that he believed he had received this good news initially; to its dissemination he must be wholly dedicated; and by its light and power he must be guided and strengthened in his total ministry. How, then, did he attempt to carry out this task?

Among the practical aspects of his apostolate we may note for our purpose certain elements that existed in unresolved tension with each other. First, there was his restless drive toward missionary outreach, coupled with a sensitive awareness of his unfinished pastoral responsibility. Clearly Paul regarded himself as a pioneer missionary preacher to the Gentiles, pressing on to cover the whole known world before the 'End.' Furthermore, his mission to the Gentiles was shaped and intensified by a heightened understanding of the eschatological age in which he had been set apart as a special agent.[1] For this he had been commissioned, and such must be his primary task. Yet supplementing this urgent pioneering phase, and not wholly reconciled with it, was the continuing pastoral phase of his ministry – the God-given task of preparing his young churches more fully for the parousia. The epistles as a whole, and their paraenetic sections in particular, witness to Paul's unrelieved concern before God for the growth and stability of the churches he had planted. His unremitting efforts to go back and visit them personally underline this concern. It is a remarkable fact that for Paul a commission to preach to all the Gentiles[2] included also pastoral responsibility for each and every Gentile church with which he had been in touch.[3]

Related to this overwhelming double burden are the signs that he wanted his churches to grow rapidly toward maturity and to become less dependent on his pastoral care. Constantly he is giving thanks for the continuing victories of his converts, praying that they increase in the graces of faith, hope, and love, and urging them to take their full share in the wider life of the whole church. His intercessory prayers seem to be closely related to a longing for the maturity of his churches, as the scope of his own mission extended.

A second area involved the tension between his clear sense of

---

[1] See below, p. 49, n. 3.
[2] Rom. 1: 13–15, 11: 13, 15: 16–23, 16: 24; Gal. 2: 2, 8f.; I Thess. 2: 16.
[3] II Cor. 11: 28.

I-2

apostolic responsibility, and his warmly personal feelings toward his churches and his fellow believers. Over and again in his letters we find his apostolic consciousness becoming transfused either by a glow of affection, or by a revulsion of hurt personal feelings. So we are warned against any purely ecclesiastical understanding of his apostolic function. His intercessions might be colored both by his official and by his personal attitudes.

A third area included the tension between his exercise of apostolic authority, and his dedication to humble service and to sharing the tribulations of his fellow believers. He believed himself to have been 'approved' and commissioned as an apostle with responsibility for preaching, teaching, warning, exhorting, guiding, and if necessary, disciplining the churches. Yet he understood this God-appointed and God-maintained authority to be most truly expressed in the lowliness and loving self-giving that had been demonstrated in the obedience of Jesus Christ. The apostle must voluntarily refrain as far as possible from exercising his rights; for he, too, must give himself in lowly service and share in the common tribulations and persecutions of the last days. Here again the mood of Paul's intercessions might be affected.

The last area to be mentioned involves one more pair of related functions – that of the missionary-pastor and that of the priestly-intercessor. Here we approach the side of Paul's ministry to which his practice of intercessory prayer more directly belongs. Signs are present throughout the letters that he believed himself appointed a mediator between God and the churches in his care,[1] charged with the priestly responsibility of

---

[1] This is described in both juridical and sacrificial or cultic imagery, the most conspicuous examples of the latter being Rom. 15: 15f. and Phil. 2: 17 (λειτουργός, -ία); see also λατρεύειν in Rom. 1: 9; δοῦλος in Rom. 1: 1, Gal. 1: 10, Phil. 1: 1, II Cor. 4: 5; παριστάνειν in II Cor. 11: 2 [Col. 1: 28]; ἱερουργεῖν in Rom. 15: 16.

For discussions of Paul as mediator or intercessor, see O. Schmitz, *Die Opferanschauung des späteren Judentums; und die Opferaussagen des Neuen Testament* (Tübingen, 1910), pp. 213–37; Sass, p. 90; N. A. Dahl, 'Paulus som Föresprakere' (Paul as Intercessor), *Svensk Theologisk Kvartalskrift*, 18 (1942), 173–82; K. Weiss, 'Paulus – Priester der christl. Kultgemeinde,' *TLZ*, 79 (1954), 355–63; K. H. Schelkle, *Jüngerschaft und Apostelamt: Eine historische Untersuchung* (Freiburg, 1957); Munck, p. 50, n. 3.

The background concept of intercessor, or 'parakletos,' was examined by N. Johansson, *Parakletoi: Vorstellungen von Fürsprechern für die Menschen vor*

presenting them blameless to God at the parousia.[1] The indications are sufficiently clear and frequent to reveal a deep intercessory sense lying behind all his preaching, teaching, prophesying, and pastoral work, adding new dimensions of meaning and urgency. While such mediation was clearly only one aspect of his complex apostolate, yet it seemed to lie near the heart of his self-understanding, a basic consequence of the intercessory act of God in Christ, an extension of the intercessory ministry of the exalted Christ[2] and of the indwelling Spirit.[3]

In the intercessory prayer passages themselves, then, we shall hope to find striking evidence about this self-understanding on the part of the apostle. By studying the passages we may discover how important intercessory prayers were within the letters themselves, what their exact significance was as a part of Paul's ministry and of his total apostolic strategy, how fully they were representative of a widespread practice of intercessions among his churches.[4]

Gott... (Lund, 1940), and O. Betz, Der Paraklet: Fürsprecher im häretischen Spätjudentum, im Johannes-Evangelium und in neu gefundenen gnostischen Schriften (Leiden, 1963); see also H. L. Strack and P. Billerbeck, Kommentar zum Neuen Testament aus Talmud und Midrash, 4 vols (München, 1922–8), II, 560–2; J. Behm, 'παράκλητος,' TWNT, v, 798–812; G. Johnston, The Spirit-Paraclete in the Gospel of John, SNTSM, 12 (Cambridge, 1970), espec. p. 80 and the literature cited there.

[1] See e.g., I Thess. 2: 19f., 3: 9–11, 5: 23f., Rom. 15: 16f., II Cor. 1: 14, 11: 2, Phil. 2: 16 [Col. 1: 28f.].

[2] Rom. 8: 34.

[3] Rom. 8: 15f., 23, 26f., Gal. 4: 6.

[4] Although we shall emphasize Paul's sense of his own special vocation on behalf of others, we shall also note his urging of others to join with him in continual intercessions.

CHAPTER 2

INTERCESSORY PRAYER MATERIAL IN PAUL'S LETTERS

SOME METHODOLOGICAL PROBLEMS

When we begin to examine those passages in the Pauline epistles which refer to intercessory prayer,[1] we confront some difficult problems. How may we recognize and select the prayer material? The more we study it, the more elusive it seems to become. So we are compelled from the start to inquire what identifying criteria of form, content, and function may be used to isolate the passages. Furthermore, can we really hope to measure their true significance? For they must be interpreted in the light of the ancient letter-writing style which many of them share, and the liturgical conventions which they seem to borrow. Yet against such formal restrictions of Paul's style must be weighed the dynamic elements of his positive spontaneity and sincerity. How far did he give to each passage a living function in relation to the main purposes of the letter and the particular epistolary situation for which he was writing? In other words, what is the real weight of these passages as evidence for Paul's use of intercessory prayer? It is to such questions that the following chapters will be addressed.

At the outset we must consider an obvious difficulty in identifying and interpreting the intercessory passages, namely that we are dealing not with liturgical texts but with letters. The canons of ancient letter style[2] prohibit the inclusion of any prayer directly addressed to God.[3] It is always the reader who

[1] For a complete listing of the various types of prayer material in the Pauline epistles, see Appendixes I, II, III.

[2] See Francis Xavier J. Exler, 'The Form of the Ancient Greek Letter; a Study in Greek Epistolography' (Diss., Catholic University of America, 1923); various other studies of ancient letter style will be cited in the pages that follow.

[3] Cf. G. Harder, *Paulus und das Gebet*, Neutestamentliche Forschungen (Gütersloh, 1936), p. 1; P. Schubert, *Form and Function of the Pauline Thanksgivings* (Berlin, 1939), p. 37; E. Orphal, *Das Paulusgebet; psychologisch-exegetische untersuchung des Paulus-gebetslebens auf grund seiner selbstzeugnisse* (Gotha, 1933), pp. 1ff.

is being addressed, and references to God or to any other third party must occur in the third person. Thus the intercessory prayers must be introduced obliquely if at all, either by re-casting direct prayers into 'wish-prayers' that mention God in the third person but are addressed formally to the readers:

Now may our God and Father himself, and our Lord Jesus, direct our way to you; and may the Lord make you increase and abound in love.... (I Thess. 3: 11f.),

or by 'prayer-reports' that claim to describe the prayers of the writer:[1]

For God is my witness...that without ceasing I mention you always in my prayers, asking that somehow by God's will I may now at last succeed in coming to you. (Rom. 1: 9f.)

In these circumstances the primary prayer material may be expected to be indirect in form and limited in range and quan-tity. It is, however, amplified by further passages in which the apostle appeals to his readers to offer intercessions, or to pray regularly. For example,

I appeal to you, brethren, by our Lord Jesus Christ and by the love of the Spirit, to strive together with me in your prayers to God on my behalf, that I may be delivered.... (Rom. 15: 30f.)

Have no anxiety about anything, but in everything by prayer and supplication with thanksgiving let your requests be made known to God. (Phil. 4: 6)[2]

Various subtle questions of interpretation result. In the first place it is difficult and perhaps arbitrary to define too narrowly the exact boundaries of some of the prayer material. For in-stance, the transition from the Pauline thanksgiving period,

---

[1] Orphal goes so far as to suggest that such a prayer-report as that in I Thess. 1: 2f. began as a personal prayer and was then recast, at the time of the writing of the letter, into the plural and the third person letter style; pp. 43f.

The names 'wish-prayers' and 'prayer-reports' are chosen for conveni-ence and will be used consistently in our analysis. 'Wish-prayer' is suggested by the frequently used German term 'Gebetswunsch.' See Harder, p. 25. 'Prayer-report,' which translates 'Gebetsbericht,' is derived from the usage of Harder (p. 26) and other scholars. For the variety of terms used to de-scribe the 'wish-prayers,' see R. Jewett, 'The Form and Function of the Homiletic Benediction,' *ATR*, 51 (1969), 18f.

[2] In addition are the few passages where Paul writes of the intercession of the Holy Spirit and the risen Christ.

which often included assurances of intercessory prayers for the readers, has been found difficult to demarcate with precision. For example, in the thanksgiving section in I Thessalonians the report of his constant thanksgiving and prayers for the readers (1: 2f.) merges at the phrase εἰδότες, ἀδελφοί into a general account of their situation (1: 4ff.).[1] We shall discover that a general mood of prayer so pervaded and lay near the surface of the letters, that the apostle could turn easily from expositional or other material into a more direct prayer form, and vice versa.[2]

It would be to err in the other direction, however, were we to include too large an amount of material within the category of prayer, simply on the basis that much of the epistles may be readily transposed into prayer. This seems to be done by Orphal and others, but it scarcely offers a sound method of investigation.[3] Thus, as far as the nature of the letters permits, we may attempt to maintain at all times a real though not too sharp distinction between the prayer passages and the other types of material. Only on this basis may well-grounded and reliable conclusions be drawn.

[1] See below, pp. 162ff. Schubert, p. 31, suggested that one regular mark of the transition from the thanksgiving to the body of the letter might be a paraenetic καθώς, as in Rom. 1: 13, I Cor. 1: 6, II Cor. 1: 5 [Eph. 1: 4], Phil. 1: 7 [Col. 1: 6, twice, and 7], I Thess. 1: 5, 2: 13 [II Thess. 1: 3]. J. T. Sanders, however, has argued for a more formally structured and recognizable transition: 'The Transition from Opening Epistolary Thanksgiving to Body in the Letters of the Pauline Corpus,' *JBL*, 81 (1962), 348–62. See also J. L. White, 'Introductory Formulae in the Body of the Pauline Letter,' *JBL*, 90 (1971), 91–7.

R. W. Funk, *Language, Hermeneutics, and Word of God* (New York, 1966), pp. 263ff., points the way towards a more complete formal analysis of the whole epistles. It is possible that a delineation of the various types of prayer material and their sequence in each letter may contribute towards this understanding. For references to previous form-critical studies in the epistles, see B. Rigaux, *Saint Paul et ses lettres, Studia Neotestamentica*; Subsidia II (1962), 163–99; P. Feine, J. Behm, W. G. Kümmel, *Introduction to the New Testament*, E.Tr., 14th rev. edn (Nashville, 1965), p. 176; J. C. Hurd, Jr, *The Origin of I Corinthians* (New York, 1965), p. 4, n. 4. See also C. J. Bjerkelund, *Parakalô: Form, Funktion und Sinn der parakalô-Sätze in der paulinischen Briefen* (Oslo, 1967).

[2] Cf. J. A. Bain, *The Prayers of the Apostle Paul* (London, n.d. [1937?]). See also D. J. Warneck, *Paulus im Lichte der heutige Heidenmission* (Berlin, 1913), pp. 36–40; cited in Orphal, pp. 140–2. Also W. Bieder, 'Gebetswirklichkeit und Gebetsmöglichkeit bei Paulus,' *TZ*, IV (1948), 22.

[3] See Orphal, *passim*, and Harder's criticism of Orphal's too loose method of selection and demarcation, p. 200.

In the second place there arises the problem of rightly interpreting and penetrating the full meaning of prayer passages
which are recast with the reader in mind rather than directly
addressed to God. Yet in spite of this apparent distortion, they
have the advantage of being first-hand reports of the apostle's
prayers, as against the second-hand reports of his prayers in
Acts, or of the prayers of Jesus in the gospel accounts.[1] In
another way, too, it has been thought that the prayers in the
Pauline corpus would lend themselves to ready understanding.
If it could be assumed that they were prepared for reading to a
church community assembled for worship, then they would
have been carefully composed by the apostle as semi-public
prayers for use on a liturgical occasion.[2]

During the past fifty years there has been a move beyond the
too simple view that Paul's letters were 'unliterary letters as
distinguished from literary epistles.'[3] We may note the special
injunction that I Thessalonians should be read 'to all the
brethren' (5: 27),[4] and that each of the epistles is addressed to
one or more churches.[5] They are, then, 'on the way to becoming literary texts with an official character.'[6] True, it was

---

[1] A. Hamman, *La Prière. I. Le Nouveau Testament* (Tournai, 1959), p. 246.

[2] O. Michel, *Der Brief an die Römer*, Meyer's Kommentar (Göttingen,
1955), p. 324.

[3] A. Deissmann's characterization: *Paul*, E.Tr. (London, 1911), p. 9. See
an early objection in P. Wendland, *Die Urchristlichen Literaturformen*, *HzNT*
(Tübingen, 1912), pp. 344f. See also W. G. Doty, 'The Classification of
Epistolary Literature,' *Catholic Biblical Quarterly*, 31 (1969), 183–99.

[4] For a similar instruction in contemporary Jewish usage, see Bar. 1: 14,
'And you shall read this book which we are sending you, to make your
confession in the house of the Lord on the days of the feasts and at appointed seasons.' Cf. Syr. Bar. 86: 1–3, 'When therefore ye receive this my
epistle, read it in your congregations with care. And meditate thereon,
above all on the days of your fasts.' R. H. Charles, ed., *The Apocrypha and
Pseudepigrapha of the Old Testament*, 2 vols, II (Oxford, 1913), 526.

[5] Colossians is to be read by the Colossian church and then exchanged
for a letter to the church at Laodicea (4: 16).

[6] Feine–Behm–Kümmel, p. 177. C. J. Bjerkelund, in 'Stilen i de paulinske formaningssetninger' (The Style of the Pauline Exhortation-Clauses),
Norsk Teologisk Tiddskrift, 61 (1960), 193–217, argues that Paul's letters are
official communications, illuminated by royal letters in Hellenistic inscriptions. Cf. U. Wickert, 'Der Philemonbrief–Privatbrief oder apostolisches
Schreiben?' *ZNW*, 52 (1961), 230–8. C. B. Welles, *Royal Correspondence of the
Hellenistic Period* (New Haven, 1934); Hurd, pp. 3–5; Funk, p. 252; see also
the literature cited below, p. 48, n. 2.

questioned by Walter Bauer whether every letter could be read *in toto* before the assembled church where unbelievers might be present.[1] But it is now generally agreed that the reading of the apostolic letters was itself an important component of the semi-public worship, perhaps followed immediately by the eucharist.[2] For this reason it is rightly claimed that the prayer passages, even though indirect in form, will repay the most careful analysis and study.[3]

Another type of problem must now be mentioned, namely that the vast and complex background which must illuminate our investigation remains relatively unexplored. To identify the intercessory passages correctly and to assess their true significance requires us to take full account of intercessory prayers used throughout the varied milieux to which Paul the Hellenistic Jew belonged. All previous and contemporary examples in liturgical texts, in letters, and in general literature, would have to be identified and analyzed. But no such comprehensive and systematic research has yet been undertaken, and to do so

---

[1] W. Bauer, *Der Wortgottesdienst der Ältesten Christen* (Tübingen, 1930), p. 62f. He thinks that Gal. and II Cor. would be unsuitable for this. Only excerpts would be read to the whole fellowship. Harnack's attractive but not generally accepted proposal that the two Thess. letters were written to separate segments of the church at Thessalonica (Gentile and Jewish) would not deny the use of these letters at church assemblies. The first epistle would be read to the whole group, the second to the Jewish segment alone. A. Harnack, 'Das Problem des Zweiten Thessalonicherbriefs,' *Sitzungsberichte der Königlich Preussischen Akademie der Wissenschaften*, 31 (1910), 560–78.

[2] R. Seeberg, *Aus Religion und Geschichte* (1906), pp. 118ff.; H. Lietzmann, *Mass and Lord's Supper*, E.Tr. (Leiden, 1953–); K. M. Hofmann, *Philema Hagion* (Gütersloh, 1938); G. Bornkamm, 'Das Anathema in der urchristlichen Abendmahlsliturgie,' *TLZ* (1950), 227–30; O. Cullmann, *Early Christian Worship*, E.Tr., *SBT*, 10 (London, 1953), p. 23; J. A. T. Robinson, 'Traces of a Liturgical Sequence in I Cor. xvi.20–24,' *JTS*, New Series, 4 (1953), 38–41; Michel, p. 5; Hamman, p. 315; J. Munck, 'I Thess. i.9–10 and the Missionary Preaching of Paul,' *NTS*, 9 (1963), 98. Cf. Rev. 1: 1–3, 'Blessed is he who reads aloud the words of the prophecy, and blessed are those who hear, and who keep what is written therein; for the time is near.' See below, pp. 42ff., etc.

Against the view that Paul was writing with the eucharist in mind, are H. Y. Gamble, 'The Textual History of the Letter to the Romans,' Diss., Yale University, 1970, p. 148; with W. Doskocil, *Der Bann in der Urkirche; ein rechtsgeschichtliche Untersuchung*, Münchener theologische Studien, 3, 11 (Munich, 1958), and G. Delling, 'Das Abendmahlsgeschehen nach Paulus,' *Kerygma und Dogma*, 10 (1964), 61–77.   [3] Harder, pp. 172f.

would carry us far beyond our present scope.[1] Therefore we must be content to cite the more significant parallels from the different backgrounds as they directly illumine the various intercessory passages in the epistles.

SELECTION AND CLASSIFICATION
OF THE PASSAGES

Moving on now to the task of identifying the passages that refer specifically to intercessory prayer, we observe first that they fall within a larger group of Pauline prayer passages. Although the activity of prayer, or communion with the divine, must be regarded as one dynamic and organic whole, we may differentiate the various kinds of prayer that Paul used or to which he referred. Thus classified lists of prayer passages have been prepared by some scholars.[2] They include the following types:[3] doxology; praise; blessing; worship; hymns, community singing, psalms, etc.; thanksgiving; 'boasting' (in Christ or before God); petition for self; intercessory prayer for others;[4] and general prayer (type not specified). It is of interest even at this stage to note that the intercessory prayer references are far more numerous than those concerning any other type of prayer.

Yet, for such a living activity as prayer, exact classification sometimes seems inappropriate. Examples of this are found in the overlapping between doxology and thanksgiving in II Cor. 4: 15, 9: 11–13 (cf. Rom. 1: 21); also between blessing and thanksgiving in I Cor. 14: 16.[5]

[1] Studies have been made which treat of prayer in general, as found in the Old Testament, the Apocrypha and Pseudepigrapha, the Jewish synagogue liturgy, and the Rabbinical literature; but only a limited amount of research has been done on intercessory prayers as such, namely in the area of the Old Testament: P. A. H. de Boer, *De Vorbede in het Oude Testament, Oudtestamentische Studiën*, III (Leiden, 1943); F. Hesse, *Die Fürbitte im Alten Testament*, Inaugural-Dissertation..., Friedrich-Alexander-Universität (Erlangen, 1949). Reference has been made earlier to work on intercessors by Johansson, Betz, and others.

[2] E. F. von der Goltz, *Das Gebet in der Ältesten Christenheit. Eine Geschichtliche Untersuchung* (Leipzig, 1901), pp. 101–16; Harder, p. 46, n. 7; see also F. L. Fisher, *Prayer in the New Testament* (Philadelphia, 1964).

[3] For a complete list, see Appendix I.

[4] For words denoting intercessory prayer, see below, pp. 18ff.

[5] See below, pp. 170f.

Of greater significance for our purpose is the close inter-weaving of intercessory prayer with thanksgiving, especially in the formal thanksgiving periods. For example,

I thank my God in all my remembrance of you, always in every prayer of mine for you all making my prayer with joy, thankful for your partnership in the gospel.... (Phil. 1: 3–5)[1]

Indeed, giving thanks on behalf of another may be viewed as a representative or intercessory activity, similar to that of sup-plicating on behalf of another.[2] However, it may be convenient for us to restrict the term 'intercessory prayer' to its more usual connotation, namely the supplications by which Paul presented the needs of others to God, rather than for the thanksgivings by which he gratefully recounted God's gifts to them. It is in this narrower sense that the term will be used in this work.[3] The important dialectical relation between intercessory suppli-cation and thanksgiving will engage our close attention later on.[4]

Of more immediate concern at this stage is the difficulty in distinguishing intercessory prayer (made specifically for others) from corporate petition (offered for members of the community to which the praying person belongs, and therefore essentially

---

[1] See below, pp. 203ff.

[2] Johansson, in his extended study of the 'parakletos-complex' in the OT and Judaism in its varied manifestations, showed that it included the mediatorial function of witnessing to the good deeds of the one being defended – pleading these before the divine court (e.g., Zech. 3: 1–5). Schubert, pp. 147–50, claims that Paul's thanksgivings resemble stylistically the official letters recorded in Greek inscriptions, praising the virtues of individuals to a king. He cites also Philo, *Quis rer. div.*, 226 and *De spec. leg.*, i. 229, where the phrase 'I give thanks on behalf of someone' (ὑπὲρ τίνος) is used in a full substitutionary sense (p. 125).

[3] Such a restriction is partly justified in the case of the apostle. For as Dahl pointed out, in his review article about Johansson's book, 'Paul's gratitude can certainly not be derived from or subordinated to any kind of intercessor complex.' 'Paul as Intercessor,' p. 179. The apostle, he con-tinues, must not be pictured as a witness to the merits of the congregations before Christ, for merits do not belong in his theology. Nevertheless, as intercessor he was bound to give thanks to God for his (God's) gracious gifts to the churches. [Cf. II Thess. 1: 3, 2: 13.]

[4] Below, pp. 166ff.; and see pp. 176f., on the merging of thanksgiving with supplication in I Thess. 1: 2f.

prayer for his own benefit). Are the prayers that Paul offered for his own mission, together with the prayers that he requested for his mission, to be regarded as primarily intercessory and for others, in that they were mainly for the benefit of the whole community – for example his prayers for a safe journey to the church to which he was writing? On the other hand, were his intercessory prayers on behalf of the churches to be considered primarily as corporate petitions for benefits in which he himself would share?[1] In other words, does intercessory prayer have a recognizably separate identity as petition on behalf of others and is this in any case a significant distinction?

Intercession in the biblical sense appears always to pre-suppose a community relation between the intercessor and those for whom he prays (whether the people of Israel, the Christian fellowship, or the wider group of 'mankind'). The two parties must in some way belong together.[2] How then may it be shown that the one making intercessory prayer is not doing this merely for his own benefit – praying for the group only because he himself is an integral part of it? Would he not then be taking part in merely corporate petition for the common needs in which he himself shares?

The answer lies in the fact that the intercessor always acknowledges not only a bridge but also a gap between himself and those for whom he prays. He stands apart from them as well as with them. He acts on their behalf, but at the same time is responsible to a God who is both against and for them, in judgment as well as in mercy. So the apostle could warmly give thanks for the love and fellowship of the Thessalonians and yet intercede about that which was still lacking in their faith.[3] The discontinuity between the intercessor and those for whom he intercedes seems to be clearest when he makes intercessory prayer for his enemies. Yet even here the bridge must be present – the bridge of love and involvement: 'But I say to

[1] E.g., compare I Thess. 3: 12–13 with 2: 19f. Cf. W. A. Beardslee, *Human Achievement and Divine Vocation in the Message of Paul*, SBT, 31 (London, 1961), pp. 108–10. He suggests that Paul's prayers are of the 'prophetic type' rather than the 'mystical type' (Friedrich Heiler's categories), and are therefore concerned with the fate of the community and the consummation of God's purpose.

[2] See de Boer, pp. 167ff.

[3] See below, pp. 183ff.

you, Love your enemies and pray for those who persecute
you...' (Matt. 5: 44f.).[1]

This paradoxical dual relation may be clearly seen in the
great intercessors of the Old Testament.[2] Moses intercedes both
against Israel and yet also on behalf of Israel (Exod. 32: 30–4).
It was against the unfaithful Israel, but on behalf of the true
Israel that Elijah at Horeb was interceding (I Kings 19: 9–14).
Thus Paul's dual intercessory attitude towards his own people,
so movingly expressed in Rom. 11: 2–5, may be compared by
him with that of Elijah:

I ask, then, has God rejected his people? By no means! I myself am
an Israelite, a descendant of Abraham, a member of the tribe of
Benjamin. God has not rejected his people whom he foreknew. Do
you not know what the scripture says of Elijah, how he pleads with
God against Israel?...But what is God's reply to him? 'I have kept
for myself seven thousand men who have not bowed the knee to
Baal.' So too at the present time there is a remnant, chosen by
grace.[3]

The most poignant of the Old Testament intercessors, Jeremiah, reveals himself as torn asunder by the unbearable tensions
of his rôle: 'My grief is beyond healing, my heart is sick within
me...."Is the Lord not in Zion? Is her King not in her?"
"Why have they provoked me to anger with their graven
images, and with their foreign idols?"'[4] The paradoxical functions of the great Old Testament intercessors, and the various
levels of their involvement with those for whom they prayed,
are illuminated by Hesse in his investigation of intercessory
prayer in the Old Testament. He suggests that in Jeremiah the
intercessor comes to identify himself so fully with those for whom
he intercedes, including even their sin as his own, that the line
between intercession and corporate petition becomes for the
first time very fluid. This may be seen in the moving prayers
recorded in Jer. 14: 7–9, and 19–22: 'Though our iniquities

[1] Cf. Lk. 23: 34; Ps. 35: 13f., 'But I, when they [the malicious enemies]
were sick – I wore sackcloth, I afflicted myself with fasting. I prayed with
my head bowed on my bosom, as though I grieved for my friend or my
brother....'
[2] See de Boer, pp. 157ff.
[3] See below, pp. 132, 253ff.
[4] Jer. 8: 18f. See the whole passage, 8: 18 – 9: 1.

testify against us, act, O Lord, for thy name's sake; for our back-slidings are many, we have sinned against thee. . . . Hast thou utterly rejected Judah? Does thy soul loathe Zion?'[1]
From the practice of community worship recorded in the Old Testament, come further instructive sidelights. The corporate petition expressed by a leader of worship ('Vorbeter'), or by a member of a group, may from another point of view be seen as intercessory petition on behalf of the needs of others within the group. Indeed, the prayer language may actually oscillate from one form to the other,[2] e.g., in Isa. 63: 7 – 64: 12. This extended liturgical passage begins in the first person (singular and plural): '*I* will recount the steadfast love of the Lord. . . according to all that the Lord has granted *us*' (63: 7a). Here the speaker is united with his fellow worshippers in a corporate prayer of praise. But immediately he changes to the third person plural: 'which he has granted *them* [the house of Israel] according to his mercy' (v. 7b), and seems now to stand apart in a representative intercessory fashion. This mood of separation continues for some time until at length the speaker addresses God directly on their behalf: 'So thou didst lead thy people. . .' (v. 14b). Finally he returns to the original mood of united corporate prayer: 'For thou art *our* Father. . .' (vv. 16ff.).

In a somewhat comparable fashion, the Psalms as cult prayers tend to be cast in the form of representative corporate petition, rather than intercessory prayer.[3] The individual 'I' of the Psalms is the representative 'I' of a worship leader, the 'Vorbeter' who speaks for the group in a liturgical sense. Yet here too the form may suddenly change to that of intercession

---

[1] Hesse, pp. 95ff.; cf. Johansson, *Parakletoi*; de Boer, *De Vorbede*, pp. 53ff.; J. Lindblom, *Prophecy in Ancient Israel* (Philadelphia, 1962), pp. 204–6.

[2] Various examples of this are pointed out by Hesse, p. 61.

[3] Hesse, pp. 64–74, following Gunkel who gives various examples including Ps. 28: 28f., and 51: 18. H. Gunkel, *Die Psalmen, übersetzst und erklärt*, Göttinger Handkommentar zum Alten Testament, 4th edn (Göttingen, 1926), pp. 14f. A similar type of representative corporate petition may be found in Hab. 1: 2–4, 12–17, and cf. IV Ezra 8: 14, 17–19, 45; Dan. 9: 9–14. In Ps. 125: 4f. we have what seems to be petition for one's own group disguised as intercession.

See also J. Heinemann, *Prayer in the Period of the Tanna'im and the Amora'im: Its Nature and its Patterns* (Jerusalem, 1964), pp. ivf., 'The Address "You" in Prayer.'

and the 'Vorbeter' becomes for the moment a 'Fürbitter.'[1] So the distinction between intercessory supplication and corporate petition in the Old Testament remains somewhat indefinite.

Turning back to the Pauline epistles in the light of this discussion, let us consider the apostle's prayer for a speedy return to the Thessalonian church:

Praying earnestly night and day that we may see you face to face and supply what is lacking in your faith.[?] Now may our God and Father himself, and our Lord Jesus, direct our way to you. (I Thess. 3: 10f.)

Was this a petition for his own well-being, or an intercessory prayer for the well-being of those who depended on his presence and counsel?

The reasons for his desiring to return were both urgent and complex, as we shall see later, centering mainly around his anxiety on their behalf.[2] Yet his interest in them was closely related to himself, as may be demonstrated by the striking way in which he links their destiny with his own (2: 17–20). His prayer for a safe journey back to them involved inextricably both their concerns and his own.[3] It functioned as a petition for himself, but included also an element of intercession.[4]

So the mutual intercessory prayers of apostle and converts might in their totality be viewed also as a kind of corporate or

---

[1] E.g., Ps. 3, which begins with representative complaint and petition for the individual's own affairs, cast in the 1st pers. (vv. 1–7). Suddenly it changes to the 3rd pers. intercessory form (v. 8), 'thy blessing be upon thy people!'

[2] Below, pp. 47ff.

[3] Cf. the prayer in Rom. 1: 10ff.; the circumstances were of course markedly different, yet the benefits to both apostle and church are kept clearly in view. See below, pp. 186ff. Similarly, Paul frequently requests, or makes reference to, the prayers of his readers, that his missionary journeys and projects might prosper: Rom. 15: 30–2, II Cor. 1: 11, Phil. 1: 19f., I Thess. 5: 25, Philem. 22 [Eph. 6: 18–20, Col. 4: 2–4, II Thess. 3: 1–3]. We shall take up these references later. It is striking that he does not mention prayers for his own personal needs, except once regarding his 'thorn in the flesh,' II Cor. 12: 7ff. See Harder, p. 194.

[4] For a different view see Schubert, p. 69, referring to I Thess. 3: 9f., 'The...participle (δεόμενος) does not express *intercessory* prayer in behalf of the addressees, but a direct petition to God on the part of Paul.'

So also Johansson rigorously excludes from consideration all intercessions which include petitions for the self (p. 11).

joint congregational praying, many of the petitions being common to apostle and converts. We may not expect always sharp differentiation at this point, since the prayers were a living action within a dynamic nexus of mutual responsibilities before God. Yet the reality of intercessory prayer as a separate and recognizable moment in the activity of prayer remains, in which one is concerned in supplication before God principally for the needs of others.

We may proceed then with our selection, on the provisional assumption that it should be possible to distinguish the Pauline intercessory prayer material.[1] But what norms are to be used? It is apparent that the basis of selection will depend in the first place on various functional considerations: does the content of any passage refer mainly to prayer and is it specifically on behalf of others? Is this initial impression confirmed when we examine its function in the letter and in the general epistolary situation that lay behind it? Our approach may be further assisted by considering the selected passages separately under more specific functional classes:

1. Intercessory wish-prayers;
2. Intercessory prayer-reports;
3. Paraenetic references to intercessory prayer (requests for and exhortations to such prayer);
4. Didactic and speculative references to intercessory prayer.

Criteria of function, however, will need to be checked by such formal and linguistic peculiarities as we may be able to discover in the passages. These may include characteristic contexts and locations in the structure of the letter, introductory formulae for the prayer passages, aspects of liturgical style such as special forms of address to God, unusual vocabulary, and peculiar grammatical or syntactical shapes. Formal and functional marks may then each in turn throw light on our search, for they are intimately related to one another, and react continually on one another.[2]

---

[1] We may expect also to find some borderline material which will be instructive for our purposes.

[2] Cf. R. Bultmann, *The History of the Synoptic Tradition*, E.Tr. (New York, 1963), p. 5. 'It is essential to realize that form-criticism is fundamentally indistinguishable from all historical work in this, that it has to move in a circle. The form of the literary tradition must be used to establish the

Employing in a preliminary way these criteria of function and form, we discover an impressive and varied range of passages for our further consideration. For convenience the material has been classified below in Appendixes II and III.

TERMS FOR INTERCESSORY PRAYER AND THE INTERCESSOR

But before we examine the various classes of intercessory passages, one formal question may be raised: whether Paul employs any special terms to distinguish intercessory from other prayer material.[1] Surprisingly enough we discover no word which by itself unequivocally denotes the act of offering intercessory prayer. Instead Paul uses general words for prayer in such a way as to imply that the prayer is on behalf of others:[2]

Words for pleading in prayer

ἐντυγχάνειν and ὑπερεντυγχάνειν are used by Paul only in Romans, where the context clearly fixes an intercessory meaning (elsewhere in the New Testament only in Acts 25: 24, Heb. 7: 25).

ἐντυγχάνειν (Rom. 8: 27, 34, 11: 2) meant originally to turn to, approach, appeal to someone. It could be used for prayer when directed to God, and took on a specifically intercessory connotation only when coupled with one of the following phrases: περί τινος, ὑπέρ τινος, or even κατά τινος, as in Rom. 11: 2.[3]

ὑπερεντυγχάνειν (Rom. 8: 26) has the same meaning, to plead or intercede.[4]

influences operating in the life of the community [in our case, the broad epistolary situation], and the life of the community must be used to render the forms themselves intelligible. There is no method of regulating or even prescribing the necessary interplay and mutual relationships of both these processes, no rule to say where the start must be made.'

[1] See Hamman, pp. 248–52, for prayer terms in the epistles; also Orphal, *Das Paulusgebet*, pp. 18–24, Bieder, 'Gebetswirklichkeit,' p. 23.

[2] In any case, terms for intercessory prayer or for the intercessor would not be expected in the wish-prayers, which are transpositions of direct prayers. See below, p. 22.

[3] See W. F. Arndt and F. W. Gingrich, *A Greek–English Lexicon of the New Testament and Other Early Christian Literature* (from W. Bauer's *Griechisch–Deutsches Wörterbuch*..., 4th edn) (Chicago, 1957), *ad loc.*

[4] *Ibid.*

General Pauline words for prayer

προσεύχεσθαι and προσευχή[1] are in frequent use throughout the New Testament with a general prayer connotation somewhat broader than their synonyms δεῖσθαι and δέησις (δέησιν ποιεῖσθαι).[2] The former words are usually preferred when no definite description of the devotional act is intended, whereas the latter usually signify asking in concrete situations.

In Paul's usage, however, the distinction often seems very slight: e.g., the two words δέησις and προσευχή are found together without apparent distinction in Phil. 4: 6 [cf. Eph. 6: 18], (LXX, III Kings 8: 45, II Chron. 6: 29). Yet it is noticeable that he does use προσεύχεσθαι, προσευχή more often for intercessions, the intercessory meaning being suggested by the context. Seven occurrences imply intercession, and eleven make the intercessory meaning possible but do not demand it:

προσεύχεσθαι has a definitely intercessory meaning in Phil. 1: 9, I Thess. 5: 25 [cf. Eph. 6: 18, Col. 1: 3, 9, 4: 3, II Thess. 1: 11, 3: 1]; it is used in a general sense, but with intercessory meaning not excluded, in Rom. 8: 26, I Cor. 11: 4, 5, 13, 14: 13, 14, 15, I Thess. 5: 17.

προσευχή suggests a specifically intercessory meaning in Rom. 1: 10, 15: 30, I Thess. 1: 2, Philem. 4 and 22 [cf. Eph. 1: 16, Col. 4: 2, 12]; it is used in a general sense, but with intercessory meaning not excluded, in Rom. 12: 12, I Cor. 7: 5, Phil. 4: 6 [cf. Eph. 6: 18].

εὔχομαι, meaning either to wish, or to pray, has a clearly intercessory prayer connotation in two of the three instances in Paul: II Cor. 13: 7 and 9. In Rom. 9: 3 ηὐχόμην may connote either wish or pray. In any case intercession is implied.

δέομαι, δέησις, as we have observed, signify request, and when used for actual prayer (comparatively rarely in Paul) they often retain the significance of petition.[3] The intercessory meaning must be indicated by the context, as in Rom. 1: 10,

---

[1] H. Greeven, *TWNT*, II, 806–8; von der Goltz, p. 141; E. von Dobschütz, *Die Thessalonicher-Briefe*, Meyer's Kommentar, 7th edn (Göttingen, 1909), p. 64.

[2] H. Greeven, *TWNT*, II, 39–41.

[3] See Bauer–Arndt–Gingrich, *ad loc.*; also *TWNT*, II, 40.

I Thess. 3: 10 (δέομαι), and in Rom. 10: 1, II Cor. 1: 11, 9: 14, Phil. 1: 4, 19 [Eph. 6: 18] (δέησις). In Phil. 4: 6, on the other hand, intercession is not clearly indicated.

αἰτήματα occurs only once, Phil. 4: 6, and means prayer-requests, without specifying intercession.

Words with other meanings, used for prayer

συναγωνίσασθαι, to fight or contend along with someone, or to assist someone, is found in an intercessory prayer sense in Rom. 15: 30 – συναγωνίσασθαί μοι ἐν ταῖς προσευχαῖς ὑπὲρ ἐμοῦ πρὸς τὸν θεόν. [Cf. ἀγωνιζόμενος in Col. 4: 12 and ἀγῶνα ἔχω in Col. 2: 1.]¹

συνυπουργέω, to join in helping,² occurs in an intercessory prayer sense in II Cor. 1: 11 – συνυπουργούντων καὶ ὑμῶν ὑπὲρ ἡμῶν τῇ δεήσει, ἵνα. . . .

μνείαν ποεῖσθαι ἐπὶ τῶν προσευχῶν, to make mention of you in my prayers, is used in Rom. 1: 9f., I Thess. 1: 2, Philem. 4 [and Eph. 1: 16], in each case shown by the context to be intercessory.³

μνημονεύειν, to remember, is used for prayer only in I Thess. 1: 3, where it seems to connote thanksgiving and intercessory petition.⁴

δεήσει ἐπιποθέω occurs only in II Cor. 9: 14 in the New Testament, where it may be translated 'while they long for you and pray for you,' in an intercessory sense.⁵

Finally it may be noted that Paul has no special term for the

---

¹ See Bauer–Arndt–Gingrich, *ad loc.*; E. Stauffer, *TWNT*, I, 134–40; V. C. Pfitzner, *Paul and the Agon Motif* (Leiden, 1967). Pfitzner, however, argues (pp. 120–9) that συναγωνίσασθαι and the cognate words do not describe the prayers themselves as a striving (agon), but rather as assisting Paul in his apostolic mission which he understood as a striving (agon) for the gospel. See below, pp. 267f.

² Bauer–Arndt–Gingrich, *ad loc.*

³ For a well-known example from the papyri, see *Ägyptische Urkunden aus den Koeniglichen Museen zu Berlin. . .Griechische Urkunden* (I–VIII, 1895–1933; Berlin: Staatliche Museen), II, 297: μνίαν σου ποιούμενος παρὰ τοῖς [ἐν]θάδε θεοῖς ἐκομισάμην [ἐ]ν ἐπιστόλιον. Cf. G. Milligan, *St. Paul's Epistle to the Thessalonians; The Greek Text with Introduction and Notes* (London, 1908), p. 5.

⁴ See below, p. 177.

⁵ [The phrase κάμπτω τὰ γόνατά μου πρὸς τὸν πατέρα. . . ἵνα. . ., occurs only in the deutero-Pauline epistles – Eph. 3: 14.]

office of the one who makes intercessory prayers. The closest he comes to such a name is λειτουργός, in a passage employing cultic language about the mediating function of his apostleship in general (Rom. 15: 16).[1] Although this does not refer only or specifically to prayer, it is placed in close relation with the two preceding wish-prayer passages.[2]

Thus for the purpose of finding marks to distinguish intercessory prayer from other prayer passages, comparatively little would seem to be gained from word studies of the prayer terms as such; attention will have to be focused rather on other identifying criteria. We are ready now to move beyond preliminary questions of selection and classification to a more extended study of the different classes of intercessory prayer material.

[1] See Beardslee, p. 103f.; W. Sanday and A. C. Headlam, *The Epistle to the Romans*, ICC (Edinburgh, 1896), p. 405; H. Strathmann, *TWNT*, IV, 236–8.
[2] See below, p. 85.

CHAPTER 3

INTERCESSORY WISH-PRAYERS:
THEIR BACKGROUND AND FORM

Our detailed examination of the material begins with the most
direct evidence, the intercessory 'wish-prayers,'[1] to which we
shall devote the next four chapters. For example,

*May the God of hope fill you with all joy and peace in believing, so that by the
power of the Holy Spirit you may abound in hope.* (Rom. 15: 13)

The general character of the wish-prayers may be described as
the expression of a desire that God take action regarding the
person(s) mentioned in the wish. Several of them would seem
to be prayers transposed for use in a letter,[2] but suitable also
for blessings to be pronounced on the congregation.[3] They
maintain the strictly epistolary form of address to the readers
current in ancient letter style, while implying that it is God
who must carry out the desired action. They may be readily
changed back into direct prayers by reversing the words for
God from the nominative into the vocative case, altering the
pronouns or nouns that name those to be benefited from the
second to the third person, and the verb back from the optative
into the imperative mood.[4]

Apart from such prayer cries as 'Abba' or 'Maranatha,' the
wish-prayers are the closest approximation to direct praying
that we find in the epistles, and are therefore among the most
important material for our investigation. Yet a whole cluster
of them seems to be so conventionalized as to retain little of

[1] For a complete list see below, Appendix III.

[2] Harder (pp. 25f.) writes, 'Zu den Gebeten selbst könnte man allenfalls
einige Gebetswünsche rechnen. Aber diese sind eben auch nur sogenannte
Gebetswünsche, also Umformungen echter Gebete, der brieflichen Über-
mittlung angepast. Es dürfte aber kein Zweifel darüber bestehen, dass sich
hinter den Gebetswünschen oder Gebetsberichten echte Gebete verbergen.'
See above, pp. 6f.

[3] See below, pp. 42ff.

[4] See Ernst von Dobschütz, p. 148, referring to the wish-prayer in
I Thess. 3: 11–13.

their true prayer character: these include the blessings which constitute the greetings at the beginning and end of each letter. So we shall do well to treat the wish-prayers in three separate (though overlapping) groups: first, eight 'principal' ones which may have been composed more or less freely;[1] second, the more conventional blessings; and third, a pronouncement blessing, and two curses which may be tentatively classed as wish-prayers of a negative character.

We begin, then, with the eight principal wish-prayers. But before examining their functional significance (in Chapters 4 and 5), we must inquire first as to their antecedents and formal characteristics. This may help us to identify the material with more certainty and to illuminate it by placing it within the broad tradition of Jewish and Hellenistic intercessory prayer language.

GENERAL LITURGICAL BACKGROUND OF THE PRINCIPAL WISH-PRAYERS

While it would be impossible within the scope of our present work to enter fully into the liturgical background,[2] we may here point out a few of the traditional elements to which we shall be referring in the course of our study of the wish-prayers. It must be recognized that behind all the prayer passages in the epistles must lie to some extent the language and structure of the prayers used by Paul in his own devotional practices. Furthermore, if these passages were intended for public and even liturgical reading, their language must have been modified by usages current in the early Christian assemblies.[3] And behind

[1] Viz., four clear examples with the aorist optative, I Thess. 3: 11–13, 5: 23f., Rom. 15: 5f., 13; one short blessing with the optative understood, Rom. 15: 33; three questionable examples with the future indicative, Rom. 16: 20a, I Cor. 1: 8f., Phil. 4: 19.

[2] See above, p. 10.

[3] See Hamman, p. 315; Jewett, 'Homiletic Benediction.' But see the earlier contrary opinion of Bauer (above, p. 10, n. 1), who claimed that Christian worship was mostly unstructured, informal, diversified, under the charismatic influence of the Spirit. (Cf. I Cor. 14.) See also the warning of W. C. van Unnik against 'a certain "panliturgism" which sees everywhere in the Pauline epistles the background of the liturgy whenever a simple parallel in wording between them and the *much later* liturgies is found,' in

the prayer language of both Paul and the churches to whom he wrote, lay not only the prayer customs of the Hellenistic world, but more directly the liturgical style of the Jewish synagogue and the Old Testament, freely adapted to new purposes by the emerging Christian Gentile communities and by the apostle himself.

By the time of Paul there seems to have been already established a prayer tradition connected with the synagogues.[1] For although the origins of the Jewish liturgy are notoriously difficult to date,[2] there is reason to believe that the Shema was already recited regularly as a duty, together with certain obligatory set prayers and benedictions – the Yotzer, Geullah and Alenu;[3] the Shemoneh Esreh, too, seems to have been in existence.[4]

'Dominus Vobiscum,' *New Testament Essays; in mem. T. W. Manson*, ed. A. J. B. Higgins (Manchester, 1959), p. 272, cited by C. F. D. Moule, *Worship in the New Testament, Ecumenical Studies in Worship*, 9 (Richmond, 1961), p. 7. In any case, we shall postpone the question of early Christian prayer language as such, dealing with it from time to time as it appears behind specified Pauline usages.

[1] See L. Zunz, *Die gottesdienstlichen Vorträge der Juden. Historisch entwickelt*, 2nd edn (Frankfurt am Main, 1892); I. Elbogen, 'Bemerkungen zur alten jüdischen Liturgie,' *Studies in Jewish Literature issued in Honour of Professor Kaufmann Köhler* (Berlin, 1913), pp. 74–81; idem, *Der jüdische Gottesdienst in seiner geschichtlichen Entwicklung*, 3rd edn (Frankfurt am Main, 1931), pp. 27–41; W. O. E. Oesterley and G. H. Box, *The Religion and Worship of the Synagogue; An Introduction to the Study of Judaism from the New Testament Period* (London, 1907), pp. 327–43; W. O. E. Oesterley, *The Jewish Background of the Christian Liturgy* (Oxford, 1925); Strack–Billerbeck, IV, 1, 153–249; Heinemann, see bibliography on pp. 196f.

[2] The problem arises partly because there was rabbinical opposition to collecting and writing down prayers until several centuries after Christ (see Zunz, pp. 382ff.).

[3] Berachoth 1 3. Some suggest that the Yotzer itself was recited already in the temple (Oesterley, p. 47), whereas Zunz thinks it was an earlier form that was used. He traced back the Geullah to 45 words parallel with Ezra 8: 22ff., used about the end of the first century. For the origins of the Alenu prayer see Oesterley, pp. 141f.

Josephus speaks of 'customary prayers,' *Ant. Jud.* XIV, 10. See also J. Jeremias, *The Prayers of Jesus*, E.Tr., *SBT*, Second Series, 6 (London, 1967), pp. 67–72.

[4] See Zunz, p. 381. Heinemann, p. x, concludes more conservatively 'that in the last two, or perhaps three, centuries before the common era a considerable number of different "orders of prayers" or even "orders of

Besides these synagogue forms, to which we shall refer from time to time, we may observe antecedents for Paul's wish-prayers in the Old Testament – especially in the Greek liturgical language of the Psalms and similar portions of the LXX. While Rabbinical strictures against praying in any language other than Hebrew may be cited, it is nevertheless likely that as a diaspora Jew the apostle would have heard synagogue prayers in Greek, based closely on Hebrew originals and shaped by the LXX. He may be thought, then, to have composed or adapted his prayers directly in Greek.[1]

To be noted at the outset are the many examples of specific blessings and curses in the Old Testament, originally 'power-laden words, spoken on cultic or other occasions and often accompanied by gestures or symbolic actions, through which the wholeness of the religious community was understood to be safeguarded or strengthened, and evil forces controlled or destroyed.'[2] Two types of blessing in the Old Testament must have made their contribution to Paul's usage: the first type lay behind the curses and 'pronouncement' blessing (I Cor. 16: 22, Gal. 1: 8f., 6: 16) that will be considered later.[3] It was in the style of a command or pronouncement which did not mention God as agent and had the verb in the imperative, e.g., 'And they blessed Rebekah, and said to her, "Our sister, be (LXX, γίνου) the mother of thousands..."' (Gen. 24: 60). The form of the blessing seemed to suggest that the spoken word itself carried power without reference to God. But, as we shall later argue, it might be interpreted as representing only a formal legacy from the earlier days of primitive magic, and in post-exilic times it was certainly understood that God was the source

---

berakhot" were current, which all had some features in common with one another....' He thinks that 'only in the third century [CE] was the standard form – the berakha – of obligatory Synagogue prayer fully established,' and that in any case 'only the opening and concluding formulas of each prayer [were fixed,] while the text itself remained "free," and many different versions continued to exist side by side' (p. ii); cf. G. J. Bahr, 'The Use of the Lord's Prayer in the Primitive Church,' JBL, 84 (1965), 156f.

[1] See Harder, pp. 29–31; Wendland, Urchristlichen Literaturformen, p. 354.

[2] W. J. Harrelson, 'Blessings and Cursings,' IDB, 1, 446f., and the bibliography there included. See also W. S. Towner, '"Blessed be YHWH" and "Blessed Art Thou, YHWH": The Modulation of a Biblical Formula,' Catholic Biblical Quarterly, 30 (1968), 386, n. 1.

[3] Chap. 6.

of all power and blessing. If the priest pronounced a blessing or a curse it was only in the name of, and not independently of, God.[1]

The second type of blessing, in the form of an intercessory petition, moved away from overtones of coercive magic. It usually had the verb in the optative, and made explicit that the blessing was requested from God, e.g., καὶ δώῃ σοι ὁ θεὸς ἀπὸ τῆς δρόσου τοῦ οὐρανοῦ (Gen. 27: 28, LXX).[2] The main Pauline wish-prayers which we are now considering stem indirectly from this second type of blessing.

Furthermore, the actual transposing of direct prayers into indirect wish-prayers or blessings finds antecedents in the Psalms. Since many of them were composed for liturgical purposes, they sometimes contain various striking changes of address within the same psalm, for instance alternation between an address to God, to the other worshippers, to the king, or to Jerusalem. In Psalm 122 (LXX, 121), verse 6a is addressed to the worshippers as a bidding prayer: ἐρωτήσατε...τὴν Ἰερουσαλήμ. But then it changes to address Jerusalem itself with a blessing: γενέσθω (imperative) δὴ εἰρήνη ἐν τῇ δυνάμει σου (v. 7).

In some of the pre-exilic psalms which included intercessions for the king, are found similar kinds of change or alternation.[3] Thus a direct intercessory prayer addressed to God about the king, may be followed by an indirect wish-form ('Wunschform'), addressed to the king and mentioning God in the third person. Psalm 20 (LXX, 19) is composed mainly of such wish-prayers for the king, with verbs couched in the desiderative optative: Ἐπακούσαι σου κύριος...ὑπερασπίσαι...ἐξαποστείλαι... ἀντιλάβοιτο...μνησθείη, etc. (vv. 1–5). Then at the end comes a sudden change to a short, explosive prayer, addressed directly and urgently to God and using the imperative: κύριε, σῶσον τὸν βασιλέα σου καὶ ἐπάκουσον ἡμῶν... (v. 9). The very indirect-

---

[1] See below, pp. 119f., for further references to this controversial question. It should be noted also that curses in the OT were usually of this first (pronouncement) type, with the verb in the imperative and no direct reference to God, e.g., Deut. 27: 15–26, 28: 16–19.

[2] Cf. the Aaronic blessing, Num. 6: 24ff., with a string of optatives; also Ps. Sol. 17: 51, 18: 6.

[3] Pss. 20, 28, 61, 72, 84, 89, 132. For a full discussion, see Hesse, pp. 64ff.

ness of the wish-form makes it less presumptuous and aggressive, permitting the lowly man to describe his petitions with more freedom and in greater detail than he would otherwise dare. The direct request to Yahweh would make the prayers more urgent.[1]

Outside of the Psalms, and apart from the many blessings and cursings already mentioned, there occur only one or two further liturgical examples of extended and freely composed wish-prayers in the Old Testament and intertestamental literature, e.g., I Kings 8: 57–61, II Chron. 30: 18f. Yet the extant occurrences are sufficient to suggest that the liturgical custom of transposing direct prayers into a wish-prayer form was well known.

Thus we shall find in the Pauline wish-prayers (as in his other prayer passages) clear indications that the Old Testament and the synagogue prayer liturgy made a significant contribution to their language and form.[2] In addition, we shall note from time to time various signs of Hellenistic prayer style that must have influenced Christian converts from the Jewish diaspora and the pagan world.

[1] See H. Gunkel, *Einleitung in die Psalmen: die Gattungen der religiösen Lyrik Israels*, Zu Ende geführt von J. Begrich, Göttinger Handkommentar zum Alten Testament (Göttingen, 1933), p. 229; *idem, Die Psalmen, übersetzt und erklärt*, p. 120, on Ps. 28: 8f. Similar though lesser changes of form are found in a number of other psalms. In Ps. 72 the prayer begins in the direct address to God (v. 1), but is continued in a long series of wish-prayers (using imperatives or future indicatives in the LXX), yet still addressed to God. So also in Ps. 61 there is a change to the wish-form in vv. 6b and 7 (future indicative in LXX).

Ps. 28 begins with direct address to God (second person, vv. 1–4), changes to the third person (vv. 5–8), and ends suddenly with a direct, ejaculatory prayer ('Stoss-seufzer'), 'O save thy people....' (v. 9). In Ps. 89 at v. 1 there is a rapid change in the Hebrew from indirect to direct address to God (LXX removes this change); so also in vv. 7f., etc. In Ps. 132 there is oscillation between direct address to God and statements about God.

It is interesting to note that Heinemann, pp. iii–v, analyzes a similar exchange between direct and indirect address to God, in the development of the 'liturgical' Beracha – a change from the 'Thou-style' to the 'He-style.'

[2] For the influence of Jewish prayer style, see Oesterley, *Jewish Background of the Christian Liturgy*; C. W. Dugmore, *The Influence of the Synagogue upon the Divine Office* (Oxford, 1944); J.-P. Audet, 'Esquisse historique du genre littéraire de la "bénédiction" juive et de l'"eucharistie" Chrétienne,' *Revue Biblique*, 65 (1958), 371–99; J. M. Robinson, 'The Historicality of

ANCIENT EPISTOLARY BACKGROUND

When we turn from the liturgical background to that of ancient letterwriting style, several possible antecedents for Paul's epistolary wish-prayers should be briefly indicated. Ernst Lohmeyer, in an important article on the background of the prescripts in Paul's letters (including the opening greetings and blessings), referred to a considerable number of short blessings or wish-prayers found in Near Eastern and Jewish letters. He believed that these had prepared the way for the form of the Pauline letter prescript, and we may add that they may also have been among the antecedents for the form of Paul's longer wish-prayers.[1]

Paul Schubert drew attention to an even more impressive prototype for Paul's epistolary wish-prayers, namely in the letter with which II Maccabees begins. Following the customary address and greetings comes an intercessory wish-prayer 'which is structurally characterised by a sequence of desiderative optatives (from ἀγαθοποιήσαι in v. 2 to ἐγκαταλίποι in v. 5)':[2] 'May God do good to you, and may he remember his covenant.... May he give you all a heart to worship him.... May he open your heart... and may he bring peace. May he hear... and be reconciled... and may he not forsake you in time of evil.' Then follows a conventional prayer-report, 'We are now praying for you here' (II Macc. 1: 2–6).

Thus Schubert sees this letter in II Maccabees as an example

Biblical Language,' *The Old Testament and Christian Faith: A Theological Discussion*, ed. B. W. Anderson (New York, 1963), pp. 131–50; Sanders; Bahr, pp. 153–9, compares model outline prayers of the Rabbis with the Lord's Prayer seen as a model outline.

For a different view, that takes account of Hellenistic influences, see Bauer, *Wortgottesdienst*. Writing in 1930, he believed that the converts in the Pauline churches would use familiar pagan rather than unfamiliar Jewish prayer forms, and that Paul would suit his prayer style to theirs.

[1] E. Lohmeyer, 'Probleme paulinischer Theologie. I. Briefliche Grussüberschriften,' *ZNW*, 26 (1927), 158–73, especially p. 160. He cites some striking examples from Babylonian and Assyrian letters; Amarna letters; Jewish letters from Elephantine; LXX Dan. 3: 98; Syr. Bar. 78: 2; and a number of rabbinic parallels, e.g., 'An unsere Brüder, die Einwohner der Babylonischen Diaspora. . .: Euer Friede gedeihe in Ewigkeit!' b. Sanhedr. 11a–11b. We shall return in Chapter 6 to the epistolary background of the opening blessings; see also pp. 158ff. below.

[2] Schubert, pp. 118f.

of a basic epistolographic pattern which pervaded the pagan–Hellenistic world and increasingly affected the Jewish diaspora. It seems then that in addition to liturgical antecedents we do have a significant epistolary convention ready to hand for the apostle's use.

FORMAL CHARACTERISTICS

We proceed now to those formal and linguistic marks that relate Paul's principal wish-prayers to the traditions and contemporary usages of general and intercessory prayer.

We begin with their basic structure.[1] This is most fully displayed in the four longer examples in I Thessalonians and Romans (I Thess. 3: 11–13, 5: 23f., Rom. 15: 5f., 13),[2] and includes four parts: (1) The prayer begins with the subject God (described with various attributes), (2) continues with a predicate having one or more verbs usually in the optative, (3) together with a noun or pronoun for the one to be benefited. (4) An 'additional benefit' is then expressed either by a purpose clause (using ἵνα, εἰς τό), or by an additional clause joined by καί, or by an adjectival or prepositional phrase. For example,

(1) May the God of steadfastness and encouragement
(2) (3) grant you to live in such harmony with one another, in accord with Christ Jesus,
(4) that (ἵνα) together you may with one voice glorify the God and Father of our Lord Jesus Christ. (Rom. 15: 5f.)[3]

The same basic structure is found in I Cor. 1: 8 and Phil. 4: 19. But the last two examples, Rom. 15: 33 and 16: 20a, are so truncated as to lack the mention of an additional benefit.[4]

---

[1] See Jewett, pp. 20ff.

[2] It is also clearly displayed in Heb. 13: 20f. Jewett, pp. 27–30.

[3] Jewett (pp. 30–4) finds the immediate liturgical background of the Pauline wish-prayers not directly in Hebrew blessings; e.g., he shows that the basic structure of the 'homiletic benedictions' differs from the threefold structure of the Aaronic blessing in Num. 6: 24–6 and its development by the Qumran community. Nor does he find elsewhere in 'Jewish, and non-Jewish materials. . .a formal prototype for the New Testament benediction' (p. 31). Rather, the background is to be found in freely composed Christian 'homiletic benedictions,' used by the early churches to end the sermon. This, he thinks, is evidenced in Heb. 13: 20f.

[4] The additional benefit is expressed as follows:
Purpose clause (ἵνα, εἰς τό), Rom. 15: 5f., 15: 13; I Thess. 3: 11–13 con-

To continue now with some more detailed observations, we notice first the characteristic introductory phrases with the special forms of address to God that belong to a widely used style of ancient prayers: αὐτὸς δὲ ὁ θεὸς καὶ πατὴρ ἡμῶν καὶ ὁ κύριος ἡμῶν Ἰησοῦς (I Thess. 3: 11); αὐτὸς δὲ ὁ θεὸς τῆς εἰρήνης (I Thess. 5: 23);[1] ὁ δὲ θεὸς τῆς ὑπομονῆς καὶ τῆς παρακλήσεως (Rom. 15: 5); ὁ δὲ θεὸς τῆς ἐλπίδος (Rom. 15: 13); ὁ δὲ θεὸς τῆς εἰρήνης (Rom. 15: 33).

To these examples must be added those in the more problematical wish-prayers with the verb in the indicative:[2] ὁ δὲ θεὸς τῆς εἰρήνης (Rom. 16: 20a); ὁ δὲ θεὸς τῆς ἀγάπης καὶ εἰρήνης (II Cor. 13: 11b); ὁ θεὸς τῆς εἰρήνης (Phil. 4: 9b); ὁ δὲ θεός μου (Phil. 4: 19); ὁ θεός (II Cor. 9: 8); ὃς καί (I Cor. 1: 8, I Thess. 5: 24); [ὁ κύριος ὅς (II Thess. 3: 3)].

The august phrase αὐτὸς δὲ θεός (but God himself) that occurs in the two wish-prayers in I Thessalonians, must have been taken over from the conventional liturgical language to which the apostle and his readers were accustomed through both their Jewish and their Hellenistic background.[3] Αὐτὸς δέ cor-

tains two petitions, the first with no additional benefit (v. 11), the second with one (v. 13).

Additional clause with καί, I Thess. 5: 23. [Cf. II Thess. 2: 16f.]

Adjectival phrase, I Cor. 1: 8 (ἀνεγκλήτους...).

Prepositional phrase, Phil. 4: 19 (ἐν δόξῃ...). [Cf. II Thess. 3: 5, 16, II Tim. 1: 18, 2: 25.]

[Participial phrase, Heb. 13: 21b (ποιῶν...).]

No additional benefit, Rom. 15: 33, 16: 20a, I Thess. 3: 11. [Cf. II Tim. 1: 16, 4: 16b.]

[1] [Compare II Thess. 2: 16f., Our Lord Jesus Christ himself, and God our Father, who loved us and gave,... αὐτὸς δὲ ὁ κύριος; also II Thess. 3: 16, The Lord of peace himself, αὐτὸς δὲ ὁ κύριος τῆς εἰρήνης.]

[2] See below, pp. 33ff.

[3] A comparable use of αὐτός occurs in other Pauline liturgical passages: e.g., II Cor. 8: 19, πρὸς τὴν αὐτοῦ τοῦ κυρίου δόξαν (αὐτοῦ is omitted in some Mss); I Cor. 15: 28, τότε καὶ αὐτὸς ὁ υἱός (Tertullian, Hippolytus, Hilary and other fathers omit ὁ υἱός, perhaps because of its subordinationist implications); cf. also αὐτὸ τὸ πνεῦμα in Rom. 8: 16, 26; and even αὐτὸς ὁ σατανᾶς in II Cor. 11: 14, although here αὐτός may have its ordinary force – 'even Satan himself.'

Yet apart from Paul, this formulation is found only once in the NT, in Rev. 21: 3. Thus it had not yet been widely adopted for use within the church at the period in which the NT was being written.

responds to the well-known prayer formula σὺ δέ. Both αὐτός,[1] and δέ,[2] whether used in combination or separately, had an accepted liturgical significance, adding a note of majesty to the address. In addition, as is argued by Jewett,[3] the particle δέ may here have a connective sense that points to a close link between the wish-prayer unit and the material that precedes it.

A feature of the address to God in the wish-prayers is the use of certain descriptive epithets: ὁ δὲ θεὸς τῆς ὑπομονῆς καὶ τῆς παρακλήσεως (Rom. 15: 5), ὁ δὲ θεὸς τῆς ἐλπίδος (Rom. 15: 13), and ὁ δὲ θεὸς τῆς εἰρήνης (Rom. 15: 33, 16: 20a, I Thess. 5: 23). In his analysis of these and similar epithets in the Pauline epistles, Harder shows that this practice also derived from the ancient Jewish prayer style.[4] Among pagans too it was customary to add a precise description of the god who was being invoked, by naming special cult words or describing his particular powers.[5] In addition, Paul's use of the title πατήρ

---

[1] M. Dibelius, *An Die Thessalonicher I II. An Die Philipper* (Tübingen, 1937), p. 14. Cf. Harder, pp. 26f., and 63, n. 1, comparing the wish-prayer expression 'God himself' with the direct address 'Thou God,' or in the Talmud 'Thou thyself,' or 'Thou, he.' He cites a number of OT and Jewish parallels from the LXX Psalms (e.g., 101: 28, 67: 36), from the (probably) Jewish prayers embedded in the Apostolic Constitutions and from the Talmud; also from pagan prayer material in Apuleius' *Metamorphosis*. Cf. the address σὺ δέ in the Mithras Liturgy; Albert Dieterich, *Eine Mithrasliturgie* (Berlin, 1923), 8, 15; 12, 13.

[2] See *Hymn Orph.* 19, 20; 16, 9; 11, 21; 10, 29; 6, 10, *inter al.* Cf. Asclepius III (32b): 'sed tibi deus summe, gratias ago...,' in *Hermetica*, I, ed. W. Scott (Oxford, 1924), 356; Josephus, *Ant.* v, 41): ἀλλὰ σύ, δέσποτα κτλ.

[3] Jewett, pp. 22f. In a context of worship the prayer would be closely connected with the preceding homily.

[4] A large number of Pauline prayer passages contain these elements: the name, or an additional name, for God (God, Father, Lord, God of our Lord Jesus, etc.), together with a descriptive phrase in Jewish style, e.g., father of mercies, father of glory, the lord of peace, God of steadfastness and encouragement, God of hope, God of peace, God of love, God of comfort, God of all grace. The genitive implied a gift which God bestowed. Harder, pp. 44f., 65f.; also Michel, *Der Brief an die Römer*, p. 320, n. 1.

[5] The same author collected an impressive number of pagan examples from the Corpus Hermeticum, Orphic hymns, Apuleius' *Metamorphosis*, and the papyri; also examples from Jewish prayer style in Josephus, Philo, the Apostolic Constitutions, the Talmud, and the Old Testament psalter. See especially p. 43, n. 1.

ἡμῶν (I Thess. 3: 11) is rooted in the traditional use of this title in Jewish prayers.[1]

A second formal characteristic of the wish-prayers to be derived from general prayer usage, is the desiderative verb in the aorist optative. This is a distinctive mark of the four main wish-prayers in the Pauline epistles: δῴη (Rom. 15: 5); πληρώσαι (Rom. 15: 13); κατευθύναι, πλεονάσαι, περισσεύσαι (I Thess. 3: 11f.); ἁγιάσαι, τηρηθείη (I Thess. 5: 23).[2] In Hellenistic Greek the use of the optative had been so much curtailed that by the time of Paul it was found mainly in prayers, formulae, and oaths.[3] Its occurrence in the New Testament is limited almost exclusively to wish-prayers or blessings,[4] where it follows the traditional

[1] It is found, for instance, in the original form of the Ahabah (according to Zunz's reconstruction): '. . .with great and overflowing pity hast Thou pitied us. O our Father, our King. . .'; it is not found, however, in his reconstruction of the Yotzer, the Geullah, nor in the Palestinian recension of the Shemoneh Esreh (see Oesterley, pp. 46–57). But it occurs in the longer and probably later Babylonian recension, in Benedictions V and VI. See G. H. Dalman, *Die Worte Jesu* (Leipzig, 1898), pp. 301–4.

[2] [Cf. also the deutero-Pauline examples in II Thess. 2: 17, παρακαλέσαι, στηρίξαι; II Thess. 3: 5, κατευθύναι; II Thess. 3: 16, δῴη; II Tim. 1: 16, 18, δῴη twice; II Tim. 4: 16, λογισθείη; see also Heb. 13: 20f., καταρτίσαι.]

Lohmeyer makes the doubtful conjecture that Phil. 4: 5a, 6, with the passive imperative verbs γνωσθήτω, γνωριζέσθω, may also be regarded as prayers. E. Lohmeyer, *Die Briefe an die Philipper, an die Kolosser und an Philemon*, Meyer's Kommentar, 10th edn (Göttingen, 1954), p. 170. For further discussion, see below, p. 287.

One or two additional examples of the optative in Pauline letters are found in some Mss which replace the future indicative with an optative reading: e.g., Rom. 16: 20 συντρίψαι; II Cor. 4: 6, λάμψαι; Phil. 4: 19, πληρώσαι; [II Thess. 2: 8, ἀνέλοι. In addition, there is one doubtful instance in Eph. 1: 17 – δῴη after ἵνα in a prayer-report (δῷ B 1739).]

[3] Moulton gives a number of examples from the papyri: ἐνορκοῦντι μέμ μοι εὖ εἴη ἐφιορκοῦντι δὲ τὰ ἐναντία (O P 240 – i/A.D.); ἢ ἔνοχοι εἴρημεν τῶι ὅρκωι (O P 715 – ii/A.D.); . . .παραδώσω. . .ἢ ἐνοχεσθείην τῶι ὅρκωι (B M 301 – ii/A.D.), etc. J. H. Moulton, *A Grammar of New Testament Greek*, I (Edinburgh, 1906), 195.

[4] Grammarians find in the NT a total of 22 (or 23) examples of the optative expressing a wish (in addition to 15 instances of the exclamation μὴ γένοιτο). They agree that in these passages the verbs should be accented as optative (acute accent) rather than as aorist infinitive (circumflex accent). See, *inter al.*, Moulton, I, 165f., 194f.; A. T. Robertson, *A Grammar of the*

liturgical and epistolary patterns that we have already noted.[1]

But besides the wish-prayers using the desiderative optative there are seven further passages in the Pauline epistles that resemble them variously in language and form, yet place the verb in the future indicative (Rom. 16: 20a, I Cor. 1: 8, II Cor. 13: 11b, Phil. 4: 7, 9b, 19, I Thess. 5: 24b, [II Thess. 3: 3]. How many of these are really wish-prayers and how many declarations?[2]

We may observe first that in three of them (Rom. 16: 20a, Phil. 4: 19 and I Thess. 5: 24b) there are significant textual variations between the optative and future indicative.[3] This would suggest that the two forms could be used interchangeably in petitionary prayer and that all the questionable passages might be interpreted as wish-prayers.

The possibility is strengthened by the use of the future indicative in both pagan and Jewish prayer forms. Some striking parallels from the magic papyri are collected by Harder.[4] In the LXX the indicative future frequently alternates in prayers with the optative or imperative, e.g., Ps. 20: 9–11, where two optatives εὑρηθείη and εὕροι are followed by several verbs in

Greek New Testament in the Light of Historical Research, 5th edn (New York, 1931), pp. 939f.; C. F. D. Moule, *An Idiom Book of New Testament Greek*, 2nd edn (Cambridge, 1960), p. 23; F. Blass and A. Debrunner, *A Greek Grammar of the New Testament and Other Early Christian Literature*, trans. and ed. R. W. Funk (Chicago, 1961), p. 194, par. 384.

[1] See above, pp. 26–9.

[2] Harder (p. 25) lists as wish-prayers using the fut. indic., Rom. 16: 20, II Cor. 13: 11b, Phil. 4: 7, 9b, 19.

[3] Rom. 16: 20a, ὁ δὲ θεὸς συντρίψει: A pc it vgᶜˡ read συντρίψαι. Phil. 4: 19, θεὸς πληρώσει: D* F G Ψ 69, 1739 pm latt Chrys Theodrt read πληρώσαι. I Thess. 5: 24b, ὃς καὶ ποιήσει: F reads ποιήσαι.

Note also that in I Thess. 5: 23, while most Mss read the optative ἁγιάσαι, G F read the fut. indic. ἁγιάσει.

For the interchangeability of optative, imperative, and future indicative, see Blass–Debrunner–Funk, p. 194, par. 384.

[4] He writes, 'Diese indikativische Form in Gebeten kann ihren Grund in der unbedingten Erhörungsgewissheit haben, also in einem psychologischen Phänomen. Sie kann das Gebet als zwingendes charakterisieren, eine dem antiken Menschen nicht unbekannte Form des Gebets' (p. 25). See K. Preisendanz, ed., *Papyri Graecae magicae*, I (Leipzig, 1928), 142. Par. 2251: τὸ Δ (δεινα) ποιήσεις, κ'ὰν θέλῃς, κ'ὰν μὴ θέλῃς, ὅτι οἶδά σου τὰ φῶτα προστίγμης, κτλ.; similarly in par. 2256, etc.

the indicative, θήσεις, συνταράξει, καταφάγεται, ἀπολεῖς.[1] That
the future indicative in these prayers does not merely describe
God's expected action, seems to be shown by the imperfect
jussive forms in the Hebrew text, which would imply a wish:
תִּמְצָא, תְּשִׁיתֵמוֹ, פְּרִימוֹ, etc.

On the other hand, we must give due weight to an argument
by van Unnik against the usual assumption that 'doxologies,
blessings, ascriptions, greetings and the like' are to be treated
as wishes rather than declarations.[2] He admits the tendency of
the LXX to translate the Hebrew jussive form יְהִי (the Lord be
with you) by a future indicative form ἔσται. This would suggest
that the Greek future indicative could be used for a wish (e.g.,
I Sam. 20: 13, I Chron. 22: 11, 16, II Chron. 19: 11, 36: 23).
But against this he points out that the Hebrew itself chooses the
future indicative in fifteen similar passages, which proves them
to be not wishes but declarations, e.g., the words spoken by the
dying Jacob to his son Joseph in Gen. 48 : 21, '' God will be with you.'

For this and other reasons he concludes that the peace blessings should usually be interpreted as declarations of the cosmic
or eschatological peace which God has already brought and is
continuing to bring: 'Peace will be with you.' Even I Thess.
5: 23, where the bulk of Mss have the optative, should be read
as 'The God of peace will sanctify you wholly.' Yet he admits
that II Thess. 3: 16, δῴη ὑμῖν τὴν εἰρήνην (may he give you
peace, cf. Num. 6: 26), presents a difficulty for the total extension of this view, and shows that in some cases the blessing was
a request for peace rather than a declaration of peace.[3]

So the utmost caution is required in generalizing about these
questionable future indicative passages. The balance of probability seems to favor Harder's view that at least some of them

[1] Cf. Ps. 7: 10, συντελεσθήτω (imperative)...καὶ κατευθυνεῖς (indicative); also Pss. 16: 7f., 30: 3–5, 51: 7, etc.

[2] van Unnik, pp. 270–302; see Moule, *Worship in the New Testament*,
pp. 78f.

[3] More recently it has been argued that in early Christian usage even the
optative in prayers and blessings might have the force of an imperative
('imperatival optative'). 'The speaker intends more than a wish...he
expresses this with a strong confidence of fulfilment.' B. Van Elderen, 'The
Verb in the Epistolary Invocation,' *Calvin Theological Journal*, 2 (1967),
46–8. Cf. the Johannine notion that what is asked for in prayer has already
been granted: I John 5: 14–16, John 11: 41.

were intended as wish-prayers, and we must proceed with considerable hesitation to decide on each one separately.

We may look first at I Cor. 1: 8, together with the verse that follows it: ὃς καὶ βεβαιώσει (fut. indic.) ὑμᾶς ἕως τέλους... πιστὸς ὁ θεὸς δι' οὗ ἐκλήθητε.... This passage may be illuminated by another closely similar one in the optative mood that must undoubtedly be a wish-prayer: I Thess. 5: 23f.: Αὐτὸς δὲ ὁ θεὸς... ἁγιάσαι[1] ὑμᾶς... καὶ... ἐν τῇ παρουσίᾳ... τηρηθείη. πιστὸς ὁ καλῶν ὑμᾶς, ὃς καὶ ποιήσει. The parallel declarations of the faithfulness of God which follow in each case, would function as an exultant 'Amen' to the prayers.[2] Furthermore, as is suggested by Schubert, this sentence in I Corinthians may act as the intercessory portion of the thanksgiving period (vv. 4–9), and replace the usual final clause that announces Paul's constant supplications for the readers.[3] Here then is a possible wish-prayer,[4] using the future indicative to express a wish: '*May he sustain* you to the end...'

Of the three passages with textual variants in the optative, the status of the first cannot be fully decided for lack of evidence, but the existence of an optative variant suggests that we examine it tentatively as a wish-prayer: Rom. 16: 20a, 'May the God of peace soon crush Satan under your feet.' The second is more

[1] For the textual evidence, see above, p. 33, n. 3.

[2] Cf. II Thess. 3: 3. The word אָמֵן meaning firmness, consistency, truthfulness, is closely related to the concept πιστός (see below, p. 68, n. 1). It was also 'a formula of confirmation.... It was, that is to say, the congregation's audible appropriation of what was said on their behalf' (cf. I Cor. 14: 16), Moule, *Worship in the N.T.*, pp. 73–6; H. Schlier, *TWNT*, I, 339–42; Harder, pp. 79–82. The LXX translated it γένοιτο, e.g., Deut. 27: 14–26. In II Cor. 1: 15–22 Paul strikingly connects the faithfulness of God (πιστὸς δὲ ὁ θεός) with saying Yes and Amen (v. 20); Moule, p. 72, and W. C. van Unnik, 'Reisepläne und Amensagen...' in *Studia Paulina* (in hon. J. de Zwann), eds. J. N. Sevenster and W. C. van Unnik (Haarlem, 1953), pp. 215–34. Sanders, however, considers these πιστός sentences not as amens, but as substitutions for the beracha (pp. 358f.); see below, p. 163, n. 3.

[3] See Schubert, pp. 45f. Yet it should be acknowledged that Paul does not usually incorporate a wish-prayer into his thanksgiving periods – not in Rom., II Cor., Phil., Philem. That he makes an exception in I Thess. 3: 11–13 is to be explained stylistically by the length and complexity of the extended thanksgiving (see below, p. 162, n. 2).

[4] This view is strengthened by the structure of the sentence which corresponds to the norm of the other wish-prayers. See above, p. 29.

doubtful: Phil. 4: 19, 'And my God will supply every need of yours according to his riches in glory in Christ Jesus.' It brings to a close Paul's acknowledgement of the Philippians' gift, 'I have received full payment, and more; I am filled....' (v. 18). Its primarily declarative character[1] may be suggested by a parallel passage, a statement rather than a prayer, made during remarks to the Corinthians (II Cor. 9: 1–15) about their part in the collection: 'God loves a cheerful giver. And God is able (δυνατεῖ δὲ ὁ θεός) to provide you with every blessing in abundance, so that you may always have enough of everything and may provide in abundance for every good work' (II Cor. 9: 7b–8). The third one, I Thess. 5: 24b, seems to be a declaration, for it corresponds, as we have just observed, to an 'Amen.' 'He who calls you is faithful, and he will do it.' The remaining passages, in the absence of optative variants or further evidence to point to a petitionary meaning for the future indicative verb, may be taken primarily as statements, but perhaps also as surrogates for peace blessings or prayers near the end of the letter, viz., II Cor. 13: 11b,[2] Phil. 4: 7, and 9b.[3]

We conclude at this stage that of the original seven passages with the future indicative, only three should be examined further as borderline wish-prayers: Rom. 16: 20a, I Cor. 1: 8f., and Phil. 4: 19.

It is convenient at this point to consider one further group of passages, where doubt is raised whether they are to be taken as a form of wish-prayer or as declarations. These are the conventional opening and closing epistolary greetings in which the verb is unexpressed: e.g., 'Grace to you and peace from God our Father and the Lord Jesus Christ.' Here, too, it is suggested by van Unnik and Moule that the verb be read not in the optative or imperative, but in the indicative mood as a declaration: 'Grace will be to you and peace....'[4]

---

[1] To indicate the dual nature of this passage, we suggest the descriptive title 'declaration-prayer'; see below, p. 102.

[2] See below, p. 107, n. 2.

[3] See below, p. 102.

[4] Thus Moule writes: '...the current habit of almost always using the optative or imperative in translations of such phrases seems to be contrary to the balance of New Testament usage...Hebrew and Biblical Greek

Yet against the quite limited number (four) of New Testament passages in the indicative which are declarations of blessings on men, must be weighed the common use of the optative or imperative which we have already noted in general liturgical style, and in epistolary prayer style both Jewish and Hellenistic. In particular there are a number of occurrences in the LXX[1] and in the New Testament[2] of the optative in greetings and blessings, liturgical and epistolary. Furthermore, even if the unexpressed verb in the Pauline blessings should be taken as indicative, this would by no means necessarily imply a merely flat statement. For we have seen that the future indicative may have been interchangeable with the optative and used on occasion to represent a Hebrew jussive form, thereby implying a confident wish.[3]

more often than not omit the verb altogether; but where a verb is supplied it is as often as not in the indicative.' (*Worship in the N.T.*, pp. 78f.)

In support of his argument Moule gives a table of greeting and blessing phrases in the NT, showing those with no main verb, with the optative, the imperative, or the indicative (p. 79, n. 1). But an important distinction needs to be observed between those phrases such as doxologies and ascriptions, which refer to the acknowledged glory and victory of God without reference to men, and those blessings and greetings addressed to men, and referring to God's aid desired for them.

It is significant that in the Lord's Prayer the ascription of power to God is in the indicative, Matt. 6: 13 (in any case a late reading), while the petition for the hallowing of God's name by men is in the imperative (ἁγιασθήτω, v. 9).

From this crucial distinction a different picture results. Of Moule's list of about sixteen such phrases with the indicative (Matt. 6: 13b, II Cor. 11: 31, Phil. 4: 7, 9b, I Pet. 4: 11, 5: 10, II John 3, Rev. 4: 11, 5: 9, 12, 11: 15, 17f., 12: 10f., 15: 3, 19: 1, 6ff.), only four are relevant as blessings offered *to men*: Phil. 4: 7 and 9b, I Pet. 5: 10, II John 3 (the John reference is striking in that it is clearly a greeting).

[1] E.g., Dan. 4: 1, 6: 26, Εἰρήνη ὑμῖν πληθυνθείη, twice as an official greeting. Ruth 2: 4, Κύριος μεθ᾽ ὑμῶν. . . Εὐλογήσαι σε κύριος, a private greeting. Cf. the optatives in the liturgical blessing, Num. 6: 24–6.

[2] I Pet. 1: 2 and II Pet. 1: 2, χάρις ὑμῖν καὶ εἰρήνη πληθυνθείη. Jude 2, ἔλεος ὑμῖν καὶ εἰρήνη καὶ ἀγάπη πληθυνθείη.

These examples are Semitic in character, for the corresponding Greek greeting would have a different form: 'The apostles say (λέγουσιν) grace to you and peace' (with χάριν and εἰρήνην in the accusative rather than in the nominative case).

[3] Cf. Van Elderen's conclusion: 'Paul expresses the greeting with such confidence and assurance that the reader can assume these elements (grace, mercy, peace) are in reality his experience' (p. 48).

Therefore while no certainty may be claimed for either interpretation, where the decision must depend on such fragmentary indications, there does not seem to be enough solid contrary evidence to change the usual assumption that the Pauline greetings should be understood in the optative or imperative, making them, at any rate formally, closer to wish-prayers than to statements.[1]

To return to the formal characteristics of the principal wish-prayers: a third characteristic is the obvious one, that they are so phrased as to indicate that intercession is being made on behalf of the readers. The second person pronoun (in the appropriate case) designates that the readers are to be recipients of the benefit prayed for, e.g., ὁ δὲ θεός...δῴη ὑμῖν (dative), Rom. 15: 5; ὁ δὲ θεός...πληρώσαι ὑμᾶς (accusative), Rom. 15: 13. This of course follows the pattern of earlier wish-prayers, e.g., II Macc. 1: 2, καὶ ἀγαθοποιήσαι ὑμῖν ὁ θεός.

Fourth, we may ask whether there are any examples of specialized vocabulary (beyond the liturgical address to God already considered) which would place Paul's intercessory wish-prayers within the Jewish tradition of the sacrificial cult and of priestly intercession. Here the evidence is sparse. In only three of the passages under consideration are there phrases which have in themselves recognizably cultic or juridical associations.

In I Thess. 3: 13 (the first passage) Paul uses the phrase ἀμέμπτους ἐν ἁγιωσύνῃ. This suggests the sanctifying prayer of a priest for his people, that they be rendered holy unto the Lord, cultically separated from the profane.[2] Cf. Phil. 2: 15,

---

[1] We assume also that (1) in the short blessing at the end of the main body of Romans (Rom. 15: 33), the unexpressed verb must be understood in the imperative or the optative (ἔστω, or εἴη), 'The God of peace be with you all. Amen.' (see below, pp. 90f.), and (2) in the blessing in Gal. 6: 16, the verb is to be understood in the same way: it corresponds to the curse found earlier in the epistle, 'Let him be (ἔστω) accursed' (see below, pp. 129ff.).

[2] ἁγιωσύνη: 'Auch hier erweist sich die Heiligkeit in der Herzensreinheit; es ist die in der sittlichen Aneignung vollendete ἁγιωσύνη, deren Ursprung in der Versöhnung gegeben ist, worin ihr kultisches Element liegt.' O. Procksch, TWNT, I, 116. For the strongly cultic origins and continued cultic significance behind the ethical value of this concept, in the Old Testament and the Rabbinic קדש, and in the words ἅγιος, ἁγιάζω,

ἄμεμπτοι καὶ ἀκέραιοι, where the apostle goes on to speak in clearly sacrificial fashion of being 'poured out as a libation upon the priestly offering of [their] faith.'

In the same passage the phrase 'before our God and Father' (ἔμπροσθεν τοῦ θεοῦ καὶ πατρὸς ἡμῶν) calls to mind the 'bema' or judgment seat in II Cor. 5: 10, ἔμπροσθεν τοῦ βήματος τοῦ Χριστοῦ, where rewards of good and evil will be received;[1] see also I Thess. 2: 19, and Rom. 14: 10. The juridical symbolism of the law court is prominently in view, with the apostle pleading the cause of the church members before the divine judge.

In I Thess. 5: 23 (the second passage), the language is clearly cultic. The words ἁγιάσαι ὑμᾶς ὁλοτελεῖς repeat the priestly connotations of the earlier wish-prayer (I Thess. 3: 13). They presage the priestly sacrificial language of Rom. 15: 16, where Paul speaks of his apostolic work of sanctification: 'to be a minister (λειτουργόν) of Christ Jesus to the Gentiles in the priestly service (ἱερουργοῦντα) of the gospel of God, so that the offering of the Gentiles may be acceptable, consecrated by the Holy Spirit (ἡγιασμένη ἐν πνεύματι ἁγίῳ).' Compare also Rom. 12: 1, 'that you present your bodies a living sacrifice (θυσίαν ζῶσαν ἁγίαν) holy and acceptable to God, which is your spiritual worship.'[2]

The expression 'your spirit and soul and body' (ὑμῶν τὸ πνεῦμα καὶ ἡ ψυχὴ καὶ τὸ σῶμα) is considered by many commentators to be borrowed from a liturgical formulation. This is because Paul seems here to depart unexpectedly from his usual anthropology (a dichotomy of spirit [or soul] and body), and teach instead a threefold division.[3] On the other hand, an

---

etc. in the LXX, apocryphal writings, and NT, see the whole article, pp. 88–115, especially pp. 107–9; see also R. Astung, *Die Heiligkeit im Urchristentum* (Göttingen, 1930); K. Weiss, 'Paulus – Priester der christl. Kultgemeinde,' p. 357.

[1] J. E. Frame, *The Epistles of St. Paul to the Thessalonians*, ICC (Edinburgh, 1912), p. 123.

[2] See K. Weiss, pp. 356f., 360f.

[3] See R. Bultmann, *Theology of the New Testament*, E.Tr., 2 vols (New York, 1951–5), II, 205f., G. Milligan, *St. Paul's Epistle to the Thessalonians*, ad loc., Dibelius, *ad loc.*, and E. Schweizer, *TWNT* VI, 433, n. 685. Yet Masson (following H. H. Wendt) finds Paul's usual dichotomy here. He would translate it as 'may *you* (i.e., your spirit; cf. Gal. 6: 18, Phil. 4: 23, Philem. 25) be kept wholly, soul and body.' See C. Masson, 'Sur I Thessa-

underlying Semitic liturgical style is suggested by van Stempvoort, who would divide the sentence after πνεῦμα, and thus
avoid the trichotomy. The first petition would then show a
synonymous parallelism, in the form of a chiasmus making use
of alliteration. The meaning would be, 'May the God of peace
sanctify you wholly, and in every part your spirit (= you)'
(ἁγιάσαι ὑμᾶς ὁλοτελεῖς – καί ὁλόκληρον ἡμῶν τό πνεῦμα).
The second petition for the 'additional benefit' would then
read, καὶ ἡ ψυχὴ καὶ τὸ σῶμα ἀμέμπτως…τηρηθείη.[1]

With regard to the words ὁλόκληρον and ἀμέμπτως, the
apparently cultic associations of ἀμέμπτως have already been
pointed out. ὁλόκληρον, meaning 'whole in all its parts, complete, intact,' cannot be said with certainty to be a cultic word.
But it does have cultic applications in the LXX,[2] and when
placed in relation to ἀμέμπτως it would seem to be used in this
sense.

Another passage (the third) in which cultic intercessory
language appears is I Cor. 1: 8:[3] ἀνεγκλήτους, clearly a juridical term, may be rendered 'unimpeachable' in the sense that
none will have the right to impeach. Cf. Rom. 8: 33, τίς
ἐγκαλέσει; and Col. 1: 22, 'to present you holy and blameless
and *irreproachable* (ἀνεγκλήτους) before him.'[4]

The sparseness of signs of specifically cultic language in the
wish-prayers in itself points to a related observation, namely
their 'remarkable flexibility in vocabulary and content.'[5] The

Ioniciens, v, 23. Note d'anthropologiè paulinienne,' *Revue de Theologie et de
Philosophie*, 135 (1945), 97–102. In any case the liturgical language may not
be intended as 'a systematic dissection of the distinct elements of personality'; H. Wheeler Robinson, *The Christian Doctrine of Man* (Edinburgh,
1952), p. 108. Cf. also W. D. Stacey, *The Pauline View of Man* (London,
1956), pp. 123f.

[1] P. A. van Stempvoort, 'Eine Stilistische Lösing einer Alten Schwierig-
keit in I. Thess. v. 23,' *NTS*, 7 (1960–1), 262–5.

[2] E.g., to describe the *unbroken* stones for an altar, Deut. 27: 6, or the *full*
week to be counted in sacred reckoning of time; cf. the cultic use in Josephus,
Ant. 3, 228, and Philo, *De Vict.*, 2, *De Off.*, 1. See von Dobschütz, *ad loc.*;
W. Foerster, *TWNT*, iii, 765f.

[3] A probable wish-prayer with fut. indic. See above, p. 35.

[4] See W. Grundmann, *TWNT*, i, 358f.

[5] Jewett, p. 22. Jewett suggests that this variability 'presents a substantial argument against an original setting within some firmly established
portion of the cultic tradition.'

wide variations of content and theme to be found within the wish-prayer form will become clear in our subsequent chapters.

We may add here one more linguistic observation. A common mark of Jewish prayer vocabulary was the concluding 'Amen.' It is therefore surprising that it occurs in none of the longer wish-prayers except (doubtfully) in I Thess. 3: 13,[1] and in the short prayer in Rom. 15: 33.[2]

A fifth formal mark, namely what Schubert called the 'eschatological climax,'[3] seems to relate some of the wish-prayers to a messianic element in Jewish prayer tradition.[4] Thus the first wish-prayer in I Thessalonians ends with the words, 'at the coming of the Lord Jesus with all his saints' (I Thess. 3: 13); the second concludes with 'at the coming of our Lord Jesus Christ' (5: 23). Such a climax, where the apostle looks forward to the consummation, occurs or is suggested in five out of the eight wish-prayers under consideration.[5]

The sixth formal characteristic involves the specific location of the wish-prayers in the letter, whereby (as we shall see in detail later on) they seem to serve a summarizing or terminating function at various transitional points in the internal structure of each letter. Sanders[6] singles out the two main prayers in I Thessalonians (3: 11–13[7] and 5: 23f.), and rightly sees them

---

[1] The Mss are divided and most commentators reject Amen as a later addition. See B. Rigaux, *Saint Paul. Les Épitres aux Thessaloniciens*, Etudes Bibliques (Paris, 1956), *ad loc*. We have already observed that the wish-prayers in I Thess. 5: 23 and I Cor. 1: 8 are followed by sentences which may substitute for an Amen (above, p. 35).

[2] We do not here include the closing grace greetings, each followed in many Mss by Amen to end the letter.

[3] Schubert, pp. 4ff., referring to the end of the thanksgiving period.

[4] See I. Elbogen, *Die messianische Idee in den alten jüdischen Gebeten* (Berlin, 1912), p. 669; also Heinemann, *Prayer in the Period of the Tanna'im and the Amora'im*, p. xii, regarding Jewish prayers of 'Bet-Midrash' origin (offered in conjunction with the public exposition of Scripture): these prayers sometimes concluded with 'a request for speedy redemption and the coming of the Messiah and the Kingdom of Heaven.' See also Sanders, 'Transition from Opening Thanksgiving.'

[5] Viz., in I Thess. 3: 13 and 5: 23f.; Rom. 15: 13 (the twice-repeated word ἐλπίς); I Cor. 1: 8f., and probably Phil. 4: 19 (ἐν δόξῃ; see below, p. 105). The climax is lacking in Rom. 15: 5f., 15: 33, and 16: 20a (see below, p. 95, n. 4) [also lacking in II Thess. 2: 16f., 3: 5, 16].

[6] Sanders, p. 359.

[7] He omits from consideration v. 13.

as examples of a closing formula which marks the end of a section of the letter: the first closes the long thanksgiving (or second thanksgiving), and the second prayer closes the main paraenetic section. Besides this, we shall see that the two principal wish-prayers in Romans (5: 5f., 13) together bring to a conclusion the main body of the letter (1: 18 – 15: 13); the two smaller wish-prayers (15: 33 and 16: 20) each conclude a shorter section; the conjectured wish-prayer in I Corinthians (1: 8f.) closes the thanksgiving period; and the one in Philippians (4: 19) comes at the end of the letter.[1]

Connected with the summarizing function of the wish-prayers is the location of several of them within a recognizable pattern that seems to occur near the end of all the Pauline epistles. Besides the customary final benediction we find one or more wish-prayers, or a curse or pronouncement blessing, loosely connected with a series of assorted items and final instructions for the readers. These form part of what appears to be a liturgically oriented closing pattern of a loosely constructed type, by means of which Paul's letters are adapted to lead into further corporate worship.[2] There is an interesting parallel from Jewish letterwriting style that may help to illustrate the general growth of this kind of variable epistolary–liturgical closing pattern. It occurs in the development that runs from the two brief instructions in the letter of Jeremiah to the captives at Babylon (Jer. 29: 7–9), through the extended series of instructions in the letter of Baruch (Bar. 1: 10–15), and finally into the briefer series in the letter to the nine-and-a-half tribes, found in a later work, the Apocalypse of Baruch (Syr. Bar. 86: 1–3).[3] While these examples do not include a wish-prayer,

---

[1] For a similar conclusion, see Jewett, p. 24.

[2] See above, p. 10, n. 2. For a tabulation of the principal features that occur at the close of the epistles, see Appendix IV. For a specimen of the epistolary–liturgical pattern as it is reflected in I Thess., see below, pp. 51f.

[3] Jer. 29: 7–9. Here are two short instructions: about 'prudential' intercessory prayer to be offered by the readers for Babylon; linked with a sharp warning against false prophets among them. 'But seek the welfare of the city where I have sent you into exile, and pray to the Lord on its behalf, for in its welfare you will find your welfare. For thus says the Lord of hosts, the God of Israel: Do not let your prophets and your diviners who are among you deceive you...for it is a lie which they prophesy to you in my name....'

Bar. 1: 10–15. Here is a longer series of instructions: about a gift of collected money (v. 10); about 'prudential' intercessory prayers by the

they do supply an antecedent for the custom of preparing an 'official' letter to be used luturgically by the readers.

The varied forms of the epistolary–liturgical closing pattern used by Paul will occupy our attention as we come to study the prayer passages at the end of each of his epistles:[1]

(1) In I Thessalonians the epistolary–liturgical pattern in 5: 12–28 (beginning perhaps with 'But we beseech you, ἐρωτῶμεν, brethren')[2] includes the wish-prayer in vv. 23f. (See below, pp. 51f. and 70f.)

readers for Babylon and her kings (vv. 11f.); linked with prayers to be offered by the readers for the writer and his companions (v. 13); in response to the prior prayers, fasting and collection, by the writer and his companions on behalf of the readers (v. 5); about the reading of the book (letter) (v. 14a); finally about using the liturgical confession contained in the letter, as an expression of the readers' own united confession, 'in the house of the Lord on the days of the feasts and at appointed seasons' (v. 14b). Then follows an extended prayer of confession that forms nearly half of the letter (1: 15 – 3: 8).

Syr. Bar. 86: 1–3. Here is a briefer series: about reading the letter 'in your congregations with care' (v. 1); about using the letter for corporate meditation 'above all on the days of your fasts' (v. 2); and finally about using the reading of the letter as a means of remembering the writer, just as the writer used it to call the readers to remembrance (v. 3).

[1] Cf. F. V. Filson, ' *Yesterday.' A study of Hebrews in the Light of Chapter 13*, *SBT*, Second Series, 4 (London, 1967), pp. 13–26. Filson finds such a pattern in the closing chapter of Hebrews and compares it with similar patterns in I Thess., II Thess., Gal., II Tim., Phil., I Pet., and Rom. (pp. 23–5). Cf. also the formal elements at the close of Rev.

G. J. Bahr, in 'The Subscriptions in the Pauline Letters,' *JBL*, 87 (1968), 27–41, has conjectured that, following contemporary letter-writing, a considerable portion of each of Paul's epistles (usually including the whole paraenetic section) should be regarded as a ὑπογραφή, written separately in the apostle's own hand, and following upon the body (σῶμα) of the letter that had been arranged to a greater or lesser degree by his secretary. The subscription would be recognizable mainly through a number of cross-references back to the body of the letter, and would perhaps reflect more authentically the work and emphases of the apostle himself.

But many of the cross-references may simply be Paul building on and applying, not necessarily in a subscription, what he had earlier written. They do not necessarily indicate where the autograph begins. In any case, the 'official' character of these apostolic letters would ensure a careful supervision of the whole letter.

[2] The precise point at which the loose pattern begins in each letter cannot be accurately defined, but the main features may be recognized (App. IV). What we shall find in this closing pattern is rather Paul's epistolary

(2) In Romans the pattern that seems to run at least through chapters 15 and 16 (perhaps beginning at 12: 12–14) includes the wish-prayers in 15: 5f., 13, 33, and 16: 20a. (See below, pp. 95f.)

(3) In Galatians the reduced pattern in 6: 11–18 (beginning with 'see with what large letters') includes the pronouncement blessing in v. 16. (See below, pp. 125f.)

(4) In I Corinthians the pattern in 16: 1–24 (beginning with, 'Now concerning the contribution') includes the curse and invocation in v. 22. (See below, pp. 151ff.)

(5) In Philippians the pattern in 4: 4–23 (beginning perhaps with 'Rejoice in the Lord always') includes the (possible) wish-prayer in v. 19. (See below, pp. 202f.)

(6) Philemon shows a reduced pattern without a wish-prayer, vv. 17–25. (See below, p. 218.)

(7) In II Corinthians the pattern in 13: 5–13 (beginning perhaps at 13: 5, 'Examine yourselves') includes the (possible) wish-prayer in v. 11b. (See below, pp. 238f.)

We may now draw this chapter to a conclusion. Our survey of the formal marks of the main intercessory wish-prayer passages in relation to their Jewish and Hellenistic background has uncovered some clear elements of a recognizable though flexible prayer style, taken over by Paul and adapted for his particular epistolary and liturgical purposes. These stylistic marks will help to confirm our selection of the passages and to illuminate the detailed functional study to which we must now turn.

adaptation of some apparently eucharistic liturgical items, together with several other features.

For a comprehensive treatment of the conclusions of Paul's letters, see Gamble, 'Textual History,' pp. 120–74. Gamble shows that several of Paul's concluding epistolary items are present in some papyrus letters (pp. 106–20). To the items listed below in Appendix IV, he would add some miscellaneous elements, including hortatory remarks, travelogue, commendation (including letter carrier remarks), and sometimes a postscript.

CHAPTER 4

FUNCTION OF THE WISH-PRAYERS
IN I THESSALONIANS

What, now, does Paul do with the liturgical or epistolary language and forms that he takes over in the wish-prayers? Does he use them to express real prayer arising spontaneously from immediate needs, and linked closely with the main concerns and themes of the letters? Do they fulfil other purposes as well? The broad question of the functioning of the eight principal wish-prayer passages is considered in this chapter and the next.[1]

BACKGROUND AND PURPOSE OF I THESSALONIANS

We may start with the two examples in I Thessalonians:

Now may our God and Father himself, and our Lord Jesus, direct our way to you; and may the Lord make you increase and abound in love to one another and to all men, as we do to you, so that he may establish your hearts unblamable in holiness before our God and Father, at the coming of our Lord Jesus with all his saints. (I Thess. 3: 11–13)

May the God of peace himself sanctify you wholly; and may your spirit and soul and body be kept sound and blameless at the coming of our Lord Jesus Christ. (I Thess. 5: 23)

This letter to Thessalonica[2] provides an appropriate beginning for our study. Besides being probably the earliest of Paul's

---

[1] Little detailed and systematic study of the content and function of the Pauline wish-prayers has been previously undertaken. But see now Jewett, 'Homiletic Benediction,' for a useful beginning.

[2] There is substantial agreement that I Thess. is a genuine single Pauline epistle. See W. G. Kümmel, 'Das Literarische und Geschichtliche Problem des Ersten Thessalonicherbriefes,' *Neotestamentica et Patristica, Freundesgabe O. Cullmann, Nov. Test.* Suppl. 6 (1962), 213–27. Recent proposals by Eckart and Schmithals to understand I Thess. as an editorial compilation have not proved convincing: K.-G. Eckart, 'Der zweite echte Brief des Apostels Paulus an die Thessalonicher,' *ZThK*, LVIII (1961), 30ff.; W. Schmithals, 'Die Thessalonicherbriefe als Briefkompositionen,' *Zeit und Geschichte. Dankesgabe an Rudolf Bultmann zum 80. Geburtstag*, ed. E. Dinkler (Tübingen, 1964),

extant letters,[1] it was occasioned and closely shaped by a congregational emergency that was causing him the deepest anxiety. Details of the founding of the church, the subsequent crisis, and the apostle's growing concern are all indirectly reflected or openly described in the letter itself.[2] Indeed, more than half of the epistle (chaps. 1–3) is taken up with discussing a chain of recent happenings in which the apostle himself is intensely involved, while the second part of the letter speaks directly to these.[3] As we shall see, the intercessory prayer passages show the closest links with this situation and may be interpreted and

pp. 295–315. Both attempts assume that the formal integrity and thematic continuity of the long thanksgiving period (I Thess. 1–3) are broken at 1:10 and 2:13. But for a defence of the integrity of chaps. 1–3, see Schubert, p. 23; cf. below, p. 162, and n. 2, pp. 175f. Various internal links throughout I Thess. will be indicated in the present work.

[1] Written probably from Corinth during Paul's first visit there, about 50 A.D. For the precariousness of the usual chronology of the Pauline epistles, which is based largely on the sequence of events described in Acts, see *inter al.*, Hurd, pp. 12–42. In view of this we shall attempt to avoid basing substantial judgments of the epistolary situations on this chronology, even though we shall tentatively adopt it for want of a more persuasive alternative. In their recent reassessment of Pauline chronology, Buck and Taylor place I Thess. after II Thess., and after Paul had left Corinth, but in any case before his other letters; C. Buck and G. Taylor, *Saint Paul: a Study of the Development of his Thought* (New York, 1969), pp. 38f., 46–52, 140–5.

[2] The question of how much the epistles are shaped respectively by Paul's immediate response to a congregational situation, by his wish to express his considered understanding of the gospel, or by his own larger missionary plans, will be considered afresh for each letter. Cf. Hurd's comment, 'Strictly speaking, there were two factors involved in the *Sitz im Leben* of each of Paul's letters. On the one hand there was the special situation of each Church...its interests, needs, questions, misunderstandings, failures, and triumphs. On the other hand there was Paul's own situation at the time he wrote: his interests, insights, needs, hopes, fears, and his maturing experience as an ambassador for Christ' (p. 5). Cf. Wendland, *Urchristlichen Literaturformen*, pp. 342–58.

[3] As long ago as 1894, Bornemann emphasized that I Thess. was molded directly by a special epistolary situation and should rightly be interpreted only within that context, not by superimposing ready-made categories and divisions. W. Bornemann, *Die Thessalonicherbriefe*, Meyer's Kommentar, 6th edn (Göttingen, 1894), pp. 40–2; cf. G. C. Findlay, *The Epistles to the Thessalonians*, Cambridge Bible for Schools and Colleges (Cambridge, 1894), and other commentators; J. Munck, 'I Thess. 1.9–10 and the Missionary Preaching of Paul,' *NTS*, 9 (1962–3), 95–110. For this reason the letter is

understood only in organic relationship with it. In addition, the intercessory prayer material is relatively extensive and appears to occupy an even more central place in the structure and thought of this letter than do the prayers in the other letters. The other epistles will all supply valuable evidence for our study, but in no other letter are these conditions combined in such a revealing way.

In attempting to assess the significance of the intercessory prayer passages in this letter, it may be well, therefore, to be reminded of the circumstances in which it was written, including the apostle's changing hopes and anxieties which had followed upon his original visit to Thessalonica.[1] The predominant theme in his recollections was thankfulness for the immediate success of his missionary preaching there. He dwells at length on the converts' eager response (1 : 4 – 2 : 1, 2 : 13–16), on the warm mutual feelings of affection between apostle and believers (1 : 9, 2 : 8f., 3 : 6b, 12), and the way in which their joyful example under persecution had communicated itself to others over a wide area (1 : 6–9).

Yet this promising start had been jeopardized by his prematurely forced departure.[2] The fear that they might after all fail in his absence was causing him unbearable concern (3 : 1,

regarded by a number of commentators as a particularly significant portrait of the apostle's understanding of his apostolic function, e.g., Milligan, p. xliii; F. Amiot, *Saint Paul, Épitre aux Galates, Épitres aux Thessaloniciens, Verbum Salutis*, xiv (Paris, 1946), 255; W. Neil, *The Epistle of Paul to the Thessalonians*, MNTC (New York, 1950), pp. xxvi–xxviii.

The account in Acts 17 : 1–10, 18 : 5, of Paul's work at Thessalonica and the subsequent movements of himself and his companions, illuminates the epistolary situation, but must be treated with some reserve. E. Haenchen, *Die Apostelgeschichte, neu übersetzst und eklärt*, Meyer's Kommentar, 13th rev. edn (Göttingen, 1961), pp. 453ff.

The complicated problem of the relation of II Thess. with our epistle finds no general agreement. As the authenticity of the second epistle is seriously questioned by many scholars, we shall examine the circumstances at Thessalonica without reference to it. For a citation of literature on this problem see Hurd, p. 27. See also above, p. 45, n. 2.

[1] Cf. Funk, *Language, Hermeneutics, and the Word of God*, pp. 237f., regarding the 'complexity of the letter and its intentionality.'

[2] This is not overtly stated in the letter, but indications are not lacking of a hurried departure such as is described in Acts 17 : 1–10. E.g., the phrase 'made orphans by separation from you' (2 : 17), and the stress laid on his desire to return after only a short time (2 : 17f.).

2, 5, 8). Would the young church be able to stand fast in love under the fires of persecution from their own countrymen (1: 6, 2: 14)?[1] He wished desperately to return to them, made several efforts to do so,[2] but in the end had to be content with sending Timothy instead (2: 17 – 3: 5).

When the good news of their continued steadfastness finally reached him (3: 6), Paul's relief was extreme; his joyful mood reflects itself throughout the long thanksgiving section of the letter that he immediately sent back to them.

Nevertheless his concern still persisted. The danger of persecution continued (1: 3, 6, 2: 14, 3: 2–4) and still posed a threat to the morale and faith of the converts (3: 2–5, 13). Attacks on the apostles themselves by a group of opponents at Thessalonica evidently threatened to undermine the very continuance of his work there, calling forth a strong counter-defense from Paul (2: 1–13 and 2: 17 – 3: 5).[3] To add to his misgivings there were problems arising from the Thessalonians'

[1] For a later sidelight on the endurance of the Macedonian churches, cf. II Cor. 8: 1–5.

[2] His vehement protestations suggest a defensive reply to accusations about his absence; but this does not remove all credence from his assertions. Funk (pp. 248, 265–70, 274, postscript) emphasizes the tremendous importance placed by the apostle on face-to-face encounter and oral communication of the gospel. Thus the 'travelogue' or reference to Paul's intended visit to his readers (his imminent presence) is a constituent element in the Pauline letter, based on the underlying theme of the 'apostolic parousia,' I Cor. 5: 3–5. Cf. *idem*, 'Saying and Seeing: Phenomenology of Language and the New Testament,' *JBR*, 34 (1966), especially pp. 209–13. See also his more recent article, 'The apostolic "*Parousia*": Form and Significance,' in *Christian History and Interpretation: Studies presented to John Knox*, ed. W. R. Farmer *et al.* (Cambridge, 1967), pp. 249–68. Paul uses letters and envoys as surrogates for his presence. Cf. H. Koskenniemi, 'Studien zur Idee und Phraseologie des griechischen Briefes bis 400 n. Chr.,' *Annales Academiae Scientiarum Fennicae*, B, 102 (Helsinki, 1965), 34–47.

It may, however, be that the apostle's continued desire to be present in his churches, rather than to rely on letters, was occasioned also by the continued threat of the opponents who dogged his footsteps and undermined his work. Their actual presence demanded his counteracting actual presence.

[3] For an account of the extensive debate on the question of Paul's opponents, see H. J. Schoeps, *Paul*, E.Tr. (Philadelphia, 1961), pp. 63–87; J. M. Robinson, 'Basic Shifts in German Theology,' *Interpretation*, 16 (1962), especially pp. 79–81; R. B. Ward, 'The Opponents of Paul,' *Restoration Quarterly*, 10 (1967), 185–95.

eschatological excitement (5: 1–11), their perplexity about those who had unexpectedly died – perhaps through persecution (4: 13–18) – and related difficulties in their Christian life and growth (4: 1–12, 5: 12–22). Evidently there still seemed to be a critical need for his return, so that anxiety alternated with his thankfulness.

In addition, all these events gained a heightened significance for Paul as foreseeable elements within God's purpose for the 'last days.' They were to be interpreted in the light of an intense eschatological hope – an imminent and dramatic consummation at the 'parousia of our Lord Jesus Christ.' A keen anticipation of this outcome seems to dominate the whole epistle.[1] Persecutions and hindrances were but the expected afflictions (θλίψεις) of the interim Age[2] (2: 14–18, 3: 2b–5). Even in their sufferings they could rejoice (1: 6, 5: 16–18), for God was biding his time (2: 16), his glorious consummation would come quickly (1: 10, 2: 19, 3: 13, etc.). Thus the final part of the thanksgiving period (2: 14 – 3: 13) presses forward to the great adventist climax of verse 13.

Paul's own ministry gained new depth and urgency as he saw himself an eschatological figure with a 'high or nearly unique position' in the divine plan.[3] His thankfulness would be increased in that the victories were but a foretaste of the final

---

[1] The adventist theme appears at frequent intervals in the letter, often at transition points: e.g., 1: 3b (hope in our Lord Jesus Christ), 1: 9f., 2: 19f., 3: 13, 4: 13 – 5:11, 5: 23f. Funk suggests that within the formal structure of the Pauline letter, an 'eschatological climax' is customarily inserted at various transitional points ('The apostolic "*Parousia*",' pp. 249, 257, 264f.). Cf. Sanders. This would follow the Christian custom of closing the hodayoth and berachoth with eschatological requests. Yet the apostle seems here, as in his other liturgical and epistolary forms, to have adapted it creatively for use in the immediate situation: see below, pp. 61ff., 67.

For a full discussion of the adventist perspective in the epistle, and reference to the literature, see Rigaux, pp. 195–280; also J. A. T. Robinson, *Jesus and His Coming* (London, 1957), pp. 104–17.

[2] See H. Schlier, *TWNT*, III, 139–48. See also below, p. 148, n. 4.

[3] Beardslee, pp. 82–94. See also *inter alia*: O. Cullmann, 'Le caractère eschatologique du dévoir missionaire et de la consciènce apostolique de S. Paul. Étude sur le κατέχον (-ων) de II Thess. 2, 6–7,' *Revue d'Histoire et de Philosophie Religieuses*, 16 (1936), 210–45; *idem, Christ and Time: The Primitive Christian Conception of Time and History*, E.Tr., rev. edn (Philadelphia, 1964), pp. 163–6, 224; P. S. Minear, 'Paul's Missionary Dynamic,' *Andover-Newton Theological School Bulletin*, 36 (1944), 1–11; A. J. Fridrichsen, *The Apostle and*

victory (2: 19f.). His concern for what was still lacking in the converts (τὰ ὑστερήματα, 3: 10) became all the more pressing through the expectation that the day of the Lord would come soon 'like a thief in the night' (5: 2; cf. 4: 6, 5: 1–11). Thus his pioneering work as apostle to the Gentiles and founder of churches involved also a more continuing phase – a responsibility before God to prepare this young church fully for the parousia. The whole letter witnesses to Paul's intense pastoral concern for them (cf. 2: 7, 11). His deep sense of accountability shines throughout the paraenetic section of the letter (chaps. 4 and 5).

Closely allied with his pastoral concern was a more personal, intimate bond of mutual love and affection which he stresses at several points in the letter.[1]

Finally, his pastoral responsibility at times takes on a representative, intercessory, or priestly character, as he looks forward to the day in the near future when he himself will jubilantly present them as an offering, or 'boast' of them to the Lord at his coming (2: 19f.). This aspect of his apostleship is brought out especially in three passages, two of them being the wish-prayers (2: 19f., 3: 9–13, 5: 23–5).[2] So his awareness of intense involvement with them as missionary, pastor, friend, and priestly representative makes him look forward to the parousia with joyous hope and exultation.

Such then, in briefest outline, was the complex situation to which Paul addressed his letter, and in relation to which we must interpret the prayer passages. It entailed a dynamic, three-way, intercessory relationship, involving Paul, the Thessalonian converts, and God (God revealed in Christ, who had entrusted Paul with the gospel in the power of the Holy Spirit, and had called the Thessalonians to respond). So their victories must be made the occasion for the sharing of continual prayers of thanksgiving; their deficiencies must become the

His Message (Uppsala, 1947); Munck, *Paul and the Salvation of Mankind*, pp. 49f., 301–8.

But for a more modest appraisal of Paul's view of himself, see J. Knox, 'Romans 15: 14–33 and Paul's conception of His Apostolic Mission,' *JBL*, 83 (1964), 5ff.

[1] See below, pp. 58f.

[2] Cf. K. Weiss, 'Paulus – Priester der christl. Kultgemeinde,' pp. 357f.; above, p. 5, n. 1.

occasion for sharing constant intercessory supplications. At this point we may turn to a preliminary survey of the prayer passages throughout the epistle.

Survey of the intercessory prayer and related prayer passages in I Thessalonians[1]

It is in the extended thanksgiving period (1: 2 – 3: 13) that the apostle emphasizes the continual occasions of his gratitude to God on their behalf: see especially 1: 2a, 2: 13, 19, 3: 9. Later he exhorts his readers, too, to be continually rejoicing and giving thanks in all circumstances (5: 16, 18).

On the other hand Paul finds it necessary more than once to refer to his unceasing intercessory supplications for them. In the customary greeting at the beginning, he prays for grace and peace upon the church at Thessalonica (1: 16). Then follows a reference to his constant mention of them in his prayers of supplication (1: 2b–3). At the end of the thanksgiving period comes another report of his constant and earnest supplications for them (3: 10), coupled with the first main intercessory wish-prayer proper (3: 11–13), which serves to bring to a close the first half of the letter.

Following out of the paraenetic section of the letter, occurs an example of the liturgically oriented closing pattern to which we have already referred (5: 12–28).[2] To draw his letter to a finish, Paul exhorts the readers to practise (among other things) constant rejoicing, continued prayer, and thanks in all circumstances (5: 16ff.). Shortly after, there follow a number of items in rapid succession: The second main wish-prayer (an adapted peace blessing) with its summarizing content and liturgical phraseology (v. 23)[3] is accompanied by an 'Amen' sentence giving an answering promise of fulfilment (v. 24).[4] These are linked with a request that the readers join Paul in an intercessory circle by praying in turn for him and his companions (v. 25). Closely associated with the prayer references are two more closing liturgical instructions, first about the holy kiss of greeting

[1] For supplication passages, see Appendix II.
[2] Above, pp. 42ff. The significance will be further discussed below, pp. 70f.
[3] See above, pp. 39f., and below pp. 63ff.   [4] See below, p. 68, n. 1.

(v. 26), and then an unexpectedly stern admonition that the letter be read to all (v. 27). Finally the letter ends with the formal blessing, 'The grace of our Lord Jesus Christ be with you' (v. 28). So the whole succession serves to bring the epistle to an impressive and prayerful conclusion.

THE FIRST WISH-PRAYER –
I THESSALONIANS 3: 11–13

Turning now to the first of the two main wish-prayers in the epistle, we may immediately see how Paul takes up the most pressing pastoral problems that filled his mind.

(For what thanksgiving can we render to God for you, for all the joy which we feel for your sake before our God, praying earnestly night and day that we may see you face to face and supply what is lacking in your faith?) (I Thess. 3: 9–10)[1]

Now may our God and Father himself, and our Lord Jesus, direct our way to you; and may the Lord make you increase and abound in love to one another and to all men, as we do to you, so that he may establish your hearts unblamable in holiness before our God and Father, at the coming of our Lord Jesus with all his saints. (I Thess. 3: 11–13)

First, and within the immediate literary context of the epistle itself, we notice that the whole prayer passage (3:9–13) sums up the mood and content of the preceding extended thanksgiving section, and brings to a close the first half of the letter (chaps. 1–3).[2] The important themes and dimensions are brought to a head in prayer. The victories are celebrated with a cry of thanksgiving: 'For what thanksgiving can we render to God for you, for all the joy which we feel for your sake before God?' (v. 9). The concerns are then focused in the intercessory passage (vv. 10–13), comprising a prayer-report, followed by a wish-prayer.[3]

[1] For convenience we quote in parentheses the prayer context that precedes the wish-prayer itself. The whole passage includes a cry of thanksgiving, a prayer-report, and a wish-prayer. See below, p. 162, n. 2.

[2] Cf. Jewett, p. 24. And see above, p. 31 on the connective significance of the particle δέ.

[3] Funk suggests that in the passage 2: 17 – 3: 13 we have an example of a Pauline epistolary form, the 'apostolic parousia' form; see 'The apostolic *"Parousia"*: Form and Significance,' in *Christian History and Interpretation*, pp. 249–68.

The wish-prayer itself (vv. 11–13) both repeats and extends the prayer-report (v. 10, 'praying earnestly night and day that we may see you face to face and supply what is lacking in your faith'), as if the apostle would say, 'I have been constantly and earnestly praying in that way for you – and now once again I do actually offer this prayer to God as I write to you.'[1] Two new notes are added in the repetition: the deficiencies (ὑστερή-ματα) are now to be supplied either by Paul's visiting them, or if not, then apart from Paul directly by the Lord ('and may the Lord make you'); and secondly, the parousia is mentioned as the goal to which everything is pointing.

Another important link between the wish-prayer and the preceding section of the letter is the striking way in which it repeats the thought pattern of an earlier 'priestly' passage that itself had formed a minor climax in the thanksgiving period:

But since we were bereft of you, brethren, for a short time, in person not in heart, we endeavored the more eagerly and with great desire to see you face to face; because we wanted to come to you – I, Paul, again and again – but Satan hindered us. For what is our hope or joy or crown of boasting before our Lord Jesus at his coming? Is it not you? For you are our glory and joy. (2: 17–20)[2]

The progression of pastoral anxieties, priestly responsibilities and parousia hopes of this earlier passage is finally transmuted into an intercessory prayer.[3]

But the wish-prayer not only serves to conclude the preceding portion of the letter; it also constitutes a transition passage into the paraenetic section of the second half of the letter. Commenting on this, Frame writes, 'The emphasis in 3: 11–13 is put less on the longing to see them (v. 11), the apologetic interest underlying 2: 17 – 3: 10, than on the shortcomings of their faith (vv. 12–13), the ὑστερήματα of verse 10. This change of emphasis prepares the way for the exhortations (4: 1ff.).'[4]

Secondly, and moving beyond the literary context to the

---

[1] Cf. Bornemann, p. 151. See also below, p. 71.

[2] Paul may here be adapting an epistolary formula of rejoicing, with a function similar to that of the thanksgiving periods. Cf. R. Webber,'The Concept of Rejoicing in the Letters of Paul,' Diss., Yale University, 1970.

[3] Bornemann draws attention to this, as does von Dobschütz, but the latter does not think it was a conscious literary device.

[4] Frame, pp. 135f.; also other commentators.

wider situation, we notice how it is the apostle's central concerns about the still undecided outcome at Thessalonica which are concentrated in the details of the intercessory wish-prayer.

(1) The first petition (3: 11),[1] 'Now may our God and Father himself, and our Lord Jesus, direct our[2] way to you,' springs as we have seen from a depth of involvement and anxious concern about the crisis, which is far beyond a merely pious epistolary wish (cf. 2: 17f., and 3: 1). The seriousness of his desire to encounter them face-to-face had been caused not only by his considerable pastoral anxiety, but by a warm personal bond of affection and a sense of priestly responsibility as he looked forward to the parousia.[3]

The opening words themselves are significant in this regard: 'Now may our God and Father himself, and our Lord Jesus.' Although, as we have seen, Paul is borrowing a conventional liturgical formula of address,[4] it must be concluded that he added to it here a new depth of meaning. For as he moves to intercede on behalf of the converts, he points away from the problems of the previous verses to invoke the august majesty and unique power of almighty God, the original creator and direct controller of events – αὐτὸς δὲ ὁ θεός. God is in command and overrides all secondary causes and lesser forces, even that of Satan the hinderer (2: 18, and 3: 5). So it is 'God himself' who must decide in what way this petition would be answered,[5] and how he would direct the path of the apostles: if possible by sending Paul back to Thessalonica (v. 11), but in any event by working his divine will among them with or without the human intervention of the apostle (v. 12).[6]

---

[1] The form of the petition is incomplete, as it omits the 'additional benefit.' See above, p. 29, n. 4.

[2] It is assumed that the plural ἡμῶν does not imply joint authorship of the epistle. For a full discussion and bibliography on the question, see Rigaux, *Thessaloniciens*, pp. 77–80.

[3] Although it is true that contemporary Jewish and Hellenistic letters often mentioned prayers for a safe journey (see e.g., Harder, p. 120), Paul, in taking over this epistolary custom, filled it with living meaning. See above, p. 48, n. 2.

[4] See above, pp. 30f.

[5] See below, p. 192 on Rom. 1: 10.

[6] The phrase ὑμᾶς δέ, answering the earlier phrase αὐτὸς δὲ ὁ θεός, may have the force, 'But as for you, may the Lord make you increase....' For a

It has already been mentioned that the title 'our Father,' καὶ πατὴρ ἡμῶν, was found in traditional Jewish prayers, and would have the most sacred liturgical connotations.[1] Yet the extraordinary new profundity and vividness with which Paul used the name Father must also be given the fullest attention. The new significance of calling upon God as Father through Jesus Christ comes to its most striking expression in his well-known passages in Galatians and Romans: 'God has sent the Spirit of his Son into our hearts, crying, "Abba! Father!"' (Gal. 4: 6); 'When we cry "Abba! Father!" it is the Spirit himself bearing witness....' (Rom. 8: 15–17).[2] To invoke God as Father in prayer was to call on the aid of one whose purpose to bless was beyond all description.[3]

(2) The second petition (3: 12) – that they increase and

similar situation, cf. Phil. 1: 27, 'so that whether I come and see you or am absent, I may hear from you that you stand firm in one spirit....' See below, p. 211.

[1] Above, p. 32, n. 1.

[2] See J. Jeremias, 'Abba,' *The Prayers of Jesus*, p. 65. If it could be proved that Paul knew the 'Lord's Prayer' as reflected in variant forms in Matt. 6: 9–13 and Luke 11: 2–4, then the immediate liturgical significance of his use of the phrase καὶ πατὴρ ἡμῶν would be further illuminated. But attempts to demonstrate this through Pauline passages which remind us of the Lord's Prayer have not been fully convincing, such as F. H. Chase, in *The Lord's Prayer in the Early Church* (Cambridge, 1891), pp. 23f., 112–23; Orphal, pp. 6–11. See Hamman, p. 328, Bauer, p. 38, and E. Lohmeyer, '*Our Father*,' E.Tr. (New York, 1965), p. 19.

Nevertheless, it seems reasonable to assume that Paul must have been aware of some form of the Lord's Prayer, and in particular of the special significance taught by Jesus to his followers in the naming of God as 'Father,' and that his prayers must be understood in this light. Cf. Ramsey's claim, 'Both S. Paul's prayers and the doxologies of the New Testament do but express what is already present in the Lord's Prayer....' A. M. Ramsey, *The Gospel and the Catholic Church*, 2nd edn (London, 1956), p. 90.

[3] The addition of the words 'and our Lord Jesus' raises the much-debated question whether Paul addressed prayers to Jesus. Cf. I Cor. 1: 2, 5: 4f., 16: 22. This phrase seems to indicate that in some way he did, yet the indirect form of the address allows ambiguity. Perhaps Jesus was re-garded as the divine agent of the requested action, as in the following verse. See below, p. 280, n. 9, on Phil. 1: 19. For literature on this question, see Harder, p. 97, n. 1; see also A. Juncker, *Das Gebet bei Paulus* (Berlin, 1905), pp. 10–22, K. L. Schmidt, 'ἐπικαλέω,' *TWNT*, III, 498–501; Hamman, p. 279; G. Delling, *Worship in the New Testament*, E.Tr. (Philadelphia, 1962), p. 117. On the linking of God and Christ in prayer language, see below, pp. 82, 112, 121, n. 4, 145f., 180.

abound in love – Paul prays both as pastor and as affectionate friend. As pastor, he is stressing precisely what he sees to be their central need. True, there was a daunting variety of problems in the Thessalonian church, including the possibility that they might even yet fail to stand firm under pressure of persecution (3: 8);[1] but at the heart of their weaknesses he saw their need to be fortified by an increase in love – 'to one another and to all men.'

Love (ἀγάπη)[2] was an essential and permanent theme in Paul's paraenesis; he saw it to be central for the continuing Christian life in *any* church fellowship. To the Galatians he wrote: 'For you were called to freedom, brethren; only do not use your freedom as an opportunity for the flesh, but through love be servants of one another. For the whole law is fulfilled in one word, "You shall love your neighbor as yourself"' (Gal. 5: 13f.; cf. also Rom. 13: 8, I Cor. 13: 13).

Among the Thessalonians, too, there were signs of a special threat to the continuation of their practice of love. Indeed, the word occurs eight times in one form or another in the letter,[3] and the theme of this love for one another appears throughout, being singled out for special mention and praise: 'remembering before our God and Father your work of faith and *labor of love*[4] and steadfastness of hope...' (1: 3); 'Timothy has...brought us the good news of your faith *and love*[5]...' (3: 6); 'But concerning love of the brethren (φιλαδελφία) you have no need to have anyone write to you, for you yourselves have been taught by God to love one another; and indeed you do love all the brethren throughout Macedonia...' (4: 9f.). So he recognizes the signs of true fellowship in the Thessalonian church – of their love to one another.

Yet he is evidently troubled at the divisive pressures exerted on them by his detractors, and he urges a still further growth of responsible love: 'but we exhort you, brethren, to do so [love

[1] Note the conditional nature of his thanksgiving, suggested by the sentence, 'For now we live, [that is] if you stand fast in the Lord' (v. 8).

[2] See G. Quell and E. Stauffer, *TWNT*, I, 20–55; also Rigaux, *Thessaloniciens*, p. 364, for a full list of the literature; and A. Nygren, *Agape and Eros*, E.Tr. (London, 1953).

[3] ἀγάπη: 1: 3, 3: 6, 12, 5: 8, 13. ἀγαπάω: 1: 4, 4: 9. ἀγαπητός: 2: 8. Cf. φιλαδελφία in 4: 9.

[4] Italics added.   [5] Italics added.

one another] more and more' (4: 10b). The letter is sent to the
entire church (1: 1) and is to be read by the entire church
(5: 27).[1] He assures them that he prays for them *all*, even his
opponents among them (1: 2), for intercession knows no limits –
all are included as far as possible within the circle of love,
within the intercessory circle.[2] He urges them to comfort one
another under the strain of persecution (4: 18); to put on the
breastplate of faith and love (5: 8); to 'encourage one another
and build one another up, just as [they] are doing' (5: 11);
'to esteem very highly in love' those who were over them in
the Lord (5: 13); to 'be at peace among [themselves]' (5: 13b);
to take responsibility for encouraging the fainthearted, helping
the weak, patient with all (5: 14); forgiving evil and doing good
to one another (5: 15); meeting together with the sign of the
kiss of peace (5: 26); sharing the burden of the apostles in
prayer (5: 25).

Hence the thought of their mutually involved responsibility
within the church was most prominently in the apostle's mind
as he wrote this letter, with thankfulness for the love they
already had, and yet with concern that it should broaden,
strengthen, increase. So his petition, 'may the Lord make you
increase and abound in love to one another,' must have held
the greatest significance for Paul as he reflected on their special
needs before God.

Yet their love must reach beyond the Christian community
'to all men' – beyond the opponents to include even their
persecutors, especially in a time of great stress. While this theme
is not fully developed – indeed hardly mentioned in the letter –
it must not be overlooked that he does in one other place enjoin
them to 'always seek to do good to one another *and to all*'
(5: 15).[3] That Paul believed it important to extend love beyond
the Christian household may be confirmed from his exhortations in other epistles, e.g., Gal. 6: 10, 'So then, as we have
opportunity, let us do good *to all men*,[4] and especially to those
who are of the household of faith'; cf. also Rom. 12: 9–14,

---

[1] See below, p. 67.

[2] Rigaux discusses fully this community aspect of Paul's exhortation
under the rubric 'Ecclesiological Paraenesis' in *Thessaloniciens*, p. 191.

[3] Italics added.

[4] Italics added. For the extravagant and all-inclusive quality in Paul's
prayers, see below, p. 60, n. 4.

17–21. What then would be the attitude of the Thessalonians towards their persecutors? Would they remain steadfast in love? It is this additional concern about these untried converts which is reflected in his prayer that their love might increase and abound even to all men.[1]

At first sight it may seem surprising that the theologically prior theme of God's initiating love is not more fully developed in the epistle.[2] Yet it is taken for granted and illustrated as the circumstances of the letter determine. God's love in Christ for them had been demonstrated through his original choosing of them in the power of the Holy Spirit (1: 4f.); so they were addressed at the outset as 'brethren beloved by God,' and his gracious and loving purpose to save them shines through the whole epistle.

Just as the particular occasions of the letter do not call forth a full, clear statement of the initiating love of God, so in the prayer Paul does not clearly base their love for one another in the fact that God had first loved them. Rather he points by way of example to a dimension of love which was more immediately to the fore, his own love for them.

Paul is writing not only as their pastor, but as their friend. The mutual affection between apostle and converts is openly discussed in the epistle. His preaching and pastoral responsibility had been rooted in love, expressed love, and could not be separated from his affectionate feelings towards them. He had been totally committed to their welfare in lowly self-giving (2: 9) and speaks of himself as 'ready to share...our own selves, because you had become very dear to us' (2: 8). His original assumption of responsibility for them under the most trying circumstances had been born of a loving concern. Even before they had been Christians, he and the other apostles had reached out to them in costly love at the risk of persecution (2: 2), and they in turn had responded by imitating the apostles: 'You know what kind of men we proved to be among you for your sake. And you became imitators of us and of the Lord' (1: 5f.).[3]

[1] Cf. Rigaux, *Thessaloniciens*, *ad loc.*

[2] Some of Paul's most characteristic themes are missing from this letter: e.g., justification by faith, freedom from the law, the equality of Gentiles and Jews in Christ.

[3] See W. P. De Boer, *The Imitation of Paul; an Exegitical Study* (Kampen,

It is therefore no merely accidental aside when he now prays that their increase in love might be as his own love for them: καθάπερ καὶ ἡμεῖς εἰς ὑμᾶς. Timothy's report of their warm remembrance of him, 'that you always remember us kindly and long to see us, as we long to see you' (3: 6b), had stirred Paul again to respond in affectionate terms. He sees this as a paradigm of the way their love should grow 'to one another and to all men' (3: 12). As his love for them enabled him to give himself to the utmost, so their own increasing and abounding love would enable them to conquer temptations of self-concern, and make them alert to help one another in crisis (5: 11, 14). Furthermore, as he had reached out to them in a time of persecution while they were still pagans, so he prays that they might show love even to their persecutors.[1]

So his prayer takes on a warm paraenetic quality; it is changed for the moment into a very personal exhortation. He attempts to kindle in them a still fuller experience of the love for which he is praying: a cordial sense of mutual responsibility for one another and for all men.

Even the structure of the prayer passage (3: 9–13) is so arranged as to lay particular emphasis on the special petition for love. This petition is placed within a triad of graces mentioned in the prayer passage: faith, love, and hope (faith in v. 10; love in v. 12; and by implication, hope in v. 13). It is true that the triad occurs three times in this epistle (1: 3, 3: 10–13, 5: 8), commonly in Paul's other letters, and in other early Christian writers, suggesting that the figure was used as a pattern of the Christian life.[2] Is the petition for love, then, merely part of a habitual train of thought that has no special significance here? On the contrary, the actual progression of

1962), pp. 92ff. For recent discussions of Paul's exhortation to his readers to imitate him, see V. P. Furnish, *Theology and Ethics in Paul* (Nashville, 1968), pp. 218ff. and the literature cited on p. 218, n. 28. Cf. I Thess. 1: 6, 3: 12b, I Cor. 4: 16, Gal. 4: 12, Phil. 3: 17, 4: 9.

[1] Paul's total mission to the Gentiles, including the Thessalonians, had implied a willingness to move out at great cost beyond the confines of the established fellowship of believers. Christ had died for all men; all men were potential converts. Cf. Rom. 5: 6–8, 'God shows his love for us in that while we were yet sinners, Christ died for us.'

[2] See A. M. Hunter, *Paul and His Predecessors* (Philadelphia, 1961), pp. 33–5.

the passage suggests that it was intended to hold the central place in the prayer.

In relation to what has preceded, the love petition finally brings into sharp focus the central aim of his constant prayers that he might come to them. In relation to what follows, it seems structurally to play an equally important part: the increase in love is the special means (εἰς τό) of preparing their hearts to be unblamable in holiness before God at the parousia – the eschatological event to which the whole passage has been moving.[1] Thus the links in both directions within the structure of the prayer passage itself seem to focus special attention on the intercessory petition for an increase in love.[2]

Characteristic of the apostle's eschatological sense of urgency was the very eagerness of his praying, expressed in the words 'increase and abound in love' (πλεονάσαι καὶ περισσεύσαι).[3] An extravagant quality marks this request, one that we shall find typical of his prayer-style, with frequent supplications for overflowing blessings, for a completion of God's gifts in the short time before the consummation, that they be poured out in full measure upon all the members of his churches without exception.[4]

---

[1] See above, p. 49, n. 1.

[2] For a contrary view, see von Dobschütz, p. 194. He suggests that the emphasis on love is only apparent, not real: Paul is using the word ἀγάπη as a *pars pro toto*, as with πίστις in v. 10. In each case the apostle uses a specific word as a symbol of their whole life in Christ.

But while Paul may not here be thinking narrowly of faith or love to the exclusion of the wider field to which they are related, his choice of a distinct word in each case cannot just be reduced to a *pars pro toto*. In the epistle as a whole it is easy to see that he deals separately and specifically with each grace.

[3] περισσεύειν occurs 39 times in the NT, of which 25 instances are in the recognized Pauline epistles.

[4] This may be noticed in most of the Pauline prayer passages: e.g., Rom. 15: 33, 'be with you *all*,' cf. II Cor. 13: 14, Gal. 6: 16; Phil. 1: 4, '*always* in *every* prayer of mine for you *all*'; 1: 9–11, '*abound more and more...filled* with the fruits'; 1: 20, 'with *full* courage, *now as always*'; 4: 6, 'but in *everything* by prayer'; 4: 19, '*every* need of yours according to his riches in glory'; I Thess. 1: 2, 'for you *all*'; 3: 10, 'supply *what is lacking*'; 3: 12, '*increase and abound* in love...and to *all* men'; 5: 23, 'sanctify you *wholly* ... spirit and soul and body'; Philem. 6, '*all* the good that is ours in Christ.' [Cf. the word '*all*' or '*every*' in II Thess. 1: 11, 2: 17, 3: 16. See also Eph. 1: 18ff., 3: 14–19, 6: 18, 24; Col. 1: 9–14, 1: 29 – 2: 3, 4: 12b.] Harder, pp. 124, 208f.

The second petition, then, brings into sharp relief Paul's central pastoral concern. Love was not merely one grace among others in the Christian life, nor one theme within the epistle, nor one petition among others in his prayer. It was the burning reality required in the Thessalonian situation, now and in preparation for the parousia. It must sum up his manifold intercessions on their behalf.

(3) The third petition (3: 13), for an 'additional benefit,'[1] brings us at last to the eschatological climax: that their hearts might be established 'unblamable in holiness before our God and Father, at the coming of the Lord Jesus with all his saints.' Once again there comes to the surface the intense adventist hope that underlies the whole epistle. Paul will shortly turn at some length to this burning expectation shared by his readers and himself (4: 13 – 5: 11). In the meantime he reveals the special urgency of his priestly solicitude as he looks forward to their standing at the imminent parousia.[2]

The language details of this final petition link closely with the wording and mood of the preceding passage. He had sent Timothy to establish (στηρίξαι) them in their faith during the tribulations of the last days (3: 2); he had been anxious about their standing firm (στήκετε) in the Lord (3: 8). He had been continually giving thanks for and praying about their 'steadfastness (ὑπομονή) of hope' (1: 3); so now he prays that the Lord might establish their hearts (στηρίξαι ὑμῶν τὰς καρδίας).[3] The addition of the word 'hearts' stresses the need for an internal strengthening which only love could effect, for the heart denoted the inner nature of man.[4] In this special testing time, when no merely outward change could give them the

---

[1] von Dobschütz, *ad loc.*, contends that this verse cannot be included as a part of the prayer because it is preceded by no verb for praying. But the construction, εἰς τὸ στηρίξαι, shows that it should be included; in any case it is part of Paul's manifest intention in praying. See above, p. 29.

[2] Cf. H. Greeven, *Gebet und Eschatologie im Neuen Testament:* Neutestamentliche Forschungen (Gütersloh, 1931). See above, pp. 49f.

[3] Cf. LXX, Ps. 111: 7f., Sir. 6: 37; also Jas. 5: 8, 'Establish your hearts, for the coming of the Lord is at hand.' See Beardslee, p. 113.

[4] Its precise meaning is difficult to define: probably will, courage, then affection. See P. Dhorme, 'L'emploi metaphorique des noms de parties du corps en Hébreu et en Akkadien, VI. – Les parties internes,' *Revue Biblique*, 31 (1922), 489–517; also F. H. van Meynenveld, *Het Hart (Leb. Lebab) in het oude Testament* (Leiden, 1950).

steadfastness they required, they must be fortified in the very center of their beings.

But the prayer gains further solemnity in that they must be prepared to stand unblamable in holiness before God as judge, the searcher of the inward motives of men, who tests and tries the hearts of men (cf. 2: 4, referring perhaps to Jer. 11: 40).[1] The apostle shows a continual awareness of their need to walk before this God in holiness,[2] and he exhorts them to live a life 'every element of which will stand his inspection and meet his approval.'[3] So his intercessory prayer concentrates this solemn concern into one pregnant phrase, ἀμέμπτους ἐν ἁγιωσύνῃ ἔμπροσθεν τοῦ θεοῦ.

Yet the God before whom they stand is not only judge. He is also the same loving Father whose purpose to save is writ large in the epistle; so the note of comfort and hope is added through the title 'our Father' (καὶ πατρὸς ἡμῶν).[4] At the beginning of the prayer God was addressed as the Father who, with the Lord Jesus, would graciously direct their steps; now at the close, it is as 'our Father' that he will judge them finally, with the Lord Jesus.

As they stand before God now (3: 9), so they will stand before Him in that day when all secrets will be revealed;[5] if they are strengthened inwardly in love now, so they will be rendered blameless in holiness at the parousia. They will find the day of the Lord a day not of wrath but of salvation (1: 10, 2: 16, 5: 9).[6] In the hopeful and joyful climax of his prayer he stretches eagerly forward to the coming of the Lord Jesus with all his saints, when all that he is now working and praying for will find its glorious completion in final triumph. Here he seems to turn again from the pastoral to the representative priestly rôle that he had anticipated earlier in the letter (2: 19f.). His presentation of them to God now in prayer is a foretaste of

[1] Cf. Neil, p. 73.

[2] See also 4: 1–8 which includes the phrases περιπατεῖν καὶ ἀρέσκειν θεῷ, ὁ ἁγιοσμὸς ὑμῶν, ἐν ἁγιασμῷ twice, and finally the naming of the Holy Spirit, πνεῦμα αὐτοῦ τὸ ἅγιον.

[3] J. Eadie, *A Commentary on the Greek Text of the Epistles to the Thessalonians* (London, 1877), p. 120.

[4] See above, p. 55.

[5] See above, p. 39, regarding the judgment seat of Christ.

[6] Frame, p. 139.

his final presenting of them as a 'crown of boasting before our Lord Jesus at his coming' (2: 20).[1]

Thus most of the pressing concerns of the apostle for his readers have been gathered up into this concentrated prayer passage, which brings to a close the communications in the first half of the letter, while serving also to introduce the exhortations of the second half. Thanksgiving for what has been accomplished is followed by a request that he may return, by mention of the difficulties which still persist, by emphasis on their continued need for love extending even to their opponents and oppressors, that they may be inwardly strengthened to meet the crisis of persecution, and finally by a prayer that they may be made ready in holiness for the imminent parousia. The apostle prays as one who is deeply involved with them as their concerned pastor, affectionate friend, and representative priest. He believes that all is taking place before God the ruler, judge, and loving Father. To him, therefore, the prayer may be confidently addressed.[2]

THE SECOND WISH-PRAYER –
I THESSALONIANS 5: 23f.

The second wish-prayer (or peace blessing) occupies a comparably strategic position in the structure of the epistle, in that it gathers up the main pastoral exhortations of the preceding paraenetic section (4:1 – 5: 22), and contributes to the liturgically oriented closing pattern.[3] As he comes to the end of his message to the Thessalonians, Paul turns once again towards God in a more directly representative way; but now he omits thanksgiving and adds a request that they in turn will present him to God in prayer (v. 25).[4]

May the God of peace himself sanctify you wholly; and may your spirit and soul and body be kept sound and blameless at the coming of our Lord Jesus Christ. He who calls you is faithful, and he will do it. (Brethren, pray for us.) (I Thess. 5: 23–5)

[1] See above, p. 50.
[2] For the note of confidence suggested by the optative verbs (κατευθύναι, πλεονάσαι, περισσεύσαι), see Van Elderen, 'The Verb in the Epistolary Invocation,' p. 48, n. 9.
[3] See above, pp. 42ff.   [4] See below, pp. 261ff.

Within the literary context of the epistle, this is the third main passage where Paul speaks as a mediator who prepares the Thessalonians for presentation to Christ at the parousia.[1] Like the second passage (3: 9–13), it serves as a small comprehensive prayer-unit to bring to a conclusion a main section of the letter. Indeed, it forms an eschatological climax to the whole epistle, followed only by the four short sentences that complete the liturgical instructions and greetings.[2]

The two wish-prayers in the epistle are closely, though not completely, similar in form, content and progression.[3] Both are oriented towards the glorious coming of the Lord Jesus and have as their object the sanctification of the believers of Thessalonica in the decisive day (cf. 'unblamable in holiness' with 'sanctify you wholly...sound and blameless'). In both prayers the apostle desires for the Thessalonians a perfection of holiness which goes far beyond and beneath merely outward ethical norms and behavior, and envisages their whole beings made ready to stand in the presence of God and Christ (cf. 'establish your hearts' with 'may your spirit and soul and body be kept sound'). There is a similarity of thought structure: in the first prayer it is an increase of love that will lead to a completion of holiness; in the second prayer it seems to be partly implied by the phrase 'the God of peace' (ὁ θεὸς τῆς εἰρήνης) that it is God's gift of peace (or wholeness and salvation)[4] which will

[1] For the first passage (2: 17–20), see above, p. 53.

[2] See below, pp. 70f.

[3] If the second prayer is taken to form part of an autograph 'subscription' (Bahr), then it may be purposely referring back to and endorsing the earlier prayer in the body of the letter. See above, p. 43, n. 1.
For alternative translations of this prayer, see above, pp. 39f.

[4] See van Stempvoort, 'Eine Stilistische Lösung...,' pp. 262f. The genitive (τῆς εἰρήνης) is a Semitism used frequently in this way of God, and seems to imply that he gives the peace that he possesses (Milligan, *ad loc.*). See above, p. 31, n. 4. Εἰρήνη, which in the LXX is used for 'shalom,' often includes such concepts as completeness, safety, soundness of body, health, wholeness, salvation, even Messianic blessings. Cf. von Dobschütz, *ad loc.*; C. Masson, *Les Deux Épitres de Saint Paul Aux Thessaloniciens*, Commentaire Du Nouveau Testament, XIa (Neuchatel, 1957), *ad loc.*

But it includes also the narrower concept of cessation of strife, and may very well refer back here to 5: 13, εἰρηνεύετε ἐν ἑαυτοῖς (so Bornemann, Frame, L. Morris, *The First and Second Epistles to the Thessalonians*, New International Commentary on the N.T. (Grand Rapids, 1959), *ad loc.*).

make them whole, complete in holiness (ἁγιάσαι ὑμᾶς ὁλοτελεῖς καὶ ὁλόκληρον).

Yet some interesting differences may be noticed. The earlier
unit springs more directly from the epistolary situation described in the preceding half of the letter, so that it expresses
Paul's more immediate dual reaction of prayerful thanksgiving
and concern. Before turning to intercession for that which is
still lacking, the apostle breaks into rejoicing and thanksgiving
at the good news (3: 9). The second prayer-unit, on the other
hand, follows upon a long paraenetic section. While it is
grounded ultimately in the same pastoral concerns, it reflects
more immediately the exhortations and warnings which have
preceded it in the epistle.[1] Thus thanksgiving is omitted in the
direct transition from exhortation to intercessory prayer, and
although the same pastoral anxieties are evident, they are not
so directly expressed.

So in spite of the extreme compactness of the second prayer
passage, it continues in a broad way the peculiar injunctions
and emphases of the paraenetic section: as the prayer for
holiness (ἁγιωσύνη) in the earlier wish-prayer has prepared the
way for an exhortation to holiness in sexual conduct (4: 1–8),
so the further exhortations converge again into the motif of
holiness in the second prayer – ἁγιάσαι ὑμᾶς. The appeals to
the converts, that in all their daily affairs they should live a
life fit for men who were already 'sons of light and sons of the
day' (e.g., 4: 1–12, 5: 1–22), are reflected in the very inclusiveness of the double supplication.[2] Thus, the sequence of πᾶς-
forms in the immediately preceding verses (14–22),[3] is focused

Cf. I Cor. 14: 33, where the God of peace is contrasted with 'confusion'
(ἀκαταστασία); cf. Rom. 4: 1–11, where peace is closely related to reconciliation. See also Rigaux, *Thessaloniciens*, p. 354 and the literature on εἰρήνη
there cited; W. Foerster, *TWNT*, II, 409–16.

It seems quite possible that Paul had both the wider and the narrower
meanings in mind. See below, p. 66, n. 1.

[1] Cf. Milligan, *ad loc.*; Rigaux, p. 594. See also above, p. 31 on the connective significance of the particle δέ.

[2] While it is not certain where the second petition (for the additional
benefit) begins, whether after ὁλοτελεῖς or after πνεῦμα, the essential meaning remains the same. See above, p. 40.

[3] v. 14, πρὸς πάντας; v. 15, πάντοτε; v. 16, εἰς πάντας; v. 17, πάντοτε;
v. 18, ἐν παντί; v. 21, πάντα; v. 22, ἀπὸ παντός. See above, p. 60, n. 4,
for the extravagant quality of Paul's prayers.

in the first petition in the comprehensive word ὁλοτελεῖς; while the negative injunction to 'abstain from every form of evil' (v. 22) is answered in the second petition, 'And may your spirit and soul and body be kept sound and blameless.'

Furthermore, we note in particular the earlier appeals for brotherly love and unity (e.g., 4: 9–10, 5: 12–15), together with the request that they 'be at peace among themselves' (v. 13). These exhortations and indeed the whole letter have emphasized unity. Now at the close the apostle prays to God as the source of the corporate unity of the congregation, choosing the traditional prayer epithet: 'the God of peace,'[1] and bids them seal their restored harmony with the rite of the kiss of peace (v. 26).[2] In the words αὐτὸς δέ he seems to point away from the weakness of the converts' own unaided efforts and to place them under the supreme power of God.

So the first part of the prayer, 'May the God of peace himself sanctify you wholly,' would envisage the healthful reuniting of the church as a whole, including hopefully even those opponents who had brought divisiveness into the community.[3] It would prepare for the surprisingly sharply worded injunction,

[1] Paul's choice of this epithet may have been influenced also by liturgical considerations; see below pp. 70f. J. A. T. Robinson, 'Traces of a Liturgical Sequence in I Cor. 16: 20–24,' p. 40, n. 2, points out that 'the frequent occurrences in the final greetings, and nowhere else, of the formula "the God of peace" (Rom. 15: 33; 16: 20; 2 Cor. 13: 11; Phil. 4: 9; I Thess. 5: 23; Heb. 13: 20; cf. 2 Thess. 3: 16 – "The Lord of peace") suggests that this...may have a liturgical origin...[perhaps] introducing the Kiss of peace itself.' Gamble finds ready analogues at the close of Jewish prayers (p. 140).

Here (as in Rom. 16: 20a, Gal. 6: 16) Paul's customary short peace blessing (see Rom. 15: 33, II Cor. 13: 11b, Phil. 4: (7), 9b; [cf. Eph. 6: 23, II Thess. 3: 16a]) has been expanded into a summarizing wish-prayer. See Appendix IV, below.

[2] The kiss, as a pre-eucharistic liturgical rite, would symbolize the restoration of harmony given by 'the God of peace.' For parallel references to the holy kiss (φίλημα ἅγιον) in Paul's closing passages, see Rom. 16: 16, I Cor. 16: 20, II Cor. 13: 12, I Thess. 5: 26, probably Phil. 4: 21 (absent from Gal. and Philem.); cf. I Pet. 5: 14, Justin, *Apology*, i, 65, and many later allusions which show this as an established rite at a later date. The kiss would come at the close of the reading of the letter. For literature, see Bauer–Arndt–Gingrich, *ad verbum*. For a contrary view, see Gamble, pp. 155–8.

[3] See above, p. 57; below, p. 180.

'I adjure you by the Lord[1] that this letter be read to all the brethren' (v. 27)[2] – it must be read to *all*, friend and antagonist alike, so that none might escape the challenge of Paul's message.[3] The second part of the prayer, which extends and further explains the first, would refer perhaps more to the believers as individuals. Their need to be soberly and completely ready to meet Christ as the eschatological judge and savior (4: 13 – 5: 11) is re-emphasized in the request that they be kept blameless at the parousia: 'and may your spirit and soul and body be kept sound (ὁλόκληρον) and blameless.'[4] The statement

[1] The invocation of 'the Lord' as witness probably refers to the sanctioning cry 'Maranatha,' customarily used before the eucharist. See below, p. 152.

[2] Probably the early Christians were accustomed to meet in small separate groups in house churches. 'Separation from Christians of somewhat different background, views, and interests must have operated to prevent the growth of mutual understanding.' F. V. Filson, 'The Significance of the Early House Churches,' *JBL*, 58 (1939), 110.

[3] In Paul's other closing sections, similarly sharp warnings are placed in juxtaposition with personal greetings and a wish-prayer or blessing. It may be conjectured that these warnings were associated with the custom of preparatory self-examination and a separation of unworthy from worthy at the Lord's supper. This will become clearer when we examine the parallels at the end of Rom. and particularly I Cor. 16: 22, where the eucharistic setting seems most striking (pp. 150ff.). Bornkamm, in discussing the addition of chaps. 10–13 at the close of II Cor., suggested a formal regulation governing many early Christian writings, namely placing the warning against false teachers at the end of a writing. G. Bornkamm, 'Der Philipperbrief als Paulinische Briefsammlung,' *Neotestamentica et Patristica, Freundesgabe O. Cullmann*, Nov. Test. Suppl. 6 (1962), 192; cf. his article, 'The History of the Origin of the So-called Second Letter to the Corinthians,' *NTS*, 8 (1961–2), 261f. This custom may have originated partly in the way we have suggested.

The warning passages (which we shall consider individually) appear as follows: I Thess. 5: 27; Rom. 16: 17–20a (pp. 93f., and 97); Gal. 6: 11–13, 17 (pp. 129, 133); I Cor. 16: 22 (cf. 5: 2ff., and 11: 28) (pp. 150ff.); II Cor., throughout chaps. 10–13 (pp. 243f.). In Phil. the warning passage comes earlier, 3: 2 and 17–19, following suddenly on the personal messages in 2: 19 – 3: 1; for a possible reason, see below, p. 203. Cf. also p. 128 on Gal. 1: 8f., and p. 143, n. 3, and 146f. on I Cor. 5: 3–8. No warning passage appears in Philemon (p. 218, n. 2).

For an illuminating epistolary antecedent, see Jer. 29: 7–9, where an exhortation to prayer is followed immediately by a sharp warning against deceiving prophets. See above, p. 42, n. 3.

[4] ὁλόκληρον meaning 'in their entirely' – that 'no part of their Christian personality should be lacking in consecration,' Frame, p. 211. See also above, pp. 40, 60, n. 4.

that God has destined the converts for salvation (5: 9) is answered by the exultant declaration of God's faithfulness – the 'Amen' sentence of verse 24, 'He who calls you is faithful, and he will do it.'[1] Thus although the various emphases and motifs of the paraenetic section are not all given separate expression in the second intercessory wish-prayer, it seems clear that they are reflected there in a compact way, both as they refer to the community and to the individual members.

VARIED PURPOSES OF THE TWO WISH-PRAYERS

We may now draw together our answers to the questions proposed at the beginning of this chapter, insofar as I Thessalonians is concerned, and review some of the main purposes of the two principal wish-prayers. In the first place it has been made abundantly evident that both prayers are flexible enough, in spite of their conventional elements, to summarize and place the spotlight on the central message of the letter.

They express Paul's vital anxieties and hopes about the Thessalonian church and its members. It is his deep love for these believers, stressed repeatedly in the letter, that forms the matrix within which his supplications on their behalf are nurtured. Through the content and mood of the prayers the apostle has shown himself, furthermore, as an eschatological figure with an urgent, representative responsibility to prepare this young church and its members for the imminent parousia when he will present them to the Lord. So there is an extrava-

---

[1] See above, p. 35, n. 2, and below, p. 163, n. 3.

As the wish-prayer began with the address αὐτὸς δὲ ὁ θεός, thus emphasizing the *power* of God to carry out his sovereign designs, so it ends with a renewed assurance of the *faithfulness* of this God who has all power. Cf. Rigaux, *Thessaloniciens*, p. 601; von Dobschütz, p. 247.

Paul appeals several times elsewhere to this faithfulness of God who has called the believers: Rom. 3: 4, 4: 21, 8: 30–9; 11: 29, I Cor. 1: 9, 10: 13, II Cor. 1: 18, Phil. 1: 6, etc. [Cf. also II Thess. 3: 3, II Tim. 2: 13, Heb. 10: 13, 11: 11.] The assurance is rooted in the OT teaching that God would keep the covenant that he had made with Israel, e.g., Deut. 7: 9. Cf. J. Moltmann, *Theology of Hope*, E.Tr. (New York, 1967), pp. 143ff., 'The God of Promise.'

As a part of an autograph to the letter, this sentence might also be regarded as a stylistic adaptation of the customary closing confirmation of a business document. Cf. Bahr, 'Subscriptions in Pauline Letters,' p. 31.

gant and all-inclusive quality about the wish-prayers. All the believers must be included, love must be shown to all, all must be made complete. As missionary, pastor, friend, and intercessor he offers the believers to God in these brief but meaningful supplications.

Next, the prayers have been seen to have a paraenetic purpose.[1] By mentioning the needs of the readers in prayers which they themselves will read together during worship, the apostle is encouraging them before God to strive still harder in critical days.[2] So there is an intentional and practical connection between the detailed exhortations and the prayer passages that sum them up.

An instructional and perhaps catechetical function may be glimpsed too.[3] Orphal points to evidence that Paul considered it an important part of his missionary duty to give instructions about prayer, e.g., the directions to the Corinthians to pray 'with the mind' rather than to use ecstatic and unintelligible prayers 'in the spirit,' so that others might understand and be edified, and an outsider might say a meaningful 'Amen' (I Cor. 14: 13–19).[4] Thus, Paul's own prayers, when written to be read by others, would have edification in view and would be composed partly as pattern prayers: 'In church I would rather speak five words with my mind, in order to instruct others, than ten thousand words in a tongue' (v. 19).[5] Seen in

---

[1] See above, p. 59. This purpose they share with the thanksgiving and the prayer-reports, see below, pp. 173f., 183, etc. Cf. Furnish, p. 95.

[2] Cf. W. Eichrodt, *Theology of the Old Testament*, E.Tr., 2 vols (Philadelphia, 1961), I, 419, 'How forcefully...intercession reminds man of his responsibilities in the sight of the righteous God....'

[3] See above, pp. 9f., and below p. 183, etc.

[4] Orphal, pp. 105ff.

[5] As he frequently called upon his readers to imitate his example in other matters (cf. above, p. 58), so we may assume they would be expected to copy his prayers. Cf. Bieder, 'Gebetswirklichkeit und Gebetsmöglichkeit bei Paulus,' pp. 26f., for the proclamation element implied by the prayer-word κράзειν, cry; also J. Coutts, 'Ephesians i. 3–14 and I Peter i. 3–12,' *NTS*, 3 (1956–7), 115–27.

We are reminded also that both John and Jesus taught their disciples how to pray (Lk. 11: 1–4) and that the Jewish rabbis composed outline patterns for the synagogue prayers (see above, p. 24, n. 4). See Bahr, 'The Use of the Lord's Prayer in the Primitive Church,' pp. 154–7, for further details. Cf. J. Jeremias, *The Prayers of Jesus*, p. 77, '...religious groups were dis-

the light of this statement, the extreme brevity of many of the prayer passages in the epistles need not be thought to detract entirely from their significance as prayer models.[1]

This leads us to the liturgical purpose that must have partly inspired the prayer passages and especially the final section of the epistle. It was in composing this early letter to be read at Thessalonica in association with the Lord's supper, that Paul may for the first time have developed such a liturgically oriented closing pattern,[2] and included an expanded peace blessing that pointed forward to the kiss of peace, and to the self-examination that must accompany and follow the reading of the letter to all. Although the actual reading of such an apostolic letter and especially its prayer passages (the opening blessing of grace and peace, the repeated thanksgiving, the various intercessory passages) would constitute a moving act of united worship and prayer, yet the final passages in particular would form a deliberate transition into the celebration of the eucharist.[3] So in this special context at the end of the letter, the second wish-prayer would be particu-

tinguished among other things by their characteristic prayers'; also p. 94. Cf. N. Perrin, *The Kingdom of God in the Teaching of Jesus* (Philadelphia, 1963), p. 191. Perrin considers that 'the Lord's Prayer is obviously one of the most important sections of teaching that we possess...it was taught to disciples of Jesus and must therefore be held to reflect those aspects of their experience which Jesus himself held to be most important, those things about which he taught them to pray.'

[1] Compare the surprising conciseness of the Lord's Prayer, and the teaching of Jesus that prayer should be brief (Matt. 6: 7–13).

[2] Cf. Filson, '*Yesterday.*' *A Study of Hebrews*, p. 82: 'Possibly Paul set this pattern. Possibly it arose without conscious literary planning as the inevitable result of preparing a message to be read aloud to a congregation (or congregations) located at a distance from the city where the writer finds himself.'

[3] See above, pp. 42ff., 51f. For literature, see p. 10, n. 2. J. A. T. Robinson concludes about I Cor. 16: 20–24 that, 'All the phrases of the final greetings take on new depths and significance. They are the language, not merely of epistolary convention, but of one worshiping community to another, the converse of the saints assembled for Eucharist. The salutations, the kiss, the peace, the grace are all rich with the overtones of worship. The last word of the letter is the first of the liturgy, the one being written to lead into the other.' 'Liturgical Sequence,' p. 40.

We have here anticipated our later discussion of the ending of I Cor. See below, pp. 150ff.

larly intended to form a part of the corporate worship of the readers.[1]

Furthermore, as we come to study the parallel, though varied, progressions that end the other letters, our impression will be strengthened that Paul was adapting elements from loosely formed eucharistic liturgical material already employed in some of his churches.[2]

But may we in addition claim with Bornemann that, in the very act of writing the wish-prayers, the apostle is thinking not only of the effect upon his readers, but is himself consciously offering up intercessory prayer to God?[3] An affirmative answer may be suggested by the ancient custom that had used the wish-prayer form to offer direct supplications. This mode of expression would therefore constitute a natural means of petition to God.[4] Furthermore, the very involvement and anxiety that so obviously filled the apostle's thoughts, together with his continued sense that all was being done under the direction of God and before God, would suggest that as he penned the wish-prayers he was turning to God in prayer. In priestly fashion he was placing the hard-pressed converts before the God of faithfulness, that they might be prepared for the great forthcoming crisis.[5]

---

[1] It is striking that Baruch contains a long prayer of corporate confession, specially composed for the use of the readers on feast days and seasons. Bar. 1: 14 and 1: 15 – 3: 8. Cf. Syr. Bar. 86: 2, where the readers are instructed to meditate on the letter, especially on fast days. See above, p. 9, n. 4, and p. 42, n. 3.

[2] J. A. T. Robinson, 'Liturgical Sequence,' p. 39. Cf. below, pp. 114f., 150ff.

[3] See above, p. 53, n. 1.

[4] See above, pp. 26f. We shall see later that the prayer-reports, too, seem to have served to offer prayers of thanksgiving and intercession; p. 186, 194, etc.

[5] Cf. Dahl, 'Paul as Intercessor,' p. 180: 'Thus also *the writing of letters* belongs to Paul's intercessory mission.' Dahl points out other intercessors as letter-writers, e.g., Jeremiah (Jer. 29), also Syr. Bar. 34, and 77–86. In his letter to the nine-and-a-half tribes the writer describes his intercessory supplications on behalf of Jerusalem, and then extends this into the ministry of letter-writing: 'For I was mourning regarding Zion, and I prayed for mercy from the Most High, and I said: "How long will these things endure for us? And will these evils come upon us always?"' (81: 1f.). Shortly after, he continues, 'Therefore, my brethren, I have written you, that ye may comfort yourselves regarding the multitude of your tribulations...' (82: 1).

CHAPTER 5

FUNCTION OF THE WISH-PRAYERS IN ROMANS, I CORINTHIANS, AND PHILIPPIANS

THE WISH-PRAYERS IN ROMANS

A continuation of our study of the main Pauline wish-prayers brings us from the comparatively slight Thessalonian document to the profound and complex theological treatise which the apostle addressed to the important church in the capital city of Rome. So we turn now to four intercessory wish-prayers found in the Roman letter: 15: 5f., 15: 13, 15: 33, 16: 20a. These all contribute to an extended liturgical pattern (in chapters 15 and 16) that would be adequate to bring this weighty epistle to a close.[1] What are the functions of these passages? Do they, like the ones in the Thessalonian letter, express real prayer arising out of the immediate circumstances and concerns of the letter? Do they, too, fulfil other purposes?

Background and purpose of the letter

We must begin, then, with the epistolary situation for which the letter was composed. The unusual nature and content of the letter as we have it[2] force the question upon the reader: was Paul mainly concerned to introduce his own missionary plans and the central elements of his own gospel to an unknown church, or was he responding to a particular situation which he believed to be present at Rome, and which the letter was designed to alleviate?[3]

On one hand the apostle seems to show unmistakably at the

[1] In the meantime we must anticipate the description of this pattern given below, pp. 95ff.

[2] We assume with the majority of scholars the authenticity of Rom. 1: 1 – 15: 33, as a document written by Paul for Rome, and sent to Rome. As for chap. 16, our conclusion will be that apart from the elaborate final doxology (vv. 25–7), it was an original part of the letter sent to Rome (see below, pp. 92ff.). For literature, see Rigaux, *St. Paul et ses lettres*, pp. 158f.

It is assumed also that the letter was sent from Corinth during Paul's last stay there, A.D. 55 or 56. But see above, p. 46, n. 1.

[3] Cf. above, p. 46, n. 2.

opening and the close of the letter that his immediate purpose is the furtherance of his own broad missionary projects (1: 8–17 and 15: 14–33).[1] The epistle is by way of introduction, and to solicit the sympathy and assistance of the important Christian community at Rome. The profound importance of this request and its extreme eschatological urgency for him may be gauged from his announced strategy to use Rome as a new base of operations for an extension of his work to the Latin half of the Roman empire, where the gospel had evidently not yet been preached (15: 20–9). For many years his thoughts have been pointing in this direction (1: 13, 15: 33 and cf. Acts 19: 21), and how the time seems ripe. He needs to ensure the help rather than the opposition of a church which he had not founded, which had not officially invited him, which would have its own theological aspect, and its own direct lines of communication with the mother church at Jerusalem.[2] He must write to introduce himself to those members who did not yet know him, and to assure them of his apostolic credentials.

On the other hand, we appear to be confronted by a strange incongruity in the content and structure of the central body of the letter (1: 16 – 15: 13).[3] It appears both too lengthy and at the same time too incomplete[4] to serve merely as a letter of introduction.[5] A more complex motivation seems to be called for, that takes into account also the specific situation that Paul envisaged in the Christian community at Rome.[6]

The very fact that he looks forward to the support of Rome for a whole new epoch of his mission work, must awaken in him a deep concern that the church be united and stable

[1] Michel, *Der Brief an die Römer*, p. 13. Cf. Funk, 'Saying and Seeing: Phenomenology of Language and the New Testament,' p. 210, 'The two passages serve as brackets which enclose and justify the body of the letter.'

[2] The tone of the letter suggests how anxious he is about the nature of the reception he will receive. On the delicacy of his position, see below, pp. 188, 191.

[3] Michel, p. 13.

[4] E.g., it neglects the Pauline doctrines of christology, eschatology, the Lord's supper, church polity.

[5] Cf. E. Trocmé, 'L'Épître aux Romains et la Méthode Missionaire de l'Apôtre Paul,' *NTS*, 7 (1960–1), 148–53.

[6] For an illuminating recent discussion of this question, see P. S. Minear, *The Obedience of Faith: The Purposes of Paul in the Epistle to the Romans, SBT*, Second Series, 19 (London, 1971).

enough to provide this strong backing. So there is warrant for the attempt to discover in the body of the epistle a message in some way related to the particular needs of his readers, even if those needs do not seem to be as precisely or personally delineated as in the Thessalonian, Galatian, and Corinthian letters.[1] At any rate he would scarcely have had the temerity to give warnings as specific as those in chapters 14–15, had he not in some way been given reason to think them particularly relevant.[2]

The letter suggests a situation of disharmony and fragmentation among the loosely associated Christian groups in the capital city.[3] A small and sensitive minority of Jewish Christians seems to have needed protection against the stronger Gentile majority (cf. Rom. 11: 1–36, 14: 1–25).[4] Such troublesome dissension would account for the various changes of front in

[1] For instance, in this letter he is content to suggest in merely vague terms that he hopes to bring to them 'some spiritual gift' (1: 11).

[2] Because of the doubtful status of chap. 16, the specific injunctions of 16: 17–20 must be used with reservation, as a clue to the nature of the letter.

Scholars who claim that Paul writes of problems known to exist at Rome include W. Lütgert, *Der Römerbrief als historisches Problem* (Gütersloh, 1913); Michel; Trocmé, with reservations. Cf. also K. H. Rengstorf, 'Paulus und die römische Christenheit,' *Studia Evangelica*, 2 (1964), 447–64; W. Marxsen, *Introduction to the New Testament*, E.Tr. (Philadelphia, 1968), pp. 95–104; K. P. Donfried, 'A Short Note on Romans 16,' *JBL*, 89 (1970), 441–9. Minear argues cogently for this claim.

Against this view are Sanday and Headlam, p. 401f.; T. W. Manson, 'St. Paul's Letter to the Romans – and Others,' *BJRL*, 31 (1948), 3–19; M.-J. Lagrange, *Saint Paul, Épître aux Romains* (Paris, 1950), p. xxxiii; F.-J. Leenhardt, *The Epistle to the Romans; a Commentary*, E.Tr., 3rd edn (London, 1964), pp. 13ff.; Munck, *Paul and the Salvation of Mankind*, pp. 197ff.; P. Althaus, *Der Brief an die Römer*, 6th edn (Göttingen, 1949), pp. 1f.; A. Roosen, 'Le genre littéraire de l'Epître aux Romains,' *Studia Evangelica*, 2 (1964), 465–71.

[3] See W. Marxsen, pp. 95–104; Minear, *Obedience of Faith*, pp. 7f.; H.-W. Bartsch, 'The Concept of Faith in Paul's Letter to the Romans,' *Biblical Research*, XIII (1968), 41–53; Filson, 'The Significance of the Early House Churches,' p. 106.

[4] We assume with Feine–Behm–Kümmel, p. 219, that both Jewish and Gentile Christians were represented; see also Sanday and Headlam, p. xxxiiif.; Leenhardt, pp. 11f.; Michel, pp. 8–13. For a contrary opinion see Munck, *Paul and the Salvation of Mankind*, pp. 201–5; T. Fahy, 'St. Paul's Romans were Jewish Converts,' *The Irish Theological Quarterly*, 26 (1959), 182–91.

the letter as Paul turns his attention to one or the other of these groups.[1] It would account also for the emphasis that his apostolic commission is to both Jew and Greek, that both groups need the gospel equally, and that both are included within its saving scope (e.g., 1: 14–16, 1: 18 – 3: 20, chaps. 9–11, etc.). It is for the same reason that in the final 'travel plan' section he highlights the central, practical symbol of unity between Gentile and Jewish Christians – the collection – and enlists the readers' prayerful involvement in that symbol (15: 25–33).

Yet although the epistle cannot be understood as merely a rounded compendium of Pauline doctrine, it does evidence a well-defined and subtly reasoned argument that progresses with a double front facing both Judaizers and antinomians. This has led some interpreters to envisage the body of the letter as a document previously crystallized out from the apostle's debates with the Galatian churches and with the Corinthian church during his last stay there (Acts 20: 2f.).[2] The use of such a tract would account for the otherwise surprising length and weight of a letter intended for a self-introduction.[3] While it is not necessary to accept the letter as constituting such a ready-made document in unaltered form, it does appear to represent the mature fruits of his long missionary experience and sustained theological reflection on the relation of the gospel of liberty to the Jewish law.[4]

We conclude that in composing the letter to the Romans, the apostle has mixed aims, involving primarily his own missionary plans, but closely tied with these, his deep interest in the unity

[1] Yet Paul's use of the diatribe style prevents our being sure of this. See R. Bultmann, *Der Stil der Paulinischen Predigt und die Kynischstoische Diatribe* (Göttingen, 1910).

Minear (*Obedience of Faith, passim*) advances a provocative analysis of these changes of front throughout the letter. Paul addresses in turn various groups whose identity is revealed in chap. 14: the weak in faith (with legalistic tendencies), the strong in faith (with libertine tendencies), the wavering doubters, sometimes the readers as a whole.

[2] 'A record made by Paul and his clerical helpers [and sent] to Rome with a statement of his future plans' (Manson, p. 18f., followed by Munck).

[3] Trocmé, pp. 151–3; C. H. Dodd, *The Epistle of Paul to the Romans*, MNTC (New York, 1932), pp. xxix–xxxi.

[4] The presence in Rome of many of Paul's friends would make it possible for him to go beyond the limits of a purely introductory letter (see below, p. 92, n. 6).

and welfare of a church with which he hopes to establish an enduring partnership. He expounds his own mature understanding of some central aspects of the gospel as these may be adapted to problems in the church to which he is writing. His letter of introduction is designed to foster a growing partnership in the gospel, of mutual benefit to the apostle with his urgent mission, and also to 'all God's beloved in Rome' (1: 7).

So it is within this many-sided network of hopes and purposes that the prayer passages must be placed. They are to be interpreted not merely in relation to the local church situation (as in the Thessalonian epistle), but in the light of the apostle's broader visions and purposes for the church at large.

Survey of the intercessory prayer and related prayer passages in Romans[1]

As a part of the epistolary salutations, he requests for his readers at the outset the gifts of grace and peace, in the standard opening benediction (1: 7b).[2] In the thanksgiving period that follows, he selects for acknowledgement the renowned faith of the church in the capital city (1: 8), adding the usual assurances about his unceasing, prayerful remembrance of them, and his requests to God that he may at length be enabled to visit them (1: 9f.).

Within the main body of the letter, there occur in the section about life in the Spirit (chap. 8), three important references to the aid of the Spirit who intercedes. The Spirit witnesses inwardly to our being truly sons of God (8: 15f.), arouses in us an inward longing for the completion of that sonship (8: 23), and intercedes for us who do not know how to pray as we ought (8: 26f.). It is in this section, too, that the apostle makes his only statement about the intercession of the risen and exalted Christ on our behalf (8: 34). In the following chapters, which treat of his perplexity about the rejection of their Christ by the Jews (chaps. 9–11), he includes two poignant reports about his intercessory attitude and his sorrowful petitions for his blind fellow countrymen (9: 1–3, 10: 1). In the same vein he refers to the intercession of Elijah against recalcitrant Israel (11: 2ff.).

---

[1] For supplication passages, see Appendix II. We omit here references to such exclamations of thanks as are found in 6: 17f., and 7: 25.

[2] Cf. below, pp. 108ff. on the opening benediction.

Yet in the end he offers up an exalted doxology before the mystery of the divine wisdom (11: 33–6).

When he moves into the paraenetic section (chaps. 12–15), he exhorts his readers to pray constantly and to bless even their persecutors (12: 12c, 14). Proceeding with the extended liturgically oriented pattern that appears in chapters 15 and 16,[1] he concludes the central body of the letter with two closely connected wish-prayers that sum up his hopes for the Roman church (15: 5f. and 15: 13); a priestly reference to his ministry to the Gentiles and his 'boasting' on their behalf (15: 15ff.); an earnest appeal that his readers, too, join him in intercessory prayers for the successful completion of his symbolic mission to Jerusalem, and his subsequent visit to themselves (15: 30–2); and a short peace blessing (15: 33). In the postscript (16: 1–23)[2] there are added the greetings, to be sealed with the holy kiss (16: 16), the stern warning (16: 17–19), a last wish-prayer (adapted peace blessing) for their victory over the intruding troublemakers (16: 20a), and the final grace benediction (16: 20b).[3]

Taken all together, the prayer passages in Romans seem to form a varied and impressive documentation of the apostle's deep reliance on a ministry of intercessory supplication.

Two related wish-prayers – Romans 15: 5f., and 15: 13

We turn now to the functional characteristics of the two intercessory wish-prayers found in close association with each other at the conclusion of the central body of the letter. For what specific purposes did Paul include them?

May the God of steadfastness and encouragement grant you to live in such harmony with one another, in accord with Christ Jesus, that together you may with one voice glorify the God and Father of our Lord Jesus Christ. (Rom. 15: 5f.)

May the God of hope fill you with all joy and peace in believing, so that by the power of the Holy Spirit you may abound in hope. (Rom. 15: 13)

At the outset it may be noted that the two prayer passages belong within a well-defined and closely knit unit of the letter

---

[1] For a fuller description of this pattern in relation to the one in I Thess., see below, pp. 95ff.

[2] See below, pp. 91ff.

[3] Omitting the doxology (16: 25–7) as a later addition; see above, p. 72, n. 2.

(14: 1 – 15: 13). A sudden change of style from the conventional paraenetic manner of the preceding chapters (12–13) indicates a transition to a new section; the apostle would now deal more directly with the particular problem that he judged to be threatening the congregations at Rome. It concerned, as we have indicated, dissensions between the 'strong' and the 'weak' in faith, those of 'robust conscience' and those of 'tender scruples.'[1] The over-scrupulousness of some members in regard to abstentions from meat and wine and the observance or non-observance of sacred days[2] led to difficulties both for themselves and their stronger brethren. These particular dissensions are, however, an example of the more general difficulties between Jewish and Gentile Christians which had occupied Paul throughout the epistle. Thus, as we have suggested, it is quite probable that the whole letter received its final shape with the special Roman difficulties in view.

Paul's counsel in this part of the letter consists of a progressive argument in which he warns both parties in the dispute. Every member, strong or weak, was accountable to his own Master and Lord alone, Christ who had died for all that he might be Lord of all. Everyone must live his life and make his decisions to the honor of the Lord alone[3] (14: 4, 6–9). But to serve and honor Christ meant also to be accountable to God, and to live in such a way as to give thanks and praise to God (14: 3b, 6, 10b, 11f., 18). It meant to be freed from the disapproval of other men (v. 18). Therefore neither side had any right to condemn the other (14: 3f., 10, 13a, 18b).

Yet they must go even further. Each side must extend the hand of positive welcome to the other, while in particular the strong must not please themselves but lend support to the weak, after the example of Jesus Christ the self-forgetting messianic

[1] NEB.

[2] Various groups, both pagan and Jewish, practised such abstentions and observances – Orphics, Pythagoreans, Philo's Therapeutae, and cf. Dan. 10: 3. See Michel, p. 297, Sanday and Headlam, pp. 399ff. But very likely a Jewish group is implicated here, particularly as Paul goes on to speak of Jews and Gentiles (15: 7–12). However, the division may not have been simply between Jewish and Gentile Christians; see Althaus, p. 117.

[3] See W. Kramer, *Christ, Lord, Son of God*, E.Tr., *SBT*, 50 (London, 1966), pp. 170f. (par. 47c).

servant (15: 1–3, 7).[1] All must strive for the harmony, peace, and mutual upbuilding of the fellowship (14: 19).

The discussion unfolds in three sections: the first emphasizes the theme that all men, weak and strong in faith, belong to and should praise the same Lord (14: 1–12). The second stresses the need to consider the interests of the other members (14: 13–23). The third (15: 1–13) develops the positive duty of the strong to bear the burdens of others, and then of both sides to welcome one another in common worship and praise. So the third section (the immediate context of our wish-prayers) divides into two paragraphs (vv. 1–6 and 7–13) which in several ways run parallel, both pointing to Christ's intercessory obedience, both quoting the Scriptures, both ending with the climax of a wish-prayer which draws together the themes of that paragraph. The latter paragraph, however, is directed to both strong and weak, calling on all to join freely in common praises, in fulfil-ment of God's long-standing purposes for all.[2] We may proceed now to examine the two prayers in the light of this context.

Romans 15: 5f.

In the first wish-prayer (15: 5f.) Paul takes up two of the main themes of his exhortation about the weak and the strong:[3] that they may be enabled to live in harmony as servants of Christ, and thus receive the additional benefit of giving united praise and glory to God.

The prayer begins with an appropriately chosen address to God as 'the God of steadfastness (or patient endurance, ὑπομονῆς) and encouragement' (παρακλήσεως),[4] echoing the words of the immediately preceding verse (διὰ τῆς ὑπομονῆς καὶ διὰ τῆς παρακλήσεως τῶν γραφῶν). Paul has just reminded his readers that these gifts are offered to them, both through the example of the Christ who did not please himself but patiently bore the reproaches of others, and through the Scriptures that

---

[1] Taking βαστάζειν (15: 1) to mean 'accept as our own burden' (cf. Gal. 6: 2); NEB, and various commentators.

[2] The connecting words between the two paragraphs (διό in v. 7, and λέγω γάρ in v. 8) suggest that the second paragraph draws and extends the conclusions of the first (cf. τί οὖν ἐροῦμεν, 8: 31; οὐ γὰρ θέλω ὑμᾶς ἀγνοεῖν ἀδελφοί, 11: 25); Sanday and Headlam, p. 397. So also Leenhardt, p. 364.

[3] For the connective significance of the particle δέ, see above, p. 31.

[4] Cf. II Cor. 1: 3, θεὸς πάσης παρακλήσεως. See above, p. 31.

had witnessed to this Christ (vv. 3f.; cf. Ps. 69: 9). The Scriptures are an additional means of suggesting patience, encouragement, and hope to them.[1] But now it is God himself who must bring these graces to fruition in them.[2]

In mentioning the grace of patient endurance (ὑπομονή)[3] Paul reinforces a theme which has appeared several times earlier in this letter and is clearly much in his thoughts as he writes (2: 7, 5: 3–5, 8: 25, 12: 12, 15: 4, 5). It is associated with θλίψις or παθήματα, both in this letter (5: 3, cf. 8: 18, 25, 35), and in his letter to the Thessalonians (I Thess. 1: 3, 6).[4] Especially during the last messianic woes it becomes an essential eschatological Christian gift – the patient, hopeful, endurance of those trials which were destined for believers in this special age.[5] But for the believers of Rome there is needed a particular kind of patience, that the strong may be enabled to bear with the failings of the weak and not to please themselves (15: 1–3).

By appealing also to 'the God of encouragement (παράκλησις),'[6] the apostle recalls a main purpose of his proposed

[1] Taking τῶν γραφῶν as governing both substantives: patience and encouragement given by the scriptures. Stylistically this appears to be a formula borrowed by Paul. Cf. II Tim. 3: 16.

[2] The Semitic prayer-style genitives suggest this: 'The God who gives patience and encouragement.' See above, p. 31, n. 4.

[3] In the NT the meaning includes patience, endurance, fortitude, steadfastness, perseverance, confidence. See C. Spicq, "Ὑπομονή, Patientia,' *RSPT*, 19 (1930), 95–105; A.-J. Festugière, "Ὑπομονή dans la tradition grecque,' *Recherches de Science Religieuse*, 21 (1931), 477–86; Bauer–Arndt–Gingrich, *ad verbum*.

[4] See below, pp. 179f.

[5] Note especially its use in Revelation (7 times) for the endurance of the saints under tribulation.

[6] The meaning here seems to include both exhortation–admonition and consolation–comfort. In the NT both meanings are found, but the former predominates. See O. Schmitz, *TWNT*, v, 790–8; T. Y. Mullins, 'Petition as a Literary Form,' *Nov. Test.* 5 (1964), 53, on the παρακαλεῖν, or personal type of petition. παράκλησις was a recognized form of early Christian ministry, see Rom. 12: 8. It applied the word of God concretely to a particular situation, and is referred to in this sense in every one of Paul's epistles (Michel, p. 259). In our passage the apostle has in mind primarily the need of the strong for admonition from the scriptures (15: 1–4); E. Gaugler, *Der Römerbrief*, 2 vols, Zürcher Bibelkommentare (Zurich, 1945–50), I, 363; cf. Phil. 4: 2.

Yet the epithet 'ὁ δὲ θεὸς τῆς παρακλήσεως' must also partly recall the God of comfort of the Old Testament (Schmitz, pp. 786f.), and is illumi-

visit to Rome and presumably of the letter: 'that is, that we may be mutually encouraged (συμπαρακληθῆναι) by each other's faith, yours and mine' (1: 12).[1] So already at the beginning of the letter there had been suggested the kind of strength which might accrue from the harmonious interchange of different understandings of the faith. Even more strikingly he echoes here the formula of 'paraclesis' which had introduced the paraenetic section of the letter (12: 1–2):[2] 'I appeal (παρακαλῶ) to you therefore, brethren, by the mercies of God, to present your bodies as a living sacrifice, holy and acceptable to God, which is your spiritual worship (τὴν λογικὴν λατρείαν ὑμῶν)...' As he had begun the paraenetic section with this all-encompassing appeal to his readers in the name of God, to present themselves as a living sacrifice of worship, so now he draws it towards a close by taking them back in prayer to the God of 'paraclesis,' who may encourage and enable them to offer their united worship of deed and word.

We turn now to the requests. The first petition (15: 5), that it be granted[3] to the Roman believers to overcome their dissensions and to live in harmony with one another (ἐν ἀλλήλοις) as servants of Christ, epitomizes in prayer the central admonition of chapters 14 and 15 to the weak and the strong in faith: that both the robust of conscience and the more scrupulous might learn to welcome one another (προσλαμβάνεσθε ἀλλήλους, 15: 7). Earlier, the apostle had given a similar injunction, 'Live in harmony with one another; do not be haughty, but associate with the lowly; never be conceited' (12: 16).[4]

The pregnant phrase, 'in accord with Christ Jesus' (κατὰ

nated especially by the blessing passage in II Cor. 1: 3–7, 'the Father of mercies and God of all comfort (παρακλήσεως).' Bauer–Arndt–Gingrich suggests consolation (for v. 4), as does Leenhardt (for v. 5). Cf. Furnish (p. 109) where it is argued that paraclesis comprises for Paul the ideas of exhortation, encouragement, and comfort.

[1] Cf. a similar reference to mutual παράκλησις in Philem. 7.

[2] This transition is itself prepared for by 6: 12–23; 8: 12f. (Michel, p. 256). For the formal aspects of the transition, see Sanders, 'Transition from Opening Thanksgiving...,' pp. 349ff.; also Bjerkelund, *Parakalô-Sätze*.

[3] For the confidence implied by the optative δῴη (may he grant), see above, p. 34, n. 3.

[4] Cf. Minear, *Obedience of Faith*, pp. 82–90. Cf. also 12: 3–13, discussed below, pp. 289f.

Χριστὸν Ἰησοῦν),[1] sums up much of the immediately preceding discussion, where the life of harmony had been grounded in Christ as Lord, and illustrated by Christ as messianic servant. Thus every member had been shown to be accountable for his own decisions only to his Master, Christ; every member must be treated in love as one for whom Christ had died; every member must follow the example of Christ, by bearing the burdens of the others as he had done who pleased not himself.

The second petition, for the additional benefit that must follow from the first, takes up several more emphases from Paul's preceding discussions and lifts the prayer to a climax of praise: 'such...that together you may with one voice glorify the God and Father of our Lord Jesus Christ' (15: 6).

The words ὁμοθυμαδὸν ἐν ἑνὶ στόματι[2] suggest that the restored harmony between the quarrelling groups might now find expression in their gatherings for worship. Their acceptable spiritual worship of living daily so as to praise God (cf. 12: 1) could now be symbolized in the united liturgical worship of their hymns. Through the overcoming of difficulties about diet and feast days, spontaneous and united praises to God would become inevitable and, together with the kiss of peace,[3] would serve to cement their renewed fellowship.

Here as in his preceding passage the apostle moves from the lordship of Christ to the lordship of God. Thus the prayer ends as it had begun, with an elevated, divine appellation, and acknowledges that 'the God of steadfastness and encouragement' is known as 'the God and Father of our Lord Jesus Christ.' It is argued by Kramer that the latter liturgical phrase 'is really a formula[4] which Paul took over together with its

---

[1] Cf. II Cor. 11: 17 [Col. 2: 8, Eph. 4: 24]; 'in accordance with the example or character of Christ,' Sanday and Headlam, p. 396.

[2] This phrase seems to have represented a stock Jewish expression for united praise or hymn singing: see Dan. 3: 51 (LXX), II Chron. 18: 12 (LXX). Harder, p. 57.

[3] As he moves into the extended liturgical ending of the letter (see below, pp. 95ff.), the apostle may already have in mind the exchanging of the holy kiss (Rom. 16: 16). Cf. the second wish-prayer in I Thess. (above, p. 66).

[4] Cf. II Cor. 11: 31 [Eph. 1: 17, I Pet. 1: 3].

original setting,' evidently from the Hellenistic Gentile Christian church.[1] Its origin, he thinks, was 'not on the basis of theological reflection, but out of liturgical necessity,' in order to enable the worshipper 'to give clear Christian expression to the designation "Father" for God...and to bring this into relationship with the Lord.'[2] But more significant for our immediate purpose is to note that these closing words confirm an important aspect of Paul's preceding discussion: that it is through honoring Christ that they may bring honor to God.[3]

Besides this, the second petition completes the theme of accountability by raising it now to the highest level – that of glorifying God in united joyful celebration. Paul had shown that to live accountably to God in accord with Christ Jesus was indeed to place their conduct beyond the judgment of others. But to live so that one's life expressed inward thankfulness and praise to God (14: 6–8, 11), would be to elevate the motivation of one's conduct to an altogether higher level; thankfulness would lift a man above mere dutiful obedience, and above the temptation to claim his freedom at the expense of others. He would be raised into the kingdom, where the important issues were not rules about food and drink, nor judging or provoking others in these matters, but the higher gifts of righteousness and peace and joy in the Holy Spirit (14: 17).[4]

Thus the prayer that they glorify God is a crowning petition that their lives be raised through thankfulness and praise above the levels of petty dissension and provocation. In addition, the exalted note of doxology would serve to introduce the following paragraph, where the Gentiles, too, are shown to praise and rejoice in their salvation – a section which will bring the whole central body of the letter to a close on a note of triumph and hope (15: 7–13).

[1] See Kramer, par. 21a, on p. 93.

[2] Par. 21 b, on p. 94. See also Michel, p. 320, n. 3, and Harder, p. 92. Confessional overtones are found by H. Lietzmann, *An die Römer*, *HzNT*, 8, 3rd edn (Tübingen, 1928), p. 113. Similar prayer phrases, linking God and Christ, are discussed above, p. 55, n. 3, and below, p. 112.

[3] See above, p. 78.

[4] An illuminating parallel is found in Gal. 5: 22–6, 'The fruit of the Spirit is love, joy, peace...gentleness, self-control....Let us have no self-conceit, no provoking one another, no envy of one another.'

Romans 15: 13

We continue now to the next paragraph (15: 7–13) and the wish-prayer that concludes it (v. 13). Here, as we have seen, Paul goes beyond his admonition to the strong in faith. Now he urges both parties, strong and weak, to welcome one another to join in the united praises to God, for both have been welcomed in turn by the same Christ (v. 7). As he had argued earlier (chaps. 9–11), he insists again that circumcised Jew and uncircumcised Gentile are bound inextricably together under the same merciful purpose of God's *Heilsgeschichte*, revealed in scripture and confirmed by Christ (vv. 8f.). Jews must realize that Gentiles are now called to join in the crescendo of rejoicing, praise, and hope (vv. 9–12),[1] so that they too may form a part of the great sacrificial offering to be made by him to God (v. 16). It is with this joyous expectation that the apostle turns to his exalted, concluding supplication: that the God who had originated this all-inclusive hope in Christ might now fulfil it for all the believers in Rome.

The prayer begins with an address to the God who can give hope;[2] it moves into the first petition – for the gifts needed immediately by the quarrelling Roman readers, joy, peace, faith; the second petition follows from the first (εἰς τὸ περισσεύειν), and requests that the God of hope now give them the final blessing of abundant hope. In this way they may be prepared to match the apostle's own hopeful plans, as he looks forward to the extension of his work beyond Rome.

By choosing to address his prayer to 'the God of hope,' Paul moves into the eschatological climax,[3] and claims the last blessing from God which he desires for his readers. Referring back to the phrase 'that we might have hope' (v. 4), he now goes on to underscore the promising elements hidden within the very problems that seem so disturbing at Rome. The very occurrence of these difficulties, indeed, points toward the dynamic fulfilment of God's promises in the eschatological era

---

[1] The quotations, with their heightening of style, are from all three sections of the OT: Torah, Nebi'im, and Kethubim; Michel, p. 322.

[2] The God of hope is the God who gives hope: see above, p. 31, n. 4. Once again we observe how appropriately the apostle selects each title of address for his prayers.

[3] See above, p. 41.

that has now dawned.[1] The coming in of the Gentiles brings many tensions, it is true, but also untold occasions for the discovery of peace, joy, and hope. Let the Roman readers go forward, then, unfettered by past scruples, and full of hope, to meet the future which God will open up before them.[2]

The words 'fill' (πληρῶσαι),[3] 'all' (πάσης), and 'abound' (περισσεύειν), typify once more that overflowing style which we have seen to characterize most of Paul's intercessory prayer requests.[4] Such is his belief in the boundless riches of God's grace in the new age, and so consuming is his passion for the complete blamelessness of all believers, Jew and Greek, that he can be satisfied with no half-measure of the gifts of the Spirit, nor that anyone in any church should fail to attain to them in the short time left before the consummation. Therefore his prayer for their abundant fullness in these gifts leads his thoughts back to the completion of his own urgent plans as priestly apostle to the Gentiles.

Indeed, he will go on immediately (15: 14ff., cf. 1: 13–15) to reiterate why, in spite of the undoubted gifts of the Roman Christians (15: 14, cf. 1: 8), he has felt bold enough to exhort, and to intercede for them in priestly fashion: 'I have written to you very boldly because of the grace given me by God to be a minister of Christ Jesus (λειτουργὸν Χριστοῦ Ἰησοῦ) to the Gentiles in the priestly service (ἱερουργοῦντα) of the Gospel of God, so that the offering of the Gentiles may be acceptable, consecrated by the Holy Spirit' (15: 15f.).[5] Paul sees himself as somehow necessary so that the Gentiles may be offered completely acceptable to God, and he is therefore so bold as to

---

[1] For the eschatological significance of the word 'hope,' see R. Bultmann and K. H. Rengstorf, *TWNT*, II, 515–30, especially 527–9. See also Moltmann, *Theology of Hope*, for an impressive emphasis on the centrality of the themes of promise and hope in biblical thought: e.g., 'The God spoken of here is no intra-worldly or extra-worldly God, but the "God of hope" (Rom. 15. 13), a God with "future as his essential nature" (as E. Bloch puts it), as made known in Exodus and in Israelite prophecy...' (p. 16, and *passim*).

[2] Leenhardt, p. 365.

[3] B and G read πληροφορησαι, fill completely. For the significance of the optative, see above, p. 34, n. 3.

[4] See above, p. 60, n. 4.

[5] Cf. Isa. 66: 20, all the nations as an offering to the Lord. See K. Weiss, 'Paulus – Priester der christl. Kultgemeinde,' pp. 355–63.

include the Romans within the scope of his intercessory ministry.[1]

In asking for 'joy' and 'peace,' he selects graces which would be most endangered by their unfortunate divisions.[2] In linking joy, peace, and hope with the power of the Holy Spirit,[3] he recalls his previous references to the kingdom of God that meant not 'food and drink but righteousness[4] and peace and joy in the Holy Spirit' (14: 17). Now in prayer he would raise his readers into this exalted kingdom. The words ἐν τῷ πιστεύειν[5] must refer back partly to the question of the weak and strong in faith (τῇ πίστει), and to that obedient faith through which a man may be approved of God in what he does (14: 1, 2, 22f.). So he prays that, as each exercises his own faith, through the Holy Spirit they may find together not the seeds of dissension, but the opposite gifts of joy and peace.

It may be noted further that the prayer draws together and applies to his readers some of the main themes of the whole preceding letter: peace and reconciliation, joy, faith, hope, the

---

[1] See R. M. Cooper, 'Leitourgos Christou Iesou. Toward a Theology of Christian Prayer,' *ATR*, 47 (1965), 263–75. We may observe a priestly, cultic train of thought appearing at intervals through the epistle: 1: 5f., Paul's commission (χάριν καὶ ἀποστολήν) to bring about obedience to the faith among all the Gentiles; 1: 9f., his cultic service in the gospel (λατρεύω), and his intercessory prayers; 1: 11–13, his mutual exhortations with them (συμπαρακληθῆναι); 11: 13, his ministry (διακονίαν) to the Gentiles; 12: 1f., his exhortation (παρακαλῶ) to them, to present their bodies as a living sacrifice, holy and acceptable to God (θυσίαν ζῶσαν ἁγίαν), which is spiritual worship (τὴν λογικὴν λατρείαν ὑμῶν); 15: 5f. – his prayer to the God of 'paraklesis' that they may offer this worship together; 15: 15ff. – his priestly work in the gospel, through offering up the Gentiles as an acceptable sacrifice (λειτουργὸν...ἱερουργοῦντα τὸ εὐαγγέλιον...ἡ προσφορὰ τῶν ἐθνῶν εὐπρόσδεκτος, ἡγιασμένη...).

[2] The heaping together of themes of salvation belongs to the regular liturgical style. Nevertheless their particular choice here ties closely with the situation. Michel, pp. 323f.

[3] The syntactically loose addition of this final phrase of the prayer, ἐν δυνάμει πνεύματος ἁγίου, is in common liturgical style, with a heaping-up of prepositional phrases; Michel, p. 324, n. 4. Cf. Eph. 1: 16–20; K. G. Kuhn, 'Der Epheserbrief im Lichte der Qumrantexte,' *NTS*, 7 (1960–1), 334ff.

[4] Although the word 'righteousness' is missing from the prayer, it may be suggested by the phrase ἐν τῷ πιστεύειν (see below, p. 87).

[5] Lacking in Western Mss D G, the phrase is otherwise strongly attested.

power of the Holy Spirit. In the fifth chapter he had described how God's love had been poured into their hearts through the Holy Spirit which had been given to them (5: 5), bringing reconciliation (5: 11). In the eighth chapter he had spoken of the Spirit's gift of peace which would accompany a life set above things of the flesh (8: 5f.). This was the peace and reconciliation that would eventually include Jew and Gentile in its scope (chaps. 9–11 in relation with 15: 7–12), lifting them above dissensions.

In the same earlier chapters he had celebrated that liberating joy of the kingdom, that must now lift them beyond their censorious judgments: 'and we rejoice (καυχώμεθα) in our hope of sharing the glory of God. More than that, we rejoice in our sufferings' (5: 2f.). With this may be compared his song of triumph over all temporary hardships (8: 35–9), and his rhapsodic praise of the hidden purposes of God to bless both Jew and Gentile (11: 33–6; cf. 15: 9–12).[1]

The phrase ἐν τῷ πιστεύειν, while recalling the obedient faith of both weak and strong, would by this stage of the letter be resonant with an extraordinary range of meaning. It would remind the readers also of a primary theme of the letter, the righteousness of God revealed through faith. Paul now prays that they themselves may be filled with that saving faith which he had earlier shown must manifest itself in obedience (cf. 1: 5, 5: 19, 6: 12–18, 16: 19, 26), and thus issue in other graces; for it is in believing, that peace, joy, and finally hope will be discovered (5: 1–2). Indeed, this whole prayer might be thought to summarize the main theological progression of the letter to the Romans: through believing (justification by faith, chaps. 1–4), come joy and peace (reconciliation, chap. 5), and hope, by the power of the Holy Spirit (chap. 8), and finally an eschatological hope for Gentiles as well as Jews (chaps. 9–11).[2] So he petitions now that, as faith leads them to joy and peace, the experience of these together may produce in them new grounds for hope even in their present difficulties.

Finally, the enabling power (δύναμις) of God had been an

[1] Cf. also the injunctions to rejoice, 12: 12, 15.

[2] Surprisingly enough the word ἐλπίς is lacking in Rom. 9–11. See E. von Dobschütz, 'Zum Wortschatz und Stil des Römerbriefs,' *ZNW*, 33 (1934), 55.

important theme in the letter,[1] beginning with the initial announcement of the power of the gospel for salvation to everyone who had faith (1: 16), and ending now with the concluding petition – 'so that by the power of the Holy Spirit you may abound in hope' (15: 13). In this phrase he recalls a great theme of chapter eight, the power of the Spirit's aid to bring hope in present distress. For the present victories are but the first fruits of the Spirit and a token of 'the glory that is to be revealed to us...the glorious liberty of the children of God' (8: 18–27). Thus the main body of the letter and the prayer end together with apostle and readers reaching forward to the final consummation of the purposes of the God of hope – an unspoken Maranatha.[2]

Yet although on one plane the reader's anticipations are directed towards the great consummation, on another, as we have seen, the apostle is preparing to bring them back to his own more problematical temporary hopes. His future plans will depend on their response to his request for assistance.[3] As they learn to rejoice fully in the hope of the Gentiles, so they will together associate themselves warmly also with the apostle to the Gentiles, and support him in his further priestly service of the gospel of God (15: 16). So the prayer functions partly in redirecting the message of the letter towards those practical missionary purposes with which it had begun.

In conclusion, then, we may summarize the purposes of the two longer wish-prayers in Romans. First it is clear that they belong together in style and content. Stylistically they correspond in their lofty liturgical language and parallel structure.[4] In content, unlike the somewhat repetitive wish-prayers in Thessalonians, they sustain a forward moving progression of thought. Together they form an important liturgical whole, which invokes the three persons of the Trinity – pleading to

---

[1] Rom. 1: 16, 20, 7: 24f., 8: 3, 32, 37, 9: 17. Cf. Gaugler, p. 371, Harder, pp. 72f.

[2] See below, p. 152.

[3] Paul may sometimes use the word 'hope' for those smaller expectations which depend on other people, e.g., I Cor. 13: 7, 'Love...hopes all things.' Cf. P. S. Minear, *Christian Hope and the Second Coming* (Philadelphia, 1954), pp. 17–29, 56–69, 85–98, regarding different levels of hope and the central hope of Christ's coming.

[4] Cf. above, p. 29.

God for the unity of all in the church including Jew and Gentile, lifting them up even in their difficulties to an exalted life in accord with Christ, and pointing them forward in hope through the Spirit to still greater blessings in the future.

Next it may be seen that together the two prayers form an impressive double coda, worthy of such a sustained and exalted epistle.[1] Like the two wish-prayers in I Thessalonians[2] these in Romans serve to bring to a climax and re-emphasize the main thrust of the letter itself.[3] They help to tie together at the end the somewhat loosely articulated major segments of the letter, the theological section (chaps. 1–11), the general paraenetic section (chaps. 12–13), and the more specific and sustained discussion on weak and strong (14: 1 – 15: 13). For beneath these discontinuities we have glimpsed a sustained theme with an undeviating paraenetic purpose: a searching analysis of the meaning of the righteousness of God revealed through faith for faith (1: 17), which would lead to the deep healing of divisions between Jewish and Gentile Christians.[4]

Within a few compact but pregnant liturgical phrases are suggested the complex anxieties, the assurances and hopes, that lie behind the writing of the letter. So he prays for a renewal in the readers of steadfast, patient, harmonious living, that they might encourage one another in mutual forbearance. There is suggested the victory of the Spirit over life in the flesh; the blessings in overflowing abundance that would follow upon faith; and the glorious hope of the entry of the Gentiles into the fullness of salvation, a hope which the Roman believers may themselves forward by their support of Paul and his future ministry.[5]

That the prayers were partly intended for instruction in how to pray would seem to be true for the same reasons as held for those in I Thessalonians.[6] The apostle felt free to counsel even

[1] Cf. the double prayer which ends the long thanksgiving section in I Thess.; see above, p. 52, and below, p. 162, n. 2.

[2] See above, pp. 68ff.

[3] Cf. Marxsen, p. 97: 'The peculiar feature of this letter is that its main message comes at the end...It is only at the end that the letter really discloses itself as a "letter."'

[4] Cf. Minear's analysis of Paul's persistent pastoral intention throughout the letter; *The Obedience of Faith, passim.* See also Gaugler, pp. 224f.

[5] For the paraenetic purpose of Paul's prayers, cf. Furnish, p. 95.

[6] See above, p. 69.

a church which he had not founded, but which came within his field of responsibility, and it was in this letter that he had specifically mentioned the need to be taught how to pray, through the Spirit's intercessory aid (8: 26f.). Furthermore, the elevated style of these closing prayers, and their location within the extended liturgical final sequence, would help to ensure their being used in the worship services of the divided community, so that 'together [they might] with one voice glorify... God.'[1]

Finally, it is difficult to avoid the opinion that in composing these wish-prayers, too, Paul was actually offering up supplications to God[2] on behalf of those Roman Christians for whom he was so concerned, and for whom he had claimed to be continually praying (1: 9f.).[3] We may picture him, then, in the very act of writing, as ministering to these believers known and unknown,[4] in priestly service offering them up confidently to the God of steadfastness, encouragement and hope, and including them once more within the scope of his daily intercessory prayers.

Romans 15: 33 and 16: 20a

We must now inquire as to the function of two more peace blessings in Romans that may be included among the wish-prayers within the closing liturgical pattern. The first, a brief benediction,[5] serves both to close the travelling-plan section of the epistle (15: 14–33) and to point forward to the greetings and the kiss of peace that will follow:

The God of peace be[6] *with you all. Amen.* (Rom. 15: 33)

[1] See above, p. 70.　　[2] Cf. above, p. 71.　　[3] See below, pp. 189ff.
[4] [Cf. Col. 2: 1f., 'For I want you to know how greatly I strive for you, and for those at Laodicea, and for all who have not seen my face, that their hearts may be encouraged. . . .']
[5] To include this short peace benediction as a penultimate 'wish-prayer,' rather than a closing epistolary blessing, must remain a doubtful classification. In favor would be our decision that the sixteenth chapter was an integral part of the original letter to Rome (see below, pp. 92ff.); the closing epistolary blessing would then appear later at 16: 20b, or at 16: 24 (the Mss are divided on this point). Cf. Gamble, p. 175. See also below, p. 129, n. 1, on the blessing in Gal. 6: 16.
[6] The missing verb must be understood as imperative or optative. See above, p. 38, n. 1.

This little prayer arises immediately out of the liturgical passage in which Paul requests his readers' prayers for his safe arrival at Rome (15: 30–2). His eager anticipation of meeting them moves him once again to add a brief supplication for them,[1] before he dictates the final chapter of personal salutations and warnings.

As in the previous wish-prayers he had called upon the God of steadfastness and encouragement, and the God of hope, so now finally he chooses to invoke the God of peace (ὁ δὲ θεὸς τῆς εἰρήνης),[2] who may bring them all within that united fellowship and wholeness that above everything he desires for the Roman believers. May that peace, then, include them *all*![3]

Romans 16: 20a

The last of the four wish-prayers in the closing liturgical progression of Romans occurs within the uniquely long appendix of extended personal greetings (16: 1–23), and forms an integral part of a sharp pastoral warning[4] against 'those who create dissensions and difficulties' (vv. 17–20). It is followed immediately by the final grace blessing (16: 20b).[5]

Then the God of peace will *soon crush* (συντρίψει) *Satan under your feet.* (The grace of our Lord Jesus Christ be with you.) (Rom. 16: 20)

Alternative optative reading:

May *the God of peace soon crush* (συντρίψαι) *Satan under your feet.*[6]

Earlier we classified this short passage in a group of two or three doubtful wish-prayers which use a future indicative verb in an

[1] See below, p. 270. Once again the connective significance of the particle δέ should be noted, linking this prayer with what has preceded.

[2] One of the recognized liturgical forms of address (above, pp. 30f.). For the meaning of this address, and its special significance in relation to the kiss of peace (16: 16), see above, p. 64, n. 4, p. 66, nn. 1 and 2, on I Thess. 5: 23. The epithet will be repeated at 16: 20a.

[3] See above, p. 60, n. 4.

[4] Its close relation to a warning passage is paralleled by Gal. 6: 16, II Cor. 13: 11b [II Thess. 3: 16]. See Appendix IV.

[5] For the divergent textual evidence about the location of this grace blessing, see *The Greek New Testament* (American Bible Society, British and Foreign Bible Society, etc., Philadelphia and Stuttgart, 1966), ed. K. Aland *et al.*, p. 576. It is generally agreed that originally it belonged here at 16: 20b (the more unusual or difficult location), rather than at 16: 24, or after v. 27.

[6] See above, p. 33, n. 3, for the textual evidence.

optative sense.[1] Although it will be treated as a wish-prayer rather than a prophetic declaration, its undecided status militates against drawing firm conclusions for our study as a whole.[2] Moreover, we are immediately confronted by the doubt as to whether the wish-prayer should be understood only within its immediate context or in relation to the whole letter, i.e., whether we are to take the greetings postscript (chap. 16) as an integral part of the letter sent by Paul to Rome. Although we cannot here enter into the details of this complex debate, we may note that it turns mainly on the evidence of textual variations[3] and on two apparent anomalies. First, the surprising number of personal greetings, and the intimate relation between Paul and so many of his readers, have seemed to point away from Rome (where the apostle had not yet been)[4] to Ephesus (where he had worked for a long period).[5] Yet against this has been the argument that it was precisely because the Roman church was strange to Paul, that he adopted the unusual device of sending so many personal salutations. His strategy was to work through friends and acquaintances, in order to introduce himself and his plans in a delicate situation.[6] Thus the post-

[1] Rom. 16: 20a, I Cor. 1: 8f., perhaps Phil. 4: 19. See above, pp. 35f.

[2] Michel interprets this passage not only as a prophecy but also as a wish-prayer, in view of the liturgical address to God (ὁ δὲ θεὸς τῆς εἰρήνης), and the alternative optative verb form in the Mss (p. 348, n. 4).

[3] We must omit discussion of the textual variations. For a summary of the textual evidence, and the extensive but undecided debate about this, see Feine–Behm–Kümmel, pp. 222–4. The textual evidence (including that of P⁴⁶) would seem to be inconclusive in itself, so that the decision must be made on other grounds. See also Gamble, 'Textual History,' pp. 3, 103.

[4] For a representative statement of this difficulty, see J. Knox, *The Epistle to the Romans, IB*, IX, 365ff.

[5] Cf. Manson's attractive hypothesis, supported by many scholars, that chap. 16 was a separate Pauline addition sent to Ephesus with a copy of the letter; 'St. Paul's Letter to the Romans – and Others.' See also J. I. H. McDonald, 'Was Romans XVI a Separate Letter?,' *NTS*, 16 (1969–70), 369–72, supporting on stylistic grounds the possibility of a separate greetings letter.

[6] See K. H. Rengstorf, 'Paulus und die römische Christenheit,' 447–61. Rengstorf argues strongly that Paul already knew personally many of the believers at Rome. Thus chap. 16, with its numerous personal greetings, would be an integral and important part of the letter. Cf. Wendland, *Urchristlichen Literaturformen*, p. 351; Dodd, pp. xixff.; C. K. Barrett, *The Epistle to the Romans*, HNTC (New York, 1957), p. 281. Many believers,

script would fulfil an important and necessary function in his total approach to an unknown church.

Of more immediate importance for our purpose is the second anomaly, namely, the severely worded warning of the paragraph in which our prayer occurs (vv. 17–20). Such a direct approach seems to cut right across the restrained, indirect style of most of the preceding letter.[1] Furthermore, it breaks unexpectedly and inappropriately into the warm personal messages to individuals and groups at Rome. The force of these considerations has buttressed the arguments of those who could not accept the postscript as an original part of the letter to Rome.[2]

Nevertheless, we have already observed that it was customary for Paul to close his letters with a surprisingly sharp warning in juxtaposition with personal greetings, and various blessings.[3] Such warnings would have in mind the separation of unworthy from worthy at the Lord's supper. Thus the inclusion of such a passage need not appear so incongruous with the total intents of the epistle. In addition it has been suggested that although he had been guarded in his approach up to this point, yet now, as he is thinking more personally of his many friends at Rome, and of the new danger which may threaten them, his strong feelings break through.[4] In taking over the pen to write the autograph sentences[5] he cannot refrain from adding the sharply worded admonition to the Roman church. They must beware of the 'opponents' who may even now be arriving

temporarily exiled from Rome by Claudius, could have met Paul and now returned to Rome; Michel, p. 345. The greetings would serve to establish wider and firmer bonds with the larger number of Roman believers still unknown to him.

If there were a number of separate congregations at Rome, the long list of greetings would be all the more readily explained. Minear, *Obedience of Faith*, pp. 7f.

[1] For the hesitancy of Paul's approach to Rome, see below, p. 191.

[2] E.g., Knox, *IB*, ix, 365, 661f. Furnish argues that the passage contains many un-Pauline features; p. 198, n. 144.

[3] See above, p. 67, n. 3, and below, pp. 150ff. on I Cor. 16: 22; also Appendix III. Gamble shows that all the epistolary and liturgical elements found in Rom. 16 are usually in the conclusions of Paul's other letters (p. 180).

[4] Dodd, p. 242; Althaus, p. 130.

[5] Lietzmann, *Römer*, pp. 121f.

there.[1] Perhaps further word about the situation at Rome, or about plans of his opponents to visit Rome, had reached him after he had completed most of the letter.[2] We assume, then, that the postscript and the warning contained in it (16: 17–20) may be regarded as an integral part of the letter as a whole.

If our opinion be justified, the wish-prayer that serves to close this final warning reflects a further grave anxiety of the apostle. Besides his general concern about disunity at Rome, he fears that the very intruders who have dogged his footsteps in the past will now from the outset hinder his new venture to Rome and into the West.

As usual, he does not name his opponents. His somewhat veiled characterization of these bringers of false doctrine (16: 17f.) leaves us in doubt as to whether they were Judaizers or quasi-Gnostic libertines.[3] But the very sharpness of his admonition would indicate the depth of his anxiety about their deceptive heresy. His earlier letter to the Galatians, warning against such intruders, had ended with the hopeful injunction, 'Henceforth let no man trouble me' (Gal. 6: 17);[4] yet now once again he must warn the Romans in advance against a similar danger.

So for the third and last time in the epistle he prepares the ground by declaring his confidence in the readers, '...your obedience is known to all, so that I rejoice over you' (16: 19; cf. 1: 8, 15: 14); and for the third and last time he continues with a note of further exhortation, 'I would have you wise (σοφούς) as to what is good and guileless (ἀκεραίους) as to what is evil' (cf. 1: 11, 15: 15). But this time the warning is far more urgent, for the situation has become more menacing.

Thus the prayer that immediately follows would be a spontaneous cry for God's power to shield the Roman believers against a new and enticing approach from the outside: 'May the very God of peace soon crush Satan under your feet.' Once again Paul chooses the liturgical phrase, the God of peace

[1] As they are to be avoided (v. 17b), they can scarcely be equated with any group already mentioned in chaps. 14–15, but must be persons coming from the outside. Gaugler, p. 407, Althaus, p. 130, Wendland, pp. 350f.

[2] So Barrett, *Romans*, pp. 284f.

[3] See above, p. 48, n. 3.

[4] See below, p. 124.

(ὁ δὲ θεὸς τῆς εἰρήνης), and for the same reasons as before.[1] It is this God of wholeness and good order who must save them from the additional dissensions and difficulties that the intruders will inevitably bring. The expected victory is described as crushing Satan under their feet, a figure which points back to the originally promised mastery over the serpent (Gen. 3: 15). Paul seems to be adapting an apocalyptic tradition witnessed to in the Testament of Levi, 'And Beliar shall be bound by him, And he shall give power to his children to tread upon evil spirits' (18: 12).[2] Yet by naming Satan in opposition to the God of peace, he is actually accusing the intruders themselves as the ministers of Satan in whose service they will bring confusion into the Roman church.[3] Thus the prayer for their speedy overthrow focuses probably upon an interim victory, more than upon the final apocalyptic conquest of Satan at the parousia.[4]

But besides being an urgent cry of the apostle himself on behalf of the Roman believers, this peace blessing may be further illuminated as an integral part of the liturgically oriented closing pattern that appears to run at least through chapters 15 and 16 – a pattern more complex than that in I Thessalonians, and extended in such a way as to prepare this long and substantial letter to be incorporated within the readers' own offering of worship to God. This may be better seen if we compare the closing passages of the two letters:[5]

Early in the paraenetic section of Romans comes a general exhortation to unceasing prayer – linked with rejoicing, patience in tribulation, and a positive attitude of blessing rather than cursing, even towards one's persecutors (Rom. 12: 12–14; cf. I Thess. 5: 14b–18). Then at the close of the main body of the

---

[1] See above, p. 91. Note once more the connective force of the particle δέ.

[2] See Strack–Billerbeck, iii, 319. Cf. Rev. 20: 1–6, 7–10.

[3] Cf. II Cor. 11: 13ff., 'For such men are false apostles, deceitful workmen, disguising themselves as apostles of Christ...for even Satan disguises himself...his servants also disguise themselves as servants of righteousness.' Sanday and Headlam, p. 431; Michel, p. 348.

[4] Lietzmann, *Römer*, p. 122, Gaugler, p. 412. Thus there would be no clearly eschatological climax in this short prayer.

[5] For the Thess. sequence, see above pp. 51f. Further confirmation will come as we examine the endings of the other epistles. Cf. Appendix IV.

letter occur the two carefully constructed wish-prayers that sum up much of the central thrust of the letter (Rom. 15: 5f., and 13; cf. I Thess. 5: 23f.). After that comes a discussion of his travel plans (15: 14–29)[1] which involves the collection of money by the writer and his companions, its transport to the poor among the saints at Jerusalem (15: 25–8), and its acceptance by them (15: 31).[2] There follows an appeal to the readers to join with him in supplications (Rom. 15: 30–2; cf. I Thess. 5: 25), which makes more specific the earlier general exhortation to prayer. This is rounded out by a brief peace blessing (Rom. 15: 33; not paralleled in I Thess.).

There now follows an extended concluding postscript conveying final messages (Rom. 16: 1–23; cf. I Thess. 5: 26–8). It begins with a personal recommendation for the bearer of the letter (Rom. 16: 1f.; lacking in I Thess.), then personal greetings to individuals at Rome (Rom. 16: 3–15; reduced in I Thess. to the greetings implied in 5: 26). Following immediately upon these comes the more formal and united salutation from 'all the churches of Christ' (Rom. 16: 16b; not appropriate in I Thess.).[3] Paul hopes that individual and united greetings would mingle because of the restored harmony of the

---

[1] Not found at this place in I Thess. While travelling arrangements and plans are mentioned at earlier points in most of Paul's letters, they occur also near the close in Rom. 15: 14–29, II Cor. 13: 10, Philem. 22.

[2] Cf. the letter in Bar. 1: 10–15, where similar instructions had been given about sending a collection to the Jews remaining at Jerusalem, and their use of it; these instructions were similarly linked with reference to intercessory supplications and the liturgical use of the letter in the house of the Lord (see above, p. 42, n. 3).

Mention of the collection is lacking in I Thess. But analagous references to a collection, or a gift or payment, do occur besides Rom. in the closing epistolary–liturgical patterns in I Cor. 16: 1–4, Philem. 18f., and Phil. 4: 10–18 (a gift to Paul). Here Bornkamm suggests that a separate letter, Phil. 4: 10–18, was placed by the editor at the close of the editorial compilation (our present Phil.); as a small personal matter it would belong at the close, where announcements were customarily placed in the Pauline letters. 'Der Phil. als paulinische Briefsammlung,' p. 201.

[3] There is a special significance in this joint salutation: it comes from the churches in the East which Paul will soon be leaving behind, to the church to which he will soon come, en route to his new work in the West. Unitedly the Eastern churches will send a collection by him back to the mother church at Jerusalem. Unitedly they will support him in his forward move to the church in the capital city of Rome. Cf. Michel, p. 345.

Roman believers, and would be liturgically symbolized in the exchanging of the holy kiss of brotherhood (Rom. 16: 16a; cf. I Thess. 5: 26).[1]

Suddenly there intrudes the sharp warning related to the eucharist, in which Paul enjoins the believers to avoid the company of the divisive opponents (ἐκκλίνετε ἀπ' αὐτῶν) (Rom. 16: 17–19; cf. the related injunction in I Thess. 5: 27). Closely attached to the warning is the short peace prayer for (or prophecy of) their victory in this threatening matter (Rom. 16: 20a; cf., perhaps, I Thess. 5: 24), and the final grace benediction as a transition to the actual breaking of bread (Rom. 16: 20b; cf. I Thess. 5: 28).[2]

In conclusion, we have understood Romans 16: 20a as essentially related to the main intent of the epistle and a part of Paul's customary warning passage. We have suggested that it may be seen more as a wish-prayer than a prophetic declaration – an urgent cry of the apostle on behalf of the Roman believers as he thinks of a new threat to their unity: 'May the God of peace soon crush Satan under your feet.' Like the other and longer wish-prayers it focuses an important epistolary concern. But also it belongs with them in the context of the carefully prepared closing liturgical–epistolary pattern, a transition into further worship.

TWO OTHER POSSIBLE WISH-PRAYERS
I Corinthians 1: 8f.

The next passage is one which may be regarded as a wish-prayer, but like the preceding one, its status remains somewhat doubtful:

Who will sustain you *to the end, guiltless in the day of our Lord Jesus Christ.*

---

[1] See above, p. 66, n. 2. We may observe a similar combination of united (official?) church greetings and the holy kiss in I and II Cor.: 'The churches of Asia send greetings. . . .Greet one another with a holy kiss' (I Cor. 16: 19f.); 'Greet one another with a holy kiss. All the saints greet you' (II Cor. 13: 12f.).

[2] Cullmann, *Early Christian Worship*, p. 23. See above, p. 70, n. 3, and below, p. 115. The few added messages from Paul's immediate companions (vv. 21–3) may for our present purpose be discarded, and the doxology falls away as a later addition (vv. 25–7).

Alternative translation:

And may he sustain you *to the end, guiltless in the day of our Lord Jesus Christ.*
God is faithful, by whom you were called into the fellowship of his Son, Jesus Christ our Lord. (I Cor. 1: 8f.)

We suggested earlier that in spite of the future indicative tense (βεβαιώσει), this sentence in a thanksgiving period might be regarded as a wish-prayer taking the place of the customary intercessory prayer-report.[1] In the thanksgiving (1: 4–9) Paul is moving from acknowledgement of the gifts of the readers, to concern for that which was still lacking in them (cf. Phil. 1: 4, 9–11; I Thess. 3: 10; Philem. 4, 6; II Cor. 1: 7). So it is within the context of the whole thanksgiving section that the significance of this short intercession may best be seen.[2]

Before beginning his warnings and instructions, the apostle singles out, in this carefully constructed thanksgiving passage, one or two of the most characteristic gifts of the Corinthian church. It is for these that he gives thanks, and it is these that will occupy much of his attention in the letter.[3] He mentions first the overall blessing of God's grace to them, joyful that they exist as a Christian community who have responded to the message of Jesus Christ (1: 4). Immediately he goes on to commend those special graces given to a church that prides itself on its spiritual enrichment (v. 5, cf. 4: 8). First comes the gift of speech. He thinks partly of their speaking in tongues (cf. 12: 10, 28, 13: 1, 8, 14: 6–40), partly of their sense of superiority over his own halting speech (e.g., 2: 1–5). Next he mentions their gift of knowledge, anticipating his frequent subsequent references to their claims to wisdom and knowledge.[4] One of the main problems he will have to face in this letter is the existence of a broad, Gnostic type of movement at Corinth,

[1] Above, p. 35.

[2] For the function of the Pauline thanksgivings and the significance of their intercessory portion, see below, Chap. 7.

[3] We must anticipate our later discussion of the background and structure of I Cor. Here we assume the integrity of I Cor. as a single letter. See below, pp. 135f.

[4] γνῶσις occurs in 1: 5, 8: 1, 7, 10, 11, 12: 8, 13: 2, 8, 14: 6. σοφός, -ία occurs 22 times in chaps. 1–3, and in 6: 5, 8: 19, 12: 8. Cf. C. K. Barrett, *A Commentary on the First Epistle to the Corinthians* (New York, 1968), p. 37.

claiming a knowledge that leads to licence and thereby threatens the unity of the church (cf. 1: 18–31, 8: 1–13, etc.).[1]

Yet it was by these gifts, he says, that the reality of the gospel message had been confirmed among them (v. 6), a reality apparently even further signified by their not lacking any spiritual gifts at all (v. 7)! Later on he will have to discuss at length their abuse of these gifts and their need to learn the more excellent way of love (chaps. 12–14). In the meantime he gives thanks for the rich graces they do already display.

But could his thanksgiving be genuine, when the gifts have served only to feed their arrogance (cf. 8: 1)? In the light of their glaring lack of love and humility, could he really intend to suggest at the outset that they are not lacking in any spiritual gift?[2] It is indeed difficult at first sight to avoid the suspicion that he is indulging either in the conventional flattery of the ancient letterwriter, or in the pungent irony of a disappointed leader. Yet in giving thanks for his readers he is in fact pleading for them as an intercessor before God, remembering sincerely the signs of grace among them, even while deeply disturbed about their aberrations. As always, the apostle witnesses both for and against them.[3] Irony would have its due place later (4: 8ff.), but hardly at the beginning of a letter composed in such a delicate situation, and one bound to prove unwelcome to a large and influential segment of the church.[4]

The solution to this dilemma seems to be that in fact he is not suggesting that the Corinthians lack no spiritual gift. Rather he is expressing a hope for their further progress: 'Even as the testimony to Christ was confirmed among you – *so that you might not be lacking*[5] *in any spiritual gift*, as you wait for the revealing of our Lord Jesus Christ' (1: 7). The Corinthians, he is saying, were challenged from the start by the very abun-

---

[1] See below, pp. 139f.

[2] The dilemma cannot be sidestepped by claiming that for Paul love is not one of the 'spiritual' gifts (χαρίσματα).

[3] See above, pp. 13f.; below, p. 173.   [4] See below, pp. 139f.

[5] ὥστε ὑμᾶς μὴ ὑστερεῖσθαι. ὥστε with inf., although usually consecutive, may sometimes be used to express purpose or intended result, e.g., Matt. 10: 1. Blass–Debrunner–Funk, 390 (3), 391 (3); Moule, *Idiom Book of the New Testament*, pp. 143f. Cf. E.-B. Allo, *Saint Paul Première Épitre aux Corinthiens*, 10th edn (Paris, 1956), p. 4. For a contrary view see H. Conzelmann, *Der erste Brief an die Korinther*, Meyer's Kommentar (Göttingen, 1969), p. 41.

dance of their endowments not to stop short while they lacked any spiritual gift,[1] but to press forward towards perfection at the coming of Christ. Thus the giving of thanks would be real, both in its appropriateness and its restraint – mentioning their undoubted gifts, omitting those which they lacked, and pointing forward to what they still needed.

So in the second half of the period (beginning with verse 7) Paul has moved over into the mood of hope and supplication. He points first (v. 7) to the high expectations that had followed from their richly endowed beginnings. Then with this hopeful thought in mind he offers his supplication (v. 8). He prays that the same Christ may indeed (καί) continue to confirm them (βεβαώσει)[2] until the end,[3] so that they may be guiltless[4] – not lacking in any spiritual gift – in the day of our Lord Jesus Christ.[5]

In this light, the supplication sentence ceases to be merely a conventional generalized prayer for the readers and takes on a more immediate relevance to the Corinthian situation.[6] His prayer is that the original intention of the preaching of Christ for them may now be brought to completion. He asks that besides the spectacular gifts of speech and knowledge which have already given ample evidence of God's grace to a dynamic church (vv. 4–6), the more excellent gifts that they still lack may be confirmed to them. So Paul may look forward to presenting them (with his other churches) guiltless at the day of judgment – a day of which he will soon be sharply warning them (3: 13, 5: 5, etc.).

All this, however, must depend on the trustworthiness of God, rather than on the undoubted gifts of the Corinthians themselves (v. 9). It was God who had called them in the first place,

---

[1] Cf. his prayer about τὰ ὑστερήματα of the Thessalonians, I Thess. 3: 10, and the customary extravagance of his prayers for his churches. See above, p. 60, n. 4.

[2] Picking up again from v. 6 the word ἐβεβαιώθη, that he had used previously about his readers. Cf. also II Cor. 1; below, p. 228, n. 4.

[3] Taking ἕως τέλους as temporal.

[4] I.e., the 'additional benefit' of the wish-prayer form. ἀνεγκλήτους used only here in Paul; in other prayers he employs a variety of parallel terms for his boundless hopes for his churches: εἰλικρινεῖς, ἀπρόσκοποι, ἀμέμπτους, -τως, ὁλοτελεῖς, ὁλόκληρον.

[5] See above, p. 41 on the eschatological climax.

[6] Cf. below, p. 173.

and only his faithful purpose would complete his work in them:
'God is faithful, by whom you were called into the fellowship
of his Son, Jesus Christ our Lord.'[1]

Having prepared the ground in a remarkably suitable passage
of thanksgiving, supplication, and trust, the apostle is now
ready to launch into his difficult pastoral appeal.[2]

Philippians 4: 19

The last example of the principal wish-prayers in the Pauline
corpus is another questionable one, occurring near the end of
the letter to the Philippians, which for the present we assume
to have been written by Paul during his captivity in Rome.[3]
Does this borderline prayer passage have intercessory significance within the letter as a whole and in relation to the
special circumstances behind the letter? Because of its problematical status, our conclusions can be only tentative.

And my God will supply *every need of yours according to his riches in glory
in Christ Jesus.* (To our God and Father be glory for ever and ever.
Amen.)[4] (Phil. 4: 19f.)

Alternative reading:[5]

And may *my God* supply *every need of yours according to his riches in glory
in Christ Jesus.*

At the outset, then, we are confronted by two debatable
questions: first, is the sentence to be understood as a declaration
or a wish-prayer? When the matter was raised earlier, we
suggested that in spite of an alternative optative reading the
sentence seemed to have a primarily declarative character,[6]

---

[1] Cf. Phil. 1: 3–6; and see above, p. 35, n. 2.

[2] The παρακαλῶ, vv. 10ff.

[3] It is appropriate to postpone our fuller examination of the letter and
its background until a later chapter (pp. 194ff.). At this stage we must
anticipate the main conclusions reached there.

[4] Context added for convenience.

[5] Reading πληρωσαι with D* F G Ψ 69 1739 pm latt Chrys Theodrt. See
above, p. 33, n. 3.

[6] Almost all commentators interpret it thus, though Harder included it
among the wish-prayers (see above, p. 33, n. 2), and Lohmeyer described
vv. 19–20 as a 'Schlussgebet.' E. Lohmeyer, *Die Briefe an die Philipper, an die
Kolosser und an Philemon*, p. 188.

after the analogy of Paul's statement in II Cor. 9: 8.[1] Yet if we place it in the context of the letter as a whole, it will now be seen to function in much the same way as the closing wish-prayers in Romans and I Thessalonians. We suggest, therefore, that it may be translated as a declaration, but with the sense also that it is a surrogate for a summarizing wish-prayer in the closing liturgical pattern of the letter.

In that case the two earlier peace-pronouncements (4: 7 and 9b) would be connected with our passage within this closing pattern. Although phrased as declarations they would correspond to the two peace blessings in Romans (15: 33, 16: 20),[2] or to the reference to 'the God of peace' in I Thessalonians (5: 23).[3] So we may examine our passage as a borderline case – a declaration which does duty also for supplication – a 'declaration-prayer.'[4]

But a further complication arises through doubts that have been raised about the integrity of the epistle in its present form. Is the passage to be construed in relation to our present letter as a whole, or to a short earlier letter of thanks sent separately by Paul in acknowledgement of the Philippians' gift and comprising only Phil. 4: 10–20, perhaps together with other material now lost? Again we may come to no categorical decision, but in anticipation of our later discussion[5] will examine the passage as if it belonged to the whole letter.

But first it must be treated as an integral part of the smaller 'thank you' section (4: 10–20), to which, indeed, it forms the denouement. Paul has been acknowledging the gift from his

---

[1] See above, p. 36.
[2] See above, pp. 90ff.   [3] See above, p. 66, n. 1.
[4] On the paradoxical relation between Paul's declarations of certainty and his supplications of faith, see below, p. 170, n. 3. At the beginning of this letter he had boldly declared in the thanksgiving period that God would assuredly complete his work for them (1: 6), and yet had found it necessary to pray that this might happen more and more in their present circumstances (1: 4, 9–11). Does he now combine the two modes in one closing declaration? This might be indicated by the close parallelism between structure and content of the two passages – the thanksgiving period and the 'thank-you' section (1: 3–11 and 4: 10–20). See Lohmeyer, *Philipper, Kolosser, Philemon*, pp. 177f.

Cf. the view of Van Elderen on the significance of the optative, above, p. 34, n. 3.
[5] Below, pp. 195ff.

friends at Philippi in a rather constrained manner – in such a way as to maintain an uneasy balance between two rather incompatible points of view. For years he has been attacked as preaching the gospel for monetary gain.[1] Even now he wishes to maintain a certain financial independence, while appreciating the help of friends who have meant so much to him. So he shifts back and forth, first joyfully expressing his indebtedness, then implying that the gift had not been really necessary (vv. 10–13). He stresses gratefully the long-standing partnership of his friends, yet assures them that he does not seek a gift in itself, but rather that their generous thoughtfulness may accrue in blessing to them (vv. 14–17). He acknowledges that he has been fully repaid for everything he has done, but immediately points out that their self-denying action must be regarded more importantly as 'a sacrifice acceptable and pleasing to God' (v. 18).[2]

It is at this point that he offers the solution by lifting the whole matter in prayer far above the level of careful calculation. The Philippians, he declares and prays with deeply rooted confidence, will be recompensed from the boundless treasury of God out of all proportion to their pains: 'And my God will supply every need of yours according to his riches in glory in Christ Jesus.'[3] Thus Paul, the prisoner who cannot hope to repay them, hands his indebtedness over to the account of the God to whom he belongs ('my God'),[4] who will repay and more than repay.

Our passage may be thought, however, to require also a wider context. When taken with the doxology and Amen that

[1] Cf. I Thess. 2: 9, I Cor. 4: 12, 9: 3–18, II Cor. 12: 13ff.

[2] Cf. J. H. Michael, *The Epistle of Paul to the Philippians*, MNTC (New York, 1927), p. 210. See also C. H. Dodd, 'The Mind of Paul: I,' *New Testament Studies* (Manchester, 1953), pp. 72f. Paul covers this embarrassment by the playful use of such technical commercial terms as καλῶς ποιεῖν (v. 14) and ἀπέχω (v. 18) for 'received.' Cf. a similar playful use of business language in Philem. See below, p. 216, n. 7.

[3] Cf. II Cor. 9: 6–15, where Paul develops earlier the reasoning that he gives here in truncated form. See below, pp. 249f. In this late epistle he tends to take for granted arguments and positions that he had earlier hammered out in full.

[4] ὁ δὲ θεός μου: a comparatively rare term of address to God, but used by Paul also in the thanksgiving, 1: 3.

complete it (v. 20), it forms a lofty liturgical climax more suitable for the whole letter than for the comparatively limited thank-you note. While sharing the basic structure of the Pauline wish-prayers,[1] it may also be seen as arranged in two halves, each consisting of three phrases that may be paired together:[2]

And my God	according to his riches
will supply	in glory
every need of yours	in Christ Jesus.

Yet it would restrict too tightly and logically the meaning of language that is essentially liturgical celebration, were we to insist on this pairing in any exact way. Instead the phrases may be understood as each contributing to the exultant totality of a passage that brings to its culmination point Paul's most joyous and triumphant letter. Various links with the preceding letter may now be noted.

In saying that God will supply (πληρώσει) every need of theirs, it is true that Paul echoes the immediately preceding context (πεπλήρωμαι), and suggests that their material sacrifices would be recompensed. But, more importantly, he picks up a central concern of the whole letter, their need to be led beyond a stagnating complacency.[3] Thus although he may not here indicate any particular grace as lacking in them,[4] his overflowing declaration implies a wish that they be content with no less than the highest possible levels of spiritual attainment.[5]

This theme is repeated in a striking way from the earlier prayer-report at the opening of the letter (1: 9–11). The second prayer passage echoes the phrasing of the first, where Paul had prayed exuberantly 'that [their] love [might] *abound more and more*,' and that they might be '*filled* (πεπληρωμένοι) with *the fruits* (καρπόν) of righteousness.'[6] Now at the end (4: 17–20)

---

[1] See above, p. 29.

[2] So Lohmeyer, *Philipper, Kolosser, Philemon*, p. 189.

[3] On the nature of this problem at Philippi, see below, pp. 200f.

[4] As he had done in the wish-prayers at the end of Romans, and perhaps I Thess.

[5] Other problems and concerns, which Paul had tried to meet in this letter and now gathers up in the all-embracing phrase 'every need of yours,' will be surveyed below, pp. 198ff. They included personal discords within the church and perhaps the threat of persecution.

[6] See below, pp. 207ff.

he 'seek[s] *the fruit* (τὸν καρπόν) *which increases* to [their] credit,' and turns again to God to '*fill* (πληρώσει) their every need,'[1] with an expectation of rich and abundant blessing, 'according to *his riches in glory* in Christ Jesus.' Furthermore, the progression of the second prayer passage and its doxology seem to echo the movement of the first, with its petitions that the readers increase more and more in love, filled with the fruits of righteousness through the mediation of Christ, and prepared for his coming; and that it all redound to the glory and praise of God.[2] These two liturgical units bracket the main part of the letter,[3] the first one anticipating rather fully the concerns and exhortations that would follow,[4] the second completing them in a soaring utterance of trust and praise, that would leave the readers with a sense of incalculable blessings still ahead.

We may accentuate one or two further links between our prayer passage and the preceding letter. In the phrase 'according to his riches' Paul introduces a metaphor that he had used in other letters to suggest the limitless reserves of God's grace available through Christ in the eschatological age.[5] Here he echoes a suggestion of his earlier prayer for the Philippians, the inexhaustibility of love (1 : 9).[6] Does he also allude indirectly to the Christ hymn: 'Who though he was in the form of God... emptied himself' (2 : 6)? This would at least be suggested by his parallel words to the Corinthians, 'though he was rich, yet for your sake he became poor, so that by his poverty you might become rich' (II Cor. 8: 9).[7]

By the addition of the resonant words ἐν δόξῃ he heightens still further the sense of rich blessings in the new age. While the

---

[1] The word πληρόω is used only 4 times in the epistle: 1: 11, 2: 2, and here in 4: 18, 19. Paul seems clearly to be taking up the thought of his earlier prayer passage in this closing one.

[2] For the parallels between the thanksgiving period and the 'thank-you' section, see above, p. 102, n. 4.

[3] It is of interest to note also a formal parallel between the structure of the thanksgiving period and the thank-you section, each leading to a liturgical passage and doxology. For details, see Lohmeyer, *Philipper, Kolosser, Philemon*, pp. 177f., 188.

[4] See below, pp. 207ff.

[5] E.g., Rom. 9: 23, 'the riches of his glory'; cf. 10: 12, 11: 12, 33; I Cor. 1: 5, 4: 8, II Cor. 9: 11.

[6] See below, p. 209.

[7] See F. Hauck and W. Kash, *TWNT*, VI, espec. 326–8.

precise reference of the phrase is difficult to decide,[1] the analogy of his other prayer passages would suggest an eschatological climax at this point.[2] It is at the return of Christ in glory that their every need will be completely met as they share in his glory.[3] This is what he had prayed for at the beginning of the letter, that they might 'be pure and blameless for the day of Christ' (1: 10, cf. 1: 6); this great day is what he had been thinking of as he exhorted them during the course of the letter (cf. 2: 16, 3: 20f., 4: 1).[4] Now in the closing liturgical passage he announces the theme for the last time.[5]

In conclusion, the 'declaration-prayer' with its accompanying doxology has given various indications that Paul composed it in relation to the opening thanksgiving and prayer-report, and as a finale to the dominant message of the whole letter. This would support the view that the whole letter was written as a unit. Moreover, the content of his hopes for his friends is somewhat differently focused from that of the wish-prayers in other epistles. It arises out of the uniquely critical situation of the apostle himself. In captivity he has learned more surely than ever the secret of overflowing sufficiency through Christ in the midst of deepest need. This he has made evident throughout the letter.[6] So at the end of the road he is moved to pray that his friends, too, be given a share in these limitless resources, both now in times of peril and in the future consummation.

For the rest, we may in this passage see purposes of a liturgical and paraenetic kind that were evident in the other wish-

[1] Commentators disagree whether it should be taken as 'glorious riches,' or 'riches made glorious in Christ,' or 'supply gloriously,' or 'supply at the glorious consummation in Christ' (this last by Lohmeyer, *Philipper, Kolosser, Philemon*; Michael, *ad loc.*).

[2] Cf. I Thess. 3: 13, 5: 23, I Cor. 1: 8, Phil. 1: 10.

[3] See G. Kittel, *TWNT*, II, 250–5. In the NT the glory of God is assigned also to Christ, and his believers will share with him in glory (cf. Dan. 12: 3), Rom. 5: 2, 8: 17f., 21; Col. 1: 27; Matt. 13: 43, 19: 28.

[4] For details, see below, pp. 210f.

[5] Yet Paul must also be partly referring to the supplying of the Philippians' immediate material needs. Elsewhere his references to the glory given to believers have a present as well as a future reference: Rom. 8: 30 (we have been given the first fruits of the Spirit, 8: 23), II Cor. 3: 18, 4: 6. 'The whole simultaneity of possession and expectation which is the basis of NT piety' (Kittel, p. 251). Cf. Moltmann, pp. 105f.

[6] See below, p. 199.

prayers. At the close of his letter Paul reinforces his exhortations, gentle rebukes, and sharp warnings, by leading the assembled church into prayer as his epistle comes to a close.[1] He has quickened their faith by the contagion of his own, kindled joy in them by his own radiant exaltation, and led them forward to intercede for himself and for themselves as they join once more in fellowship with him in his prison ordeal (1 : 19f.), and in the presence of one who would supply their every need.

Our study of the eight principal wish-prayers is completed.[2] But before drawing our conclusions together in summary form,[3] we must turn in the next chapter to two other groups of intercessory prayer passages that may be classified with the wish-prayers.

[1] See below, pp. 202f.

[2] We may add a reference to one more doubtful blessing-wish, at the close of II Cor., 'And the God of love and peace will be with you' (13: 11b). While we decided for want of evidence to regard this primarily as a declaration (p. 36), yet its situation at the end of a warning passage points to its being a surrogate for a peace-prayer in the closing liturgical pattern, in preparation for the holy kiss (v. 12). See pp. 66, nn. 1, 2.

[3] See below, pp. 154f.

CHAPTER 6

BLESSINGS AND CURSES

EPISTOLARY GREETINGS

Linked with the eight principal wish-prayers are two further types of prayer passages in the Pauline epistles, namely the epistolary greetings or blessings at the beginning and end of each letter, together with a curse and a pronouncement blessing in Galatians (1: 8f. and 6: 16) and two curse passages in I Corinthians (5: 3–5 and 16: 22).[1] We consider first the opening and closing epistolary greetings:

Grace to you and peace from God our Father and the Lord Jesus Christ.

The grace of our Lord Jesus Christ be with you.[2]

What significance, if any, do these have as intercessory prayers?

We are confronted initially by the problem that the verb is unexpressed; but as we have argued, it should be understood in the optative or imperative, and we should take the greetings as closer to wish-prayers than to declarations.[3] Yet, even so, are these benedictions any more than pure formalities?

The opening benedictions

Grace to you and peace from God our Father and the Lord Jesus Christ.

At first sight the answer to our question would seem to be no. The blessings at the beginning of each letter are quite stylized[4] – they remain unchanged in wording throughout the Pauline

---

[1] See above, pp. 22f.

[2] The closing greeting varies considerably from letter to letter; see Appendix III.

[3] See above, pp. 36f.

[4] See e.g., F. Ziemann, *De epistolarum graecorum formulis solemnibus questiones selectae* (Halle, 1911), pp. 334–65; O. Roller, *Das Formular der Paulinischen Briefe; ein Beitrag zur Lehre vom antiken Briefe* (Stuttgart, 1933); A. Pujol, 'De salutatione Apostolorum "Gratia vobis et pax,"' *Verbum Domini*, 12 (1932), 38–42, 76–82; L. G. Champion, *Benedictions and Doxologies in the*

epistles,[1] and are therefore thought by some to have been either conventional adaptations from general epistolary usage,[2] or borrowed from an early Christian benediction.[3] Strikingly different are the creative variations of the opening formula of authorship, where Paul adapts his description of himself and his credentials to the circumstances of each particular letter.[4] By contrast, then, does the stereotyped nature of the opening blessings allow any living meaning in Paul's use of it?

With regard first to their derivation from ancient letter style, it has been suggested by Friedrich (following Lohmeyer) that their form is dependent on Near Eastern epistolary antecedents. But he rejects Lohmeyer's claim that in wording and content they represent a traditional early church formula used to introduce a service of worship.[5]

We may, however, seek further light from the use of the words χάρις and εἰρήνη in ancient greetings. First, what was the relation of the Christian χάρις greeting to the usual Greek

Epistles of Paul (Oxford, 1934); R. Gyllenberg, 'De inledande hälsningsformlerna i de paulinska breven' (The introductory greetings formula in the Pauline letters), *Svensk Exegetisch Arsbok*, XVI (1951–2), 21f.; G. Friedrich, 'Lohmeyers These über "Das paulinische Briefpräskript" kritisch beleuchtet,' *ZNW*, 46 (1955), 272–4; Kramer, par. 42 (pp. 151–6).

[1] Except for the I Thess. formula, shortened in most Mss to avoid repetition of the phrase ἐν θεῷ πατρὶ καὶ κυρίῳ Ἰησοῦ Χριστῷ.

[2] Kramer, par. 42b. Cf. Ziemann, pp. 302ff.; Roller, pp. 62ff.; Koskenniemi, pp. 130–9.

[3] Lohmeyer, 'Briefliche Grussüberschriften,' pp. 161–4.

[4] Gyllenberg (pp. 28–31). See also T. Y. Mullins, 'Greeting as a New Testament Form,' *JBL*, 87 (1968), 418–26.

[5] Lohmeyer (*Philipper, Kolosser, Philemon*, pp. 158–64; see above, p. 28, n. 1) had pointed to the strange dual sentence form of the Pauline prescript, with a change from the impersonal or 3rd person address of ordinary Greek epistolary usage, to the more personal blessing in the 2nd pers. The model for this complex form he saw in various Near Eastern letters. But the actual content and wording of the Pauline blessing with its elevated liturgical style must, he thought, have come directly from early Church usage.

Friedrich, on the other hand, denies the liturgical borrowing. For neither did Paul himself maintain the blessing formula always unchanged (I Thess. 1: 1), nor did the writers of the post-Pauline letters: I and II Pet. 1: 2, II John 3, Rev. 1: 4. Therefore Friedrich believes that the Near Eastern epistolary antecedents pointed out by Lohmeyer were the true source. (Friedrich, 'Lohmeyers These,' pp. 272–4; see Kramer, par. 42b.)

greeting χαίρειν?[1] It is suggested by some that Paul's use of χάρις was simply a play on words, a substitution for χαίρειν.[2] True, the external change involved is small, and the striking similarity of sound can hardly be ignored. Yet the difference in connotation is considerable,[3] and indeed the papyri show that the two words may be used together with separate meanings – to express both greeting and thanksgiving.[4] Hence others justifiably doubt whether there is any simple relation or equivalence between the Greek χαίρειν and Paul's radically richer χάρις greeting.[5]

In any case Paul's use of χάρις would introduce a completely new note into a greeting.[6] A concept fundamentally characteristic of his gospel message,[7] χάρις was his regular expression for God's free and gracious purpose to save men through the gift of Christ (cf. Rom. 3: 23f.). Of course this full theological meaning must have been partially muted, even for Paul, in a formalized epistolary greeting. And Paul himself sometimes restricted the word to denote a particular gift or commissioning: e.g., Rom. 1: 5.[8]

A further clue may perhaps be found in a significant church custom described in Acts, of commissioning and commending members 'to the grace of God' as they were being sent on an important mission (Acts 14: 26, 15: 40), or during a solemn

[1] Found customarily in the papyrus letters, and meaning literally 'rejoice!' See von Dobschütz, *Die Thessalonicher-Briefe*, p. 59, and Roller, pp. 61ff. Cf. Jas. 1: 1, Acts 15: 23, 23: 26, II Macc. 11: 34.

[2] So von Dobschütz, *Thessalonicher-Briefe*, p. 59, and Rigaux, *Thessaloniciens, ad loc.*

[3] For the differences between the cognates χαίρειν, χάρα, χάρις, χαρίзεσθαι, see Bauer–Arndt–Gingrich; Liddell, H. G., and Scott, R., *A Greek–English Lexicon*, rev. edn (Oxford, 1951), *ad verbum*.

[4] See an example from *Epistolae privatae graecae*, ed. S. Witkowski (Leipzig, 1906), pp. 30f., Ἀλκαῖος Σωσιφάνει χαίρειν. χάρις τοῖς θεοῖς πολλή. . . . See Frame, *Commentary on Thessalonians*, p. 72.

[5] Frame, *ibid.*; J. Armitage Robinson, *St. Paul's Epistle to the Ephesians*, 2nd edn (London, 1914), p. 141; W. Foerster, *TWNT*, II, 412, n. 78; also Lohmeyer, *Philipper, Kolosser, Philemon*, p. 159.

[6] Lohmeyer, pp. 163f. For reference to the more important studies on χάρις see Rigaux, *Thessaloniciens*, p. 353, and Bauer–Arndt–Gingrich, p. 886.

[7] Occurring 100 times in the Pauline and deutero-Pauline letters.

[8] Cf. the particularizing of grace in the movement from I Cor. 1: 3 to vv. 4f. See also Rom. 12: 3, 6; 15: 15; I Cor. 15: 10, etc. (Lohmeyer, *Philipper, Kolosser, Philemon*, p. 164, n. 2.)

occasion of farewell, when the elders of a church were commended 'to the Lord and to the word of his grace' (20: 32).[1]
This striking triple use of the word 'grace' suggests that in
certain circles by the time of the writing of Acts, believers were
in the habit of placing one another under the grace of God, or
of the Lord, as a form of farewell greeting. The theological
meaning of the word grace would be adapted to immediate
practical concerns of the work of spreading the gospel (Acts
14: 26, 15: 40), or of standing fast under affliction in Ephesus
(Acts 20: 32).

It is possible that here we have an indication of a rich church
background for Paul's use of the word χάρις in his greetings,
and an insight into the vital though somewhat reduced theological significance of the word in this context.[2] It seems to
express a deeply prayerful concern and perhaps a commissioning of his readers, as individuals and as a church, to renewed
Christian living under grace appropriate to the immediate
circumstances.

The second main word in the Pauline blessing, εἰρήνη, suggests Jewish influence, from the customary greeting שלם. This
links with the fact that the blessing has a Semitic rather than a
Greek syntactical form.[3] Moreover in the LXX the epistolary
greeting 'shalom' is rendered by εἰρήνη.[4] In Jewish travel-
prayers there is a predilection for the word שלם, as in Jewish
prayer language generally.[5] Furthermore the joining of the
Greek χαίρειν and the Jewish 'shalom' would be a natural
usage for bilingual Jewish communities of the diaspora;[6] cf. the
letter in II Macc. 1: 1, 'to their Jewish brethren in Egypt,
χαίρειν...καί...εἰρήνην ἀγαθήν. Thus a complex background
of epistolary greetings, Christian commissionings, Jewish
prayers and salutations may all have prepared for the Pauline

[1] See Rigaux, *Thessaloniciens*, pp. 352f.

[2] Yet the post-Pauline date of Acts, and the lack of further evidence
about the spread of this custom, suggest caution in drawing firm conclusions.

[3] See above, p. 37, n. 2.

[4] Ezra 4: 17, 'To Rehum the commander...and the rest of their associates...peace' (εἰρήνη); Ezra 5: 7, 'To Darius the king, all peace.'

[5] A number of examples from the Talmud are collected by Harder, p. 29,
n. 2; and see Strack–Billerbeck, I, 380–5.

[6] See Wendland, *Urchristlichen Literaturformen*, p. 413 (see Harder, *ibid.*).

opening greeting of grace and peace; it is difficult and probably wrong to pin-point any single derivation.

We may now ask whether Paul himself coined the exact wording of this blessing, or took it over ready-made. His unvarying use of the same words in every letter (apart from the shorter form in I Thess.) would point to his having borrowed it. The absence of this formula from general Christian usage in ordinary letters might indicate that it was a recognized expression reserved for liturgical use.[1] Moreover the liturgical nature of the language, especially the words 'from God our Father and the Lord Jesus Christ,' might at first seem to support Lohmeyer's view that Paul borrowed it directly from a church blessing.[2] Thus Cullmann, too, argues that 'the benediction formulae at the beginning...are probably the liturgical introductory formulae which were spoken at the beginning of the service.'[3]

Yet, in the light of the variety of available epistolary antecedents and parallels, there is no compelling reason to accept this view. Indeed, the expression 'from God our Father and the Lord Jesus Christ,' may seem actually to favor Pauline authorship of the precise wording.[4] It must be noted further that the earliest attestation of this blessing as such is in the Pauline epistles themselves. In line with this it has been suggested that the blessing itself 'summarizes well his theological and apostolic preoccupations,'[5] that the two concepts of grace and peace are not just mechanically added together from Jewish and Greek antecedents, but from an organic association within his par-

---

[1] Compare a somewhat similar restriction in the use of the Jewish synagogue beracha. 'Once the "liturgical *berakha*" had become the established norm in the synagogue, it was considered illicit to recite a "*berakha* which is not necessary," i.e., to use the *berakha* outside the sphere of obligatory prayer proper,' Heinemann, *Prayer*, p. xiv.

[2] 'Briefliche Grussüberschriften,' pp. 164ff. See also above, p. 82 on the similar prayer phrase, 'the God and Father of our Lord Jesus Christ.'

[3] Cullmann, *Early Christian Worship*, p. 23 (following Lietzmann); cf. Hamman, p. 315.

[4] See the persuasive argument of Kramer that this is a characteristically Pauline addition, par. 42c (pp. 152ff.). For the deep significance of these names, see above, p. 55.

[5] Rigaux, *Thessaloniciens*, *ad loc.*

ticular understanding of the gospel.[1] With grace and peace everything is given.[2]

Thus the greeting would be a thoroughly appropriate one for Paul's special use as an apostolic salutation[3] and might well have been his own formulation.

In summary, it seems that Paul himself was responsible for the exact character of the opening salutation, although the form and ingredients were suggested to him both from epistolary and liturgical usage. On one hand, this blessing need not be reduced to a merely conventional use by Paul, either of a stock epistolary greeting, or of a ready-made liturgical formula. On the other, it need not be regarded as expressing fully his highest theology of God's grace in its majestic freedom, and the readers' salvation which would flow from it. Whether original or borrowed, the apostolic salutation would serve a more limited epistolary and liturgical purpose. It would help to adapt the letter right at the start for reading during the eucharist.[4] In the light of the enlarged and deepened significance which had come into the life of all who were in Christ, Paul's salutation would point toward that particular range of blessings which were most needed by his readers and which the letter would be intended to convey.

---

[1] Cf. von Dobschütz, *Thessalonicher-Briefe*, p. 59.

[2] Findlay, *Thessalonians*, p. 47: '*Grace* is the sum of all blessings that God bestows through Christ. *Peace* is the sum of all spiritual blessings that man receives and experiences; it is Grace in its fruit and realization.' Paul does not wish joy (χάρα) and peace to them, for this would have narrowed the blessing to their subjective response to God's grace. We do find this more subjective emphasis in the prayer-wish in Rom. 15: 13 (all joy and peace in believing); cf. Rom. 14: 17, Gal. 5: 22.

[3] It has been suggested that this was rooted partly in the Israelite royal salutation of which numerous echoes are found in the Psalms. P. Bonnard, *L'Épître de Saint Paul aux Galates* (Neuchâtel, 1953), p. 21, citing N. A. Dahl, *Das Volk Gottes* (Oslo, 1941), pp. 8ff. The attempt to link the Pauline greeting directly back to the Aaronic priestly blessing (Num. 6: 26) has not been generally accepted, von Dobschütz, *Thessalonicher-Briefe*, p. 59, and von der Goltz, *Das Gebet*, p. 115. Yet see E. Best, 'Spiritual Sacrifice, General Priesthood in the New Testament,' *Interpretation*, 14 (1960), 273–99. He notes the act of blessing as a function of the priesthood at Qumran, and argues that this liturgical function was taken over as part of the office of priest in the NT.

[4] Cf. above, p. 9.

The element of intercession is by no means lacking. But the unchanging character of the formula denies it the spontaneous intercessory value of the main wish-prayers, and places it in a borderline category.

The closing benedictions

Unlike the uniformity of the opening greetings, variations are found in the wording of the final grace-wish, ranging from the shortest form,

The grace of the Lord Jesus be with you (I Cor. 16: 24),

to the long 'trinitarian' form,

The grace of the Lord Jesus Christ and the love of God and the fellowship of the Holy Spirit be with you all (II Cor. 13: 14).[1]

But except for this long form[2] the gift which is offered is always limited to one – grace, and the impression is still that of a formula used with variation.[3]

Much of what has been said about the opening greetings applies also to the closing ones and need not be repeated. These final benedictions replace a customary Greek epistolary salutation meaning 'farewell!'[4] But as we have seen, their position in the liturgically oriented closing section of the letters may give them a special significance as a 'transition to the actual breaking of the bread,'[5] and here indeed the apostle seems to have adopted and varied a formula 'of pre-Pauline liturgical origin.'[6]

[1] See Appendix III. Similar grace blessings are found at the close of the deutero-Pauline letters, and Heb. 13: 25, Rev, 22: 21. In I Pet. and III John, grace is replaced by peace. Closing blessings are lacking in James, II Pet., and I and II John, Jude.

[2] And perhaps Rom. 15: 33; but see above, p. 90, n. 5.

[3] Cf. Kramer, par. 20a (p. 90), 'The farewell formula in the Pauline epistles is largely stereotype.'

[4] Usually ἔρρωσο, ἔρρωσθε, or ἔρρωσθαί σε (ὑμᾶς) εὔχομαι. Rigaux, *Thessaloniciens*, p. 718; Ziemann, *Epistolarum graecorum*, 334–46; Koskenniemi, pp. 151–4.

[5] Cullmann, *Early Christian Worship*, p. 23; see also Kramer, par. 20 (pp. 90f.).

[6] J. A. T. Robinson, writing about I Cor. 16: 23, states, 'And, finally, Paul's closing greeting echoes the words with which the president [of the eucharist] begins: "The grace of the Lord Jesus Christ be with you."' 'Traces of a Liturgical Sequence...,' p. 40. Cf. Kramer, *ibid.*, referring also to Rev. 22: 17–21. But, for a cautionary opinion, see Gamble, p. 129.

Yet the use of such a formula may have enabled Paul to utter a genuine wish-prayer that grace, the most precious blessing of the new life in Christ, be not taken from the community and each of its members.[1] The fact that he felt at liberty to vary the wording more freely – even as far as the threefold form in II Corinthians – may imply a greater element of the purposeful adapting of a formula. By the end of a deeply spiritual and personally felt pastoral letter, written usually at a time of threatening crisis, with the outpouring of prayerful and concerned interest on behalf of the readers, a richer level of spontaneous communication would be reached. Even the words of a well-known blessing would gain immeasurably in significance both for the writer and for his readers, gathered together in eucharistic worship.[2]

But as with the opening blessings, we remain partly in the realm of conjecture. Although the closing blessings may with some reservation also be classed with the principal wish-prayers, they suggest a reduced level of spontaneous intercessory significance.

[1] Rigaux, *Thessaloniciens*, p. 606.

[2] In this connection it is worth remarking that the 'trinitarian' benediction (II Cor. 13: 14) is used by Paul to close his 'severe letter' (see below, p. 238), as if he would pronounce the richest blessing especially on those he had reprimanded so sternly. The impression is strengthened by the phrase 'with you all,' not found elsewhere in Paul's benedictions.

That he himself authored this blessing may be indicated with some probability. He seems to have developed it from his usual shorter liturgical form, 'The grace of the Lord Jesus Christ be with you,' by adding 'the love of God and the fellowship of the Holy Spirit,' and thereby arriving at an unexpected order that begins with the grace of Christ. It would, of course, be fitting also for the sequence of the New Testament Christians' experience of salvation through Christ.

While the blessing with its familiar liturgical threefold cadence gives no formal statement of the doctrine of the Trinity, it reflects the trinitarian habit of Paul's thought (cf., for example I Cor. 12: 4ff., II Cor. 1: 21f.). This in turn reflects his own Christian experience and his theological reflection on that experience: the grace available in and through Christ (subj. gen.), was initiated by and grounded in the originating love of God (subj. gen.), mediated and sustained by the Christian's participation in the Holy Spirit (gen. of participation). But for alternative interpretations of this compressed formula (especially the difficult phrase ἡ κοινωνία τοῦ ἁγίου πνεύματος), see the commentaries, together with J. Y. Campbell, 'KOINⲰNIA and its cognates in the New Testament,' *JBL*, 51 (1932), 378ff.; H. Seesemann, *Der Begriff* Κοινωνία *im Neuen Testament* (Giessen, 1933); F. Hauck, *TWNT*, III, 807.

CURSES AND A 'PRONOUNCEMENT BLESSING'

We turn now to a third group of passages which may be tentatively regarded as a type of wish-prayer.[1] In Galatians Paul utters a forceful imprecation[2] balanced by an answering 'pronouncement blessing':

> But even if we, or an angel from heaven, should preach to you a gospel contrary to that which we preached to you, let him be accursed. As we have said before, so now I say again, If any one is preaching to you a gospel contrary to that which you received, let him be accursed. (Gal. 1:8f.)

> Peace and mercy be upon all who walk by this rule, and upon the Israel of God. (Gal. 6:16)

In I Corinthians he utters a curse in the closing sentences of the letter:

> If any one has no love for the Lord, let him be accursed. Our Lord, come! (I Cor. 16:22)

Again we must inquire as to the function of these sentences. What do they contribute to our understanding of the intercessory ministry of the apostle? Before making a detailed study of each one, it will clarify our undertaking to survey some preliminary questions about the peculiar form and origin of this type of sentence.

At the outset we notice that these passages share a distinctive form which sets them apart from the more freely composed main wish-prayers, while distinguishing the pronouncement blessing from the opening and closing epistolary greetings.[3] The two imprecations consist of a conditional sentence with the verb of the apodosis in the imperative mood, ἀνάθεμα ἔστω, or ἤτω. Being in the passive voice they make no direct reference to the agency of God. The pronouncement blessing has a similar form: the conditional aspect is expressed in the word ὅσοι, and the main verb must be understood in the imperative, ἔστωσαν.[4] The blessing is in the passive voice, without naming

---

[1] See Appendix III, p. 300.
[2] The terms curse, imprecation, execration, and malediction will be used interchangeably.
[3] See also below, p. 129, n. 1.
[4] Cf. above, pp. 25f.

God. For convenience we may consider also at this time a fourth passage, an injunction to the Corinthians to pronounce a curse on Paul's behalf (I Cor. 5: 3–5):[1]

For though absent in body I am present in spirit, and as if present, I have already pronounced judgment in the name of the Lord Jesus on the man who has done such a thing. When you are assembled, and my spirit is present, with the power of our Lord Jesus, you are to deliver this man to Satan for the destruction of the flesh, that his spirit may be saved in the day of the Lord Jesus.

These four passages may be seen as related closely in form and function[2] to a number of apparently juridical or legislative pronouncements in Paul's epistles and elsewhere in the New Testament, which have a similar conditional cast, e.g., 'If any one (εἴ τις) destroys God's temple, God will destroy him' (I Cor. 3: 17); 'All who (ὅσοι) have sinned without the law will also perish without the law' (Rom. 2: 12). These pronouncements seem to reflect a *Sitz im Leben* in the very early Christian prophetic rulings uttered probably at the eucharist, to guide the earliest church during its still fluid and unorganized period.[3] An element of paraenesis is not lacking,[4] but the pronouncements are clothed in a Jewish casuistical law-style, a decretal form suitable for congregational guidance and warning.[5] Their prophetic claim is grounded in the authority of the

---

[1] It might be thought to belong more precisely to the paraenetic references, class III.

[2] The I Cor. 5: 3–5 passage is related in function though not in form.

[3] See E. Käsemann, 'Sentences of Holy Law in the New Testament,' *New Testament Questions of Today*, E.Tr. (London, 1969), pp. 66–81 (an essay published originally in 1955); Bornkamm, 'Das Anathema in der frühchristlichen Abendmahlsliturgie'; H. Frhr. von Campenhausen, *Die Begründung kirchlicher Entscheidungen beim Apostel Paulus. Zur Grundlegung des Kirchenrechts* (Heidelberg, 1957), and the literature cited on p. 5, n. 1.
For a different view which objects to classifying these sentences as law, and grounds them (with only partial success) in Wisdom literature and in a teaching situation, see K. Berger, 'Zu Den Sogennanten Sätzen Heiligen Rechts,' *NTS*, 17 (1970–1), 10–40.

[4] For an emphasis on the hortatory aspect of Paul's judgment passages, see C. Roetzel, 'The Judgment Form in Paul's Letters,' *JBL*, 88 (1969), 305–12.

[5] Among further examples of this style in the NT, Käsemann, 'Sentences of Holy Law,' includes Rom. 10: 11, 13, I Cor. 14: 38, II Cor. 9: 6, Gal. 3: 12, Matt. 5: 19, 6: 14f., 10: 32f., Mk. 4: 24f., 8: 38, Rev. 22: 18f.

Holy Spirit, given as one of the expected accompaniments of the new age.[1]

Many of them indicate a strongly eschatological background from an early Christian period when rewards and sanctions were still expected at the immediate future coming of Christ, so that it was God himself who would execute the judgment. Several of them actually state such a divine eschatological sanction or reward, as do our four passages: 'Let him be accursed' (I Cor. 16: 22, Gal. 1: 8f.); 'for the destruction of the flesh, that his spirit may be saved in the day of the Lord Jesus' (an immediate sanction with an eschatological reward, I Cor. 5: 5); 'Peace and mercy be upon all who' (Gal. 6: 16).[2] With these we may compare such examples as I Cor. 3: 17, 'If any one destroys God's temple, God will destroy him'; II Cor. 9: 6, including both a sanction and a reward, 'will also reap sparingly ...will also reap bountifully'; Rom. 2: 12, 'All who have sinned without the law will also perish without the law....'[3]

Most of these eschatological judgment pronouncements[4] have the sanctioning verb in the present or future indicative and

Cf. the famous temple inscription, ὃς δ' ἂν ληφθῇ ἑαυτῷ αἴτιος ἔσται διὰ τὸ ἐξακολουθεῖν θάνατον. A. Deissmann, *Light from the Ancient East; the New Testament illustrated by recently discovered texts of the Graeco-Roman world*, E.Tr. (New York, 1927), p. 80.

[1] Cf. Joel 2: 28f. (Acts 2: 14ff.), Mal. 4: 5f., Test. Lev. 8: 14, Test. Benj. 9: 2. See Friedrich, 'Propheten und Prophezien im Neuen Testament,' *TWNT*, VI, espec. 849–58; H. A. Guy, *New Testament Prophecy, Its Origin and Significance* (London, 1947), pp. 90ff.

[2] Here the eschatological character is implicit.

[3] These sentences depend partly on the eschatological oracles of blessing and doom in the OT prophets, related in turn to the blessings and curses attached to the keeping or breaking of Israel's covenantal laws; see D. R. Hillers, *Treaty-Curses and the Old Testament Prophets* (Rome, 1964), and the literature therein cited. Cf. Jer. 34: 18 and Isa. 34: 16 with Josh. 8: 34, Deut. 28 (blessings for obedience, curses for disobedience), Lev. 26 (blessings for obedience, curses for disobedience, and a final promise of hope should the disobedient repent, vv. 40–5). Cf. the treaty-curses attached to the widely used international treaties of the Near East. For further literature, see P. B. Harner, 'Exodus, Sinai, and Hittite Prologues,' *JBL*, 75 (1966), 234, n. 4.

Cf. the recitation of blessings and curses with which the initiates into the Qumran community were warned of the consequences of keeping or breaking their vow; Manual of Discipline, 1QS 2: 2–18.

[4] A descriptive phrase used by N. Perrin, *Rediscovering the Teaching of Jesus* (New York, 1967), p. 22.

should therefore probably be taken as juridical decisions or statements. Others, however, have a more directly paraenetic cast and are modified so as to omit the divine sanction or reward, although it may sometimes lurk in the background, e.g., I Cor. 14: 13, 28, 30, 35, 37, culminating finally in v. 38, 'If anyone does not recognize this, he is not recognized.'[1]

Among these sentences, however, the four under consideration express the sanction or reward not as a casuistical decision (indicative verb), but as the pronouncement of a curse or blessing (imperative verb), and are therefore of immediate relevance for our study, since they approximate the form of negative intercessory prayers rather than statements.[2] Yet they differ from the ordinary wish-prayers in being conditionally applicable only to certain individuals, should these persist in a certain course of action, whereas the other wish-prayers refer unconditionally to all the readers. So they retain their juridical aspect even while verging on intercessory prayer.

They differ from the usual wish-prayers also in not referring overtly to God as agent, being couched in the passive voice. Does this imply that along with their apparently magical form they retained some of the magical nature of a spell, so that the curse or blessing is in itself effective apart from the will and disposal of God? Does Paul in his zeal assume here some kind of independent apostolic or prophetic authority, with the power to pronounce irresistible blessings and curses, rather than to place his requests in God's hands?[3]

Now it is true that behind these curse formulae there may be seen the form and cadence of pagan execrations, e.g., 'but if anyone shall attempt to take away a stone...let him be accursed with the inscriptions written above,' εἴ τις δὲ...ἤτω ἐπικατάρατος (second or third century A.D.), and 'cursed whoever doth not spare this place of work,' ἐπικατάρατος ὅστις

---

[1] See Käsemann, 'Sentences of Holy Law,' p. 74. For a discussion of the paraenetic aspects of many sentences of this type as found in the synoptic gospels, and their dependence on Wisdom, or Apocalyptic Wisdom literature, see Berger, pp. 19ff.

[2] The fourth passage (I Cor. 5: 3–5), being an injunction, is of course differently phrased, and many of the stylistic observations on the next few pages apply only indirectly to that passage.

[3] See below, pp. 192, 268, n. 4.

μή... (second century A.D.).[1] But if we turn to the Old Testament, we shall find numerous prototypes of blessings and curses couched also in the same conditional and passive form, without naming God as agent.[2]

Some scholars have suggested that in the rhythmic incantational style of the Old Testament curses, in their repetition, and in various accompanying gestures there is to be seen the remains of a magical view of their inexorable potency.[3] Against them, however, Brichto has argued that 'traces of magical thought in the Bible are one thing, the assumption that the operation of curses is magical and independent of the Deity is quite another.'[4] The passive construction of the curse formula ארור does not make it 'automatic and self-fulfilling,' but may originate from a stylistic accident.[5] In support of this he points out the long and intense struggle of Israel to root out all forms of magic before a 'Deity [who] is supremely independent of outside power, Himself the source of all power.'[6] He concludes, 'In the Bible, good fortune and misfortune (beraka and qelala respectively) are traceable to God, and prayers or imprecations invoking these are, even when not made explicit in the text, addressed to the Deity.'[7]

We may assume, then, that while the wording of Paul's imprecations and pronouncement blessing reflects not only an

[1] See Deissmann, *Light from Ancient East*, pp. 97 and 96. The words ἀνάθεμα, ἀναθεματίζομεν τούτους are also attested in pagan curses, *ibid.* p. 95. See also below, p. 128, n. 3.

[2] E.g., Deut. 28: 3–6, 16–19. See above, pp. 25f.

[3] See above, pp. 25f. See the literature cited by H. C. Brichto, *The Problem of Curse in the Hebrew Bible* (Philadelphia, 1963), pp. 3–13.

[4] P. 210. See also Towner, '"Blessed be YHWH"...,' p. 387, n. 3.

[5] Brichto, pp. 211f.   [6] *Ibid.* pp. 212f. Cf. W. Eichrodt, I, 172–6.

[7] Brichto, p. 218. See also Hillers, p. 28, note. Eichrodt (I, 173) points to 'instances...which show how Yahweh became Lord over the blessing and the curse and stripped them of their original character. Because the curse is uttered in the name of Yahweh (I Sam. 26. 19, II Kings 2. 24 [etc.]) it is he who carries it out (Judg. 9. 57; Deut. 28. 20); but equally this means that he has the power to apply the curse to a different object or to make it ineffective (Deut. 30. 7; II Sam. 16. 12).' See also II, 449, '...even the most outstanding man of God is always subject to the will of the divine majesty, and...the hearing of his prayer is strictly the gift of God's free condescension...the unseen corrective when at any given time the limit is overstepped.'

Old Testament and Jewish but also a pagan usage, it does not in itself necessarily imply a magical concept nor a departure from his usual understanding of the limits of his own power and authority under God.[1]

Yet in these sentences he does speak with the prophetic authority of an agent of God.[2] It is against those whom he judges to be undermining his churches that he assumes this authority. So in Galatians (1: 8f.) he uses the curse essentially as a 'protective device' against a specific danger, which it had usually been in the Old Testament.[3] While the malediction is in God's hands to carry out, the apostle believes that in these special circumstances of threat to the wellbeing of the church, he is speaking as a prophet under the Spirit's guidance, according to God's will, and therefore on behalf of God.[4] Unlike the large element of uncertainty found in the intercessory wish-prayers, where he does not claim to know the designs of God in detail, there is shown in this curse the fullest assurance, in that he is defending his church members against particular enemies of the gospel who would destroy it from within.[5] The troublemakers at Galatia have been identified and judged as damaging those weaker than themselves, and the apostle therefore feels no hesitance in pronouncing their doom.[6] The same assurance in using a protective device against a limited group who are harming the church at Corinth may be seen in the curse

[1] Perrin, *Teaching of Jesus*, p. 22, interprets the passive judgment-pronouncement, 'he is not recognized' (I Cor. 14: 38), as 'referring to the eschatological activity of God...an Aramaism frequently to be found in the New Testament.' Cf. *ibid.* pp. 37, 145, 189. Also Blass–Debrunner–Funk, 130 (1), 313, on the use of the passive to avoid the divine name. For a contrary view see R. T. Stamm, *The Epistle to the Galatians*, IB, x, 452.

[2] Käsemann, 'Sentences of Holy Law,' p. 70; Eichrodt, II, 450. For recent emphases on the prophetic mold of Paul's call and mission, see Roetzel, p. 305, n. 2; A.-M. Denis, 'L'Apôtre Paul, Prophète "Messianique" des Gentils,' *EphTL*, 33 (1957), 245–318. See also Schmithals, *The Office of the Apostle*, pp. 51–3. [3] S. Gevirtz, *IDB*, I, 749.

[4] See W. Grundmann, *TWNT*, II, 312, 'Es ist die Kraft des Christus, die Paulus in seiner apostolischen Wirksamkeit hat und über die nichter, sondern der Christus frei verfügt. Es ist nötig dass sich Paulus mit dieser Kraft zusammentut.' See below, pp. 145f.

[5] P. Althaus, *Der Brief an die Galater*, 5th edn (Göttingen, 1949), p. 7.

[6] See below, pp. 126ff. Cf. the curses and woes elsewhere in the NT against those who hinder others weaker than themselves, e.g., Matt. 18: 6f.

enjoined in I Cor. 5: 5, and the associated curse which follows in I Cor. 16: 22. There, too, his imprecations must take effect.[1]

Thus we conclude that although the curses may be seen as a type of negative intercession,[2] they were pronounced only in specially threatening circumstances and in a prophetic juridical manner against particular offenders, with a solemn conviction that their sanction would be implemented under the hand of God. Similarly, the pronouncement blessing (Gal. 6: 16), directed only to those who accept the true gospel, manifests a juridical quality, with the same assurance of its fulfilment.

A curse and a pronouncement blessing in Galatians

Coming now to a more detailed study of the curse and the pronouncement blessing in Galatians, we begin with the epistolary background in which they occur. The letter was written probably not long before Romans,[3] and had actually prepared the way for the larger epistle.[4] It was in the main an impassioned defense of justification through faith in Jesus Christ alone rather than by works of the law (2: 16).[5] But compared with the network of competing interests that lay behind Romans, the relations between the apostle and his Galatian churches were

and parallels, Matt. 23: 13ff. and parallels. The apparently conflicting instruction in Rom. 12: 14 (to bless and not curse those who persecute you, cf., Matt. 5: 44, Luke 6: 28), referred to vengeful reactions against persecutors, rather than to juridical pronouncements against those who were judged to be corrupting the church from within.

[1] See below, pp. 142ff. [2] Cf. below, p. 254.

[3] The long-debated question of the dating of the epistle and the location of the Galatian churches is still undecided. See Feine–Behm–Kümmel, pp. 192–8 and the authorities there cited; see above, p. 46, n. 1. As the answer to these complex problems does not profoundly affect our study, we will assume that Paul was addressing a homogeneous group of churches in the northern territory of Galatia; also that he wrote the letter either during his lengthy stay in Ephesus (Acts 19: 1 – 20: 1, I Cor. 15: 32, II Cor. 1: 8), or shortly thereafter in Macedonia, on the way to his last visit to Corinth, about 53–55 A.D. (Acts 20: 21, II Cor. 2: 12f., 7: 5, 8: 1).

[4] See above, p. 75; M.-J. Lagrange, *Saint Paul, Épître aux Galates* (Paris, 1950), pp. lxiiiff., and Dodd, *The Epistle to the Romans*, p. xxx.

[5] Yet 'the apparent presence of libertinistic tendencies in the Galatian congregation is difficult to reconcile with the main arguments of the letter directed against an orthodox nomism.' R. Jewett, 'The Agitators and the Galatian Congregation,' *NTS*, 17 (1970–1), 198.

more clearly established; although threatening, the circumstances were less complicated.[1]

A group of intruders (1: 7, 4: 17, 5: 10, 12, 6: 12)[2] were demanding that the Gentile Christians submit themselves to Jewish law (2: 16, 3: 21b, 4: 21, 5: 4), particularly the rite of circumcision, and to other external legal observances (5: 2, 6: 12f., 4: 8–11),[3] in addition to their faith in Christ. They supported their attacks on Paul's gospel of liberty by undermining his apostolic authority (1: 1, 11ff.). So persuasive were they that the Galatian believers were rapidly surrendering to their blandishments (1: 6, 3: 1–5, 4: 9, 17, 5: 1, 6: 12). A fundamentally 'different gospel' threatened to destroy all that Paul had taught (1: 6–9, 5: 1, 7f.).

Against this threat the apostle reacts violently with an angry letter couched in an unusually official style,[4] that begins with a polemical note in the address (1: 1) and ends without the customary personal greetings. So narrowly is his attention concentrated on the crisis at Galatia that his agitated thoughts do not for a moment broaden to include wider concerns. Everything else is secondary to the one immediate problem.[5] In contrast to his other extant letters, no mention is

---

[1] That is, as far as we may reconstruct them from the letter itself, for we have little other evidence.

[2] For our purpose it does not seem necessary to decide exactly who these agitators were – whether Jewish Christians (Judaizers from Jerusalem), Judaizing Gentile Christians, syncretistic Jews, Gnostic Jewish Christians, or two separate groups (Judaizing and libertine). From the general antilegalistic argument of this letter we assume that Paul is here contending mainly against a group who advocated a Jewish type of legalism, centered in but not confined to circumcision. For a recent discussion, see Jewett, 'The Agitators and the Galatian Congregation,' and the literature cited there.

[3] See Althaus, *Galater*, p. 2. Gentile Christians among the believers would be retreating to their earlier reliance on the observance of feasts (4: 9–11), but adding the rite of circumcision (5: 1–8).

[4] H. Schlier, *Der Brief an die Galater*, Meyer's Kommentar, 12th edn (Göttingen, 1951), pp. 1f. Cf. Wendland, *Urchristliche Literaturformen*, pp. 346f. The authenticity and integrity of this letter are not seriously debated. We have here an original composition, written at white heat, affording us in the prayer passages, as in other sections, first-hand insights into Paul's inner understanding of his gospel ministry.

[5] We may of course envisage other letters and communications between Paul and the Galatians of an entirely different character, cf. I Cor. 16: 1.

made here of his own current personal circumstances and anxieties although we know from the Corinthian letters how pressing they were,[1] nor of his future travelling plans perhaps involving his readers.[2] Even about his large-scale projects which must already have been maturing, he is silent – the taking of the collection to Jerusalem, the visit to the capital city of Rome and beyond.[3] In the unusually extensive autobiographical section (1: 11 – 2: 21), he selects only those incidents crucial for proving his authentic and independent apostleship.[4] The references to his previously cordial relations with the Galatian churches (4: 12–15) do but serve the same purpose – to re-establish his standing among them and regain credence for his gospel. He is fighting for speedy control over the situation, as if out of all patience that so late in his Western ministry his ubiquitous opponents should once again have moved in to hinder his plans.

So it is the intruders rather than the Galatians who are the focal point of the apostle's attention. While he may address the believers themselves (1: 6–10, 3: 1–5, 4: 8–20, 5: 7–10), it is the agitators whom he is mainly answering.[5] Nowhere does he seem to take the readers themselves into his personal confidence, nor seek to enlist their interest in his own larger designs for the gospel, nor to include them in an active partnership with himself through contributions to the collection or through their prayers. As he prepares to wind up his affairs in the West, he seems impatient only to have his present churches in order, and his relations with the conservative wing sufficiently settled (6: 17). Then he may feel free to move on. The difference of all this from his carefully hesitant appeal to Rome for help and co-operation, could scarcely be more striking.

So J. B. Lightfoot, *St. Paul's Epistle to the Galatians*, 7th edn (London, 1881), p. 25.

[1] See I Cor. 15: 30–32, II Cor. 1: 8–11, 2: 12f., 7: 5ff.

[2] Contrast the frequency of such travel references in all the other epistles: e.g., I Thess. 2: 17, I Cor. 4: 19–21, 5: 3, II Cor. 1: 15ff., 23, 12: 14, etc. See above, p. 48, n. 2.

[3] Cf. Rom. 15: 22–33. See below, p. 270. He does actually mention the matter of the collection to them (2: 10), but not in regard to themselves, although we know they were included in the scheme, I Cor. 16: 1.

[4] For a strong statement of this view, see J. T. Sanders, 'Paul's "Autobiographical" Statements in Galatians 1 – 2,' *JBL*, 85 (1966), 335–43.

[5] Cf. A. Oepke, *Der Brief des Paulus an die Galater*, 3rd edn (Berlin, 1964), p. 10.

*Survey of the intercessory prayer and related prayer
passages in Galatians*[1]

In line with such fiercely narrowed concentration upon the
immediate problem at Galatia, is a noticeable constriction in
the prayer passages of the epistle. While the opening grace
greeting (1: 3) is standard, the other prayer references are
reduced to a minimum. They are infrequent, short and pointed,
closely reflecting the sombre mood of the letter in what they
say and what they omit.

Gone are both the individually tailored thanksgiving and the
opening assurance of Paul's constant supplications for the
readers, a formula that would have served at the outset to lift
their errors into the circle of his prayers and hopes. In their
place we find first, a formal doxology that refers to the gift of
Christ and avoids giving thanks for any victories at Galatia
(1: 4–5);[2] second, a vehement apostolic curse upon those who
are misleading them (1: 8f.), that directs attention away from
the Galatians themselves to the troublemakers. Instead of the
prayer for a speedy journey to see them, is a silence, broken
only later when the apostle has come around to consider his
earlier affectionate dealings with them. 'I could wish to be
present with you now and to change my tone, for I am per-
plexed about you' (4: 19f.).[3]

In the main body of the epistle there appears one fleeting
though triumphant reference to the Spirit's intercession (4: 6).
But missing from the paraenetic section is the expected
exhortation to the readers to pray constantly with joy and
thanksgiving.[4]

In the autograph section (6: 11–18)[5] we find a drastically
reduced variation of the liturgically oriented pattern. The
sudden warning is there (6: 12–15), but the various greetings

[1] For supplication passages, see Appendix II.   [2] See below, pp. 172f.
[3] This expression falls far short of his usual travel plans; see above, p. 124,
n. 2. But for an alternative explanation, see Funk, 'The apostolic "*Parousia*,"'
pp. 266f.
[4] In its place we may find an angry echo of the earlier curse, directed
again not to the Galatians but to the opponents: 'I wish those who unsettle
you would mutilate themselves!' (5: 12).
[5] Assuming tentatively that it begins at 6: 11. But see Bahr, 'Subscriptions in Pauline Letters,' pp. 34f.

and the kiss of peace are lacking. The summarizing wish-prayer has been contracted from a warm intercession for all the readers, to a formal blessing pronouncement (an adapted peace blessing), restricted to those who accept the apostle's exposition of the gospel, and also to 'the Israel of God' (6: 16). Finally, in lieu of a positive request for their prayers, we find only a restraining injunction upon his opponents, 'Henceforth let no man trouble me' (6: 17).[1] The only note of increased cordiality and fellowship seems to be the addition of the irenic word ἀδελφοί to the closing blessing: 'The grace of our Lord Jesus Christ be with your spirit, brethren. Amen' (6: 18).

Galatians 1: 8f.

We may now ask what was the apostle's precise intention in uttering a curse that lends such a dark tone to the epistle:

But even if we, or an angel from heaven, should preach to you a gospel contrary to that which we preached to you, let him be accursed. As we have said before, so now I say again, If any one is preaching to you a gospel contrary to that which you received, let him be accursed. (Gal. 1: 8f.)

The body of the letter begins bluntly with a strong exclamation of astonishment at the Galatians' rapid desertion of God and his gospel of free grace in Christ, and at their weak submission under certain unnamed persons who are perverting the true gospel (1: 6–9). Furthermore, he makes it clear that he considers their defection not merely an unfortunate mistake, nor primarily a disloyalty to himself, but a quite fundamental apostasy from those central truths apart from which there can be no real gospel at all – no gospel of Christ.[2] Having established the radical seriousness of a situation which was beyond

[1] The request for prayer is lacking also from I Cor., probably for somewhat similar reasons, in a letter which ends with a severe curse injunction (see below, p. 142, n. 1); and from the 'severe letter,' II Cor. 10–13 (see below, p. 239).

[2] Taking τοῦ Χριστοῦ (v. 7) as an objective genitive, the gospel concerning Christ, or grounded in Christ.

Attempts have been made to soften the words παρ' ὅ (vv. 8 and 9), so as to mean 'an additional gospel besides or beyond that which we preached and you received' – i.e., including additions to the basic gospel. But Paul's view was clearly that the troublers were attempting to preach a *different* and *contrary* gospel (vv. 6–7). For the meaning of παρ' ὅ as 'other than,' see Moule, *Idiom Book*, p. 51.

appeasement, he proceeds immediately to give his official apostolic judgment on the matter – a juridical curse of eschatological doom on the troublemakers – underlining its weight and authority by a legal style and solemn repetition.

The first version of the curse (v. 8) is worded in such a way as to be a general apostolic and prophetic ruling about the unalterable nature of the gospel, rather than a judgment on particular individuals. The generalized nature of the maxim is indicated by its hypothetical syntax, 'But even if we, or an angel...should preach,'[1] and by the two highly improbable instances adduced for consideration (apostle and angel). Furthermore, the possible omission of the first ὑμῖν[2] would serve to make the form still more general. The judgment is based ultimately not in Paul's apostolic authority, but in the authority of the unchangeable gospel itself, which had been delivered to him together with his apostleship (1: 1, 11f.), and which in turn he had preached to them (1: 8f.).[3] His own apostolic authority is derived from the authority of the gospel, which he may prophetically interpret and apply, but not basically change. Such is the stable permanence and finality of that gospel of Christ (v. 7), that neither he nor even a heavenly messenger, have either the power or the authority to alter it.[4]

In the second version of the curse (v. 9), Paul goes on to apply the general ruling to the actual Galatian crisis. The words 'as we have said before' probably refer to some earlier statement given by the apostle, perhaps in anticipation of the very situation which had now arisen.[5] Thus the imprecation is claimed to be no merely hasty reaction to the immediate problem.[6] The conditional clause is recast so as to suggest an actual happening: 'If anyone is preaching to you,'[7] and the word τις may refer back to his description of the troublemakers them-

---

[1] ἀλλὰ καὶ ἐὰν ἡμεῖς...εὐαγγελίσηται, aorist subjunctive, indicating an unlikely condition.

[2] The first ὑμῖν in v. 8 is omitted in ℵ* G^gr* Ψ it^ar it^g and several fathers. It may have been wrongly added by assimilation to the next verse.

[3] See Althaus, *Galater*, p. 7, and Bonnard, p. 24.   [4] Cf. I Cor. 3: 11.

[5] Opinions differ about this reference: whether the earlier statement had been made on some previous occasion, or referred merely to the previous verse (v. 8). There can be no certain decision, but it would seem to refer to some earlier occasion.

[6] See below, pp. 144, 146, n. 7.   [7] εἰ with present indicative.

selves as τίνες οἱ ταράσσοντες ὑμᾶς.[1] The gravity of their defection from the true gospel is further underlined by the word παρελάβετε, an almost technical term in Pauline usage for the receiving of the traditional gospel message (cf. I Cor. 11: 23, 15: 1, 3, etc.).[2]

Both versions include the authoritative traditional words ἀνάθεμα ἔστω.[3] In writing this grave juridical imprecation, Paul is assuming his full apostolic authority to apply a previously uttered ruling to a current crisis, and to take the sternest measures to protect the gospel against those who would distort it and mislead others. Certainly he intends at least excommunication from the church, although more than that would be included here.[4] The curse must be read out liturgically at the eucharist[5] in the Galatian churches, and the troublemakers solemnly handed over to the eschatological judgment and

---

[1] τινες is a frequently used term for his adversaries whom he seldom named, e.g., Gal. 2: 12, Rom. 3: 8, I Cor. 4: 18, 15: 12, Phil. 1: 15, etc. Rather than listing their precise names from a distance in such a serious and delicate matter, he may prefer that those on the spot act in the matter, and resist or expel any to whom the warning might apply.

[2] See G. Delling, *TWNT*, IV, 14f.

[3] For the imperative see Blass–Debrunner–Funk, p. 194, par. 384; in classical Greek, imprecations had used the optative, but in the Old Testament, blessings and curses tended to be stated more strongly than wishes (see above, pp. 25f.).

ἀνάθεμα (Attic ἀνάθημα) represented something devoted to a deity and given up to destruction. In the LXX it is one of the words used for חֵרֶם (e.g., Lev. 27: 28f., Num. 21: 3, etc.). Paul follows LXX usage – the word denotes the object of a curse in Rom. 9: 3, I Cor. 12: 3, 16: 22, Gal. 1: 8; the sinner must be delivered up to the judicial wrath of God. See J. Behm, *TWNT*, I, 356f.

For the significance of the passive voice, and the omission of the name of God, see above, pp. 119ff.

[4] Cf. Gal. 5: 4, 'You are severed from Christ, you who would be justified by the law.' See J. Jeremias, *TWNT*, III, 752, 'Die Übung der Bindegewalt in der ältesten Christenheit,' where the different forms that excommunication might take are pointed out. See Acts 8: 20f., Gal. 1: 8f., I Cor. 16: 22, 5: 3–5 (see below, pp. 147ff.), I Tim. 1: 20, etc.

The phrase ἀνάθεμα ἔστω probably corresponded to a formula of exclusion from the synagogue (Strack–Billerbeck, IV, 293ff.). Yet here as elsewhere it goes beyond church discipline, as it includes 'an angel from heaven'; elsewhere it is applied to Jesus himself (I Cor. 12: 3), while in Rom. 9: 3 it involves being expelled from fellowship with Christ.

[5] See above, p. 67, n. 3, and the further references given there.

wrath of God, in the full assurance that they have been rightly judged.

Yet even so, the final responsibility must remain in God's hands. Paul himself immediately goes on to suggest this, using the very forthrightness of his curse to prove that he is responsible to God, a slave of Christ, not a pleaser of men (v. 10). Even here he remains an intercessor before God.

Galatians 6: 16

As a direct counterweight to the force of the curse passage that had imparted such a polemical thrust to the epistle, comes the positive word of the pronouncement blessing near the end. What did Paul mean by it, and for whom did he intend it?

Peace and mercy be upon all who walk by this rule, and upon the Israel of God. (Gal. 6: 16)[1]

In the first place this short benediction forms a dramatic climax for the autograph section of the letter, which in itself would be assigned a special emphasis (6: 11–18). Once again we find a direct warning at the end of a letter, that will polarize his readers, compel them to re-examine themselves as they come to the Lord's table, and to purge out the unworthy ones from their midst. Closely attached to the warning is the peace blessing.[2]

In this final autograph résumé he has summarized in the sharpest possible way the radical opposition between the two camps. On one side are those who, with the agitators, glory in human righteousness symbolized by circumcision and other legal observances (v. 12). On the other are those who, with the apostle, reckon all such human endeavors completely indifferent to salvation, and glory only in the cross of Christ,[3] by faith dying with Christ to the flesh, renouncing all human pre-

---

[1] This penultimate blessing is not to be confused with the regular final epistolary greeting which follows it at v. 18. It differs from the closing greetings in wording, form, and the fact that it is not addressed to the readers as a whole, but is a conditional blessing.

[2] For its close relation to a warning passage, see above, p. 91, n. 4, and Appendix IV.

[3] The cross being, for Paul, the instrument of condemnation of 'the world,' i.e., of the arena of spiritual egotism. Bonnard, p. 130; cf. I Cor. 1: 18ff.

tension and rising with him to a completely new existence (vv. 14f.).¹ With the pregnant phrase καίνη κτίσις Paul has reached the very epitome of the letter; he has enunciated a fundamental rule of freedom from the old, and freedom for the new, in Christ. 'For neither is circumcision anything, nor un-circumcision, but a new creation.'²

Finally, upon those who follow this rule (τῷ κανόνι τούτῳ), he pronounces his special apostolic blessing, bringing to a cul-mination in prayer the autograph section with its stern warning, and indeed the whole letter. The rule implies not some new moral or cultic law, but rather a new regulative principle of their whole relationship with God, based in faith, and working out in love (Gal. 5: 6).³ To 'walk,' στοιχεῖν,⁴ by this rule means, then, to live a life whose basis is founded in a totally new spiritual understanding. It will work out in new levels of ethical living, whose norm will be love, and which will mani-fest the fruit of the Spirit (cf. 5: 16–25). So it is upon all those (ὅσοι), circumcised or uncircumcised, who may walk by this rule, that he now proclaims the twofold gifts of peace and mercy.

The formal character of this apostolic pronouncement is suggested in two ways. While the gift of peace (often linked

---

¹ Cf. Gal. 5: 6, also 2: 19f., I Cor. 1: 17–31, II Cor. 11: 16 – 12: 10.

² In Gal. 5: 6 and I Cor. 7: 19 he gives variant forms of the rule.

The background of this radical concept καινὴ κτίσις lay in the eschato-logical expectations of the OT and Jewish apocalyptic traditions. For references see Schlier, *Galater*, p. 208, n. 2; Strack–Billerbeck, II, 421f. and III, 519; also W. Foerster in *TWNT*, III, 1032ff., and E. Stauffer, *New Testament Theology*, E.Tr. (New York, 1956), pp. 141f.

In Paul the phrase itself occurs only once again, II Cor. 5: 17, and means for him the divine eschatological act of creating man and nature completely anew in Christ, 'the old has passed away, behold, the new has come.' In Romans he will explain his meaning more fully, pointing especially to the first-fruits of this new spiritual creation, Rom. 8: 18–25 [cf. Eph. 2: 10, 15, 4: 24, Col. 3: 10].

³ Bauer–Arndt–Gingrich; Oepke, p. 162; H. W. Beyer, 'κανών,' *TWNT*, III, espec. pp. 602f.

⁴ στοιχέω implies here to conform to the basic understanding of the gospel which Paul has described. See G. Delling in *TWNT*, VII, 668. The preferred fut. reading, στοιχησουιν (over -σωσιν, -χουσιν), with ὅσοι may have a hortatory thrust (equivalent to the pres. with ἄν) – 'whoever may walk by this rule.' Cf. Blass–Debrunner–Funk, par. 380; N. A. Dahl, 'Zur Auslegung von Gal. 6: 16,' *Jud.* 6 (1950), 161–70.

with other graces)[1] is a frequent subject of the apostle's wish-prayers and blessings, it is only here that he employs the particular combination 'peace and mercy,'[2] which finds a background in Jewish blessings and greetings.[3] Jewish worship is echoed further as he goes on to include 'the Israel of God' within the scope of his blessing. Formal synagogue prayers tended similarly to see individuals as integrally related to the whole house of Israel.[4]

But whom does Paul include in the phrase 'and upon the Israel of God'? Is it limited to those who walk by his gospel of grace, the new Israel which is the church of Christ? Or does he include also the old Israel – the Jews, or perhaps even Judaizing Christians?

The answer is obscured by the ambiguity of the conjunction καί. Most commentators adopt the first and restricting view in one or other form, some by translating the καί as '*that is to say*, upon the Israel of God.'[5] He would then be referring to the earlier curse (1: 8f.)[6] and adding to it the complementary blessing: 'Cursed be those who distort the gospel and teach others so, but blessed be all who walk by the true gospel of grace, those who form the whole church of Christ, the true

---

[1] Rom. 15: 13, joy, peace, (faith), hope; Rom. 15: 33, peace; I Thess. 5: 23, peace; in the opening greetings throughout, grace and peace.

[2] εἰρήνη, meaning wholeness, healing (see above, p. 64, n. 4). ἔλεος, here denoting the grace of God, his compassion in judgment (cf. חֶסֶד); Bultmann, *TWNT*, II, 474–82.

[3] See Syr. Bar., 78: 2; Ps. Sol. 4: 29, 6: 9, 7: 9, 9: 20, 11: 9, 13: 11; Shemoneh Esreh 19. Bultmann, *ibid.* p. 481. In the NT, see I Tim. 1: 2, II Tim. 1: 2, II John 3, Jude 2, where mercy and peace are combined with grace and love; Ign. Sm. 11: 2.

[4] E.g., two synagogue inscriptions reading 'Peace be upon this place of worship and upon all places of worship of Israel'; E. L. Sukenik, *Ancient Synagogues in Palestine and Greece* (London, 1934), p. 71, n. 2. (See T. W. Manson in 'St. Paul in Ephesus: (3) the Corinthian Correspondence,' *BJRL*, 26 (1941–2), 21.) Cf. Shemoneh Esreh 19, 'Bestow peace, happiness, and blessing, grace, loving kindness, and mercy upon us and upon all Israel thy People....'

[5] An epexegetic sense. So Lightfoot, p. 221, Bonnard, p. 131, n. 2. See Blass–Debrunner–Funk, Sec. 442, 9. καί might then be omitted as redundant in English translation, cf. RSV.

[6] We may take it that the blessing does refer back to the curse, in that there are no intervening prayers in the letter. Cf. the frequent association of blessings and curses as in Deut. 12: 26, 27: 12f., Lk. 6: 20–6, etc.

Israel of God.'[1] Others take καί in its simple copulative sense, to include not only the circle of believing Galatians, but the whole Christian church: 'But blessed be all those in Galatia who may walk by the true gospel of grace, and indeed also the whole church of Christ.'[2]

Yet nowhere else does Paul actually refer to the church as the Israel of God.[3] Thus others take him here to be extending his blessing rather to those Jews 'who even though as yet un-enlightened are the true Israel of God.'[4] Thereby he would be softening the effect of his earlier curse upon his Judaizing opponents. As he recalls the frequent synagogue prayers for the peace of the house of Israel, he is moved himself to add, 'And may God's peace and mercy extend beyond those who now walk by this rule, even to the Israel of God.'[5]

It is tempting to observe that not long afterwards, during the progress of his letter to the Romans, he would show a similar softening of attitude towards the Jews. The harsh judgments of Romans 2: 17–24 would give way to the sympathetic attempts to understand of chapters 9–11, as he prays, 'Brethren, my heart's desire and prayer to God for them is that they may be saved' (10: 1). In these chapters is developed that paradoxical

[1] Similarly, in a number of places Paul indicates that Israel according to the flesh is not the true Israel of God; the true children of Abraham are those who believe in Christ (Gal. 3: 16, 19, 29, 4: 21–31; cf. Rom. 2: 29, 9: 6, I Cor. 10: 1–12, Phil. 3: 3). Cf. N. A. Dahl, *Das Volk Gottes*, pp. 212–17; see also his later article, 'Zur Auslegung von Gal. 6.16.'

[2] Cf. the inclusive address in I Cor. 1: 2. Dahl, 'Zur Auslegung von Gal. 6: 16,' p. 166. Oepke, p. 163, Lagrange, *Galates*, p. 166, Schlier, *Galater*, p. 209.

[3] Cf. P. Richardson's contention 'that Justin Martyr was the first to identify the church with Israel'; *Israel in the Apostolic Church*, SNTSM, 10 (Cambridge, 1969), p. 74, etc.

[4] E.g., E. DeW. Burton, *Syntax of New Testament Moods and Tenses*, 3rd edn (Chicago, 1898), p. 358; G. Schrenk, 'Was bedeutet "Israel Gottes"?', *Jud.*, 5 (1949), 81–94, and 'Der Segenswunsch nach der Kampfepistel,' *Jud.*, 6 (1950), 170–90.

[5] Cf. the closing prayers for the peace of Israel in Ps. 125: 5, 128: 6 (LXX) εἰρήνη ἐπὶ τὸν Ἰσραήλ, cf. Ps. 122: 6–9. W. D. Davies argues for 'an inconsistency in the Apostle's theology....Despite his noble universalism he finds it impossible not to assign a special place to his own people.' *Paul and Rabbinic Judaism* (London, 1948), pp. 75–85. Richardson proposes that Paul 'expects that only a part, *Israēl tou theou*, will be blessed in the way he prays. There is an Israel (of God) within (all) Israel' (p. 82; cf. pp. 146f.).

double rôle of the apostolic intercessor that we have already
noted, interceding both against and for his own people, in
discontinuity and in continuity with them.[1] In the light of the
hopeful attitude in Romans of Paul towards his own countrymen, it is not impossible that he would express a like hopefulness toward them at the close of the Galatian letter. If that is
so, then we might accept the revised punctuation offered by
Richardson,[2] εἰρήνη ἐπ' αὐτούς, καὶ ἔλεος καὶ ἐπὶ τὸν Ἰσραὴλ
τοῦ θεοῦ – and the sense of his paraphrase, 'May God give
peace to all who will walk according to this criterion, and
mercy also [even] to his faithful people Israel' [that portion of
Israel still to become believers].

Nevertheless, because of the considerable differences between
the purposes of the two letters,[3] we may not so readily use
Romans 9–11 to interpret Galatians 6: 16.[4] It seems more likely
that, at the end of such a single-minded epistle as Galatians
with its clear-cut dichotomy between two groups, Paul is once
more hammering home his message with a simple blessing on
all who will walk by his rule, whether they be in Galatia or
elsewhere – that is, on the whole, true church of Christ.[5]

Finally, we may note that within the liturgically shaped
ending of the epistle (6: 12–18),[6] the blessing pronouncement
gains further significance from its juxtaposition with the succeeding two verses. Together they form a solemn unit to close
the epistle and lead into further worship: thus the blessing of
peace and mercy points forward to the ritual kiss of peace that
would follow the reading of the letter;[7] then follows a last restraining injunction ('henceforth let no man trouble me') that
may substitute for his usual request for prayer;[8] finally the

[1] See above, pp. 13f., below, pp. 255ff.

[2] Richardson, pp. 81–4. The second καί would have the ascensive significance 'even,' p. 82. Cf. a somewhat similar use of καί in I Thess. 5: 25,
'Brethren, pray also (καί) for us.' See below, p. 262.

[3] See above, pp. 122ff.

[4] Dahl, 'Zur Auslegung von Gal. 6: 16,' p. 169.

[5] Ibid. pp. 164f.

[6] Drastically reduced and camouflaged in this pungent letter. See above,
pp. 125f.   [7] See above, p. 66.

[8] Bonnard (p. 131) sees this verse as an interruption; but in the light of
I Thess. and Rom. we may see it rather as an integral part of Paul's closing
style. If he does not ask for their prayers, he does to this extent seek their

benediction adds a word of healing, ἀδελφοί,[1] reminding his readers that underneath all his stringency there remains the deep ground of mutual love.

We may now summarize our conclusions about the intercessory significance of the curse and the pronouncement blessing in Galatians. In the first place it is clear that they do function as a type of intercessory prayer. Although they reflect the language of the more primitive incantations of pagan and some Old Testament usage, yet in the final instance the apostle as prophet remains responsible to the sovereign will of God in Christ, while he intercedes against his opponents and for his converts. In presenting to God those whom he curses and those whom he blesses, he understands himself to be under the guidance and power of the Holy Spirit.

But the very certainty of these pronouncements sets them also somewhat apart from the less assertive wish-prayers. The curse is not only an intercessory but also a protective and juridical device, to be used only in special circumstances against such flagrantly threatening attacks as would destroy the church from within. The imminence of the return of Christ added force to these solemn utterances. Paul shows no hesitancy about the fact that both curse and blessing must take effect under the hand of God.

Within the structure of the letter they (like the wish-prayers) serve to focus the apostle's profound disturbance about the major crisis in the Galatian churches. Indeed, he uses them as a twin lightning rod to discharge in one double flash all the conflicting forces that have been generated.

Considering the severe tension under which he was writing, it is doubtful that he intended these apostolic pronouncements to instruct his readers in the practice of prayer. Yet their paraenetic force is obvious in that they underline the whole message of the document.[2] Their liturgical and juridical pur-

co-operation: he makes a solemn request through them that no one lay any further burdens on him, by attacking his gospel and his authority. For he bears the authentic marks of ownership by Jesus, and from now on must be left free to carry out his further tasks for the gospel without hindrance.

[1] For the significance of ἀδελφοί in relation to membership of religious communities, see Rigaux, *Thessaloniciens*, pp. 370f.; also H. von Soden in *TWNT*, I, 144–6.   [2] See above, pp. 119, n. 1, 130, n. 4.

poses may be gauged as we imagine the stunning impact of this apostolic letter with its curse and its blessing, upon the congregation assembled for the Lord's supper. Those cursed ones who preach a contrary gospel are to be excluded; those blessed ones who accept the gospel of freedom are to come.[1] So in the act of writing, and in the act of reading and hearing, apostle and believers would be aware that though absent in body, he was indeed present in spirit,[2] both pronouncing judgment through them, and interceding for and with them, in the name of their common Lord Jesus.

Two curse passages in I Corinthians

When we move to I Corinthians we are confronted by two forthright imprecations: the injunction against an individual moral offender (5: 3–5), and the more general anathema in the epistolary conclusion (16: 22). By contrast with most of Paul's epistles, this extended letter is notably deficient in intercessory prayer passages; even those that do occur remind us of the Galatian letter in their restrained or negative emphasis.

As we attempt at the outset to place the two curse passages within their original epistolary context, immediately the much debated question of the integrity of the letter arises. Do they belong within the framework of the present total document as substantially an original letter, or must each be located separately in one or other of several reconstructed Pauline letters lying behind the present I Corinthians?[3]

It is pointed out by Hurd[4] that most of the principal attempts to partition the document are in relative agreement in reconstructing those letters (A, B, and C): letter A comprises II Cor. 6: 14 – 7: 1, I Cor. 10: 1–23, 6: 12–20, 11: 2–34, 9: 24–7; letter B comprises I Cor. 5: 1 – 6: 11, 7–8, 9: 1–23, 10: 24 – 11: 1, 12 – 15; and letter C, I Cor. 1–4. To one or more of these three letters we should add portions of I Cor. 16. Within these

---

[1] See below, pp. 151f., on I Cor. 16: 19–24.

[2] See below, pp. 142ff. on I Cor. 5: 3–5.

[3] Incompatibilities or contradictions in the letter have been thought to point to its composite nature. For a survey of the debate, see B. Rigaux, *Saint Paul et ses lettres*, pp. 153ff.; and Hurd, *The Origin of I Corinthians*, pp. 44–7. [4] Hurd, *ibid.*

hypothetical letters our prayer passages would lie as follows: The opening blessing and the thanksgiving might be seen either as the introductory section of the short letter C (chaps. 1–4), or of our present I Corinthians.[1] The imprecation passage (5: 3–5) would be located in letter B.[2] The final anathema and the closing epistolary blessing (16: 22f.) (both within the autograph section, 16: 1–24) might be the ending of one of the reconstructed letters, or of the whole epistle. Because it is probable that this anathema echoes the earlier curse, we should attach the autograph either to letter B, or to I Corinthians as a whole.[3] Any decision would be no more than conjectural.

Although we shall take account of the possibility that our epistle may be an editorial compilation, we shall proceed mainly on the assumption that we have here one letter substantially in its original form.[4] Our analysis of the function of the curse passages and related warning sentences within the structure of the letter will tend to confirm this assumption.

Nevertheless, an apparent diffuseness of structure and theme presents us with new difficulties. By contrast, the letters so far examined (I Thessalonians, Romans, and Galatians) have each shown a comparatively well-integrated structure and a uniform approach to the readers, making it feasible to interpret the prayer passages within the total epistle.[5] But the varieties of content and approach that mark the present letter seem at

---

[1] See above, pp. 97ff.   [2] See below, p. 150, n. 1.

[3] See below, pp. 153f.

[4] While the apparent contradictions or incompatibilities might suggest an editorial compilation, they may more readily be explained away, or seen as signs that the letter was dictated over a period, during which further news from Corinth caused Paul to modify his earlier statements. See Allo, *Saint Paul Première Épitre aux Corinthiens*, pp. lxxxiiiff.; and C. K. Barrett, *First Corinthians*, pp. 15–17.

Cf. Hurd's cautious conclusion against theories that attempt to partition I Corinthians: 'Most scholars and the present writer. . .do not believe that the evidence is strong enough to support the burden of proof which this kind of theory must always bear' (p. 47, cf. pp. 131–42).

The letter is usually dated in A.D. 54 or 55 and was written in Ephesus (I Cor. 16: 8), i.e., about the same time as or shortly before Galatians, one or two years before Romans, and four or five years after the founding of the Corinthian church about A.D. 50. But see above, p. 46, n. 1.

[5] This will be found true also of Philemon and with less certainty of Philippians.

first to militate against the prayer passages being closely related to any central epistolary theme.

All commentators observe that the first part of the letter (1: 10 – 6: 20, with 11: 17–34) contains the apostle's volunteered advice about several Corinthian problems brought to his attention by word of mouth (1: 11, 16: 17). The second part is made up of replies to a wide variety of questions specifically addressed to him or implied in a letter from the Corinthians (7: 1 – 11: 16 and 12: 1 – 16: 4). These inquiries he answers one by one, pausing from time to time to digress in an extended excursus. So the epistle does not initially seem to be concerned with any one central theological or practical question nor to follow any connected train of thought.[1]

Yet can there be discovered any central theme beneath the looseness of the surface structure, to impart underlying coherence to the whole letter? The problem of contentiousness might be taken as the hidden source behind the varied concerns of the letter. Although Paul does not seem particularly interested in the exact theological opinions of the different groupings at Corinth,[2] he is anxious about 'the quarrelsome spirit which they bred.'[3] It is this theme with its attendant problems that occupies the first four chapters;[4] it may lie behind the question of lawsuits (6: 1–11), the problems at the Lord's supper

[1] Karl Barth has attempted unsuccessfully to interpret the whole letter around the theme of the resurrection, so that '1 Cor. i–xiv [is] in fact the authentic commentary upon 1 Cor. xv,' K. Barth, *The Resurrection of the Dead*, E.Tr. (New York, 1933), p. 7.

[2] See e.g., Munck, *Paul and the Salvation of Mankind*, pp. 135–67; '. . .the matter dealt with is one of bickering between the Corinthians, but not of factions or of clear points of view as to doctrine and practice. . .' (*ibid.* p. 166).

[3] J. Moffatt, *The First Epistle of Paul to the Corinthians*, MNTC (London, 1938), p. 9.

[4] N. A. Dahl argues that the quarrels centered largely around the opposition of some members to Paul; especially, they objected to seeking his advice when in any case he did not intend to return to Corinth. So Dahl sees the entire opening section as an apology for Paul and his authority and as a preparatory basis for the delicate task of answering the official letter of inquiry from Corinth. His thesis gives strong support to the unity of the epistle. 'Paul and the Church in Corinth in I Cor. 1: 10 – 4: 21,' in *Christian History and Interpretation: Studies presented to John Knox*, ed. W. R. Farmer *et al.* (Cambridge, 1967), pp. 313–35.

(11: 17–34), and the various disorders that plagued their services of worship (chaps. 12–14). It might also be involved in several of the other questions asked of Paul, and would explain particularly why he included the hymn in praise of love (chap. 13).[1]

To claim, however, that the spirit of contentiousness was the one central problem underlying and explaining all the others, would surely be to oversimplify a complex situation. If Paul is not concerned to distinguish the positions of the various groups, may he be reacting throughout the letter against one major segment of the congregation? Again we meet a much-debated question,[2] in that each of the three named groups (apart from the Paul group!) has been cast in the rôle of the primary opposition: the Apollos party, the Peter party,[3] and the Christ party. But for our purpose the important thing is not so much to name the opposition as to recognize its general character.[4]

[1] Hurd, pp. 112f.; it has often been remarked that the converts at Corinth reflected the social, ethical, religious, and cultural tensions of a large cosmopolitan city. See W. Meyer, *Der erste Brief an die Korinther*, 1 (Zürich, 1947), 3–6.

[2] For a clear and recent summary of the wide range of conflicting opinions, see Hurd, pp. 96–107.

[3] We assume with Hurd (p. 110) that 'since the violent attacks against outsiders found in II Cor. 10–13 are absent from I Corinthians, it seems probable that the "apostles" in question arrived in Corinth some time after I Corinthians had been sent, and that the problems of II Cor. 10–13 do not underlie I Corinthians.'

[4] Cf. H. Conzelmann, *Der erste Brief an die Korinther*, p. 28. Various scholars have seen the opponents at Corinth in different guises, e.g., as followers of Apollos and his 'cultured Christianity of eloquent wisdom' (a phrase in Feine–Behm–Kümmel, p. 201), or 'spirituals,' πνευματικοί (e.g., K. Lake, *The Earlier Epistles of St. Paul; their Motive and Origin*, 2nd edn (London, 1914), pp. 227–32), or even as radical Judaizing Christians (Schoeps). For details see Hurd, pp. 97–107.

Their Hellenistic Gnostic aspect has been emphasized recently in various ways by R. Bultmann, *Exegetische Probleme des zweiten Korintherbriefes* (Uppsala, 1947); E. Käsemann, *Die Legitimität des Apostels*; E. Dinkler 'Zum Problem der Ethik bei Paulus. Rechtsnahme und Rechtsverzicht (I Kor. 6: 1–11),' *ZThK*, 49 (1952), 167–200; U. Wilckens, *Weisheit und Torheit* (Tübingen, 1959). W. Schmithals, *Die Gnosis in Korinth: Eine Untersuchung zu den Korintherbriefen*, 2nd edn (Göttingen, 1965), has proposed an extreme view that in every epistle Paul was fighting Gnosticism in the same form – involving a pre-Christian Gnostic redeemer-myth. For a survey of varied

Throughout the epistle Paul seems to have faced mainly a broad, libertine, Gnostic type of front, claiming unconditional moral freedom through the slogan, 'All things are lawful for me' (6: 12, 10: 23). As spiritual men, *pneumatikoi*, they were released from all considerations of the flesh.[1] It is this type of attitude that Paul is countering in his treatment of many problems throughout the epistle[2] and which, in addition to his polemic against dissensions, would help to give a central thrust to the letter.[3]

Evidently Paul's relations with the Corinthians were mixed, showing incipient undertones of strain, although at this period the church as a whole does not seem to have questioned his jurisdiction.[4] Indeed, some of them have written to him for advice, and he gives it freely and for the most part calmly, as he answers their written inquiries (chaps. 7–15).[5] He compli-

reactions to this position, see J. M. Robinson, 'Basic Shifts in German Theology,' espec. pp. 79ff.

Hurd (pp. 289–96) offers a bold but debatable alternative theory that the questions addressed to Paul by the Corinthians actually originate in their legitimate understanding of his own earlier teaching. From this Paul himself has suddenly moved away because of his recent acceptance of the Apostolic Decree. It is, however, probable that Paul's previous teaching at Corinth had been somewhat distorted or misconstrued by the Corinthians. Cf. also Barrett, *First Corinthians*, pp. 6–8.

[1] In addition to the works already cited as emphasizing the libertine Gnostic aspect of Paul's opponents, see *inter alia* W. Lütgert, *Freiheitspredigt und Schwarmgeister in Korinth* (Gütersloh, 1908), pp. 62ff.; A. Schlatter, *Paulus, der Bote Jesu* (Stuttgart, 1934); M. S. Enslin, *The Ethics of Paul* (Nashville, 1957), pp. 125ff., 244; Munck, *Paul and the Salvation of Mankind*, pp. 161–6.

[2] This attitude is reflected in the problems of dissension, human pride and boasting, arrogant claims to spiritual wisdom (chaps. 1–4); an arrogant libertine attitude (chap. 5); a loose attitude towards prostitution, etc. (6: 9–20); an inconsiderate freedom about food offered to idols (chaps. 8–10); an undisciplined use of spiritual gifts (chaps. 12–14); a claim that they had already been delivered from the body, the resurrection was past already (chap. 15, cf. 4: 8ff.).

[3] Yet a perhaps inconsistently ascetic undercurrent may appear in the written questions about marriage, beginning, 'It is good for a man not to touch a woman.' (7: 1–40.)

[4] As they would do later on under the instigation of the 'superlative apostles' (II Cor. 11: 5, 12: 11). See below, pp. 231ff.

[5] See Hurd's summary, p. 74. The possibility must not be overlooked that their letter represented only one faction of the church (Dahl, 'Paul and the Church in Corinth').

ments them in the opening thanksgiving period, and later on when he writes, 'I speak as to sensible men; judge for yourselves what I say' (10: 15).

Yet there are others who do not accept his authority. As he responds to the further difficulties mentioned by Chloe's people (1: 10 – 6: 20, 11: 17–34), his tone is less relaxed.[1] Here his authoritative directness betokens a far more anxious concern about conditions at Corinth. He speaks as a father whom they should imitate, and as one who exercises discipline over them (4: 14–21, 5: 1–5, 11: 34b). He addresses them as infants (νήπιοι, 3: 1) and sarcastically unmasks their pretensions (4: 8ff.).[2] There are signs that he thinks it necessary to defend his own apostolic position (9: 1–27;[3] cf. 15: 8–11), for he is finding them arrogant, self-complacent, and difficult to deal with (4: 6 – 5: 6). 'What! Did the word of God originate with you, or are you the only ones it has reached?' (14: 36).[4]

So he approaches them in a somewhat ambivalent way that foreshadows the open hostilities soon to break out. He writes without the warmly affectionate solicitude of his letter to the Thessalonians, without the hesitantly apologetic and friendly tone of Romans, yet also without the unyielding official severity of Galatians.

It is within this context, then, that we must endeavor to locate and interpret the few scattered intercessory passages in the epistle.[5]

Survey of the intercessory prayer and related prayer passages in I Corinthians

The opening blessing adheres strictly to the standard formula (1 : 3); but as we have seen, the thanksgiving (1 : 4–8) is a carefully constructed period that singles out for commendation the

---

[1] Dahl, *ibid.* p. 82.   [2] Allo, pp. xlixf.

[3] See, e.g., Manson, 'The Corinthian Correspondence,' p. 4. The main purpose of this excursus is to use his voluntary abstinence from his apostolic rights as an example to the Corinthians. But a related purpose would be defense against a growing current of attacks against himself.

[4] For further examples see Hurd, pp. 108–13, 'The Relationship between Paul and the Corinthian Church,' to which I am here indebted.

[5] Assuming in the meantime that the letter is an integral whole. For supplication passages, see Appendix II. We omit references to such exclamations of thanks as are found in 1: 14, 14: 18, 15: 57.

Corinthians' most characteristic graces and prepares for his subsequent warnings against the very difficulties that accompany such spiritual richness. To close the thanksgiving, instead of the usual assurance of unceasing intercessory prayers on their behalf, we find a brief supplication for them, that asks their still further growth in spiritual gifts (1: 8f.).[1]

In the body of the letter the main intercessory type of passage is the solemn prophetic injunction that a curse be pronounced on an offender (5: 3–5). Here the apostle deals forthrightly with a problem that he believes has reached the critical point. Although the curse arises out of a particular situation, its pronouncement may also reflect a wider attitude of stern intercessory judgment upon his libertine spiritual opponents as a whole. As we noted earlier, he had refrained in the thanksgiving period from his usual assurances of petitions for all the readers; his supplications at this time are mostly negative, focused against those who are harming the congregation.

Yet he is not unmindful of the continual thanksgivings, blessings, supplications, hymns, together with prophesying and speaking in tongues, that go on continually at Corinth (chap. 14). In his prescriptions about these practices he is concerned not so much that they be curtailed, but that they be made more effective within the prayerful life of the community (chap. 14, especially vv. 13–19, 24–8).[2]

Finally in the autograph section at the end of the letter (probably 16: 1–24), there comes the second negative intercessory passage, a curse formula coupled with the cry 'Maranatha' that invokes the coming of the Lord (16: 22).[3] It is placed in the context of a closing liturgical passage (16: 19–24) more condensed than in the other three epistles we have

[1] For details, see above, pp. 97ff.

[2] In addition, we find that three problematical didactic references in the body of the letter have an oblique bearing on intercessory prayer; the first (2: 9–16) refers to the aid of the Spirit in searching the depths of God (cf. 14: 2ff.), and seems to prefigure the related teaching on the Spirit's intercession in Romans 8: 12–27. Yet in the I Corinthians passages the direct application is to the searching out and interpreting of spiritual truths, rather than to intercession. The second passage (11: 10) offers an extremely problematical allusion to angel intercessors. The third (15: 29) is the still more obscure reference to baptism on behalf of the dead.

[3] See below, pp. 150ff.

studied,[1] and for that reason all the more striking in its clear progression.[2] In echoing the earlier imprecation, this closing anathema underlines and reinforces his judgment of exclusion. But now it is extended to all who have no love for the Lord. Again we seem to have a negative substitute for the warm wish-prayers at the close of I Thessalonians and Romans, and a counterpart to the stern warnings at the close of several of his letters. As in Galatians, so here, the attention is turned towards those who Paul knows are causing deep injury within the church.

Brief as they are, the intercessory prayer passages in this epistle seem to make clearer, both by their sparseness and their character, something of the general mood and purpose of the letter. They reveal an even deeper concern on Paul's part about the crisis at Corinth than might otherwise appear from the letter. To a detailed examination of the two curse passages we may now turn.

I Corinthians 5: 3–5

The first imprecation passage concerns a grave sexual problem that Paul believes is threatening to spoil the whole church.

For though absent in body I am present in spirit, and as if present, I have already pronounced judgment in the name of the Lord Jesus on the man who has done such a thing. When you are assembled, and my spirit is present, with the power of our Lord Jesus, you are to deliver this man to Satan for the destruction of the flesh, that his spirit may be saved in the day of the Lord Jesus. (I Cor. 5: 3–5)

The immediate occasion was a particularly brazen form of sexual aberration (πορνεία) persisted in by a church member who was flouting not only the Old Testament law, but over-stepping even the customary standards acceptable to pagans. Paul omits the details, known well enough to his readers, and says merely, 'a man is living with his father's wife.'[3]

---

[1] Notably absent besides the peace blessing, is the request for the prayers of the readers, as being inappropriate for the present context. See above, p. 126, n. 1, and below, Chap. 10.

[2] See below, p. 151.

[3] Probably his stepmother. This was forbidden in Lev. 18: 8, 21: 11, cf. Deut. 22: 30, 27: 20, and carried the death penalty. Yet for proselytes this law came to be relaxed in majority rabbinical opinion, and Paul may

We notice first that the apostle is concerned more about the tolerant and even defiant attitude of the Corinthians than about the offense itself: 'And you are arrogant![1] Ought you not rather to mourn? Let him who has done this be removed from among you' (v. 2). 'Your boasting[2] is not good. Do you not know that a little leaven ferments the whole lump of dough? Cleanse out the old leaven....'[3] (vv. 6f.; cf. vv. 9–13). Paul believes that corruption from within the community is even more dangerous than pressures from without (v. 10).[4] But behind this conviction lies his awareness of the crude standards of a licentious cosmopolitan city, from which most of the converts have but recently emerged, and into which they may easily fall back (6: 9–11).[5] The 'spirituals' among them have evidently never agreed with the apostle that such standards must be completely shunned by the Christian in his new life, for they are above these ethical considerations.

Here then is a crucial instance of that easy-going, libertine attitude at Corinth that gives the apostle so much anxiety.[6]

therefore have been contending for a position on which there was a difference of opinion in Judaism; C. T. Craig, in *IB*, x, 60. For the pagan view, see E. von Dobschütz, *Christian Life in the Primitive Church*, E.Tr. (London, 1904), pp. 387f.

[1] πεφυσιωμένοι, probably referring to earlier occurrences of the word in his description of those who consider themselves wise, 4: 6, 18, 19, and forward to 8: 1, 13: 4. For this word occurs only once in the NT outside of I Cor. (Col. 2: 18; φυσιώσεις occurs in II Cor. 12: 20, see Hurd, p. 76). This would support a link between chapters 4, 5, 8, and 13, suggesting that letter C (chaps. 1–4) should be attached as part of letter B (see above, p. 135).

[2] καύχημα, linking back probably with καυχάομαι in 1: 29, 31, 3: 21, 4: 7. This would further indicate the joining of letters C and B.

[3] The custom of removing every trace of leaven in preparation for the passover (Exod. 12: 15ff.) suggests the need to excise the corrupting effects of sin and laxity through the whole community. The allusion to Christ as paschal lamb and to the passover festival (I Cor. 5: 7f.) points to the observance of the Lord's supper, and the need for those who partake to purge themselves in preparation (see chap. 11). Cf. J. Héring, *The First Epistle of St. Paul to the Corinthians*, E.Tr. (London, 1964), p. 36, and other commentators; see below, p. 146.

[4] For a clear analysis of the context (5: 1–13), see J. Cambier, 'La Chair et l'Esprit en I Cor. v. 5,' *NTS*, 15 (1968–9), 221ff.

[5] Cf. Meyer, pp. 4–6.

[6] Cf. Barrett, *First Corinthians*, p. 120.

Indeed, it is not the Corinthians who have troubled to approach him about this problem, but it is he who must take the initiative, for they have forfeited their responsibility by default (v. 1). So he begins his juridical proclamation by emphasizing himself and his own action (ἐγὼ μὲν γάρ) as if to say, 'Therefore [because of your arrogance] I myself have already pronounced judgment.'[1] Once again Paul finds it necessary to apply to a particular case a more general prophetic ruling which he had enunciated earlier. He had warned them in an earlier letter about associating with immoral brethren (5: 9), but they had mistakenly or deliberately misunderstood his intent (vv. 10–13). Now he must apply this ruling to a specific situation that calls for the drastic action of expulsion.[2]

The measure of his grave concern is shown both by his forthright rebuke to them for their careless tolerance, and even more by the unusual severity of his ban upon the offender.[3] In the circumstances, only stringent disassociation from immoral brethren can stem the contagion, and only the 'protective device'[4] of excommunication can effect this (5: 2b, 13b).[5]

While the general meaning of the passage is clear enough, an exact translation cannot be determined because of the numerous possible alternatives in punctuation.[6] It seems advisable, with the RSV and most commentators, to make a break either before or after the phrase ἐν τῷ ὀνόματι τοῦ κυρίου 'Ἰησοῦ. Thereby κέκρικα governs τὸν οὕτως τοῦτο κατεργασάμενον (I have pronounced judgment on the man),[7] and a new start is

---

[1] See A. Robertson and A. Plummer, *First Epistle of St. Paul to the Corinthians*, ICC (Edinburgh, 1911), p. 97; Allo, p. 120.

[2] See above, p. 127, on Gal. 1: 9. See von Campenhausen, *Die Begründung kirchlicher Entscheidungen*, p. 15; Conzelmann, p. 115.

[3] Contrast, for instance, his later intervention on behalf of an offender at Corinth (II Cor. 2: 5–11), and his counsel to the Galatians (Gal. 6: 1f.); cf. Jas. 5: 16, Matt. 18: 15–17.

[4] See above, pp. 121f.

[5] An anticipation of this judgment is to be found earlier in the letter, I Cor. 3: 16f. Cf. also the related judgments in 11: 27, 14: 38, and, of course, 16: 22.

[6] For a clear analysis of these, see Allo, pp. 120f. The textual variations do not significantly alter the sense and may therefore be ignored.

[7] The progress of the sentence might be eased if we take τὸν... κατεργασάμενον as 'in the case of the man...,' Barrett, *First Corinthians*, p. 124.

made with the solemn formula that will explain the nature of Paul's judgment to be carried out by the church:[1] 'When you are assembled...you are to deliver....' A related question is where to attach the two important phrases, 'in the name of the Lord Jesus' and 'with the power of our Lord Jesus.' It seems redundant to attach them both together either to 'when you are assembled,' or to 'you are to deliver.' Out of various possible arrangements, Allo chooses to make the break before ἐν τῷ ὀνόματι, so as to make Paul give a solemn formula to explain his judgment as follows: 'In the name of the Lord Jesus, when you are assembled and my spirit is present with the power of our Lord Jesus, you are to deliver this man to Satan....'[2]

At any rate, we may take it that Paul has made his prophetic judgment of the culprit in advance, and now calls upon the Corinthians to carry out his sentence of excommunication at an assembly duly convened.

Although his judgment has been made *in absentia* (ἀπὼν τῷ σώματι), he emphasizes that somehow he is present with them 'in spirit (παρὼν δὲ τῷ πνεύματι).'[3] He repeats this claim twice more: 'as if present,' and 'when you are assembled and my spirit is present with the power of our Lord Jesus.' This striking threefold emphasis on his presence must mean more than a conventional epistolary formula that he would be thinking about them,[4] or that his judgment would be taken over by the church as if he were present. Rather, his spirit is mediated to them σὺν τῇ δυνάμει τοῦ κυρίου ἡμῶν Ἰησοῦ. It is with the help of (σύν)[5] the power of the Lord that there is a constantly effective intercessory link between himself and them. Even in

[1] παραδοῦναι is then understood as an injunction to the readers to be carried out – 'you (or we) are to deliver.'

[2] Here 'in the name of the Lord Jesus' qualifies loosely both their assembling, and their delivering the culprit to Satan; 'with the power of the Lord Jesus' refers to their assembling and his presence with them.

[3] This phrase may be regarded as an intercessory prayer-report of a negative character. [Cf. the parallel in Col. 2: 5, '...yet I am present in spirit, rejoicing to see your good order....']

[4] Conzelmann, p. 117. Bultmann, *Theology of the New Testament*, I, 208, suggests that 'for Paul it is not a matter of "mental" presence in his thoughts, but that his *pneuma* will be present as an active "power."'

[5] Cf. the phrase σὺν θεῷ (with God's help). Barrett, *First Corinthians*, p. 125.

ordinary times of bodily separation, Christ's power is released by the network of mutual intercessory prayers,[1] but on this critical occasion it is the power of the Lord as judge which is brought into operation in a special way through Paul's pronouncement.[2]

Thus, however the two phrases 'in the name of the Lord Jesus,' and 'with the power of our Lord Jesus' may be placed in the sentence, they underline the claim of the apostle to be pronouncing judgment as a prophet on behalf of Christ and according to the will of Christ.[3] Through the help of Christ he may be 'present' with them,[4] and through the effective power of Christ apostle and congregation take juridical action together.[5]

The execution of his judgment is to take place at a solemn meeting of the church assembled with the power of the Lord Jesus, and under obligation to carry out the ban. As the whole Corinthian church has been affected by the libertine threat to its life, so the whole church must be unitedly associated in purging this evil from its midst.[6] Surprisingly,[7] however, no further trial on their part is suggested, but simply a carrying out of his sentence; for they have already limited their responsi-

[1] Cf., for instance, his request to the Romans (15: 30–2) to strive together with him in their prayers. See below, pp. 267f.

[2] See Harder, *Paulus und das Gebet*, pp. 71, and 196, n. 2. Cf. Käsemann, 'Sentences of Holy Law,' p. 71. Paul is present 'with the power of the Lord Jesus,' so his physical presence is not relevant. For a contrary, but undefended, opinion, see Allo, p. 120: 'πνεύματι signifies "in spirit," a presence in thought and intention, nothing more.'

[3] See Kramer, par. 17b (p. 77), on the use of the title *Lord* in church functions. Cf. par. 52.2 (p. 181), the *Lord* is the authority to whom men are accountable; par. 18e (p. 82), the *Lord* gives power 'in baptism, in expulsion, in exorcism, against negative powers and influences.' Cf. below, p. 152 on the sanctioning invocation of the Lord in the cry 'Maranatha' at the eucharist.

[4] See above, p. 55, n. 3.

[5] Thus παραδοῦναι may mean 'we (rather than you) are to hand over.'

[6] Allo thinks, however, that Paul intends a special closed meeting of leaders and a few selected members (p. 122). Héring points out that in the synagogue it was the elders who formed the tribunal, p. 35.

[7] Jeremias (*TWNT*, III, 752) points out that in the usual case careful provisions would be adopted to prevent a too hasty resort to excommunication; see Matt. 18: 15–17; cf. Tit. 3: 10, II Tim. 2: 24–6, Gal. 6: 1. See above, p. 127.

bility through failure to take earlier action. It is when they prepare for the Lord's supper that the occasion will arise during the self-examination by each member – a solemn 'cleansing out of the old leaven' so that they may celebrate the festival, 'with the unleavened bread of sincerity and truth' (5: 7f.). Later on he will again emphasize that the Lord's supper calls for individual self-examination (11: 27–32),[1] and will point out the grave danger of partaking in an unworthy manner, so as to bring judgment on oneself (11: 27–32). Finally he will remind them that, if necessary, those who 'have no love for the Lord' must be formally excluded from the supper (16: 21).[2]

Yet with all his apparent severity, Paul shows concern for the offender himself. Had there been either some signs of repentance on the part of the culprit, or of condemnation on the part of the church, his judgment might have been more lenient. In the absence of these, the offender must be handed over to Satan 'for the destruction of the flesh,' but this is in order 'that his spirit may be saved in the day of the Lord Jesus.' At the price of comparatively short immediate suffering,[3] there would follow not only renewal for the threatened Corinthian church, but also ultimate salvation for the culprit. The double nature of this sentence, offering both immediate sanction and final reward, serves to give a remedial and hopeful intent to what would otherwise be but a harsh and vindictive judgment.[4] Here its imminent eschatological fulfilment must be taken with the utmost seriousness.[5] Once again, as in his prayers for his other churches, the apostle in priestly fashion envisages the rapidly approaching day when he will present the believers 'kept sound and blameless at the coming of our Lord Jesus Christ' (I Thess.

[1] Cf. the prayer of confession in the letter of Baruch, designed to bring the reader to self-examination and repentance through corporate confession. See above, p. 71, n. 1.

[2] See below, pp. 150ff. Jeremias has argued that already at the time of I Cor. the Eucharist may have been separated from the Agape. See *The Eucharistic Words of Jesus*, E.Tr. (London, 1966), p. 121.

[3] Cf. II Cor. 4: 16–18.

[4] Cf. the remedial element in many OT prophetic oracles of doom, e.g., Hos. 2: 14–23; cf. Lev. 26: 40–5.

[5] Cf. Paul's claim in the next section, 'Do you not know that the saints will judge the world? Do you not know that we are to judge angels?' (6: 2f.). See above, pp. 118f.

5: 23). It is only in the light of this imminent eschatological certainty of Paul and his readers that the purpose of the imprecation may be rightly understood. To judge it as a merely angry or over-anxious reaction on the part of the apostle, would be to miss its true intent.

Handing over the culprit to Satan involved, first, excommunication from the protection of the church fellowship.[1] Beyond that we can only conjecture what Paul envisaged.[2] At any rate, it meant that the man was being 'devoted' or exposed to the direct assaults of the powers of evil of this present age, powers which momentarily held men in bondage.[3] Satan was the supreme agent or head of these temporary powers, through whom hindrances and sicknesses were inflicted on men (e.g., I Thess. 2: 18, II Cor. 12: 7).[4]

By the words 'for the destruction of the flesh' (σάρξ), Paul intended at least the possibility, or even the probability, of death.[5] Yet he believed that Satan had no power to hinder the

---

[1] Vv. 2b, 13b, and see above, p. 128, n. 4.

[2] For pagan parallels to 'delivering this man to Satan,' see Deissmann, *Light from the Ancient East*, pp. 301–3, referring to 'the ancient custom of execration, i.e., devoting a person to the gods of the lower world.' In Jewish cursing, Satan took the place of the gods of the lower world. In the Old Testament, God hands over Job to Satan (Job 2: 6). See also, Harder, pp. 122f.; B. Noack, *Satanás und Sotería* (Kobenhavn, 1948), p. 97f.; H. Frhr. von Campenhausen, *Kirchliches Amt und Geistliche Vollmacht*. . . . (Tübingen, 1953), p. 147, n. 1; E. Schweizer, *TWNT*, VI, 434.

[3] Cf. above, p. 49. These powers, given a temporary freedom, would themselves all be subdued when 'the end' came, I Cor. 15: 24–8, 54–8. See W. Grundmann, *TWNT*, II, 313: 'Bedeutungsvoll für die gesamt-paulinische Anschauung ist an dieser Stelle folgendes: der Satan hat über den an Christus Gläubigen keine Macht. Er muss ihm erst förmlich übergeben werden. . .die Ubergabe an den Satan nur den Zweck der augenblichlichen, aber nicht endgültigen Vernichtung hat.'

[4] See W. Foerster, *TWNT*, VII, 161f.; T. H. Gaster in *IDB*, IV, 224–8 and the literature there cited; D. E. H. Whiteley, *The Theology of St. Paul* (Philadelphia, 1964), pp. 21ff.

[5] Some scholars (e.g., Käsemann, 'Sentences of Holy Law,' p. 71) equate this with a direct sentence of death; cf. Acts 5: 5, 9f. When Job is delivered to Satan, the wording suggests that it is exceptional that his life should be spared: 'and the Lord said to Satan, "Behold he is in your power; only spare his life."' Job 2: 6. Others (e.g., Robertson–Plummer) believe that Paul would envisage the possibility, though not the necessity, of death. A still milder view of Paul's meaning, is that the culprit in his exclusion from

man's final salvation, for his spirit (πνεῦμα) would be in the hands of God in Christ. So death (the destruction of the flesh) would only release the man from the sphere of his persistent sinning and place his spirit directly before the final, merciful judgment of God.[1] Later in the epistle we shall find Paul applying similar reasoning. He attributes the sickness and even the death of some members to their misuse of the Lord's supper, and to the consequent judgment of God upon them as they persist in their blindness (11: 29–32). But this immediate judgment of God is seen by the apostle as in some way a merciful chastening that cuts short their sinning and will finally save them from the condemnation that awaits the world (11: 32).[2] If in our present passage he uses language common to many pagan and Jewish curses, yet his imprecation is a guarded one; it avoids both the vengeful intent of many pagan execrations, and the purpose of sacred destruction of the Old Testament *cherem*.[3] It is done 'in the name of the Lord Jesus' and 'with the power of our Lord Jesus'; therefore it must represent him who died for the weak man (8: 11), and whose grace is present with them (1: 3, 16: 23). Its outcome is in the hands of the God whose final judgment will be made only through the merciful agency of this same Christ (1: 8; cf. II Cor. 5: 10).

In summary, the imprecation passage in chapter five dramatizes sharply a central theme of the whole letter, namely Paul's

the fellowship would be exposed to greater trials (but not death), and be led thereby to repent. The destruction of the flesh would then mean destruction of evil fleshly instincts (φρόνημα τῆς σαρκός, Origen). See, e.g., Cambier. For a description of the various views see Allo, pp. 123f.

[1] For Paul, *sarx* is usually that aspect of man which is exposed to the attacks of sin and through which he is held in bondage (Rom. 7: 5ff., 18, 8: 3ff.). See Bultmann, *Theology of the NT*, I, 232–46. It probably includes here man's body. *Pneuma* has various fluid meanings in Paul, but implies here probably the man's real self and that aspect which is capable of salvation. See Bultmann, *ibid.* pp. 205–9, espec. p. 208.

[2] Cf. I Tim. 1: 20, and the somewhat later Jewish prayer that a man's death may be an atonement for his sins (Tos. Ber. VII, 17. See Harder, p. 123). Although this prayer sees death as atonement rather than chastening and release, it does suggest a common view lying behind the apostle's execration, with its final goal of salvation.

[3] Allo, p. 123. Robertson–Plummer, p. 100, point out the 'fundamental difference' between the evil intent of magic spells and curses and the apostle's attempt to rescue both offender and church in the name of Christ.

anxiety about the dangerously libertine attitude at Corinth. The passage focuses an underlying coherence and drive in a long and loosely structured epistle, partly reflected in the repeated use of the words φυσιόω and καυχάομαι. Furthermore, only in the light of this pervasive anxiety may we properly assess the close links between the imprecation passage (5: 3–5), the judgment about destroying God's temple (3: 16f.), the instructions about self-examination before the Lord's supper (11: 27–32), and the final demand for a purging of the church before partaking of this feast (16: 22). It is, then, the context of the total and undivided letter that seems to supply the most adequate background in which to understand our imprecation passage, together with its occasion, necessity, purpose, and intended method of implementation.[1]

Paul saw in Corinth, as in Galatia, a particularly dangerous situation threatening a church from within. Therefore he claimed quite dogmatically to make a prophetic eschatological judgment according to God's will and on behalf of God, assured that his juridical pronouncement would be carried out under the divine hand. Confident that no other protective course could be taken, he acted as apostolic intercessor with a certainty that went far beyond his usual intercessory practice.

I Corinthians 16: 22

The second imprecation passage in I Corinthians occurs in the autograph section and contributes to the epistolary–liturgical pattern in chapter 16.[2]

---

[1] If we should prefer to place the imprecation passage in the smaller context of the reconstructed letter B, its connections would still include many sections that deal with libertinism. Of the passages comprising letter B (p. 135, above), the following sections would be related to the theme of libertinism (p. 139, n. 2, above): 6: 9–11, 8: 1–9: 23, 10: 24–33, 12: 1–15: 58. And assuming that the autograph (16: 21–4) belonged to letter B, then the imprecation would also be linked with the final demand for purging (16: 22).

But there would be lacking a link with the important discussion of human pride, boasting, and arrogant claims to spiritual wisdom (chaps. 1–4), and also the important link with the regulation about the Lord's supper (chap. 11).

[2] Significant elements in the pattern are the instructions about the collection in 16: 1–4 (see above, p. 96, n. 2), and the other instructions in vv. 19–24. Missing are the admonitions to prayer, the peace blessing, and the request for prayer.

If anyone has no love for the Lord, let him be accursed. Our Lord come!
(I Cor. 16: 22)

As we have already noted, the earlier judgment passages
(5: 3–5, 3: 16f., 11: 27, and 14: 38) presaged this general one
at the close of the letter; here Paul is underlining and rein-
forcing those prior injunctions,[1] by excluding all who have no
love for the Lord.

At previous stages of our study it was suggested that in
shaping the endings of his epistles for use at the Lord's supper,
Paul was partly adapting elements from early Christian
liturgy.[2] The most striking evidence for this borrowing is now
before us at the close of I Corinthians, where the liturgically oriented material assumes a specially compact shape
(16: 19–24).[3] As Bornkamm has pointed out, a whole series of
liturgical forms, when compared with the similar series in
Didache 10: 6, appears to derive from a eucharistic celebration:[4]

(1) The exchange of mutual greetings would be sealed by
the rite of the holy kiss, in itself part of the communion rite, and
an act of reconciliation;[5] then follow in succession: (2) the
formal anathema upon those who do not love the Lord; (3) the
Aramaic exclamation or prayer for the coming of the Lord;
(4) the customary grace blessing; (5) the apostle's personal
message of love in Christ Jesus. Items (2) and (3) would be
adapted from an older formula that might be reconstructed as

---

[1] The emphasis would be heightened by its location next to Paul's autograph signature, endorsing and making binding all that had been written.
Bahr, 'Subscriptions in Pauline Letters,' p. 31.

[2] Above, p. 43, n. 2, p. 70, etc.

[3] Leitzmann, *Mass and Lord's Supper*, p. 193; Bornkamm, 'Das Anathema
in der urchristlichen Abendmahlsliturgie,' pp. 227–30; J. A. T. Robinson,
'Traces of a Liturgical Sequence in I Cor. 16: 20–24'; C. F. D. Moule,
'A Reconsideration of the Context of *Maranatha*,' *NTS*, 6 (1959–60), 307–10;
Kramer, par. 23 (pp. 99ff.), par. 45 (pp. 161ff.).

[4] 'Abendmahlsliturgie,' p. 227, citing earlier suggestions by Seeberg,
Lietzmann, and Hofmann. J. A. T. Robinson came independently to similar
conclusions: 'We have in I Cor. 16: 22 (which at all events appears to be
pre-Pauline in origin) the remains of the earliest Christian liturgical
sequences we possess' ('Liturgical Sequence,' p. 41). Cf. also Käsemann,
'Sentences of Holy Law,' pp. 70f.

[5] Meyer, pp. 330f.; see above, p. 66, n. 2.

follows: 'If any one loves the Lord, let him come; if anyone does not love the Lord, let him be anathema; our Lord, come!'[1]

Within this eucharistic framework the anathema pronouncement[2] appears to have been closely linked with the 'Maranatha' cry, an Aramaic exclamation that would solemnly invoke the eschatological presence of their future judge.[3] While it is agreed that the cry was customarily associated with the eucharist,[4] Moule has argued persuasively that it was not in the first place a eucharistic invocation, but an invocation used generally 'to reinforce and sanction the curse or ban.'[5] In any case, the particular eucharistic invocation of the unseen Lord as witness would underline both the seriousness of their self-examination and the weight of the anathema upon all who might seek to partake of the supper in an unworthy manner.[6]

[1] A similar liturgical situation may lie behind Rev. 22: 17–19, with the separation of those within and without, in vv. 14–15; E. Lohmeyer, *Die Offenbarung des Johannes*, HzNT, enlarged 2nd edn (Tübingen, 1953), p. 179. But see Moule, 'Maranatha,' p. 309, for a contrary opinion.

Further evidence that Paul was using a borrowed formula is his use of three unaccustomed words: φιλεῖ (used elsewhere in the NT for believers – Tit. 3: 15; cf. III John 15, but Paul prefers ἀγαπάω – Rom. 8: 28, I Cor. 2: 9, 8: 3 [Eph. 6: 24], etc.); also ἤτω and μαρανα θα.

[2] The formula belongs within the category of prophetic judgments, with the sanction expressed in the imperative. See above, p. 117.

[3] Although Maranatha may mean 'Our Lord, come' (cf. Rev. 22: 20), or 'Our Lord is coming' (Phil. 4: 5), or 'Our Lord has come,' the first seems to be preferable. See above, pp. 32ff.; also K. G. Kuhn, *TWNT*, IV, 470ff., espec. p. 474; Moffatt, pp. 282–6; Lietzmann, 'Mass and Lord's Supper,' p. 193; Kramer, par. 23 (pp. 100–7), Barrett, *First Corinthians*, pp. 397f., Conzelmann, *ad loc.*

[4] See the literature cited in Moule, 'Maranatha,' p. 307; also Kramer, par. 23b (p. 100), par. 55d (p. 164).

[5] 'Maranatha,' p. 307. Cf. the 'sanctioning' invocations used by Paul; see above, pp. 145f. on I Cor. 5: 4f.; p. 67, n. 1, on I Thess. 5: 27.

[6] I Cor. 11: 27. On this view the invocation would seek to anticipate the Last Day – 'the delinquent is faced by the presence of the Judge, yet with time to repent' (Moule, 'Maranatha,' p. 310, n. 2). Both Moule and Kramer, however, prefer to interpret it as an appeal for the speedy coming of the parousia. Either way, the Lord's coming would be in judgment and in ultimate mercy.

For a recent attempt to avoid the seeming incongruity of such a harsh judgment, see the brilliant but speculative reconstruction of the text in W. F. Albright and C. S. Mann, 'Two Texts in I Corinthians,' *NTS*, 16 (1969–70), 271–6.

It is the solemn language of eucharistic rite, then, that Paul uses to bring his letter to a close. In the sharp anathema pronouncement, he looks back not only to the previous curse injunction (5: 3–5), but also to the special warnings about partaking of the supper unworthily (11: 27–34). There, too, he must have been using recognizable eucharistic language to describe the process of examination and separation at the supper.[1]

So a common purpose ties together the warning about destroying the temple (3: 16f.), the specific curse on a particular offender (5: 3–5), the careful instruction about exclusion of the unworthy from the Lord's supper (11: 27–32), the pronouncement about those who do not acknowledge Paul's prophetic authority (14: 37), and finally the eucharistic liturgy of preparation and exclusion that closes the letter (16: 22). In each of these passages the apostle returns to his grave polemic against the libertine front at Corinth, the major concern that gives unity to the whole epistle. He has adapted his apostolic letter for solemn reading before a congregation who must carry out his sentence against the unworthy.[2] Yet all must 'be done in love' (16: 14). Thus he believes that he himself is 'speaking the truth in love'[3] to those who would show tolerance at any price, reminding them that although 'love is patient and kind,...it does not rejoice at wrong, but rejoices in the right' (13: 4–6). In spite of his harshness, then, he may end with a word of personal affection, 'My love be with you all in Christ Jesus' (16: 24).[4] Even so, as with the Galatian epistle we may guess

---

[1] Cf. his claim in 11: 23 to be handing on traditional usage, followed by a prophetic formula, 'For any one who eats and drinks without discerning the body eats and drinks judgment upon himself.' Bornkamm points also to parallels in Heb. 6: 6, 10: 29, 13: 10–15, I Clem. 34, and perhaps even in Lk. 22: 21–3, regarding the presence of the betrayer at the table. 'Abendmahlsliturgie,' p. 230. The division is not between baptized and unbaptized, but between those who do and do not love the Lord; Barrett, *First Corinthians*, p. 397, Conzelmann, p. 360.

[2] In the closing pattern of this letter, both the customary 'sharp warning' and the negative wish-prayer are expressed together in the curse passage.

[3] Eph. 4: 15.

[4] Cf. the word ἀδελφοί at the end of Galatians, which fulfils the same irenic function, and stands in the same place between the grace and the final Amen. See above, p. 126. But here the note of healing warmth seems to include all, with nobody beyond its reach.

at the jolting impact of such a letter upon the assembled church at Corinth.[1]

What, then, was the intercessory significance of the two curse passages in this letter? We may regard them like the corresponding passage in Galatians, as a type of negative intercessory wish-prayer. With all his bold prophetic assurance, the apostle must make his pronouncements 'in the name of the Lord Jesus Christ,' 'with the power of our Lord Jesus,' and it is to God's merciful judgment in Christ that he entrusts the culprit. In spite of its sternness his intercession is meant to bring immediate blessing to the church and ultimate blessing to the offender.[2]

Like the more positive wish-prayers in I Thessalonians and Romans, the sharply cutting pronouncements in I Corinthians underscore the numerous exhortations in the letter. In addition, they guide the members in a difficult juridical decision to be carried out at the eucharist. Like those other prayers, they aim to include the readers with him before the Lord as they gather around the reading of his letter. In the act of writing he intercedes for them, and in the act of reading and hearing they will be involved in joint intercessory action. Here again Paul is revealed as apostolic intercessor both for and against them, thankful for their rich gifts, yet praying that they may be sustained 'to the end, guiltless in the day of our Lord Jesus Christ' (1: 8).

Our extended examination of the various groups of wish-prayers is now complete. In briefest recapitulation it may be said that the eight principal wish-prayers, especially the more expanded ones in I Thessalonians and Romans, are sufficiently flexible in spite of their compact, formal character, to give living expression to the apostle's deeply responsible love – to his vital anxieties and burning hopes for each particular church. In offering these intercessory supplications Paul was conscious of a priestly accountability, the more urgent in that he must shortly present his churches to the Lord at the expected parousia. So by these prayers he sought to reinforce his earnest exhortations to the readers, kindling their aspirations, teaching

[1] See below, p. 231, n. 3.
[2] Cf. Dahl, 'Paulus som Föresprakere' (Paul as Intercessor), p. 178.

them how to pray, and finally (through the liturgically oriented closing passages) inviting them in their eucharistic worship to make his prayers their own. Thus the ministry of letter-writing and reading would be deepened and extended by a reciprocal priestly ministry of intercessory supplications, while they responded to his further invitation that they in turn pray for him.[1]

The opening and closing blessings proved to be more formalized, yet a living intercessory function was not wholly absent. Within their special context they would contribute toward the network of intercessory prayer that undergirded the apostle's ministry and the life of his churches.

Finally, the startling curse passages and the blessing pronouncement in Galatians and I Corinthians, were seen to concentrate Paul's intense feelings about the special emergencies that had arisen in these two churches. They showed the apostle as prophetic and priestly intercessor powerfully involved in tension with his churches in the name of the Lord Jesus, willing to polarize, to separate, and to exclude where need be, and pressing the faithful converts to join with him in even the most stringent aspects of his intercessory ministry.

[1] See Chapter 10.

CHAPTER 7

INTERCESSORY PRAYER-REPORTS:
THEIR FORM AND FUNCTION

We proceed now to the second major class of intercessory prayer passages, the 'prayer-reports,'[1] to which the next two chapters will be devoted. At the beginning of most of his letters, in the formal thanksgiving period, the apostle assures his readers not only of his continual thanksgivings for them, but also of his constant intercessions on their behalf, and he indicates briefly some of the contents of his prayers; for example:

I thank my God always when I remember you in my prayers,...and I pray that the sharing of your faith may promote the knowledge of all the good that is ours in Christ. (Philem. 4–6)[2]

In the body of the letters[3] there are reports of prayers by the writer(s) for the readers, by the writer for a third party, or by a third party for the readers; for example:

But we pray God that you may do no wrong....What we pray for is your improvement. (II Cor. 13: 7, 9b)

Brethren, my heart's desire and prayer to God for them is that they may be saved. (Rom. 10: 1)

While they long for you and pray for you, because of the surpassing grace of God in you. (II Cor. 9: 14)

Although the prayer-reports offer somewhat less direct evidence of the apostle's intercessions than do the main wish-prayers, they nevertheless form an important element in our study.

---

[1] See Appendix III, p. 300.

[2] Prayer-reports in the thanksgiving periods: I Thess. 1: 2b–3, 3: 10, Rom. 1: 9f., Phil. 1: 4, 9–11, Philem. 4b, 6; also a borderline example, II Cor. 1: 7. [Cf. Eph. 1: 16–23, Col. 1: 3b, 9–14, II Thess. 1: 11f.]

[3] Prayer-reports in the body of the letters: prayers by the writer(s) for readers, II Cor. 13: 7, 9b, I Cor. 5: 3 (?) [Eph. 3: 14–19, Col. 1: 29 – 2: 3, 2: 5]; prayers by writer for a third party, Rom. 9: 3 (?), 10: 1; prayers by a third party for the readers, II Cor. 9: 14 [Col. 4: 12].

Before considering their functional significance, we may find it useful to survey their general stylistic peculiarities and the particular features of those occurring in the thanksgiving periods.

FORMAL CHARACTERISTICS OF THE PRAYER-REPORTS

First, the prayer-reports offer an alternative method from the wish-prayers for adapting prayer to fit into a letter, while maintaining the strictly epistolary form of address to the readers. Like the wish-prayers, they may easily be transposed back into direct prayers by adding the address to God in the vocative case, changing the pronouns or nouns for those to be benefitted from second to third person, and the verb from the subjunctive or infinitive into the imperative mood.

So they display a characteristic form that makes them comparatively easy to identify: They are introduced by verbs for praying that we have already discussed.[1] The verb occurs usually as a participle, but sometimes in the indicative mood, depending upon the context,[2] and is followed in appropriate syntactical construction by the mention of the one prayed for and the content of the prayer.[3]

Second, the prayer-reports like the wish-prayers include a prepositional phrase or a pronoun which shows that they are made on behalf of others; for example: ὑπὲρ αὐτῶν (Rom. 10: 1); μνείαν ὑμῶν ποιοῦμαι (Rom. 1: 9); τὴν ὑμῶν κατάρτισιν (II Cor. 13: 9).

It may be added here that instances of cultic or juridical vocabulary are almost wholly lacking, which might relate the prayer-reports to the Jewish sacrificial cult. Only in Romans 1: 9f. does Paul use the cultic word λατρεύειν, bringing this prayer-report into close relation with the concept of priestly service.[4]

---

[1] See above, pp. 18ff.   [2] See below, p. 162.

[3] For a list of prayer-words and syntactical constructions used in the prayer-reports, see the appended note on p. 173 below.

[4] H. Strathmann, *TWNT*, IV, 58–65, espec. p. 64, stresses the cultic significance of λατρεύειν in the LXX, and its close relation with λειτουργεῖν. See below, p. 190.

Cultic language may perhaps be seen in the petition in Phil. 1: 10,

When we turn to the intercessory prayer-reports incorporated in the thanksgiving periods,[1] we note one or two additional features. In several of them (as in the wish-prayers) there occurs an eschatological climax that points to Jewish prayer style:[2] for example, Phil. 1: 6, 'bring it to completion at the day of Jesus Christ'; 1: 10, 'so that you may... be pure and blameless for the day of Christ'; I Thess. 1: 3, 'steadfastness of hope in our Lord Jesus Christ'; 3: 10, postponed to verse 13, 'so that he may establish your hearts... at the coming of our Lord Jesus with all his saints'; I Cor. 1: 8, 'who will sustain you to the end, guiltless in the day of our Lord Jesus Christ.' The climax is lacking, however, in the prayer-reports in Rom. 1: 9f., Philem. 6,[3] and the prayer-report surrogate in II Cor. 1: 7,[4] as in the prayer-reports scattered in the body of the letters (Rom. 9: 3, 10: 1, II Cor. 9: 14, 13: 7, 9b).[5]

Another stylistic feature of the prayer-reports in Paul's thanksgiving periods is the very fact that assurances of thanksgiving should be linked with assurances of unceasing intercessory prayers. What antecedents may be found for this practice, and for the emphasis on the frequency and urgency of his prayers?

It has long been recognized that the complex prescripts in Paul's letters, including the thanksgiving and assurances of constant prayer are closely related to a well-attested conventional letter style.[6] Scores of Greek papyrus letters contain

εἰλικρινεῖς καὶ ἀπρόσκοποι. [Striking vocabulary parallels with the language of the synagogue liturgy and the Qumran writings may be seen in the deutero-Pauline prayer-reports, Eph. 1: 16–23, 3: 14–20, Col. 1: 9–14, 2: 1–3. See K. G. Kuhn, 'Der Epheserbrief im lichte der Qumrantexte,' pp. 334–45.]

¹ See Appendix III, p. 300.   ² See above, p. 41.

³ But see below, p. 225, n. 1.

⁴ [Lacking in the deutero-Pauline prayer-reports, Col. 1: 3b, 9–14, II Thess. 1: 11f., but present in Eph. 1: 21b.]

⁵ [But see in Col. 1: 28 an eschatological emphasis leading into the prayer-report 1: 29 – 2: 3, and a similar emphasis in 4: 12.]

⁶ See above, pp. 34f., and 108, n. 4, with the literature on ancient letter style cited there. For a full bibliography of related studies, see Rigaux, *Thessaloniciens*, p. 358, and note in particular O. Gerhardt, *Studien zur Geschichte des griechischen Briefes*, I: *Die Anfangsformel* (Tübingen, 1903); Ziemann, *De epistolarum graecorum formulis solemnibus quaestiones selectae*, p. 319; Roller, *Das Formular der Paulinischen Briefe*, pp. 53f.; Harder, p. 78, n. 1: Schubert, *passim*.

introductory assurances of the writer's constant prayers for the health and general welfare of the readers.[1] But although the practice is found in Babylonian and Assyrian letters,[2] those described in the Old Testament all lack this convention.[3] It is not until the second century B.C., when Greek influence has made itself felt, that we find in II Maccabees a Jewish prototype of Paul's custom, 'We are now praying for you here' (II Macc. 1: 2–6).[4] A similar assurance occurs in I Maccabees, 'We therefore remember you constantly on every occasion...at the sacrifices...and in our prayers....' (I Macc. 12: 11).[5]

A number of other Greek letters contain introductory thanksgivings, but those which link thanksgiving with prayer assurances are rare.[6] A political inscription noted by Schubert contains the equivalent of intercessory prayer in addition to commemorative praise for Verus,[7] and a religious inscription links intercessory prayer with thanksgiving.[8] In the II Maccabees opening letters, thanksgiving which is missing from the first letter with its extended wish-prayer (1: 1–10) is placed at the beginning of the second letter which immediately follows, 'Having been saved by God out of grave dangers we thank him greatly....' (v. 11). In the I Maccabees letter the assurances

---

[1] E.g., the *proskynema* prayer, καὶ τὸ προσκύνημά σου ποιῶ παρὰ τοῖς ἔνθαδε θεοῖς (Class. Phil. xxii, 243), or an alternative form, μνίαν σου ποιούμενος παρὰ τοῖς [ἐν]θαδε θεοῖς (Papyrus BGU, II, 632). Cf. Koskenniemi, pp. 139–45.

[2] See M. Jastrow, *Die Religion Babyloniens und Assyriens* (Giessen, 1912), II, 521, '...so meldet der Schreiber dem König, dass er zu den Göttern für ihm beten werde und das Ritual zur Versöhnung des erzürnten Hauptgottes des Pantheons und seiner Gemahlin verrichten werde.' Hesse, *Die Fürbitte*, p. 84, n. 2. Cf. also Lohmeyer, 'Briefliche Grussüberschriften,' p. 160.

[3] See II Sam. 11: 14f., I Kings 21: 8f., II Kings 5: 6, Jer. 29: 4–28.

[4] As we noted above (p. 28), these letters in II Macc. offer precedents for both the Pauline prayer-report and the wish-prayer.

[5] Cf. Syr. Bar. 86: 2f.

[6] Of the fifteen extant papyrus letters (260 B.C. to the 8th century A.D.) in which he found the thanksgiving formula εὐχαριστῶ τοῖς θεοῖς or its equivalent, Schubert found four which link thanksgiving and assurances of prayers for the health of the reader: pap. Lond. 42 (*c.* 168 B.C.); pap. Vat. 2289 (*c.* 168 B.C.); *BGU*, II, 423 (2nd cent. A.D., from Apion); pap. Giessen, no. 85 (A.D. 98–138). Pp. 160–8.

[7] *Ibid.* pp. 152f., referring to CIG 1318 (A.D. 161–80).

[8] S.B. 4117 (A.D. 117); see also Epictetus, *Diss.* IV, 1.104f., cited in Schubert, p. 135.

of intercession (12: 11) are followed directly by an equivalent of thanksgiving, 'And we rejoice in your glory' (v. 12). Although these instances are comparatively rare, Schubert concludes that their occurrence in widely separated eras and places is significant, and that the apostle made use of an epistolary convention which had been well established.[1]

Yet Paul's linking of thanksgiving with supplication or intercession was based not only in epistolary convention, but more fundamentally in Jewish liturgical practice. This may be seen in a number of Psalms, where petitions are sometimes preceded by praise, sometimes followed by praise, sometimes placed in between sections of praise, as in Psalm 9:

'*I will give thanks* (literally, I will praise, אוֹדֶה; in LXX ἐξομολογήσο-μαι) to the Lord with my whole heart; *I will tell of all thy wonderful deeds* (v. 1)....*Be gracious to me, O Lord!* Behold what I suffer from those who hate me. O thou who liftest me up from the gates of death, *that I may recount all thy praises* (vv. 13f.)....*Arise, O Lord!*' (v. 19).[2]

The opening praises were predicated upon the *Heilsgeschichte* of God's glorious deeds which showed that he *had* helped before.[3] So petitions and intercessions calling for similar help in the present might be added, and would lead in turn to more praise for contemporary mercies. Robinson points out an example in I Maccabees 4: 30–3: 'Blessed art thou, O Savior of Israel, who didst crush the attack of the mighty warrior by the hand of thy servant David, and didst give the camp of the Philistines into the hands of Jonathan....So do thou hem in this army by the hand of thy people Israel...and let all who know thy name praise thee with hymns.'[4]

---

[1] Schubert, p. 168. But for a contrary opinion, see Rigaux, *Thessaloniciens*, p. 357.

[2] Cf. Pss. 29, 30, 57, 59, 69, 71, 89, 106, 109, 144, I Chron. 16: 7–36. The psalms in the Thanksgiving Scrolls of the DSS, however, developed more in the direction of praises (hodayoth), confession, and meditation; intercessory and other petitions are rare – but see Pss. XVI, XVII, XVIII, where petitions do occur. *RGG*, II (3rd edn, 1958), 1215f.

[3] Cf. de Boer, *De Vorbede in het Oude Testament*, pp. 153ff.

[4] J. M. Robinson, 'The Historicality of Biblical Language,' espec. pp. 131–50. He cites also Sir. 51: 1–12, Jth. 13: 18–20. Cf. also *idem*, 'Die Hodajot-Formel in Gebet und Hymnus des Frühchristentums,' *Apophoreta. Festschrift für Ernst Haenschen*, ed. W. Eltester (Berlin, 1964), pp. 204ff.

In synagogue liturgy, too, petitions and intercessions were enclosed with praises and blessings to God, as in most of the Eighteen Benedictions, in the Ahabah, Geullah, and Hashkibenu: e.g., 'Blessed art thou, O Lord, the holy God. Bless us, our Father, with the knowledge that cometh from thee, and with intelligence and understanding from thy Law. Blessed art thou, O Lord, gracious giver of knowledge!'[1] This pattern was taken over into Christian liturgy, as may be seen partially in the prayer in Acts 4: 24–30,[2] and fully in the eucharistic prayers in Didache 9–10.[3] Finally, it contributed to the structure of the Pauline thanksgivings, which begin with an expression of thanks (reflecting the somewhat different Jewish hodaya),[4] may continue with a report of petition and intercession (reflecting Jewish petition), and may end with some feature which serves to replace the traditional closing beracha.[5]

---

[1] Shemoneh Esreh, 1–4. See Oesterley, *The Jewish Background of the Christian Liturgy*, pp. 126–36; Heinemann, *Prayer*, pp. iiif., and xi; Funk, *Language, Hermeneutics, and Word of God*, pp. 256f.; Bahr, 'Use of the Lord's Prayer,' pp. 158f.; M. Kadushin, *Worship and Ethics, A Study in Rabbinic Judaism* (Northwestern Univ. Press, 1963), pp. 105ff.

For the growth of the synagogue blessing, see J.-P. Audet, 'Esquisse historique du genre litteraire de la "benediction" juive, etc.' A number of elements came eventually to make up the beracha: the initial blessing (beracha, εὐλογέω, -ία) or praise (hodaya, ἐξομολογέομαι, ἐξομολογήσις), involving a confession of faith in God's power; the expression of wonder at his marvellous past acts, together with the sentiment of gratitude; often supplication regarding present needs and relying on the faithfulness of God; perhaps a note of exhortation (e.g., Ps. 107: 43); finally a closing section of praise or doxology.

For a somewhat similar structure in early Christian hymns, see R. Deichgräber, *Gotteshymnus und Christushymnus in der frühen Christenheit* (Göttingen, 1967).

[2] 'Sovereign Lord, who didst make the heaven and the earth...And now, Lord, look upon their threats....' (Praise at beginning and end is lacking.)

[3] 'We thank thee, our Father, for the holy vine of David...which thou hast made known...to thee be glory forever....So let thy church be gathered together from the ends of the earth into thy kingdom; for thine is the glory and the power through Jesus Christ forever.' Didache, chap. 9. A similar pattern is used in chap. 10. (See Audet, p. 395.) Cf. the structure of the Lord's Prayer: that God's name be hallowed...; supplications for present needs; a final doxology (probably added later). See C. E. B. Cranfield, 'Hebrews 13. 20–21,' *Scot. Journ. Theol.*, 20 (1967), 437–41. Cf. J. M. Robinson, 'Die Hodajot-Formel,' pp. 209f.

[4] See below, pp. 170ff.   [5] See below, p. 163.

So Paul's incorporation of an intercessory petition within his thanksgivings is a product of several interacting backgrounds, epistolary and liturgical, Hellenistic, Jewish, and Christian.[1]

We may now ask what is the precise grammatical connection between the thanksgiving and its petitionary component (the prayer-report). In his structural analysis of the Pauline thanksgiving periods, Schubert displayed a pattern of close yet varied syntactical relations between the report of thanksgiving and the report of intercessory prayer. The simplest construction used a participle for the verb of petition: e.g., μνείαν ποιούμενος.... (Philem. 4–6). Next we have seen that the prayer-report might be replaced by another type of clause with the verb in the indicative, which would function as a wish-prayer or declaration: ὃς καὶ βεβαιώσει.... (I Cor. 1: 4–8). A third type of construction occurred in the more elaborate and extended thanksgivings, when a fresh start is made one or more times, e.g., in I Thess. 1: 2 – 3: 13. Here we find two widely separated participial phrases, μνείαν ποιούμενοι...μνημονεύοντες... (1: 2), and δεόμενοι.... (3: 10). In the elaborate thanksgiving in Philippians we find both a participial phrase, τὴν δέησιν ποιούμενος.... (1: 4), and an indicative verb, προσεύχομαι.... (1: 9).[2]

[1] J. M. Robinson, 'The Historicality of Biblical Language,' pp. 148, 149, n. 29.

[2] See Schubert's table of constructions, pp. 54f. He points out that in the extended thanksgiving in I Thess., the final intercessory clause is postponed right until the end of the period at 3: 10: 'We give thanks to God always, constantly mentioning you in our prayers (1: 2f.)...And we also thank God constantly for this (2: 13)....For what thanksgiving can we render... praying earnestly...that we may see your face (3: 9f.)....Now may our God and Father....(3: 11–13).'

Here (as in Phil. and Col.), we have the stylistic device of repeating the basic formula to preserve the formal unity of the thanksgiving and complete its basic structural pattern with the intercessory portion. The final intercessory unit (3: 10–13) contains both the usual prayer-report and a wish-prayer. 'It predicates Paul's highly developed sense of form. This long drawn-out thanksgiving very much needed some such double climax' (Schubert, p. 23). Cf. II Macc. 1: 2–6 containing both a wish-prayer (vv. 2–5) and a prayer-report (v. 6).

But Sanders ('Transition from Opening Thanksgiving,' pp. 355f.) suggests two thanksgiving periods (1: 2–10 and 2: 13 – 3:13). In any case, the double climax at the end would be stylistically fitting.

The variety of syntactical constructions used within the prayer-report to give the content of the petition[1] caused Schubert to think that 'the point is here reached [in the thanksgiving period] where the specific epistolary situation begins to influence form and content more strongly....'[2] Sanders brought further understanding to the varied forms of the closing portion of the thanksgiving period. He explained them as a reflection of or a substitute for the Jewish beracha.[3] Yet we should also notice the petitionary or intercessory aspect of these transition forms, where it occurs. It must be seen in the light of both the epistolary and liturgical backgrounds that we have sketched, and of the distinctive identity and importance of petition in the Pauline letters.[4] Thus the intercessory prayer-reports and wish-prayers, insofar as they do occur in the thanksgiving periods, cannot be explained merely as replacements of the beracha, but rather as corresponding to the separate petitionary element in Jewish prayer.

The prayer-report may often (though not invariably) lead into or be followed by a liturgical element of praise or positive encouragement. In each instance the transition is fairly clearly marked:

E.g., in Rom. 1: 9f., the prayer-report ends clearly with the words 'now at last succeed in coming to you,' and a new beginning is made in v. 11, 'For I long to see you' (a formula of mutual encouragement, perhaps a surrogate for praise); in Phil. 1: 11 the prayer-report ends on a note of praise, 'to the glory and praise of God,' and a new start is made in v. 12, 'I want you to know, brethren...'; in I Thess. 1: 3, the break is not quite so sharp, yet it is evident that with the

[1] See below, Appended Note 1, pp. 173f.

[2] Schubert, p. 62. He does not, however, subject these clauses to detailed scrutiny.

[3] He classified these closing forms as follows: a doxology (I Tim. 1: 17, Phil. 1: 11, Eph. 1: 14, I Pet. 1: 7); a 'πιστός-surrogate' for the beracha (I Cor. 1: 9, II Thess. 3: 3, cf. I Thess. 5: 24b); an oblique petition for aid (I Thess. 3: 11–13, cf. 5: 23f.); a liturgical unit of mutual *paraklesis* (Philem. 7, II Thess. 1: 12; he omits Rom. 1: 12); and an inverted thanksgiving (II Cor. 1: 11).

[4] Cf. also Audet, p. 395, referring to the need to distinguish between εὐχαριστίαι and προσευχαί in the Didache prayers.

6-2

words in v. 4, 'For we know brethren' (εἰδότες, ἀδελφοί), he passes beyond the specific subject matter of his prayers of remembrance, and begins a long descriptive statement of the coming of the gospel to the Thessalonians. In the other examples the demarcation is clear in each case: the intercessory prayer-report breaks off with Phil. 1: 4, I Thess. 3: 10, Philem. 6 (I Cor. 1: 8, II Cor. 1: 7) [II Thess. 1: 12].[1]

The endings of those prayer-reports which occur less formally in the body of the letters, are also comparatively easy to determine:

No difficulty is presented by the endings of the brief reports in Rom. 9: 3, 10: 1, II Cor. 9: 14, each of which is followed by an obviously new beginning. The divided report in II Cor. 13: 7, 9b presents some problems of strict demarcation because of the ambiguity of the two ἵνα constructions in v. 7; also vv. 8–9a, while closely associated with the prayer-report, must be taken as intervening additional explanation: 'For we cannot do...' (οὐ γὰρ δυνάμεθα).[2]

One further stylistic observation: The surprising fact that the intercessory portion is usually introduced so unemphatically by a participial phrase (e.g., 'praying earnestly night and day that we may see you,' I Thess. 3: 10), need not imply that this was of little significance for the apostle compared with the forcible *eucharisto* (I Thank God) which usually began the period.[3] Indeed, in the Thessalonian epistle the participle

---

[1] [It is only in the deutero-Pauline epistles that some of the transitions are doubtful – Eph. 1: 16–23, Col. 1: 9–14, where the prayer passages gradually shade into statements.]

These endings precede the endings of the thanksgiving periods shown by Sanders, 'Transition from Opening Thanksgiving' (except II Thess. 1: 12, where they coincide). J. L. White, 'Introductory Formulae in the Body of the Pauline Letter,' finds introductory formulae to the body of the letter as follows: Rom. 1: 13–15 (following the formula of mutual encouragement); I Thess. 2: 1–4 (well along in the thanksgiving period); Phil. 1: 12–18, Philem. 7–14, I Cor. 1: 10–16, II Cor. 1: 8–12 (in each case immediately after the prayer-report or equivalent).

[2] See below, pp. 244, n. 7, 246, n. 7.

[3] A partic. is used in the thanksgivings in I Thess. 1: 2f., 3: 10, Phil. 1: 5, Philem. 4 [cf. Eph. 1: 16, Col. 1: 3]; but an indic. in the mixed type thanksgivings, Rom. 1: 9, Phil. 1: 9 (II Cor. 1: 7) [cf. Col. 1: 9, II Thess. 1: 11].

δεόμενοι actually marks a watershed for the whole letter. It introduces the second half of Paul's message, marking a transition from thanksgiving for what had already transpired, to intercession for the further blessings that he still desires for his readers.[1]

In conclusion, we have seen that the Pauline intercessory prayer-reports in general have a characteristic though elastic form, easy to recognize and demarcate, whether located in the thanksgivings or in the body of the letters. Their principal distinguishing formal features involve the transposition of capsule intercessory prayers into an epistolary mode, through the use of a prayer verb in the indicative or participial form, followed usually by an appropriate final clause or a nominal phrase to express the substance of the prayer and mention the one prayed for. Those intercessory reports which constitute a part of the thanksgiving period adopt a well-attested epistolary convention, but their linking of thanksgiving and intercession is based also in Old Testament and Jewish liturgical practices. The emphasis on the frequency of the supplications, an emphasis found in nearly all Paul's prayer-reports,[2] also reflects epistolary and liturgical custom. Liturgical practice is followed in the eschatological climax found in several of the introductory prayer-reports. Yet their syntactical variety seems to allow the apostle some freedom in expressing the particular supplications required for each letter, a question to which we shall turn in the next chapter.

PRELIMINARY FUNCTIONAL CONSIDERATIONS ABOUT THE PRAYER-REPORTS

Before we proceed to a detailed functional study of the individual intercessory prayer-reports, one or two general questions demand our attention. First, is the apostle's joining of thanks-

In the reports in the body of the letters (App. III, p. 300) the indic. is preferred, Rom. 9: 3, 10: 1, II Cor. 13: 7, 9 [cf. Eph. 3: 14, Col. 1: 29, 2: 1, 5]; but a partic. with prep. occurs in II Cor. 9: 14 [cf. Col. 4: 12].

[1] Cf. Sanders' comment that the lack of prominence of the liturgical ending at the close of the epistolary thanksgiving is related to its function of introducing the body of the letter; 'Transition from Opening Thanksgiving,' p. 361, n. 18.   [2] See below, p. 182, n. 1.

givings and supplications merely the result of epistolary and liturgical custom, or does it also express an inner necessity of his intercessory relation with his churches before God?[1]

To begin with we note that the pattern linking supplication and thanksgiving was not invariably followed by the apostle. Thus outside of the thanksgiving period he makes a number of thanksgiving exclamations not closely associated with petition or intercession.[2] As far as the prayer-reports are concerned, only one out of five in the body of the letters is closely linked with thanksgiving – II Cor. 9: 14.[3] The wish-prayers are inconclusive, only two being related to thanksgiving – I Thess. 3: 11–13 and the doubtful one in I Cor. 1: 8.[4] Moreover, of the five requests for prayer in the Pauline epistles, only one is closely coupled with thanksgiving – II Cor. 1: 11.[5] His didactic references to intercessory prayer in the eighth chapter of Romans (vv. 15f., 23, 26f., 34) are not directly related to thanksgiving, although placed within a broad context of hope and victory. Nor are the other didactic passages linked with thanksgiving.[6] In the apostle's exhortations to prayer,[7] however, three out of the four examples (those in the closing section of the letter) join petitionary prayer with rejoicing or thanksgiving – I Thess. 5: 16–18, Rom. 12: 12–14, Phil. 4: 6, but not I Cor. 7: 5.

So Paul follows no merely set pattern. Rather his usage reflects an underlying sense of a double situation that he does not always express in so many words – a situation in which

[1] Cf. Schubert's judgment, '...intercessory prayer...and thanksgiving ...are not only syntactically related, but Paul considers them two inseparable aspects of the same religious and liturgical act.' P. 67. See also above, p. 12.

[2] Rom. 6: 17f., I Cor. 1: 14, 14: 18, 15: 57, II Cor. 2: 14, 8: 16. See Appendix I.

[3] The others are I Cor. 5: 3; II Cor. 13: 7, 9b; Rom. 9: 3; 10: 1. See Appendix III, p. 300. [Cf. Col. 2: 1–3 and 5.]

[4] Rom. 15: 5 and 15: 13 are associated with the praises in vv. 9–12. Rom. 15: 33 and 16: 20 are negative. I Thess. 5: 23 follows at some distance the thanksgiving reference in 5: 18. Phil. 4: 19 is followed by a doxology.

[5] For list, see Appendix III, p. 301. [In the deutero-Pauline letters, one out of three is so linked, viz. Col. 4: 2–4, 'Continue steadfastly in prayer, being watchful with thanksgiving; and pray for us also' (request and exhortation).]

[6] For list, see Appendix III, p. 301.   [7] See *ibid.*

victories are continually associated with new occasions of need. The Thessalonian letter was seen to illustrate this clearly: a joyful celebration of the extraordinary blessings of the gospel already bestowed was balanced by an anxious sense of continuing dangers outward and inward. Much remained uncertain in a time of persecution crisis.[1]

Of course, prayer has always tended to involve both acknowledgement of gifts received and requests for blessings still hoped for. But this double character became intensified in the eschatological era, with its overlapping 'inaugurated' and 'futurist' aspects.[2] Throughout all Paul's letters shines a vivid sense of the glory and yet the incompleteness of his own position and that of his fellow Christians: 'Not that I have already obtained this or am already perfect; but I press on to make it my own, because Christ Jesus has made me his own' (Phil. 3: 12).[3] Although he is thankful for past blessings, he will permit no mere satisfaction with them, but constantly in every letter exhorts and urges the churches to move forward in their Christian life.

Closely allied with thanksgiving (εὐχαριστία) was his practice of exultation or 'boasting' (καύχησις).[4] While he attacked all boasting based in self-trust (Rom. 3: 21–6, 5: 11, I Cor. 1: 29, II Cor. 10: 17, Phil. 3: 3, Gal. 6: 14), he himself could glory in his congregations (e.g., Rom. 15: 17, I Cor. 15: 31, II Cor. 7: 4, 14, 8: 24, 9: 2f., etc.). In so doing he was confidently exulting in the work already done for them through Christ in the new age.[5] Yet his glorying, too, had an element of incompleteness in it, so that he looked forward to the day of the parousia when he could boast of his churches as fully acceptable (I Thess. 2: 19, Rom. 15: 16f., II Cor. 1: 14, 11: 2, Phil. 2: 16 [Col. 1: 28f.]).[6] And because of their mutual inter-

---

[1] See above, pp. 47ff. Cf. Rigaux, *Thessaloniciens*, p. 483.

[2] See Greeven, *Gebet und Eschatologie im Neuen Testament*; Harder, pp. 110f.; R. Kerkhoff, *Das Unablässige Gebet. Beiträge zur Lehre von immerwährende Beten im Neuen Testament* (München, 1954). Cf. also Moltmann, *Theology of Hope, passim*; P. R. Baelz, *Prayer and Providence* (New York, 1968), pp. 100f.

[3] Cf. below, p. 200.

[4] A characteristic Pauline word taken over from the LXX. See R. Bultmann, *TWNT*, III, 646–54, and the literature there cited.

[5] Cf. above, p. 12, n. 3.

[6] See above, p. 5, n. 1. Cf. Bultmann, *TWNT*, III, 652.

cessory relationship, Paul would also be *their* boast – they must thank God that he had given *Paul* to *them* (II Cor. 1: 14, 5: 12, Phil. 1: 26). Each would celebrate the gift of the other.

It is, then, against the heightened eschatological situation as Paul sees it, that we must interpret the double movement in his prayers: boasting and thanksgiving must be augmented by petition and intercession. This duality may be described in three ways.

First, Paul's thanksgiving alternated with his intercessory prayer in a reciprocal manner. Thankfulness for past and present blessings uncovered needs still remaining and gave him boldness to pray. As he gives constant thanks for the Thessalonians, so he becomes ever more aware of new possibilities for them.[1] Remembering before God their 'work of faith and labor of love and steadfastness of hope' (I Thess. 1: 3), he is constrained to pray that their deficiencies may be supplied (3: 10). On the other hand, the discipline of constant prayer leads him to give thanks for them in a continuous, alternating movement. So he writes to the Corinthians, 'You also must help us by prayer, so that many will give thanks on our behalf for the blessing granted us in answer to many prayers' (II Cor. 1: 11).[2]

Second, the duality in Paul's prayers is paradoxical. Even the negative aspects of the eschatological age have their positive value; affliction and testing are interpreted as belonging to the loving purpose of God in the last days and therefore as an occasion for thanksgiving.[3] This is shown especially in the apostle's exhortations to prayer, e.g., 'Rejoice always, pray constantly, give thanks in all circumstances; for this is the will of God in Christ Jesus for you' (I Thess. 5: 16–18; cf. Rom. 12: 12, Phil. 4: 6f.).[4] The Thessalonian passage offers an example that sums up Paul's fundamentally paradoxical understanding of the Christian's living.[5] It forms a closely knit parae-

---

[1] Cf. Harder, p. 205, 'Die Gabe Gottes ermöglicht erst das richtige Beten und gibt dem Gebet neue Ziele.' See also Moltmann, p. 105ff.: 'Hence every reality in which a fulfillment is already taking place now, becomes the confirmation, exposition, and liberation of a greater hope.'

[2] See below, p. 274.   [3] See above, pp. 49f.

[4] [Cf. also Eph. 5: 4b and Col. 2: 7b.]

[5] It is convenient to discuss this passage prematurely at this point; see also below, pp. 285f.

netic unit in which joy, constancy in prayer, thanksgiving in all circumstances, are joined together by a final statement that such was the will of God in Christ for them. The theme of rejoicing under great difficulty had appeared several times already in the epistle (1: 6, 2: 2, 2: 19f., 3: 9). Now for the last time he exhorts the converts to continue to rejoice always. Nowhere is the duty to celebrate in the midst of suffering more cogently stated.[1] A practical and continuous means for the believers to express and renew their joy would be found in constant supplication associated with thanksgiving ('pray constantly, give thanks in all circumstances,' vv. 5: 17f.). Through remembering one another constantly (ἀδιαλείπτως) in prayer, their joy would be renewed, and their thanksgiving.[2]

But the paradox of rejoicing in afflictions is even more strongly suggested in the phrase ἐν παντί, 'in all circumstances.'[3] True, the believer must share outwardly in the difficulties common to all men, but inwardly he may transcend these sufferings by interpreting every event as a gift of God, seeing blessings hidden within all things.[4] This goes much farther than giving thanks *in spite of* adverse conditions. So ἐν παντί brings the paradox to its sharpest expression. It is a victory of the spirit that is both privilege and duty;[5] and it is possible only 'in Christ' – the believer finds strength for this only through the reconciliation which has come through Christ – 'for this is the will of God in Christ Jesus for you' (v. 18).

[1] Cf. II Cor. 6: 4–10, 12: 10, Phil. 1: 18, 2: 18, 3: 1, 4: 4, 10. Of course Paul shared this with other NT writers and the early Church: e.g., Matt. 5: 10–12, John 15: 11, 16: 33, 17: 13, Eph. 5: 19–20, Heb. 12: 2, I Pet. 4: 12–14, etc. See Beardslee, *Human Achievement and Divine Vocation in the Message of Paul*, pp. 111–15. See also below, pp. 199f. on the note of joy in Phil.

[2] Frame, p. 201. For further discussion of 'constant' prayer, see below, pp. 182f.

[3] Taking ἐν παντί not as temporal (πάντοτε), but of circumstances; Vulgate, 'in omnibus gratias agete.' The balance of probability seems strongly to favor this view. See, e.g., II Cor. 9: 8 where ἐν παντί is found in addition to, and probably in distinction from, πάντοτε. Schubert, p. 92, renders it 'for everything.'

[4] Rigaux, *Thessaloniciens*, p. 589, and Morris, p. 173.

[5] Cf. Fisher, *Prayer in the New Testament*, p. 61. 'To refuse to give thanks to God is considered to be one of the characteristic marks of men in their sin and rebellion...(Rom. 1: 21).'

Thus the very circumstances about which intercession was made should also be regarded as the subject of thanksgiving.[1] Related to this was the fact that thanksgiving had for Paul its representative aspect: in boasting and giving thanks about the churches, he was actually rejoicing before God on their behalf, pleading their cause by describing what had already been done for them.[2]

Third, the blessings and promises of the eschatological era far exceeded its hardships and anxieties. To eyes of faith all was seen in the light of God's revealed plan to save, the present lordship of Jesus Christ, and the certainty of final victory. Prayers of hope must be complemented by declarations of certainty.[3] Every intercession could end with the 'Amen' which expressed the unshakable faithfulness of God: 'He who calls you is faithful and he will do it' (I Thess. 5: 24).[4] Thus thanksgivings exceeded intercessory petitions, for thankfulness was the more basic Pauline response to God's great saving acts in the new age.[5]

A somewhat different question may here be touched upon. Various commentators have believed it was the widely spread Hellenistic concept εὐχαριστία that prepared the ground for a peculiarly intimate Christian note of gratitude to God stemming from a deepened sense of sonship through Christ.[6] The increasing substitution by the early Christian church and the New Testament of εὐχαριστέω, -ία for the LXX εὐλογέω, -ία (beracha) and for ἐξομολογέομαι, -ήσις (hodaya),[7] indicated a

[1] Would Paul include even human sin and failure as a subject of thankfulness? Perhaps even these might be included, if repented of and transformed by God into occasions for grace (Rom. 5: 20b). But Paul was fully aware of the danger of this (Rom. 6: 1, etc.).

[2] See above, p. 12. The word εὐχαριστία is later attested in the papyri as meaning something very close to 'prayer' in the sense of petition. Milligan, *Thessalonians*, p. 75; also Schubert, pp. 165ff.

[3] For examples of this relationship see Phil. 4: 19 (above, p. 102, n. 4); II Cor. 1: 7 (below, pp. 226ff.); II Cor. 1: 10f. (p. 273, and n. 2); Phil. 1: 19f. (pp. 279f.).   [4] See above, pp. 35, n. 2, 68, n. 1.

[5] Just as praise had been the basic response to God's great acts under the old covenant; see above, pp. 160f. Cf. Bauer, *Der Wortgottesdienst der Ältesten Christen*, pp. 35ff.; Audet, pp. 380f., 395f.; Jeremias, *The Prayers of Jesus*, p. 87.   [6] Schubert, pp. 121f.

[7] εὐχαριστέω, -ία occurs very rarely in the LXX (10 times in all). But in Aquila εὐχαριστία substitutes in a number of places for ἐξομολόγησις as

profoundly new kind of thankfulness.[1] Throughout his letters
Paul repeatedly uses 'give thanks,' where we might have expected to find the LXX words for 'bless,' 'give praise,' 'glorify.'[2]
On this view, εὐχαριστία is to be seen as a newly transformed
attitude of the Christian in his deepened existence as a child
before God.[3] More recently, however, it has been argued that
εὐχαριστεῖν in the New Testament reproduces the lofty connotations of the Old Testament and Jewish blessings and praises,
although deepening their content in the light of the marvelous
acts of God in Christ. It was only in the second century under
the increasing impact of Gentile Christianity, that the meaning
moved towards gratitude, at the expense of wonder and adora-
tion – the focus was transferred from the marvels wrought by
God to the benefits received by man.[4]

a translation of *toda*; so also in Philo. For examples of this and for the
increasing use of εὐχαριστέω, -ία in early Christian writings, see J. M.
Robinson, 'Die Hodajot-Formel,' pp. 198ff.

[1] A parallel transition of terms may be seen in the free interchange of
'give thanks' (εὐχαριστεῖν) and 'bless' (εὐλογεῖν) in the gospel accounts of
Jesus distributing bread: 'bless' is used in Mk. 6: 41 = Matt. 14: 19 = Lk.
9: 16. In the doublet account, we find both 'give thanks' and 'bless' in
Mk. 8: 6f., only 'give thanks' in Matt. 15: 36, while Lk. is lacking. In the
Last Supper account we find in Mk. 14: 22f. that Jesus 'blesses' before the
bread and 'gives thanks' before the wine; the same in Matt.; in Lk.
22: 17–20 he 'gives thanks' before the first cup, and before the bread (the
doubtful reading that includes a second cup merely says 'likewise'). See
J. M. Robinson, 'Die Hodajot-Formel,' pp. 202f.

[2] See Appendix I, below, under 'Thanksgiving'; and note the sudden
shift from 'bless' to 'thanksgiving' in I Cor. 14: 16; also the shift from thanks-
giving to giving glory in II Cor. 9: 11–13, see below, p. 250, n. 3.
Jeremias mentions 'an important linguistic observation: Hebrew, Ara-
maic, and Syriac have no word for "thank" and "thankfulness".' J.
Jeremias, *The Parables of Jesus*, E.Tr. (New York, 1962), p. 127, citing
P. Joüon, 'Reconnaissance et action de grace dans le Nouveau Testament,'
RSR, 29 (1939), 112–14.

[3] So Hamman, *La Prière*, pp. 292–7; von der Goltz, in a section 'Lobpreis
und Dank,' draws a similar distinction between εὐλογεῖν (bless) and
εὐχαριστεῖν (thank): Before, there had been praise; now there was a more
personal giving of thanks (*Das Gebet*, p. 105); cf. Harder, pp. 130–8 and
163–214; and Juncker, *Das Gebet bei Paulus*, p. 23.

[4] Audet, pp. 396–8; C. F. D. Moule, *The Birth of the New Testament*,
HNTC (New York, 1962), pp. 19f. J. M. Robinson, 'The Historicality of
Biblical Language,' p. 132, points out the increasing preference of Judaism
for Berachoth over Hodayoth, whereas primitive Christianity increasingly

But however the new term εὐχαριστεῖν may have been understood generally in the earliest Christian church, for Paul it indicated a mood not only of ceaseless wonder and praise, but also of intimate gratitude to God. It was only within this prior consciousness of particular gifts and graces received, that particular intercessory supplications could be offered. We conclude that the formal and syntactical linking of thanksgivings and intercessory prayer-reports represented a profound dialectic of the human spirit before the God who had so graciously acted in Jesus Christ.[1]

One further preliminary task remains, namely to outline the function of the thanksgiving periods that incorporate several of the intercessory prayer-reports. The custom of starting letters with a thanksgiving may have originated in 'a superstitious desire to begin every message with a good omen.'[2] If that is so, there is a suggestion that in Paul's epistolary thanksgivings we have an actual offering of prayer.[3] In addition, the thanksgiving period enables him to begin with a *captatio benevolentiae*, to 'approach his readers in a spirit of good will, with the assurance that he recognizes in them the fruits of divine grace.... If he has criticisms to offer, the hostility which they might provoke is disarmed in advance by warm words of praise and regard';[4] thanks to God may be used to express thanks and praise to the recipients of the letter also.[5]

Moreover, by naming victories and blessings Paul is offering kindly encouragement to the readers in the presence of God to continue and strive still harder.[6] An opportunity is afforded to

preferred Hodayoth, and replaced the verb 'bless' by the verb 'thank'; Cf. *idem*, 'Die Hodajot-Formel,' pp. 203f.; also Sanders, 'Transition from Opening Thanksgiving,' pp. 358, 361f.

[1] '...thanksgiving and supplication, joy and care, peace and passion flow together and ever and again spring in two.' K. Barth, *The Epistle to the Philippians*, E.Tr. (London, 1962), p. 23.

[2] F. W. Beare, *IB*, xi, 149f.

[3] See below, p. 186, etc.   [4] Beare, p. 149.

[5] Cf. M. Dibelius, *A Fresh Approach to the New Testament and Early Christian Literature*, E.Tr. (New York, 1936), p. 143; also J. M. Robinson, 'The Historicality of Biblical Language,' p. 137, n. 2, 'a blessing on a person's God functions as a blessing upon the person. A similar role is played in epistolary thanksgivings....' Cf. Schubert, pp. 59, 150, 169, etc.

[6] Cf. Barth, *Philippians*, p. 14; Schubert, p. 67; Furnish, *Theology and Ethics*, p. 94.

acknowledge those special eschatological mercies which have been shown to the readers of that letter, and in the light of which further blessings may be expected.[1] As intercessor he witnesses to their victories so that he may move into supplication for more victories. Finally, the thanksgiving periods give an indication of the main interests and mood of the letter which follows.[2]

It is in relation to these varied purposes of the opening thanksgiving that the intercessory portion is best understood. We shall find, however, that the intercessory portion tends to focus even more closely than does the general thanksgiving the immediate occasion of the letter, somewhat like a subtitle following a broad newspaper headline.[3]

Having surveyed in this chapter the stylistic peculiarities of the various intercessory prayer-reports, and examined the general relation of a group of them to the introductory thanksgiving periods, we are now ready to make a more detailed functional study of the individual passages.

APPENDED NOTE I

Prayer-words and syntactical constructions in the prayer-reports

(a) *Words and phrases for praying which use* ἵνα, εἴ πως, ὅπως, *and a final clause to express the content of the prayer*

προσεύχομαι ἵνα. See Phil. 1: 9–11 [Col. 1: 9, προσευχόμενοι καὶ αἰτούμενοι ἵνα. II Thess. 1: 11f.] Cf. I Cor. 14: 13.

εὐχόμεθα ἵνα. II Cor. 13: 7.

μνείαν ποιοῦμαι ἐπὶ τῶν προσευχῶν. In Rom. 1: 9f. the phrase is followed by δεόμενος with εἴ πως, where Paul is hesitant in writing to a church which he had not founded. See below, p. 191. In Philem. 4 and 6, the phrase takes ὅπως directly. [In

---

[1] See above, pp. 16of.

[2] See Schubert, p. 77: '. . .each thanksgiving not only announces clearly the subject matter of the letter, but also foreshadows unmistakably its stylistic qualities, the degree of intimacy and other important characteristics.' Cf. *ibid.* pp. 26f. and 168. Harder, pp. 200–4. Funk, *Language, Hermeneutics, and Word of God*, p. 249.

[3] An analogue used by Sanders in another connection ('Transition from Opening Thanksgiving,' p. 354).

Eph. 1: 16–23, it takes ἵνα, 'remembering you in my prayers that....']

[ἀγῶνα ἔχω, ἀγωνίζομαι, ἵνα. Col. 1: 29, 2: 1–3, 4: 12.]

[κάμπτειν τὰ γόνατα ἵνα. Eph. 3: 14ff.]

(b) *Words and phrases for praying which use the infinitive and* εἰς τό, *or* μή

δεόμενοι εἰς τὸ ἰδεῖν. I Thess. 3: 10.

ηὐχόμην ἀνάθεμα εἶναι. (See above, p. 19 on the meaning of εὔχομαι.) Cf. II Cor. 13: 7, 'We pray to God that,' εὐχόμεθα... μὴ ποιῆσαι.

(c) *Words for praying which use a nominal phrase for the prayer content*

ἡ δέησις...εἰς σωτηρίαν. Rom. 10: 1.

τοῦτο εὐχόμεθα, τὴν ὑμῶν κατάρτισιν. II Cor. 13: 9b.

(d) *Words for praying, with the prayer content postponed*

Phil. 1: 4, τὴν δέησιν ποιούμενος. The construction is broken off and completed in v. 9, προσεύχομαι ἵνα (Schubert, *Pauline Thanksgivings*, pp. 14 and 66).

I Thess. 1: 2, μνείαν ποιούμενοι. The construction is finally completed at 3: 10, δεόμενοι εἰς τὸ ἰδεῖν (Schubert, pp. 16–27. See above, p. 162, n. 2).

(e) *Words for praying with no content given*

II Cor. 9: 14, δεήσει ὑπὲρ ὑμῶν ἐπιποθούντων ὑμᾶς.

(f) *A problematical example*

I Cor. 5: 3–5, 'For though absent in body I am present in spirit,' followed by an injunction which gives the content of his negative prayer (curse), 'you are to deliver....' See above, p. 145.

CHAPTER 8

FUNCTION OF THE PRAYER-REPORTS IN THE THANKSGIVING PERIODS

The questions that were asked earlier about the wish-prayers must now be addressed to the individual prayer-reports: What new depth of meaning does the apostle add, in adapting a conventional epistolary formula to his own purposes? And how much evidence is there that he used each prayer-report to express the concerns that were the specific occasion for the letter? We shall start with seven prayer-reports in the thanksgiving periods,[1] following later with the less formal ones in the body of the letter to Romans and the two to Corinth.

I THESSALONIANS 1: 2b–3

We begin with two prayer-reports at the opening and close of the thanksgiving section of I Thessalonians. The first one reads as follows:

(We give thanks to God always for you all,)[2] *constantly mentioning you in our prayers, remembering before our God and Father your work of faith and labor of love and steadfastness of hope in our Lord Jesus Christ.* (I Thess. 1: 2b–3)

The purpose of this prayer-report may first be assessed through its location in a uniquely long thanksgiving (chaps. 1–3).[3] The thanksgiving in I Thessalonians not only announces the main subject matter of the letter, but actually develops it *in extenso*, in its positive and negative aspects.[4] Within this broad

[1] For list, see Appendix III. As with the wish-prayers, little detailed study has been done in this area.

[2] Context added in parentheses.

[3] For the possibility that this section may be regarded formally as two thanksgiving periods, see above, p. 162, n. 2. But in either case the function of the material remains unchanged.

[4] J. M. Robinson ('The Historicality of Biblical Language,' p. 142) shows that 'Already in the Old Testament historical books Berachoth seem to provide a setting for historical narration, which tends to overflow the original

literary context the first prayer-report (1: 2b–3) prepares the way for a gradual unfolding throughout the thanksgiving of all the reasons for Paul's gratitude and anxious praying.[1] Indeed this advance prayer-summary shades off naturally by means of the participial phrase εἰδότες, κτλ. (v. 4), into a long account of the many details of his constant remembering:[2] their election, joyful acceptance of the gospel, expectancy of the parousia, the triumph of the gospel among them, the spread of the news of their faith far and wide, their willingness to suffer persecution, and yet the continued doubt about their stability under afflic-tion and temptation. All these details are foreshadowed in the pregnant threefold summary of his constant thanksgivings and supplications about their 'work of faith and labor of love and steadfastness of hope in our Lord Jesus Christ.'

An unusual problem of identification arises in this particular passage: how far are we dealing with thanksgiving and how far with petition? Because the clearly petitionary sentence in this elaborate thanksgiving section is postponed until 3: 9ff., the line between thanksgiving and petitionary intercession is blurred at this earlier point (in the other thanksgiving periods it is more clearly drawn). The syntactical shape of the passage seems to lead the opening thanksgiving statement into a de-veloping exposition of reasons for thanksgiving only. In his joy the apostle composes a sentence which, in Jowett's words, seems 'to grow under his hands':[3] 'We give thanks...men-tioning you in our prayers, remembering your work...knowing that he has chosen you...as you know what kind of men we proved....' By this time he is well into the long account of the call of the Thessalonians and the founding of their church. Strictly speaking, then, the phrase 'remembering your work of faith and labor of love, etc.' would qualify 'we give thanks.' So the prayer-report would describe only the apostle's thanks-

limits of the formula; i.e., there is a tendency to produce a narrative form of the formula,' e.g., I Kings 5: 21, II Chron. 2: 12. See above, pp. 160f.

[1] For the situation at Thessalonica, see above, pp. 47ff.

[2] Schubert, however, continues the basic thanksgiving structure through to the middle of v. 5, where there is a transition from 'we know' to 'you know' (p. 17).

[3] B. Jowett, *The Epistles of St. Paul to the Thessalonians, Galatians, Romans*, vol. I, 2nd edn (London, 1859), pp. 44f.

givings and lead on to further grounds of thankfulness, 'knowing that he has chosen you....'[1]

But in such a loosely growing sentence, probably he is referring both to the thanksgivings and to the supplications that arise as he remembers the Thessalonians: μνημονεύοντες refers both to εὐχαριστοῦμεν and to μνείαν ποιούμενοι ἐπὶ τῶν προσευχῶν ἡμῶν. The word μνημονεύω probably indicates not so much a formal and dutiful calling to mind of the converts, but a continual, almost involuntary remembering that betokens his unfailing sense of pastoral responsibility for them.[2] And in remembering them, he finds occasion both to give thanks and to lift them up to God in supplication.[3] Paul the loving pastor makes Paul the intercessor.

It should be noted that in this instance the blurring of intercessory petition with thanksgiving prevents the intercessory phrases from focusing the immediate occasion of the letter. This matter is postponed until the second prayer-report (3: 10–11).

As we turn to examine the relation between the prayer-report and the Thessalonian situation, it is striking to observe the warmth of thankfulness conveyed by the wording of the passage.[4] The emphatic position of ὑμῶν serves to mark the depth of Paul's interest in them.[5] A similar emphasis is found in 2: 19f., 'Is it not *you*? For *you* are our glory and joy.'[6] In

---

[1] Cf. Frame, *Thessalonians*, p. 65.

[2] The use of the genitives (τοῦ ἔργου, etc.) suggests this: cf. Gal. 2: 10, Col. 4: 18, Heb. 11: 15. Cf. the Vulgate, 'memor esse,' and other ancient versions. The accusative would suggest 'hold in remembrance,' e.g., I Thess. 2: 9, Matt. 16: 9, II Tim. 2: 8, Rev. 18: 5. So von Dobschütz, *Thessalonicher-Briefe*, Rigaux, *Thessaloniciens*, Dibelius, *Thessalonicher, et al.*; against is G. Lünemann, *Kritisch exegetisches Handbuch über die Briefe an die Thessalonicher...*, 3rd edn (Göttingen, 1867), *ad loc.* See below, p. 181, n. 1, on 'remembering before God....'   [3] Cf. above, p. 170.

[4] See above, p. 47; surpassed only by the thanksgiving in Phil.; below, p. 205, n. 5. The plural εὐχαριστοῦμεν suggests that Paul includes witnesses who share in the message of the latters and in the prayers that lie behind them. A concerned intercessory community is implied (cf. Neil, *Thessalonians*, p. 9), but not necessarily 'joint authorship' of the letter. For a full bibliography, see Rigaux, pp. 77–80.

[5] Syr pesh and Luther rightly repeat the translation of ὑμῶν three times: your work of faith, and your labor of love, and your steadfastness of hope, Rigaux, *Thessaloniciens*, p. 367.   [6] See above, p. 53, n. 2.

addition, the reality of his concern is suggested by the pertinence of his constant thanksgivings and petitions.

To describe these he employs a complex aggregation of three pairs of concepts, forming a double triad joined by the use of a string of genitives (τοῦ ἔργου τῆς πίστεως, τοῦ κόπου τῆς ἀγάπης, τῆς ὑπομονῆς τῆς ἐλπίδος). Yet, complex and ambiguous as is the language, its general meaning and main emphasis are unmistakable. The stress in the prayer passage lies where the apostle will place it throughout the epistle, not directly on the graces of faith, love, hope (important as these are in this and in the other letters),[1] but on the costly day-to-day activity that gives expression to them.[2] So we may paraphrase with Bicknell, 'We constantly remember your active work that is the fruit and evidence of your faith, your toil for others that only love could inspire, and your perseverance that nothing could sustain but hope in the coming of our Lord Jesus Christ....'[3]

Πίστις, a central concept for Paul, stood always at the head of the triad of Christian graces. As the indispensable condition of the Christian life, its very centrality caused the word to be used for a variety of connected aspects of man's response to God in Christ.[4] It could refer not only to the initial act of believing, but to the state and continuing life of the believer: thus there are growth in faith (II Cor. 10: 15), fullness of conviction and faith (I Thess. 1: 5, cf. Rom. 4: 21, 14: 5), deficiencies of faith (I Thess. 3: 10), etc.[5] In the present passage

[1] See above, p. 59.

[2] Thus the translation 'active faith' and 'patient hope' (Moffatt) places the stress wrongly.

[3] E. J. Bicknell, *The First and Second Epistles to the Thessalonians*, Westminster Commentaries (London, 1932), p. 5. The genitives (πίστεως, ἀγάπης, ἐλπίδος) are usually taken in this way as subjective; cf. Milligan's version, 'remmebering how your faith works (the working of your faith), and your love toils, and your hope endures' (p. 6).

The first triad is found also in Rev. 2: 2, ἔργα (plural), κόπον, ὑπομονήν; but the linking together of the two triads seems peculiar to Paul (Frame, p. 76).

[4] Cf. R. Bultmann, *TWNT*, VI, espec. 218–24; also his *Theology of the New Testament*, I, 314–30. Already in the LXX and in Judaism πίστις had become a broad expression for the religious attitude.

[5] '...being a believer is not a static affair. It takes place in the flux of individual life. It has to be maintained constantly in face of the danger of πίπτειν...It has to establish itself continually against assaults as an attitude which controls all life.' Bultmann in *TWNT*, VI, 219.

the word seems to carry this general meaning as it does through-out the letter – it was their total Christian life of trust in God about which the apostle was concerned (1: 3, 8, 3: 2, 5, 7, 10).

In speaking of their 'work' of faith (τοῦ ἔργου τῆς πίστεως), Paul is not here preoccupied with the question of faith versus works as a means of justification,[1] but is referring to their Christian life in all its range of activities as energized by faith (cf. Gal. 5: 6, 'faith working through love'; II Thess. 1: 11, 'every good resolve and work of faith'; Jas. 2: 18ff.).[2] Accordingly he constantly gives thanks and intercedes about their active work, the fruit and evidence of their continuing inner Christian life.

But while faith stands at the head in the prayer-report, costly love is the immediate need of the Thessalonians. This will be stressed in the main wish-prayer (3: 12) and throughout the epistle.[3] So the central pair in the triad, τοῦ κόπου τῆς ἀγάπης, emphasizes both the practical expression of love, and its pain and costliness.[4] It is the special discipline of continuing to practise love under the harsh pressures of persecution that occupies the apostle's thoughts. How deeply he cares that this be no merely transient feeling of goodwill is shown by his stress upon the labor which love must entail.

The final phrase of the triad (τῆς ὑπομονῆς τῆς ἐλπίδος) anticipates one of the most urgent purposes of the epistle. It brings us to the 'eschatological climax' and introduces the adventist emphasis of the letter. Clearly the hope referred to here was the Thessalonians' fervid expectation of the parousia (e.g., 1: 10, 4: 13, 5: 8b).[5] It could be a steadfast hope because grounded in God's faithful purpose to complete his work of salvation in Christ (1: 10, 2: 19, 3: 13, 4: 17f., 5: 9–11, 23f.).

---

[1] Against Calvin and others who laboriously render it 'God's work in you of faith,' or 'your work which consists of faith'; e.g., J. Ch. K. von Hofmann, *Die Heilige Schrift Neuen Testaments zusammenhängend untersucht...*, vol. 1: *Die Briefe Pauli an die Thessalonicher* (Nördlingen, 1862); *ad loc.*, P. W. Schmiedel, *Die Briefe an die Thessalonicher, HzNT*, II, 1 (Freiburg, 1898), *ad loc.*

[2] So von Dobschütz, *Thessalonicher-Briefe*, Milligan, *et al.*

[3] For details, see above, pp. 55ff.

[4] See F. Hauck, *TWNT*, III, 827–9. The word is used several times in the NT for the labor of Christians, e.g., I Cor. 3: 8, 15: 58, II Cor. 10: 15.

[5] See above, p. 49, n. 1; p. 85, n. 1.

As God was faithful,[1] so their hope could be steadfast (τῆς ὑπομονῆς).[2] Once again Paul is stressing the immediate need for the converts to give practical expression to a central Christian grace: inspired by their great hope of the parousia, may they stand fast under the difficulties of the last days, and 'wait for his Son from heaven' (1: 10).[3]

Accordingly the threefold prayer-report is seen to epitomize clearly the pastoral concerns of the epistle: 'work of faith' points to their total daily Christian activity; 'labor of love' summarizes their costly and sacrificial living under the limitless demands of *agape*; and 'steadfastness of hope' indicates a standing fast under critical persecution in the assured expectancy that God in Christ would speedily complete his purposes. All three graces are 'in our Lord Jesus Christ' (1: 3) who makes them possible.[4] And they are lived out 'before our God and Father' (1: 3), the searcher of hearts (2: 4) and the judge (3: 13), yet the one who as the Father will give us salvation through Christ (5: 9).[5] So at the beginning of the letter Paul has placed his most pressing interests within the nexus of thanksgiving and intercessory prayer.

We may now consider some further questions of the relation between the prayer-report and the Thessalonian situation. First, who are meant to be included in these constant thanksgivings and intercessions? The phrase περὶ παντῶν ὑμῶν shows that he prays not only for his faithful supporters, but for the idle, faint-hearted, weak (5: 14), and the ones who actually oppose him.[6] His loving responsibility reaches out to them all without distinction.[7]

---

[1] See above, p. 68, n. 1. [2] See above, p. 80, n. 3. [3] Cf. above, pp. 61f.

[4] Taking the phrase τοῦ κυρίου ἡμῶν. . . as qualifying all three members of the triad, rather than the last only: so J. Wohlenberg, *Der erste und zweite Thessalonicherbrief* (Leipzig, 1903), *ad loc.*, von Dobschütz, *Thessalonicher-Briefe, ad loc.*, Rigaux, *Thessaloniciens*, etc. Others attach it only to the word 'hope' – hope in Christ.

[5] The phrase ἔμπροσθεν τοῦ θεοῦ will be repeated in the prayer language of 3: 9 and 13; cf. above, p. 62. For the liturgical origin, yet deep Pauline significance, of the title 'our God and Father' (τοῦ θεοῦ καὶ πατρὸς ἡμῶν), see above, pp. 32, n. 1, and 55.

[6] So Milligan, p. 5. Cf. above, pp. 57f., 66f.

[7] At the end of the letter he enjoins that it be read to *all* the brethren. On the all-inclusive quality of Paul's prayers, see above, p. 60, n. 4.

But how can we rightly assess the weight of Paul's assurance that he gives thanks and prays for them πάντοτε and ἀδια-λείπτως (1 : 2) ?[1] It is true, as we have seen, that he is using a regular epistolary convention, so that we should heed Schubert's warning against giving too much weight to these assertions of unceasing prayer.[2] Hence it is only by considering the context of the whole letter and its prayer passages, that we conclude a conventional phrase is being used to describe his actual practice of frequent and earnest prayer. His claim appears even stronger in the light of the striking list of references to constantly prac-tised and urgent prayer by the apostles and others, that occur in various parts of his epistles.[3] It has been repeatedly drawn to our attention in the prayer passages that the apostle's eschato-logical understanding had added a powerful new impetus for continual priestly intercession, an insatiable longing that

[1] The exact punctuation is debated. Perhaps the text should be divided after πάντοτε (so Schubert, p. 54, against most commentators), and again before ἀδιαλείπτως (so Bornemann, von Dobschütz, Dibelius, et al.), thus reading, 'We give thanks to God always when (i.e., whenever) we mention you all in our prayers, without ceasing remembering before God. . .your work of faith, etc.' See Harder, pp. 15f. The phrase ἔμπροσθεν τοῦ θεοῦ. . . might be taken with μνημονεύοντες, rather than with one or all of the triad of graces (Wohlenberg, Schmiedel, Amiot, RSV, etc.). Perhaps the exact meaning is left vague: both Thessalonians in their actions, and the apostle in his prayers, stand ἔμπροσθεν τοῦ θεοῦ; cf. von Dobschütz, Thessalonicher-Briefe, p. 65, Rigaux, Thessaloniciens, p. 367.
In any case the statement is being made that the apostles pray 'without ceasing' (ἀδιαλείπτως), in thanksgiving and in intercessory supplication. The claim is made even more directly in other places, as in I Thess. 2: 13, 'we earnestly thank God without ceasing for this,' and 3: 10, 'praying earnestly night and day'; and see below, p. 185.

[2] Schubert, p. 52. Cf. pap. Giessen, no. 85, for a typical example.

[3] References in the Pauline epistles to 'unceasing' or constantly practised prayer (cf. Harder, pp. 8–19):
In the opening thanksgivings: Rom. 1: 9, I Cor. 1: 4, Phil. 1: 3f., I Thess. 1: 2, 3: 10, Philem. 4. [Cf. Eph. 1: 15, Col. 1: 3, 9, II Thess. 1: 3, 11.]
Other references (requests and exhortations): Rom. 12: 12, Phil. 4: 6, I Thess. 5: 17. Cf. I Cor. 7: 5. [Cf. Eph. 6: 18–20, Col. 4: 2–4, 12.]
References to the urgent character of the prayers: Rom. 9: 3, 10: 1, 15: 30–3 (συναγωνίσασθαι), II Cor. 9: 14 (ἐπιποθούντων), I Thess. 3: 10 (ὑπερεκπερισσοῦ). [Cf. Col. 1: 29 – 2: 2, 5.] See also the references to 'watchings' (ἐν ἀγρυπνίαις), II Cor. 6: 5, 11: 27 [cf. Eph. 6: 18, Lk. 21: 36]; and to groanings or sighs (στενάζειν, στεναγμοί) as we wait for full redemp-tion: Rom. 8: 23, 26, II Cor. 5: 2.

the gifts of the Spirit might be poured out fully on all believers.

Yet how literally need his claims be taken when he speaks of unceasing, constant prayer, practised 'night and day' (I Thess. 3: 10)? The contemporary Jewish and Christian practice of regular prayers three times a day[1] suggests that he implied regularly practised prayer. As Origen pointed out, the apostle who gave instructions to the readers to work with their hands as he himself had done night and day (cf. 4: 11 with 2: 9), could hardly have intended them to be consciously praying at every moment (4: 17), nor that his own thoughts were uninterruptedly on the readers in prayer.[2] Rather he seems to have believed that their whole life should be lived as if standing prayerfully 'before God,' but be punctuated by frequent acts of consciously turning back to Him. Indeed, the very structure of the letter illustrates this alternation between unconscious and conscious prayer, by the way in which the prayers are interspersed throughout the epistle (1: 1b–3, 2: 13, 3: 9–13, 5: 23f., 28). So an undercurrent of thanksgiving and supplication imparts direction and tone to the whole letter.[3]

Furthermore, the prominent position of this prayer-report at the head of the letter, assuring the readers of the writer's constant prayers, would tend to suggest that they in turn reciprocate by offering thanksgiving and supplication for the apostle and for one another. Thus the way is prepared for Paul's later injunctions that they pray constantly (5: 16–18), and pray also for him (5: 25). The opening assurances of prayer together

[1] See above, p. 24; cf. Harder's examination of the evidence in Berachoth, Didache, etc. (pp. 8–19); also Strack–Billerbeck, II, 237f.; Orphal, *Das Paulusgebet*, p. 13; Hamman, pp. 250ff.; Jeremias, *The Prayers of Jesus*, pp. 67–72, 79; von der Goltz took the phrase 'night and day' to refer to the Jewish custom of saying prayers at morning and night; but Paul must have meant a higher level of continuous prayer; so von Dobschütz, *Thessalonicher-Briefe*, p. 146. Cf. II Macc. 13: 10–12, 'Judas. . .ordered the people to call upon the Lord day and night, now if ever to help. . .When they had all joined in the same petition and had besought the merciful Lord with weeping and fasting and lying prostrate for three days without ceasing. . . .'

[2] Origenes, *de Oratione Liber*, ed. Guilielmo Reading (London, 1728), XXXI, 2.

[3] Cf. Findlay, *Thessalonians*, p. 119. See above, p. 7f. For a list of the intercessory prayer passages interspersed throughout the other epistles, see Appendix II.

with these later injunctions make a powerful appeal to the readers to complete the network of intercessions.[1]

Whether such a brief prayer-report would have been consciously intended for instruction in the content and method of praying is difficult to say. Yet in any case it would serve as an example for the readers. The prayer-report and the wish-prayers together would instruct them as to the priorities in their own thanksgiving, petition, and intercession.[2] In addition, the compact prayer-summary of the apostle's desires for the Thessalonian church clearly anticipates the paraenetic thrust of the whole letter, and itself serves to exhort the readers to further endeavor. It is given detailed application by the exhortations in the second half of the letter, just as these in turn will be underlined by the wish-prayer that follows them.[3] No definite clue is given as to whether the prayer-report constitutes not only an assurance of his constant prayers, but also the actual offering of a prayer to God. But a positive answer will be suggested by the question-form of the second prayer-report in the epistle (3: 9f.).[4]

Short and compact as is the first prayer-report in the Thessalonian epistle, and conventional in its form, it nevertheless opens a window upon a background of intense, purposeful, and constant intercessory prayers undergirding the more public activities of the apostle.

I THESSALONIANS 3: 10

We move on to the intercessory significance of the second prayer-report at the end of the thanksgiving section:

(For what thanksgiving can we render to God for you, for all the joy which we feel for your sake before our God,)[5] *praying earnestly night and day that we may see you face to face and supply what is lacking in your faith?* (I Thess. 3: 10)

---

[1] Cf. Bar. 1: 5, where the writers are described as weeping, fasting, and praying before the Lord, on behalf of the readers at Jerusalem. In v. 13 comes the request for the prayers of the readers. See also Syr. Bar. 86: 3, where reciprocal remembrance is also enjoined, 'And bear me in mind by means of this epistle, as I also bear you in mind in it, and always.' See also below, pp. 259ff.   [2] See above, p. 69.   [3] See above, *ibid.*   [4] See below, p. 186.   [5] Context added in parentheses.

The report must be seen as part of a larger prayer unit
(3: 9–13) that includes an intercessory wish-prayer that we
have already studied.[1] Within this larger unit is a characteristic
progression from the victories of the past through the anxieties
of the present to the hopes for a speedy future culmination.[2]
In this way, as we observed before, an adequate and well-
rounded coda is formed for the first half of the letter, and a
transition into the paraenetic second half. The earlier prayer-
report (1: 2f.) is answered by this longer passage which summarizes once again the apostle's thanksgivings, his joyful feelings, his pastoral concerns, and his constant petitions.

The prayer-report itself (v. 10) takes up what had been postponed from the earlier one – it indicates more precisely the
immediate occasion of the letter,[3] his frustrated longing to visit
the Thessalonians and help them in their time of crisis. While
its participial syntax ties it with the preceding thanksgiving[4]
yet it may be contrasted with it, being linked in content with
the following wish-prayer that repeats and extends it.

Once again it is the warmth of the apostle's thanksgiving
'for joy' that supplies a vivid background against which the
intercessory prayer may be understood in its true urgency. In
the preceding verses there has been a crescendo of jubilation at
the good news brought by Timothy: the news of their faith
and loyal affection has brought him comfort (vv. 6f.), a renewal
of life (v. 8), and an outburst of indescribable joy and thankfulness to God (v. 9). Over and again he has stressed his profound
interest in their particular welfare – the pronoun 'you' has
been repeated ten times with growing emphasis in these verses
(6–10),[5] and echoes the earlier sentence, 'For you are our
glory and joy' (2: 20). So it is against this background of
celebration for joy (v. 9) that the earnestness of the intercessory
phrases (v. 10) must be read.

[1] Above, pp. 52f.
[2] The eschatological climax is omitted from the prayer-report and given
at the end of the wish-prayer (v. 13).   [3] See above, p. 177.
[4] See above, pp. 186f. The participle 'praying' should probably be read
in a temporal sense: 'What thanks can we return to God...*while we pray*
most earnestly night and day...?' See, *inter al.*, C. J. Ellicott, *A Critical and
Grammatical Commentary on St. Paul's Epistles to the Thessalonians* (Andover,
1864), *ad loc.*, Dibelius, *An die Thessalonicher*, *ad loc.*, and Schubert, pp. 54f.
[5] See also above, p. 177, n. 5.

The apostle's desperate longing 'to see them face to face' and 'to supply what was lacking,'[1] was rooted, as we saw earlier, not only in his personal affection for them, but in his intense anxiety about conditions at Thessalonica.[2] The deficiencies[3] in their faith would include those difficulties and problems suggested by his detailed exhortations in the second half of the letter; in the wish-prayer itself they would be focused as a need to be fortified by an increase in love. That he speaks of deficiencies of their *faith*, but then in the wish-prayer asks for an increase in their *love* (3: 12), may be explained in that the word faith refers to the continuing life of the believer.[4] Here, as in the first prayer-report, Paul prays that their total Christian life of trust in God may function through an increasing practice of love to men, and prepare them in hope for the parousia (3: 13).

Taken with its accompanying wish-prayer, the second intercessory prayer-report continues the shape of the first, while in itself it points up the immediate occasion of the letter. Furthermore, it underlines in several ways the thrust of the preceding report. For example, the earlier assurances of constant prayers are confirmed in new words, 'praying earnestly night and day.' Usually the phrase νυκτὸς καὶ ἡμέρας is taken to qualify the following word δεόμενοι, rather than the preceding words of rendering thanks.[5] Thus it would make the strongest claim to intense and constant supplications.[6] The urgency is further stressed by the powerful word ὑπερεκπερισσοῦ,[7] which denotes

---

[1] The close syntactical connection of the verbs ἰδεῖν and καταρτίσαι after εἰς τό suggests that the visit and its pastoral purpose were inseparable in Paul's thought.

[2] For details, see above, pp. 47ff.

[3] ὑστερήματα, used frequently by Paul, is found in the NT with the general meaning 'that which is missing'; the context would suggest that meaning here, where Paul is seeking to encourage rather than to chide. Frame, pp. 134f.; Findlay, p. 87; von Dobschütz, *Thessalonicher-Briefe*, p. 147.

[4] See above, pp. 178f.

[5] Schubert, pp. 23, 57.

[6] Once again we should note the conventional side of this assurance, suggested by the parallel in *BGU*, I, 246, 12f.: 'I intercede night and day to God on your behalf.' Harder, p. 16, n. 6. But see above, pp. 181f.

[7] One of the few descriptive phrases which Paul uses about his intercessory prayer practice; we may link it with his word in Rom. 15: 30, συναγωνίσασθαι (see below, pp. 267ff.).

an extreme intensity of praying on Paul's part. So once more Paul prepares for his request at the close of the letter, that they in turn should join in intercession for him.

Again, the paraenetic thrust of the earlier prayer-report is reinforced: the apostle now refers to what is lacking in that faith which earlier he had commended in his prayers, and so prepares for the exhortations of the second half of the letter.

Next, the question-form in which the thanksgiving is cast indicates that we do have here, and so also in the earlier prayer-report, an actual offering of prayer to God. This is suggested by the close parallel with Psalm 116: 12, 'What shall I render to the Lord for all his bounty shown to me?' – a liturgical utterance which may well have been in the background of Paul's rhetorical question.[1] Likewise, intercessory prayers in the Old Testament are sometimes phrased as questions to God, e.g., Num. 16: 22, 'O God, the God of the spirits of all flesh, shall one man sin, and wilt thou be angry with all the congregation?'[2] So the intercessory portion of our prayer-report (v. 10), being closely linked with the thanksgiving prayer question (v. 9) and leading into the subsequent offering of prayer in the wish-prayer (vv. 11–13), itself involves an actual supplication to God on behalf of the readers.

In sum, the two prayer-reports in the Thessalonian thanksgiving section have been seen to strengthen the sense of vital intercessory significance revealed in our earlier study of the wish-prayers in this letter; in spite of their conventional form they have further illuminated the mediatorial aspects of Paul's apostleship.

ROMANS 1: 9f.

The third intercessory prayer-report occurs in the thanksgiving period of the epistle to the Romans.

(First, I thank my God through Jesus Christ for all of you, because your faith is proclaimed in all the world.)[3] *For God is my witness, whom I serve with my spirit in the gospel of his Son, that without ceasing I mention*

---

[1] Cf. Pss. 13: 1f., 35: 17, 42: 2, 9, 43: 2; Rev. 6: 10.
[2] Cf. II Sam. 24: 17 and Isa. 6: 11; see Hesse, *Die Fürbitte*, p. 30. Also the intercessory prayer in question-form, in Syr. Bar. 81: 1f. (see above, p. 71, n. 5).
[3] Context included for convenience.

you always in my prayers, asking that somehow by God's will I may now at last succeed in coming to you. (For I long to see you....) (Rom. 1: 8–11a)

We may recall that in writing this letter Paul was concerned about his future missionary plans, about the unity of the congregations at Rome, and about the need to introduce himself and his gospel to those who did not yet know him, in order to gain their confidence and support.[1]

The thanksgiving period (vv. 8–17)[2] in which our intercessory report occurs, follows a typical progression: the *eucharisto* statement (v. 8), assurances of the writer's constant prayers for the readers (v. 9) that center round his petition for a safe journey to visit them (v. 10), an anticipation of mutual encouragement (vv. 11–15), and a climax that anticipates the main epistolary theme and leads into the body of the letter (vv. 16–17).[3] The whole passage forms a proemium designed to establish immediate personal rapport with all the Roman readers.[4]

Important for our evaluation of the prayer-report is the close parallelism between the thanksgiving and the corresponding passage in chapter fifteen (cf. 1: 7–17 with 15: 13–33).[5] These two units belong together, enclosing the body of the letter and justifying it.[6] Each begins with an intercessory blessing or wish-prayer for the readers (1: 7b and 15: 13), continues with a

---

[1] Above, pp. 72ff.

[2] According to Schubert, pp. 31ff., the thanksgiving must be taken as extending to v. 17, which substitutes for an eschatological climax. Sanders, 'Transition from Opening Thanksgiving,' however, suggests that it may end at v. 12, because of the new beginning (opening formula) at v. 13 (p. 360).

[3] Schubert suggests that the unusual syntactical breaks in the sentence show Paul struggling to be tactful; thus he departs somewhat from the normal thanksgiving syntax (*ibid.*).

[4] O. Kuss, *Der Römerbrief*, 1 (Regensburg, 1957), 15; Michel, *Der Brief an die Römer*, p. 36. Funk finds here an example of Paul's apostolic parousia form; see 'The apostolic "*Parousia*,"' p. 253.

[5] See Cooper, 'Leitourgos Christou Iesou...,' p. 266, and the commentators there cited.

[6] See above, p. 73, n. 1. We may compare a similar parallelism in Phil. between the opening thanksgiving (1: 3–11) and the closing thank-you passage (4: 10–20), which enclose the body of that letter and justify it. See above, p. 102, n. 4.

thankful acknowledgement of their undoubted Christian graces (1: 8 and 15: 14), then broaches the more difficult matter of Paul's proposed apostolic ministry to them (1: 9ff. and 15: 15ff.). The first unit mentions a ministry of intercessory prayer, the second a ministry of writing and reminding ('I have written... by way of reminder');[1] in each case he bases his claim on his priestly commission to the Gentiles – a commission that will include the readers in its scope (1: 5f., 13b–15 and 15: 16). The apostle continues with his personal plan to visit them (1: 10 and 15: 24a), which has been prevented for many years (1: 13a and 15: 17–23); now he looks forward to preaching to them, encouraging and being encouraged by them (1: 11f., 15 and 15: 24b, 29, and 32). But the further details of his plans to go first to Jerusalem, and afterwards with their assistance to venture as far as Spain, are tactfully postponed until the second passage.[2] By the end of the letter he hopes to have overcome any opposition to his special gospel (1: 16f.), and to succeed in engaging their active interest (15: 24–33). The parallelism is so striking that it must reflect a deliberate composition; each unit reinforces the epistolary importance of, and illuminates, the other.

Proceeding now to some details of the thanksgiving and the prayer-report, we see that the initial statement of thanksgiving is extremely concise and apparently quite general: 'First, I thank my God through Jesus Christ for all of you, because your faith is proclaimed in all the world' (v. 8). It lacks the expansive affection of the Philippians one, and the joyous recounting of details of the one in I Thessalonians, but its implied praise serves as a suitable *captatio benevolentiae* in an uncertain situation. Although there is 'doubtless a natural exaggeration in these words,'[3] they do select precisely that strategic aspect of the Roman situation which must have been of most concern to the apostle.[4] The significance of a Christian community in the capital city could hardly be overstressed, and the news of their

---

[1] For letter-writing as an intercessory activity, cf. above, p. 71, n.5.

[2] In any case, the matter of the collection would belong in the closing part of the letter. See above, p. 96, n. 2.

[3] Barrett, *Romans*, p. 24.

[4] So Leenhardt, *Romans*, Lagrange, *Romains*, Althaus, *Römer*, Michel, *et al.*

successes and failures would travel in every direction among the scattered Christian communities, and wield considerable influence. As he contemplated his future missionary plans the apostle could not fail to recognize the special importance of favorable reports from Rome (cf. 15: 14). It is quite appropriate, then, that his thanksgiving should mention their wide reputation as the most immediate cause for his gratitude. He knew their potential for aiding or hindering his own projects in the years to come.[1]

Following upon this fitting affirmation of Paul's thankfulness, there is a preliminary statement of the immediate occasion for the letter, given in the intercessory prayer-report (vv. 9–10). He assures them of his constant prayers for the continuance of their welfare, but in particular he prays that at long last the way might be opened for him to come to them.

The prayer-report begins with a solemn calling on God to bear witness to his unceasing intercessions. Here as in the other prayer-reports, we must weigh the conventional nature of such an assurance, and the ambiguity of the language,[2] against the wider evidence for his constant practice of intercessory prayer. Yet why the extravagant emphasis of an oath? Does not the very vehemence remove credence from the claim?

In the first place, Paul had for some time been deeply involved in his own mind with the Roman church,[3] though until now there had been no occasion to demonstrate this openly. His long-standing personal ties with some of the believers there[4] had been gaining new importance with the maturing of his plans for the West. Yet he was painfully aware that his profession of intercessory concern for Rome might readily be twisted against him by sceptics or opponents in the church there, as had happened at Thessalonica, Corinth and Galatia.

[1] The address 'my God' (τῷ θεῷ μου) reflects Jewish prayer-style and thus suggests an actual offering of thankful prayer. Michel, p. 37. Cf. I Cor. 1: 4 (some Mss), Phil. 1: 3 (most Mss), and Philem. 4.

[2] An alternative translation would be: 'God is my witness...that whenever I mention you in my prayers, I always ask that somehow...I may now at last succeed in coming to you' (see Harder, p. 15).

[3] See above, pp. 73ff.

[4] The fact of his constant prayers for Rome may presuppose close acquaintance with some of the believers; Rengstorf, 'Paulus und die römische Christenheit,' p. 452. See above, p. 92.

So he calls God to witness to the genuineness of that prayerful interest.[1]

In addition, by referring in this oath to his service 'in the gospel of [God's] Son' he is appealing to a central commitment and legitimization of his apostleship that the whole letter will be designed to confirm.[2] He recalls the opening description of himself as 'a slave of Jesus Christ, called to be an apostle, set apart for the gospel of God,' and foreshadows the assertions that he is 'eager to preach the gospel' (v. 15), and 'not ashamed of the gospel' which the letter will expound (vv. 16ff., cf. 2: 16). At the close of the epistle he will return to this theme of his unremitting 'priestly service of the gospel of God' (15: 16), which he has 'fully preached' in pioneering fashion in the East (15: 18–21), and which he now proposes to carry as far as possible in the West.

Finally, his use in the oath of the cultic word λατρεύειν links his intercessory prayers with the priestly understanding of his apostolic commission[3] that will appear again at various points in the letter, and especially in chapter fifteen.[4] It is this representative function before God that particularly obliges him to minister to the Romans by prayer, by letter, and eventually by personal encounter. Indeed, Strathmann suggests that Paul was here thinking of his priestly service in the gospel in two senses, his outer missionary preaching and his inner intercessory prayer life (ἐν τῷ πνεύματί μου), of which the main subject was the gospel mission.[5] So he must call God to witness to the hidden

---

[1] He often called God to witness to personal assertions which might be questioned, e.g., I Thess. 2: 5, 10, Gal. 1: 20, II Cor. 1: 18, 23, 2: 17, 11: 31, 12: 19; cf. Rom. 9: 1, Phil. 1: 8.

[2] Cf. the oath by which Elijah legitimizes himself at the outset of his prophetic work (I Kings 17: 1). Later in this letter Paul compares himself directly with Elijah in his pleading with God against Israel (Rom. 11: 1–5). See above, pp. 14, 253f.

[3] See above, p. 157, n. 4.   [4] See above, p. 86, n. 1.

[5] 'Paulus dient, verehrt Gott, übt Gottesdienst, einmal tätig in der Ausrichtung der Botschaft, zugleich aber innerlich, in der Fürbitte für die Gemeinden und den Lauf des Evangeliums.' Strathmann, *TWNT*, IV, 65. So also Michel, p. 38. In similar vein, Deut. 11: 13, 'to serve him with all your heart' was interpreted by the Rabbis as meaning prayer: 'Dienst im Herzen = Gebetsdienst.' Strack–Billerbeck, III, 26.

Others, however, make λατρεύειν refer to the preaching of the gospel only: K. Weiss, 'Paulus – Priester der christl. Kultgemeinde,' Kuss, Barrett,

representative service of his prayers for them – for it was God alone who might know of that inner activity in his spirit.

We may conclude, then, that Paul's fervent emphasis on his constant prayers for the Roman church was doubtless intended to be taken factually. He was continually returning to them 'in spirit' as he considered not only the needs of his friends at Rome, but also the importance of Rome for his bold forward missionary thrust.[1] Thus he hopes that the readers, too, will join him in thanksgiving and supplication.[2]

The passage goes on (v. 10) to state more precisely that every time he remembers them in prayer he makes a special request for God to open a path that will take him to Rome.[3] Here, then, Paul partially unveils the purpose of the letter,[4] for which he had already prepared the way by claiming Rome as within the field of his apostleship (vv. 5f.). The very wording of the petition (εἴ πως ἤδη ποτὲ εὐοδωθήσομαι...πρὸς ὑμᾶς)[5] shows both the delicacy of the situation and the eager impatience of the apostle. He hesitates to take too much for granted at the beginning of the letter. So the mixture of boldness and restraint in the prayer-report presages the tone of a crucial but difficult letter,[6] while its conciseness suggests that he does not wish to say too much at this stage.[7]

Romans. On the other hand, Cooper suggests the reductionist view that Paul, like Anselm, regarded theology as being a form of prayer (p. 264).

'In my spirit' has been variously interpreted: as the inner life (Strathmann, Kuss, Althaus, *Römer*), the spiritual side of his nature (Barrett, *Romans*), the whole person (Michel), or the organ of service (Sanday and Headlam, Lagrange, *Romains, et al.*); see Kuss, p. 17.

[1] Cf. Leenhardt, p. 43, 'the idea of going to Rome has not ceased to ferment in his mind and has mastered him in his prayers which are the crucible in which his missionary projects come to birth.'

[2] Cf. above, p. 183, n. 1.

[3] With a pause after ποιοῦμαι: 'always in my prayers asking that somehow by God's will I may now at last succeed in coming to you.' So Kuss, Barrett, *Romans*, NEB. Regarding Paul's use of the conventional 'safe journey' petition, see above, p. 48, n. 2. Here again he fills the epistolary form with urgency.

[4] But postponing the full import.   [5] See above, p. 173, sec. *a*.

[6] Cf. 15: 15, 'But on some points I have written to you very boldly.' The general tone of the letter is apologetic, reflective, rather than polemical; contrast Galatians. Michel, p. 2.

[7] Contrast the much fuller prayer-report(s) in Phil. 1: 4, 9–11, and the somewhat fuller one in I Thess. 1: 2b–3.

The hint of impatience in the wording suggests the frustration of his plans because of previous missionary commitments (v. 13 and 15: 22),[1] although in any case, we may have to reckon here partly with the influence of Jewish prayer style.[2] Furthermore, there is a strong hint of the grave uncertainty about the outcome of the journey that will come to light at the end of the letter. For the apostle, all lies ἐν τῷ θελήματι θεοῦ. While this phrase was common in Jewish and pagan usage,[3] here it seemed to be more than the pious addition of a 'Deo volente.'[4] Paul would later confirm its true import by begging the prayerful aid of the Romans for his dangerous interim journey to Jerusalem – 'to strive together with me in your prayers to God...so that by God's will (διὰ θελήματος θεοῦ) I may come to you' (15: 30–2).[5]

Although the actual prayer-report ends here (v. 10), it will be useful to glance at the conclusion of the thanksgiving (vv. 11–17), where the apostle elaborates the major concerns of his intercessory prayers for the readers.[6] He goes on: 'For I long to see you,[7] that I may impart to you some spiritual gift to strengthen you' (v. 11, cf. 15: 29). Here again he shows some hesitation in advancing his apostolic claim. He had written boldly to the Thessalonians that his visit would supply their

[1] Cf. the similar impatience suggested in Galatians; see above, p. 124.

[2] E.g., Ber. 29b, 'the prayer before setting forth on a journey...May it be Thy will, O Lord my God, to lead me forth in peace, and direct my steps in peace...' Cf. Michel, p. 39.

[3] Michel, *ibid*. Cf. James, 4: 15.

[4] Sanday and Headlam, p. 21; Harder, p. 120.

[5] See below, pp. 263ff. Cf. I Cor. 4: 19, 16: 7, Acts 18: 21.

Surprisingly enough, there is no eschatological climax in this prayer-report (see above, p. 158) in spite of the emphasis on looking forward in hope that will follow in the letter, e.g., 5: 2–5, 8: 15–25, chap. 11; 12: 12, 15: 4, 7–16.

[6] In the two prayer-reports in I Thess., Paul both states the immediate occasion of the letter and characterizes his major pastoral concerns. Here he limits the report itself to the immediate occasion, while giving a broader explanation in the verses that follow.

[7] The use of the word ἰδεῖν (to see) instead of ἱστορεῖν (to visit for the purpose of coming to know someone – Bauer–Arndt–Gingrich) suggests that Paul is here thinking of those already known to him at Rome, and for whom particularly he intercedes. Rengstorf, 'Paulus und die römische Christenheit,' p. 453.

deficiencies (I Thess. 3: 10), and similarly to the Corinthians (II Cor. 1: 15ff., 13: 2, etc.), yet he is careful here not to suggest any such level of apostolic authority. He expresses only a general hope that he may strengthen them with some further spiritual gift. Even this offer seems too bold for a start, and he immediately makes a modification,[1] at any rate for the duration of the next sentence (!) (v. 12): 'that is, that we may be mutually encouraged....' (συμπαρακλη-θῆναι).[2]

Then he begins again (v. 13) with an emphatic explanation that his delay in coming to them had not been of his own choosing, but because of prior duties (cf. 15: 18–22). The introductory phrase, οὐ θέλω δὲ ὑμᾶς ἀγνοεῖν ἀδελφοί, shows that the explanation is of great importance to him.[3] Following as it does upon the oath (v. 9), it may further reveal his suspicion that his opponents are already questioning the genuineness of his interest and the reality of his courage.[4] Yet whatever his detractors may say, he is indeed eager to visit Rome (v. 15) and not ashamed of the gospel (v. 16). For he has an apostolic obligation (ὀφειλέτης εἰμί) to the Gentile world in its totality (vv. 14–15, cf. v. 5). Not only does he feel obligated to preach at Rome and reap some harvest there,[5] but perhaps he is already hinting at plans to move beyond the boundaries of Romans and Greeks to the barbarians on the fringes of the empire, even as far as Spain (v. 14, cf. 15: 24, 28).[6]

All this serves to confirm and elaborate the mood and con-

---

[1] τοῦτο δέ ἐστιν is usually taken thus, as implying a correction; but perhaps it meant more an addition. Leenhardt, p. 44.

[2] Perhaps an example of a 'formula of mutual encouragement,' see above, p. 163, n. 3. Regarding the theme of *paraklesis* that runs through the epistle, see above, p. 81.

[3] Cf. Rom. 11: 25, I Cor. 10: 1, II Cor. 1: 8, I Thess. 4: 13.

[4] Cf. his similar defense in I Thess. 2: 17f., I Cor. 5: 3, II Cor. 1: 17, etc.

[5] Funk suggests that 'Paul is eager to preach the gospel in Rome, but that he can do so only when he arrives in person...in contrast with the written word.' 'Saying and Seeing: Phenomenology of Language and the New Testament,' p. 211.

[6] H. Windisch, 'βάρβαρος,' *TWNT*, I, 549f. Yet possibly the reference does not go beyond the cosmopolitan character of the city of Rome; Michel, *et al.*

tents of the preceding intercessory prayer-report, and to show how it has indicated the immediate occasion and the tone of the letter, and anticipated its broader concerns. The prayer passage has included all the readers known and unknown within the circle of intercessory thanksgiving and supplication. The note of priestly urgency and impatience has prepared the way for exhortations and injunctions that will follow in the letter, and for his subsequent appeal that they join him in the intercessory circle and uphold him in the dangers that loom ahead. The unusual language, εἴ πως ἤδη ποτὲ εὐοδωθήσομαι, may suggest not only tactful hesitance, but a prayer in question-form: 'When shall I be able to come?' This would indicate once again the use of a prayer-report for the actual offering up of prayer by the apostle as he writes.[1]

THE DIVIDED PRAYER-REPORT IN PHILIPPIANS –
I : 4 AND I : 9–II

In continuing our study of the prayer-reports in the thanksgiving periods, we turn next to one at the beginning of an epistle that reflects all the warmth of the apostle toward a small church which over the years had remained uniquely close to him. We may begin by examining the circumstances and content of the letter before seeing how far these are reflected in the prayer itself.

The epistle to the Philippians differs considerably from those we have so far discussed in detail. Paul is neither facing a crisis of disaffection against himself, nor composing a weighty treatise of introduction and self-explanation. Instead, 'in an intimate, personal, and informal manner Paul puts down thoughts about his own and the Philippians' concerns of the moment, in the warm light of their common experience and faith.'[2] Furthermore, he is writing under the shadow of probable execution, and the letter may be seen partly as 'a

---

[1] Cf. above, p. 186. Harder draws attention to this question form which he sees as a hesitant 'prayer-sigh,' a *Gebetseufzer*, or *Frageseufzer* (p. 32). We note also that the report follows a thanksgiving which also, by its style, suggests actual prayer; see above, p. 189, n. 1.

[2] An unpublished characterization by Paul Schubert. In many ways Phil. is closest in mood and style to I Thess.

classic utterance of the mind of the martyr,'[1] written to prepare his friends to continue their conflict, if necessary without him (2: 12–18).

But once again the question must be considered as to whether we have a single letter or an editorial compilation[2] within which to place the prayer passages.[3] The three segments into which the letter is usually divided by proponents of its composite nature are, with some variations, as follows:[4]

Letter A, 4: 10–20. This short letter or fragment of thanks would have been written first, soon after the arrival of Epaphroditus. It acknowledged the gift from Philippi, and made no reference to any troubles there. It would include in its short closing section only one (possible) intercessory prayer passage (4: 19), linked with a doxology and an Amen (4: 20).[5]

[1] F. W. Beare, *The Epistle to the Philippians*, HNTC (New York, 1959), p. 26. In suggesting this we do not imply the specific understanding of martyrdom developed in the second century A.D. See R. Jewett, 'The Epistolary Thanksgiving and the Integrity of Philippians,' *Nov. Test*, 12 (1970), 49f.

[2] Various interruptions in the continuity cast doubt on the integrity of the letter, especially the sudden break and alteration of tone after 3: 1. The comparative tolerance in 1: 15–18 gives way to the sharp attacks in 3: 2f., 18f. Another break occurs after 4: 9. These anomalies, together with such questions as the apparently inexplicable delay in Paul's acknowledgement of the gift brought by Epaphroditus, have prompted a number of different theories of the composite nature of the letter.

For literature and survey of the debate, see Rigaux, *Saint Paul et ses lettres*, p. 157; Feine–Behm–Kümmel, *Introduction*, pp. 226, 235f.; more recently, T. E. Pollard, 'The Integrity of Philippians,' *NTS*, 13 (1966–7), 57–66; Jewett, 'Epistolary Thanksgiving,' pp. 40–53.

[3] For list of intercessory prayer passages in Phil., see Appendix II.

[4] E.g., by Beare, *Philippians*, pp. 24ff., 100–2; W. Schmithals, 'Die Irrlehrer des Philipperbriefes,' *ZThK*, 54 (1957), 297–341; *idem*, 'Zur Abfassung und ältesten Sammlung des paulinischen Hauptbriefe,' *ZNW*, 51 (1960), 225–45; B. D. Rahtjen, 'The Three Letters of Paul to the Philippians,' *NTS*, 6 (1959–60), 167–73; see also G. Bornkamm, 'Der Phil. als paulinische Briefsammlung,' pp. 192–202. It would take us too far afield to consider more complex reconstructions that have been proposed, e.g., by J. Müller-Bardoff, 'Zur Frage der literarischen Einheit des Philipperbriefes,' *Wissenschaftl. Zeitschrift*, Jena, 7 (1957–8), 591ff.

[5] See above, pp. 101ff. Schmithals 'Die Irrlehrer,' would add also to A the final greeting and grace blessing (4: 21–3).

Letter B, 1: 1 – 3: 1 with 4: 4–7 and 21–3. This letter, written perhaps soon after the recovery of Epaphroditus from severe illness, would be a more substantial pastoral type of letter, encouraging them, acknowledging in more general terms their 'partnership in the gospel.' Gently but firmly they were exhorted to resolve their discords, to move on towards maturity in preparation for the day of Christ, and to resist their opponents. It would include all except one (4: 19) of the intercessory prayer passages from our present letter.[1]

Letter C, 3: 2 – 4: 1 (or 4: 3). This fragment, written after the receipt of further news from Philippi, would be a sharp warning against new dangers to the church.[2] In this form it would include no intercessory prayer passages.[3] Yet in view of Paul's practice in other letters, of including such a warning (in line with epistolary precedents), it is doubtful whether this need be taken as a separate fragment.[4]

The outcome for us is to note that if we should be dealing with a composite document, letter B would refer (directly or indirectly) to nearly all the major concerns[5] of our present letter, and also probably include the bulk of the intercessory prayer passages. Hence our estimate of the intercessory sig-

---

[1] For a survey of these prayer passages, see below, pp. 202f. Schmithals' version of B (1: 1 – 3: 1, with 4: 4–7) would omit also the final greetings and grace blessing (4: 21–3). Rahtjen's reconstruction of B (1: 1 – 2: 30; 4: 21–3 – omitting 4: 2–9) would omit the prayer exhortation (4: 6) and the two (doubtful) peace blessings (4: 7, 9).

[2] Cf. above, p. 94, for a similar situation in the writing of Romans (16: 17–20).

[3] But Schmithals' version of C (3: 2 – 4: 3 and 8f.) would attach at the end the (doubtful) peace blessing (4: 9b). Rahtjen's version (3: 1 – 4: 9) would add the prayer exhortation (4: 6) and the two (doubtful) peace blessings (4: 7, 9).

[4] See above, p. 67, n. 3. For a detailed discussion of the passage, see H. Koester, 'The Purpose of the Polemic of a Pauline Fragment (Philippians III),' *NTS*, 8 (1961–2), 317–32; see also A. F. J. Klijn, 'Paul's opponents in Philippians iii,' *Nov. Test.* 7 (1965), 278–84.

[5] These are outlined below, pp. 197ff. An exception might be the polemic against 'the dogs,' 'those who mutilate the flesh' (3: 2f. in letter C); yet even this is probably referred to in the reconstructed letter B at 1: 28. Also the acknowledgement of the gift (letter A) has oblique mention in letter B at 1: 5ff., which refers tactfully to the spirit of partnership behind the gift.

nificance of most of the prayer passages would not be greatly affected whether we placed them in the context of the present letter, or of letter B.[1]

But none of the difficulties raised against accepting the epistle as a unity appear to be insurmountable, nor does the evidence seem sufficient to bear the burden of proof for dividing the letter.[2] We may furthermore take note of various inter-related themes and interests that link the different sections of the epistle,[3] and, as we shall see, are reflected in the opening thanksgiving and prayer-report, and in the other prayer passages.

To begin with, the general tone of the letter emphasizes that he was on long-standing and familiar terms with the church at Philippi.[4] Hence he could assume their genuine interest in the details of his imprisonment and the progress of his trial. He describes with joy how his imprisonment had resulted in spreading the gospel even in the capital city of Rome (1: 7, 12–18).[5] And he shares with them his mixed hopes and appre-

---

[1] Or we might consider letter A (4: 10–20) as a separate document, treating B and C as a unit in which to place most of the prayer passages. This 'B and C' document would for our purpose very closely resemble the letter as a whole, and our main conclusions would not be much affected thereby.

[2] See e.g., Jewett, 'Epistolary Thanksgiving,' pp. 40–9. See also above, pp. 104–6.

[3] See Pollard; earlier, W. Michaelis, 'Teilungshypothesen bei Paulus-briefen,' *TZ*, 14 (1958), 321–6, B. S. Mackay, 'Further Thoughts on Philippians,' *NTS*, 7 (1960–1), 161–70. Common language, vocabulary, tone, and themes all point to one letter. Jewett ('Epistolary Thanksgiving,' pp. 49–53) has argued for the position taken independently in this work, that the thanksgiving anticipates the main themes of the total Philippian letter. See below, pp. 203–14.

[4] E.g., 1: 5, 7f., 19, 25, 30; 2: 12, 17f., 24, 25b, 28–30; 4: 1, 3, 10, 14–18.

[5] A judgment must be made on two undecided questions, the place and the date of the letter. (For the principal literature, see Feine–Behm–Kümmel, p. 226.) Although there can be no certainty among Ephesus, Caesarea, and Rome, it seems most probable that he wrote from Rome toward the end of his life (*c.* A.D. 60–3). Without entering into the debate we must assume this to be the case. The objections to the Roman venue are not insurmountable, and the situation described in the letter best suits the church at Rome, the trial in that city, and the conditions of his imprisonment there. He takes for granted, now, the theological truths for which earlier he had argued so thoroughly.

hensions about the impending trial verdict (1: 19–26, 2: 12, 17f., 23) and his victorious reconciliation to whatever may come, 'through him that strengthens me' (4: 11–13, 2: 16–18). He hopes that the verdict will go in his favor and looks forward to visiting his old friends before too long (1: 26, 2: 24). In the meantime he relies on their intercessory prayers in his behalf (1: 19f.).

Throughout most of the letter he refers gratefully to their never-failing and thoughtful support of him in their 'partnership in the gospel,' in repeated tangible gifts and now in the sending of Epaphroditus.[1] He refers appreciatively to their latest gift, indirectly in the opening thanksgiving (1: 5 and perhaps 11), but postponing specific mention of it until the middle and end of the letter (2: 25b, 30b, 4: 14–18). Thus the thanking for their gift is hardly a primary occasion for the letter, and it would seem that he had already sent an acknowledgement at an earlier time.[2] Rather, he has in mind more general encouragement of the Philippians, by expressing his warm sense of all they were doing for the gospel and for himself.[3] He wishes also to reassure them of his own deep and unabating commitment to them whether in life or death (1: 3, 7f., 24–6, 2: 17, 19, 24), and speaks of his responsibility for them at the judgment day of Christ (2: 16).[4]

On the other hand he has cause to be anxious about his friends. In the first place, personal discords have arisen between members of the church in spite of their loyalty. Again and again he returns to this problem and tries to counter it in different ways. He entreats them to live in love, affection and sympathy (2: 1f.), in lowliness and mutual forbearance (2: 2–14, 4: 2, 5). He points to the example of Christ Jesus (the Lord who is at hand), 'who, though he was in the form of God,...emptied himself, taking the form of a servant,...obedient unto death' (2: 5–11). Let his friends adopt that divine pattern (2: 5).

---

[1] Phil. 1: 5–7, 19, 30; 2: 1, 18, 25b, 30; 4: 3, 10, 14–18. For an account of their close and continuous relationship (their gifts, leadership in the collection, and his return visits to them), see Beare, *Philippians*, pp. 13f.

[2] Michael, *Philippians*, pp. 209–12.

[3] Cf. his similar warm encouragement of his friends at Thessalonica; above, p. 47.

[4] See below, pp. 210f.

He appeals also to his own human example, reminding them of their partnership in his imprisonment and possible martyrdom for the gospel (1: 7). Now let them imitate him (2: 12, 3: 17, 4: 9a), and follow him in the self-emptying involved in his own suffering for Christ (1: 29f.).[1] Repeatedly he returns to describe his own reconciliation in Christ to humbling situations of loss (1: 18, 20f., 2: 17f., 4: 11–13). The thought of suffering the loss of all things gladly for Christ's sake inspires one of his most moving passages (3: 3–11), as he consciously parallels his own despoilment with that of his Master described in the previous chapter:[2] 'For his sake I have suffered the loss of all things, and count them as refuse, in order that I may gain Christ and be found in him. . . .' (3: 8). 'Paul has set before them the example of Jesus in his humility and obedience, and his own example of humility and obedience; now he urges the Philippians to imitate these examples, his and Christ's.'[3]

Closely allied with his experience of humble reconciliation, is the recurrent note of joyousness that forms so remarkable a feature in a letter emanating from prison and under the shadow of martyrdom.[4] In learning contentment under the will of God, he himself has been able to discover joy in all circumstances (1: 4, 18f., 2: 2, 17, 19; 4: 1, 10).[5] And he repeatedly urges them to be glad and rejoice with him (2: 18, 3: 1, 4: 4;[6] cf. 1: 25, 2: 29).

The notable emphasis on joy in suffering has been thought by some to imply a severe crisis of persecution at Philippi.[7] Yet it is hard to think that if this were so, Paul's allusions to their

[1] For Paul's frequent exhortations to his churches to imitate him, see above, p. 58, n. 3.

[2] For a perceptive analysis of the parallels between the 'despoliation' of Paul in chap. 3 with that of Christ in chap. 2, see Pollard, pp. 58ff. A thematic link is thus constituted between 'Letter C' and 'Letter B'; see above, p. 196.

[3] Pollard, p. 63.

[4] Lohmeyer, *Die Briefe an die Philipper, an die Kolosser und an Philemon*, p. 50.

[5] See above, pp. 168f., on giving thanks in all circumstances.

[6] It is just possible, however, that χαίρετε in 3: 1 and 4: 4 means farewell: Bauer–Arndt–Gingrich, p. 882; Rahtjen, p. 171, n. 3. But see the rebuttal in Mackay, p. 167.

[7] Lohmeyer understands the whole epistle as essentially that of a martyr speaking to martyrs, and its fundamental unity in the relation between the martyrdom of Paul and that of his readers. *Philipper, Kolosser, Philemon*, pp. 3–7, 26f., 29, 36, etc.

conflict would have occupied so small a place in the letter in comparison with his own.[1] But their partnership in the gospel does of necessity involve shared suffering (1: 29f.), the predestined woes of the messianic age before the consummation.[2] So in the question of their discords, linked with their need to be reconciled to suffering, we have a central occasion for the epistle.

There are, however, other problems about which Paul wishes to address his friends.[3] He is concerned that the Philippians are in danger of succumbing to a form of perfectionism by claiming that they have already received all the blessings of the new age. So he reminds them that it is only at the parousia that they will be made perfect (1: 6; cf. 1: 9f., 2: 16, 3: 20f.), and that he too has not yet attained to perfection (3: 13–15).[4] He bids them 'work out [their] own salvation with fear and trembling' (2: 12f.), and looks for their 'progress and joy in the faith' (1: 25). Towards the end of the letter he urges his readers to lift their thoughts to all that is excellent and worthy of praise (4: 8f., cf. 1: 9f.), manifesting that extravagant level of expectation that we have noted before (e.g., 4: 4–7, 13, 19),[5] and concluding with a doxology of praise to God (4: 20).

A closely related anxiety of the apostle appears at first sight to stand apart from the rest of the letter (3: 2–21). The harsh polemic against apparent legalists, 'those who mutilate the flesh' (3: 2f.), and against apparent libertines whose 'god is the belly' (3: 19),[6] has seemed to many to indicate a letter written

[1] Contrast the recurrent indications in I Thessalonians of Paul's deep concern at the persecution crisis among his readers (I Thess. 1: 6, 2: 14b, 3: 3–5), and the repeated mention of his desperate anxiety to be with them. See above, pp. 47f.

[2] See above, pp. 49f.; also Jewett, 'Epistolary Thanksgiving,' pp. 50f.

[3] Contrast the single-minded intensity of the Galatian epistle; see above, pp. 123f.

[4] Köster (p. 329) renders this sentence as follows: 'If we call ourselves perfect (as you do) let us take this attitude, i.e., that we have not yet arrived, but are still on our way.' Cf. Moltmann's emphasis: 'Hence [the Pauline call to new obedience] ought not to be rendered merely by saying: "Become what you are!", but emphatically also by saying: "Become what you will be!"' (*Theology of Hope*, p. 162.)

[5] See above, pp. 105f.

[6] No consensus has been reached as to who these opponents were, whether libertine 'Gnostic pneumatics' who claimed to be perfected

for another occasion.[1] However, as we have already suggested, this portion of the letter may represent the kind of sharp warning characteristic of Paul's letter style, perhaps accentuated by further news from Philippi that reached him during the writing of the letter. Furthermore, there are associations with other parts of the letter that lessen its apparent incompatibility.

Köster has argued that Paul is here attacking a complex form of religious perfectionism 'based on the law and a "realized" eschatological experience of the Spirit.'[2] If, however, there were two sets of opponents, the first group, the Jews or Judaizers of 3: 2, would claim to offer a way of legalistic perfection that Paul goes on to attack (3: 3–16). Their perfection, he suggests, was but 'in the flesh,' whereas true perfection is 'in spirit' (3: 3), is a goal to be striven for (3: 11–16), and must await the coming of Christ (3: 20f.).[3] The second group, the Gnostic libertines 'who glory in their shame, with minds set on earthly things' (3: 18f.), would also miss the higher reach of those whose 'commonwealth is in heaven,' who 'await a Savior,' and whose lowly bodies will be changed 'to be like his glorious body' (3: 20f.). In any case it is the anti-perfectionist thrust of the whole letter that receives its sharpest statement in this section, both negatively through his attack on the perfectionist opponents (3: 2, 18f.) and positively in the rest of the section where he describes his own reaching forward to what lies ahead (vv. 3–17, 20f.). A foreshadowing of this sharp attack may be seen in his earlier word of encouragement to his friends to stand firm against their opponents. 'This is a clear omen to them of their destruction, but of your salvation' (1: 27f.).[4]

So we have here a single, joyous, intimate, comparatively loosly knit letter, composed at a time of extreme anxiety, to

(Schmithals), or Jewish Christian Gnostics preaching a doctrine of perfection based on the Jewish law (Köster), or Jewish proselytizers (Beare; A. F. J. Klijn). Jewett argues for two different sets of opponents: Judaizing missionaries (3: 2ff.) and Gnostic libertines (3: 18ff.); 'Epistolary Thanksgiving,' pp. 48f.   [1] See above, p. 195, n. 2.
[2] Köster, p. 331.   [3] Klijn, p. 284.
[4] See Mackay, p. 163. Schmithals points out this foreshadowing, but nevertheless proposes two separate letters in which the second illuminates the meaning of the first; 'Die Irrlehrer des Philipperbriefes,' p. 339. Bornkamm, however, does not think that the opponents of 1: 27f. are the same as those of chap. 3 ('Der Phil. als paulinische Briefsammlung,' p. 198).

convey to his friends at Philippi what might be his last messages of thankfulness, encouragement, and warning. How well do the intercessory prayer passages reflect the mood and content of such an epistle?

Survey of the intercessory prayer and related prayer
passages in Philippians[1]

As we should expect, the general tone of the prayer passages is one of thankfulness, trust and exalted expectation even in the midst of anxiety, with a warm personal interest in the welfare of the Philippians. Even the absence of wish-prayers[2] is counterbalanced by the radiant character of the other prayer passages.

The letter begins with the customary grace blessing (1: 2), followed by a glowing thanksgiving period that dwells upon his sense of intimate fellowship with his friends at Philippi (1: 3–11). In the first part of his prayer-report (v. 4) he assures them that his prayers for them are always made with joy. They have been his loyal partners in the gospel from the first and he is filled with affectionate Christian yearning for them (vv. 5, 7f.). Thus he is sure that God will complete the work that he had begun in them (v. 6). This certainty is associated with his constant supplications for them which he now describes in the second part of the prayer-report (vv. 9–11), spelling out his exalted hopes for them, 'that [their] love may abound more and more . . . to the glory and praise of God.'

In the central part of the letter there occurs only one directly intercessory prayer passage, but one which strengthens the mood of intercessory involvement between church and apostle (1: 19ff.). Paul takes for granted the continued supplications of his friends at this critical moment in his trial, and suggests the lines along which they should pray. Their prayers will result in his strengthening and perhaps even his release to be with them (1: 26).

Toward the end of the letter in what seems to be the liturgically oriented closing section (4: 4–23), we find several prayer passages. First comes the exhortation to his readers to practise

---

[1] For supplication passages, see Appendix II.
[2] Except for the doubtful example at 4: 19. See above, pp. 101ff.

prayer and supplication with thanksgiving (4: 6), coupled with an affirmation of the peace of God (4: 7).[1] Another peace-affirmation follows at verse 9b, probably anticipating the kiss of peace that will follow the reading of the letter.[2] Then comes the main reference to their gift, the result of a collection for him at Philippi (vv. 10–18).[3] This leads into a final confident affirmation (a 'declaration-prayer' with an ascription of glory – 4: 19f.)[4] that God will supply every need (material and spiritual) of his readers, as they have supplied his (4: 19f.). So at the end he re-echoes the substance of his prayer-report at the beginning of the letter (1: 9–11).

In customary fashion this declaration-prayer is followed by the instructions for greetings (envisioning the rite of the holy kiss). The request for the readers' prayers is lacking at this point, having been included within the personal communications early in the letter (1: 19f.). Similarly, the sharp warning is lacking, but this too has been introduced at an earlier stage (3: 2–21). Perhaps the apostle desires to forgo any bitterness at the close of what may be his final message to beloved friends at Philippi. So from the greetings he moves straight into the closing grace blessing (4: 23).

Philippians 1: 4 and 1: 9–11

We move on now to a closer look at the divided prayer-report and the thanksgiving period of which it forms a substantial part (1: 3–11).

(I thank my God in all my remembrance of you,) (v. 3)[5] *always in every prayer of mine for you all making my prayer with joy,* (v. 4) (thankful for your partnership in the gospel from the first day until now.) (v. 5) (And I am sure...I hold you all in my heart...how I yearn for you all with the affection of Christ Jesus.) (vv. 6–8) *And it is my prayer that your love may abound more and more, with knowledge and all discernment, so that you may approve what is excellent, and may be*

---

[1] For our decision to regard the peace sentences 4: 7 and 9b as affirmations rather than short wish-prayers or blessings, see above, p. 36.

[2] See above, p. 66, n. 1.

[3] For the apparently liturgically oriented character of Paul's collection references, see above, p. 96, n. 2.

[4] See above, pp. 101ff.

[5] The context, given in part, is placed in parentheses.

pure and blameless for the day of Christ, filled with the fruits of righteousness which come through Jesus Christ, to the glory and praise of God. (vv. 9–11)

In the divided prayer-report we find the customary assurance of the apostle's constant supplications for his friends (v. 4) and an impressive intercessory passage, the longest prayer-report in the Pauline corpus (vv. 9–11):[1]

We begin with a short review of the thanksgiving period and its functional significance, with prior attention to those parts other than the prayer-report. The thanksgiving falls into three sections, each carefully shaped and integrated.[2] The first (vv. 3–5) announces the apostle's continual prayers of thanksgiving and supplication for those who are his partners; the second (vv. 6–8) breaks in with[3] a personal statement of encouragement, stressing the intimate partnership that inspires his prayers (vv. 7–8);[4] this leads back into the third section, describing the main content of his intercessions, and bringing the thanksgiving period to a fitting close in a doxology of praise to God (vv. 9–11).[5] Expressions of thanksgiving, personal affection, pastoral concern, supplication, and praise all are knit closely together in a prayer passage that typifies the mood and style of what is to come.[6]

It is further noteworthy how in this proemium Paul's glance moves rapidly back and forth in time. He looks back with joy to the beginning of their common life in Christ (vv. 5, 6a); he moves into a consideration of their present sharing of his grace (vv.

[1] [The deutero-Pauline letters go far beyond Paul in this respect; Eph. 1: 15ff., 3: 14–19; Col. 1: 9ff.]

[2] See the penetrating analysis of form and content in Lohmeyer, *Philipper, Kolosser, Philemon*, pp. 13ff.

[3] The thanksgiving and prayer-report are broken off after v. 5, to be taken up again at v. 9, a broken construction classified by Schubert as a mixed type, where a fresh start is made one or more times, as in I Thess., and Rom. See above, p. 162.

[4] Perhaps another example of a 'formula of mutual encouragement'; see above, pp. 163, n. 3, 193, n. 2.

[5] See above, pp. 160f. See G. Heinzelmann, *Der Brief an die Philipper* (Göttingen, 1949), p. 86.

[6] Bonnard characterizes it as having 'une richesse de pensée surprenante en même temps qu'une profonde unité littéraire et théologique.' P. Bonnard, *L'Épître de Saint Paul aux Philippiens* (Neuchâtel, 1950), p. 15.

5 and 7); and hastens in thought to the future day (vv. 6b and 10b) when he himself expects to rejoice with them.[1] Under the clarifying light shed by impending death, he sees past, present, and future in a unifying flash of insight that seems to foreshorten the rapid progression of the eschatological age. Hence, they must avoid all temptations to perfectionism and press urgently onward in the short time that lies ahead. 'And I am sure that he who began a good work in you will bring it to completion at the day of Jesus Christ' (v. 6). Right at the start he directs the readers' thoughts to expectations of richer blessings.[2] No hint is given, however, of the stinging attack on his perfectionist opponents in chapter 3. Such sharp warnings must be reserved for later insertion – they do not belong in the thanksgiving.[3]

The thanksgiving begins with an unusually demonstrative assurance of his continued thankfulness. 'I thank my God in all my remembrance of you[4]...making my prayer with joy, thankful for your partnership... (1: 3–5).[5] It is with unusual pleasure that he mentions the continued support of these special friends, and in this way he introduces another major theme of the epistle.[6] Moreover, the phrase τῇ κοινωνίᾳ ὑμῶν εἰς τὸ εὐαγγελίον (v. 5) shows a practical cast to his thoughts. Their association is an active alliance in the work of the gospel.[7]

---

[1] Cf. 2: 16, 'So that in the day of Christ I may be proud that I did not run in vain or labor in vain.'

[2] See above, pp. 200f.

[3] The only sharp attack in a Pauline thanksgiving is in the long descriptive one in I Thess.: see 2: 14–16. Usually such attacks occur rather in the closing sections of the letters. See above, p. 67, n. 3.

[4] ἐπὶ πάσῃ τῇ μνείᾳ ὑμῶν might be translated 'for all your remembrance of me' (ὑμῶν as subj. gen.). Paul would then mention the readers' monetary support at the beginning of the thanksgiving. But against this is the lack of μου, the object of remembrance; also the use of μνείαν in several other epistolary thanksgivings in the sense of mentioning in prayer (μνείαν ποιοῦμαι), Rom. 1: 9, I Thess. 1: 2, Philem. 4 [Eph. 1: 16, II Tim. 1: 3]. See M. R. Vincent, *The Epistles to the Philippians and to Philemon*, ICC (Edinburgh, 1902), p. 6; Michael, p. 10.

[5] Compare the more restrained character of the corresponding statements in Rom. 1: 8, I Cor. 1: 4–8, Philem. 4f. The extended thanksgiving in I Thess. is equally joyful but more defensive and less intimate.

[6] See above, p. 198.

[7] εἰς τὸ εὐαγγελίον means that they share in actively supporting (εἰς) the spreading of the gospel, as the following verses will show. Bonnard, *Philip-*

Besides referring to this in a general sense, he may be making an oblique allusion to the gift from Philippi,[1] to be mentioned openly at a more appropriate place near the end of the letter.

Not only is he thankful, but particularly at this time he feels the seriousness of his accountability for them in the light of that rapidly approaching day when he will present them to Christ (v. 6). He trusts (πεποιθώς) that God will not abandon that good work which he had begun in them, but will bring it to full fruition (v. 6).[2] This sense of accountability presages a pastoral concern that will be evident throughout the whole epistle.[3]

Before he describes his intercessions more fully (1: 9–11), he must underline the deeply felt reasons for his thankfulness and joyful petitions (vv. 7–8). Warm feelings for his friends break through as he thinks of their partnership in costly support of the gospel, and their sharing with him in the grace of Christ. More than in any other Pauline thanksgiving period[4] we find the related emphases of warm personal feelings and spiritual fervor, affectionate comradeship and apostolic concern, gratitude to his friends and gratitude to God, anxiety about their continuing progress and concern about his own immediate fate. More than in any other Pauline letter these concerns will be mingled throughout the letter.

It is clear, then, that the whole thanksgiving period arises straight out of the unusual situation of apostle and congregation. And although couched in elevated and carefully structured language, and confined by liturgical idiom and epistolary convention for the most part to generalized statement, it nevertheless functions as a prologue to a drama, setting the tone and

piens, p. 16, Barth, *Philippians*, p. 16. (But see Blass–Debrunner–Funk, sec. 205, on the substitution of εἰς for ἐν.)

Cf. the practical emphasis in the prayer-report in I Thess. 1: 3; see above, p. 178.

[1] κοινωνία could mean an active tangible sharing with others in the form of a gift, especially in reference to the collection that Paul was organizing: Rom. 15: 26, II Cor. 9: 13, cf. 8: 4, and perhaps Philem. 6. See K. F. Nickle, *The Collection, A Study in Pauline Strategy, SBT*, 48 (London, 1966), pp. 105f. and 122–5; F. Hauck, *TWNT*, III, 808f.

[2] An example of reliance on past mercies as a surety for future blessings. See above, p. 68, n. 1, on I Thess. 5: 24.

[3] See above, p. 198, below, pp. 210f.

[4] The nearest in this regard is I Thess.

anticipating some of the major themes that we have seen to bind the whole letter together.[1]

Within the context of the thanksgiving period we may now focus upon the prayer-report itself (1: 4 and 9–11), in particular the second part (9–11). What special features relate it to the immediate situation of the apostle and his friends, and provide the clue to the epistle which follows?

The extravagant wording of his assurance of constant prayers (v. 4) underlines his warm and grateful feelings for the Philippians: 'always in every prayer of mine for you all making my prayer with joy.'[2] The jubilant note that will sound through the whole letter is struck right at the beginning in the words μετὰ χαρᾶς. While the distinct element of supplication is stressed through the unusual double use of δέησις,[3] the customary participial construction, ποιούμενος, indicates his petitions to be closely related to a prior act of thanksgiving, εὐχαριστῶ.[4] Finally, the comparatively rare and intimate form of address, τῷ θεῷ μου,[5] helps to accentuate the fact that even in his present crisis everything begins for Paul with a personal and vivid sense of gratitude to God.

In the second part of the prayer-report (vv. 9–11), we note again that it is with the fervor of a prisoner facing death for the sake of the gospel (vv. 7f.), that he outlines the gist of his lofty hopes for the Philippians. It is to implement these hopes that he is writing the letter and planning to send messengers to urge them 'to press on toward the goal for the prize of the upward call of God in Christ Jesus' (3: 14).

This supplication passage[6] is constructed so as to forecast the general upward movement of the letter,[7] mounting through a

---

[1] Lohmeyer, *Philipper, Kolosser, Philemon*, p. 14.

[2] Note the words πάντοτε, πάσῃ, πάντων. For the extravagant style of Paul's prayers, see above, p. 60, n. 4.

[3] See above, pp. 19f. In the corresponding prayer-report in I Thess. 1: 2f., the line between thanksgiving and petition is blurred at this point. Above, p. 176.   [4] See above, p. 170.

[5] Preferring this reading with the majority of Mss. Used also in Rom. 1: 8, Philem. 4, and reminiscent of the Psalms. Paul will use it again in his closing prayer passage, Phil. 4: 19. See above, p. 103, n. 4.

[6] It is clearly identified through its decisive opening καὶ τοῦτο προσεύχομαι, that picks up the thought of δέησιν in v. 4. For the construction, see above, Appended Note 1, p. 173, sec. *d*.   [7] See above, pp. 200f.

progression of elevated petitions, to the goal in the closing doxology. This is achieved through an arrangement of two balancing sections, each with an opening clause, a dependent clause, and a clause of purpose:

And it is my prayer:
  1. (ἵνα) that your love may abound more and more,
        (ἐν) with knowledge and all discernment,
        (εἰς τό) so that you may approve what is excellent,
  2. (ἵνα) so that you may be pure and blameless for the day of Christ,
        (πεπληρωμένοι) filled with the fruits of righteousness which come through Jesus Christ,
        (εἰς) to the glory and praise of God.

So the very movement of the language suggests the sense of constant pressing forward from the first day until now, and on to the day of Jesus Christ, which we have observed in the thanksgiving and the epistle.

The first section plunges characteristically into the heart of the Christian life: 'And it is my prayer that your love may abound more and more' (v. 9). He brushes aside all limits, praying that they may overflow with the central grace from which all the others follow.[1] He finds no need to describe love at this point,[2] for as the letter unfolds its meaning will be fully illustrated.[3] In the meantime it is sufficient that love be placed at the forefront of his prayer. More and deeper love is what they will need to overcome the discordant tendencies that have caused him such anxiety, and which he will try to counteract throughout the letter.

He asks for them what he had once asked for the neighboring church at Thessalonica in the days of its infancy. Perhaps this typical petition for love to abound might recall to some of his Philippian readers that earlier wish-prayer for their sister Macedonian church.[4] Yet there are important differences that reflect some further problems in the Philippian situation. In asking that their love might abound, he uses the same word as before, περισσεύειν, but now he adds the phrase 'more and

---

[1] See above, p. 56.   [2] Cf. Michael, p. 19.   [3] See above, pp. 198f.
[4] I Thess. 3: 12. See above, pp. 56ff. Had some of the Philippians who had kept in touch with Paul at Thessalonica read his letter to the Thessalonians?

more,' thus accentuating their need for unremitting progress.[1] And he goes on to stress a different aspect of love from that which he had asked for the Thessalonians: a love that will abound ἐν ἐπιγνώσει καὶ πάσῃ αἰσθήσει. In that earlier situation of fierce persecution the primary requirement had been a 'strengthening of their hearts' so that they might 'stand fast in the Lord.'[2] But for the more experienced Philippians with their temptations to perfectionism, the need is rather for a continuous growth in the kind of knowledge (ἐπίγνωσις)[3] and discernment (αἴσθησις)[4] that love alone can bring. It is love that can guide the believer into ever newer insights and possibilities, for, to Paul, 'love is the fulfilling of the (whole) law' (Rom. 13: 10, cf. Gal. 5: 14).[5]

The next phrase, εἰς τὸ δοκιμάζειν ὑμᾶς τὰ διαφέροντα (v. 10), continues his preliminary reply to the opponents who 'put their confidence in the flesh,' or 'whose god is the belly,' and whom he will later attack so sharply (3: 2–21). So he prays that his friends on the contrary, through the knowledge and insight which love alone will give, may be enabled to judge (δοκιμάζειν, judge, test, approve)[6] what really matters (τὰ διαφέροντα, what is worthwhile, excellent, vital).[7]

---

[1] Cf. above, pp. 200f.   [2] I Thess. 3: 8, 18.

[3] ἐπίγνωσις: '*knowledge, recognition* in our lit. limited to relig. or moral things…consciousness of sin…knowledge of God and Christ,' Bauer–Arndt–Gingrich. See also R. Bultmann, *TWNT*, I, 707. 'Phil. 1, 9f zeigt deutlich, dass es sich um ein nachdenkendes Forschen handelt; aber wie es in der Liebe fundiert ist, so führt es zum rechten Tun.' ἐπίγνωσις is asked for also in the prayer-report in Philem. 6 (see below, p. 224, n. 1 [and Eph. 1: 17, Col. 1: 9]).

[4] αἴσθησις (דַּעַת) = '*insight, experience*, denoting moral understanding,' Bauer–Arndt–Gingrich. See also G. Delling, *TWNT*, I, 188, 'Unter αἴσθησις ist Phil 1, 9 das sittliche Unterscheidungsvermögen, die ethische Urteilsfähigkeit…verstanden….' It suggests insight in concrete situations, Michael, p. 21.

[5] Elsewhere he had written that through the perfection of love, 'I shall understand fully (ἐπιγνώσομαι), even as I have been fully understood' (ἐπεγνώσθην), I Cor. 13: 12. See also Furnish, *Theology and Ethics*, pp. 235–7.

[6] A Christian duty often referred to by Paul. See W. Grundmann, *TWNT*, II, espec. 263. See below, p. 243, n. 6.

[7] 'Das, worauf es in der jeweiligen Situation ankommt,' Grundmann, *ibid.* We take this to apply more to judging ethical matters than to deciding about doctrinal questions. So Bonnard, *Philippiens*, p. 19. Moffatt's transation renders it 'what is vital.'

According to the antagonists, then, the norm for choosing what is excellent or what really matters is found either in the attainable standards of the law, or in behavior that does not rise above 'earthly things.'[1] But according to Paul, it is found in the new and deeper insights brought by love (1: 9), a love exemplified by Christ himself (2: 1ff.).[2] He himself has learned this secret of judging what is vital, as he will go on to show: 'For his sake I have suffered the loss of all things...But one thing I do...I press on toward the goal for the prize of the upward call of God in Christ Jesus' (3: 8, 13f.). So he prays now that his friends too may judge what is excellent, and he anticipates his later exhortations to them, 'Have this mind among yourselves (τοῦτο φρονεῖτε ἐν ὑμῖν), which you have in Christ Jesus' (2: 5), and 'Finally, brethren, whatever is true ...honorable...lovely...if there is any excellence, anything worthy of praise, think about these things' (4: 8).

In the second section of the prayer[3] Paul takes up another characteristic intercessory theme, preparation of his churches for the judgment day of Christ.[4] Though for many years this thought has spurred him on, it has become even more urgent as he confronts the final test of having to leave his friends behind. The fact that he mentions the parousia for a second time in the thanksgiving period suggests that his mind is turned intently in that direction. First he had expressed his trust that God would bring to completion, at the day of Jesus Christ, the good work he had begun in them (v. 6). Now he prays that they 'may be

[1] See above, pp. 200f.

[2] An illuminating parallel may be found in Romans: early in that letter Paul had questioned the Gentile who 'did not see fit to acknowledge God' (οὐκ ἐδοκίμασεν τὸν θεὸν ἔχειν ἐν ἐπιγνώσει), and the Jew who boasts that he 'knows God's will and approves what is excellent (καὶ γινώσκεις τὸ θέλημα καὶ δοκιμάζεις τὰ διαφέροντα), because he is instructed in the law' (2: 18). Paul's own summary answer was postponed until the beginning of the ethical section of the letter: 'but be transformed by the renewal of your mind, that you may prove what is the will of God (εἰς τὸ δοκιμάζειν ὑμᾶς τί τὸ θέλημα τοῦ θεοῦ), what is good and acceptable and perfect' (12: 2). But now in the Philippian letter he reverses the order and summarizes his answer at the beginning of the letter in his introductory prayer-report.

[3] Marked by a second ἵνα clause.

[4] On the eschatological climax in the thanksgiving periods, see above, p. 158.

pure (εἰλικρινεῖς)[1] and blameless (or without stumbling) (ἀπρόσκοποι),[2] for (εἰς)[3] the day of Christ' (v. 10). In the epistle he will several times reveal this burning sense of account-ability at the parousia. When he pleads about their manner of life 'in the midst of a crooked and perverse generation,' he supports his appeal with the words, 'so that in the day of Christ I may be proud that I did not run in vain or labor in vain' (2: 15f.). Speaking of them as 'my joy and crown' (4: 1), he looks forward to their bringing a crown of joy to him at the parousia (cf. I Thess. 2: 19).[4] In another section he will remind them that 'our commonwealth is in heaven, and from it we await a Savior...who will change our lowly bodies to be like his glorious body...' (3: 20f.).

How deeply this sense of responsibility for the Philippians weighs upon him, is shown by his indecision between the alternatives of life or death that the trial must soon decide: 'I am hard pressed between the two. My desire is to depart and be with Christ, for that is far better. But to remain in the flesh is more necessary on your account...for your progress and joy in the faith...' (1: 23ff.). A little later this anxiety will again rise to the surface: 'Therefore, my beloved, as you have always obeyed, so now, not only in my presence but much more in my absence, work out your own salvation with fear and trembling...' (2: 12).[5] Accordingly, his constant prayer for them is that even if he should leave them, they continue to grow in love, so gaining those deeper insights and experiences

[1] εἰλικρινεῖς: completely pure (tested in the light of the sun) – used in a moral sense. F. Büchsel, *TWNT*, II, 396; Lohmeyer, *Philipper, Kolosser, Philemon*, p. 33, n. 5.

[2] G. Stählin, 'ἀπρόσκοπον εἶναι als eschatologisches Ziel (Phil. 1: 10),' *TWNT*, VI, 757, suggests three possible senses for ἀπρόσκοπος: (1) the con-ventional sense, blameless (Lohmeyer); (2) without offense before God, cf., 'pleasing to God' in Phil. 4: 18, a common Pauline theme; (3) the preferred sense, reaching the goal without stumbling in their faith. Cf. Gal. 5: 4, Jude 24, 'him who is able to keep you from falling and to present you without blemish.'

It can also mean 'not causing others to stumble,' or 'no harm to anyone' (Moffatt); but the link with 'for the day of Christ,' counts against this.

[3] Taking εἰς to mean 'in preparation for,' Stählin, *ibid.* But, in the light of I Thess. 3: 13, 5: 23 (ἐν τῇ παρουσίᾳ), εἰς may be equivalent to a dative, 'in the day of Christ.' Cf. Moule, *Idiom Book*, p. 69.

[4] See above, p. 53.   [5] See above, p. 54, n. 6.

that will make them 'pure and blameless in preparation for the day of Christ' (1: 10).

Typically, he goes on to pray that they demonstrate their increasing love in a practical way (cf. I Thess. 1: 3);[1] that the result be shown in their being 'filled[2] with the fruits[3] of righteousness which come through Jesus Christ' (v. 11). The metaphor of fruit (καρπόν) foreshadows the theme of demonstrable results that will recur in the letter, both about himself as he hopes for further 'fruitful labor' (1: 22), and about his friends as he hopes that their gift may bring results in blessing to them ('the fruit which increases to their credit') (4: 7).[4] Thus he may be alluding a second time to their gift,[5] as he had already done in verse 5.

But with the addition of the pregnant phrase, 'which come through Jesus Christ,' there occurs a characteristic twist of direction that prepares for other central developments in the letter. Up to this point he has been emphasizing the need for his friends to press forward, even if he is not to be with them, until they attain to the full fruits of righteousness. Now he reminds them that such fruits can come only through Jesus Christ.[6] In this way the whole meaning of the phrase 'fruits of righteousness' is turned from self-effort to dependence on Jesus Christ.[7]

[1] See above, p. 178.

[2] πεπληρωμένοι expresses once again the apostle's overflowing prayer-style and great expectation. Cf. G. Delling, *TWNT*, vi, 290.

[3] See F. Hauck, *TWNT*, iii, 617–19. καρπός is used in the NT in the general figurative sense, as consequence, result, or profit from an action. So good fruits are the outer test of genuineness of the action of repentance, Matt. 3: 8, or the outer manifestation of men's inner nature, Matt. 7: 15–20. Thus here the phrase means the fruit resulting from and demonstrating righteousness (obj. genitive) rather than the fruit which is righteousness; Beare, Heinzelmann, Michael, etc.   [4] See above, pp. 104f.

[5] Cf. Rom. 15: 28, where the collection is referred to as τὸν καρπὸν τοῦτον and see above, p. 198.

[6] τὸν διὰ 'Ιησοῦ Χριστοῦ: in this phrase it is the fruit of righteousness rather than righteousness itself that is said to come through Jesus Christ (Michael); thereby stress is laid again on the practical aspect of their spiritual growth.

[7] Near the close of the letter, he will once again make this sudden correction as he boasts of having learned the secret of reconciliation – at the end he will add the phrase, ἐν τῷ ἐνδυναμοῦντί με (4: 13).

So in the prayer he anticipates exactly his important exhortation in chapter 2: that especially when they may no longer depend on his presence, they work out their own salvation, yet not in the arrogance of self-achievement nor claims to perfection, but 'with fear and trembling,' mindful always that the outcome is not finally in their hands, 'for God is at work in you, both to will and to work for his good pleasure' (2: 13f.). In chapter 3 he will emphasize this again: 'Not having a righteousness of my own, based on law, but that which is through faith in Christ....' (3: 9). Self-achievement and self-assurance are further cautioned against in the hesitancy of the words, 'that if possible I may attain (εἰ πῶς καταντήσω) the resurrection from the dead' (3: 11).

In his supplications, therefore, he prays that they be released from easy contentment with humanly attainable standards, conscious always of their need to rely on the power of Christ. So they may be enabled to resist the perfectionist claims of their legalistic and libertine antagonists.

Finally he reaches the culmination to which the prayer and indeed the whole thanksgiving period have been pointing – an ascription of glory and praise to God (v. 11b).[1] His thanksgiving returns to the divine ground from which it had begun (v. 3). God's saving work among the Philippians, begun and continued in times of trial, will eventually redound to the divine glory.[2] In this way he prefigures the climax of the great 'Christ-hymn,' when 'at the name of Jesus every knee should bow...and every tongue confess that Jesus Christ is Lord, to the glory of God the Father' (2: 10f.); he anticipates also the climactic doxology at the close of the letter, 'To our God and Father be glory forever and ever, Amen' (4: 20).

Once more we have seen how an opening intercessory prayer-report introduces the immediate concerns that prompt the

[1] Cf. the return to God near the close of the wish-prayers in I Thess. 3: 13, and Rom. 15: 6.
We read καὶ επαινον θεου, with the majority of Mss. The three alternative readings καὶ επαινον Χριστου, D*; καὶ επαινον μοι, G; θεου καὶ επαινον εμοι, P46, are all unlikely in view of the Jewish prayer custom of ending with praise to God; see above, pp. 160f. But the last two readings reflect the understanding that Paul expected to 'boast' of his churches at the parousia.

[2] Cf. Matt. 5: 16; a theme that Paul refers to several times, e.g., II Cor. 1: 11. See below, pp. 274f.

writing of a letter. Indeed, the whole thanksgiving period has been shown to do this in an unusually comprehensive way, setting the tone and suggesting much of the content of the letter that is to follow. It is the intercessory portion, however, that indicates more precisely the anxieties and hopes that motivate Paul as he writes.[1]

Other significant aspects of this prayer-report may be touched upon shortly. As in the corresponding passages in I Thessalonians and Romans, but more emphatically in this cordial letter to friends, the apostle includes all his readers in his prayers, joyfully breaking down all barriers and all limits. As a prisoner awaiting sentence, his motives for reconciling intercession have been refined and made even more urgent than before. We must conclude that at this time of crisis especially, his assurances of constant intercession mean much more than conventional phrasing.

Next, it is clear that in writing to friends and close partners, Paul is counting on their supplications for himself. His revealing description of his own prayers would make the strongest appeal to them to continue to intercede for him. He is sure that they are already praying for him (vv. 19f.)[2] and knows that they will turn once again to united supplication whenever they read his epistle.

The elevated prayer style of this beautifully composed intercessory passage would make it eminently suitable for adaptation by the congregation at Philippi. In association with the 'Christ-hymn' it would add to their service of praise a note of profound commitment to their common Lord – a legacy from Paul to his friends as he seeks to teach them to aspire in prayer. It would focus and reinforce the exhortations of the letter[3] and give the believers an opportunity to ally themselves with his highest hopes for themselves.

As in the other prayer-reports, so in this we may see an actual offering of prayer by the apostle. This he states directly, 'And

[1] In this letter, as we have argued (pp. 197ff. above), there are several rather than one primary occasion for the writing.

[2] See below, p. 277.

[3] Bonnard, *Philippiens*, p. 18; cf. Stählin, p. 757; Barth, *Philippians*, p. 23, 'the urgent admonition which here turns out to be the content of the apostolic intercession....' Cf. Furnish, p. 95.

it is my prayer that your love may abound. . . .' Both in the writing of the letter and in the composing of the prayer[1] he holds them up before that God to whom (as he is persuaded) he will soon present them finally. So at the beginning of this affectionate epistle, writer and readers are brought together in thanksgiving and supplication, a joyful partnership not only in the grace of active service, but in the grace of concerned intercession.

THE DIVIDED PRAYER-REPORT IN PHILEMON –
vv. 4b and 6

When we turn to the next prayer-report in a Pauline thanksgiving, we move into another letter written from captivity, perhaps near the time of the epistle to the church at Philippi,[2] but addressed mainly to one individual and concerned with what seems at first to be a merely personal matter. Although a brief little document that offers no directly theological or ethical instruction, it is unique among his letters in revealing a more personal side of the apostle's Christian understanding and character,[3] and may help to round out our study of his intercessory prayer passages.

The well-known background of the epistle may be reconstructed from the document itself, at least in its essential outlines. The letter is addressed primarily to Philemon, a Christian leader at Colossae. A runaway slave of his called Onesimus (vv. 12, 16, 18) had in some way become associated with Paul during his imprisonment (v. 10). He had been converted to Christianity by the apostle (v. 10) and had become very useful as his personal attendant, and presumably also in the work of preaching the gospel (vv. 11, 13). Paul had formed a close and affectionate attachment to him and would very much have liked him to remain as his helper (vv. 12, 13, 16). But reluctantly he had decided to return Onesimus to his master Philemon so that things might be put right (vv. 12, 15). So now

[1] See above, p. 71, n. 5.

[2] See above, p. 197, n. 5. It is unimportant for our purposes to determine the place and date of Philem.

[3] See E. F. Scott, *The Epistles of Paul to the Colossians, to Philemon, and to the Ephesians*, MNTC (New York, 1930), p. 97.

Paul sends him back (perhaps with Tychicus),[1] supported by this most skillful and persuasive letter on his behalf. Apparently he had known Philemon for some time; he writes as to an old friend (vv. 7, 17, 19b) on whom he would have considerable claim as he pleads for Onesimus (vv. 20–1).[2]

What precisely is Paul asking for in this carefully indirect appeal? Certainly he is requesting that Onesimus be received with forgiveness and kindness (vv. 16–18). This in itself would be a vital matter in view of the harsh fate that threatened every fugitive slave.[3] Yet various hints and implications in the letter show that he is asking for more than the kindly reception of the slave.[4] Perhaps he wishes Philemon to grant Onesimus his legal freedom,[5] but more urgently he wants Onesimus released from household service and sent back to him for the service of the gospel (vv. 13f., 21).[6] Perhaps the half-playful use of commercial terms[7] throughout the letter is Paul's tactful way of reminding Philemon that, as a servant of Christ, all his possessions should be made over into the possession of Christ and for his service.[8] The obvious care with which the document has been penned reveals how urgently the apostle desires the success of his appeal.

[1] According to the deutero-Pauline Col. 4: 7–9.

[2] But see below, p. 221, n. 1.

[3] See, inter al., E. R. Goodenough, 'Paul and Onesimus,' HTR, 22 (1929), 181–3; W. J. Richardson, 'Principle and Context in the Ethics of the Epistle to Philemon,' Interpretation, 22 (1968), p. 302.

[4] See, e.g., J. Knox, Philemon Among the Letters of Paul, rev. 3rd edn (Nashville, 1959), pp. 18–32. Paul himself implies that he wants more than he says: 'knowing that you will do even more than I say' (v. 21). For a contrary view, see Wickert, 'Der Philemonbrief – Privatbrief oder apostolisches Schreiben?', pp. 230ff.

[5] Lohmeyer, Philipper, Kolosser, Philemon; see also P. N. Harrison, 'Onesimus and Philemon,' ATR, 32 (1950), 277f.

[6] Cf. Knox, Philemon Among the Letters, Richardson, pp. 307ff., C. F. D. Moule, The Epistles of Paul the Apostle to the Colossians and Philemon, CGTC (Cambridge, 1962), p. 21.

[7] 'On your behalf,' v. 13; 'without your consent,' v. 14; 'that you might have him back forever,' v. 15; 'if you consider me your partner, receive him as you would receive me,' v. 17; 'charge that to my account. I, Paul, write this with my own hand, I will repay it,' vv. 18f. See Deissmann, Light from the Ancient East, pp. 84, 332, 335.

[8] T. Preiss, 'Life in Christ and Social Ethics in the Epistle of Philemon,' in Life in Christ, E.Tr., SBT, 13 (London, 1954), pp. 39ff.

Can the epistle, then, be regarded as a private letter? Although addressed in the first place to an individual and treating what seems a personal matter, it bears many of the marks of Paul's 'apostolic' epistles.[1] Paul employs the full address and blessing, the thanksgiving with intercession, and the formal liturgical conclusion that characterize his more extended epistles.[2] Timothy is included with himself as a signatory and the letter is addressed to Philemon with Apphia, Archippus, and the church in his house. In asking that Onesimus be sent back to work with himself, he writes with the authority of 'an ambassador[3] but (δέ) now a prisoner also[4] for Christ Jesus' (v. 9). Thus he makes it clear that he regards this personal request as a matter also for the Christian fellowship,[5] and he places his request within the new context of the life 'in Christ.'[6]

What part, then, do the prayer passages play in this carefully planned appeal?

Survey of the intercessory prayer and related
prayer passages in Philemon

In a letter that exhibits in brief compass so many of the marks of an apostolic epistle, we may expect to find the customary prayer passages. By and large they are all there, aptly phrased and planned, except for the wish-prayers and the exhortation to the readers to pray constantly. Indeed they seem to exhibit

[1] See Wickert, pp. 230f.

[2] Lohmeyer, *Philipper, Kolosser, Philemon*, p. 174.

[3] Assuming that either variant reading πρεσβυτης or πρεσβευτης could mean ambassador. *Ibid.* p. 185; cf. Knox, *Philemon Among the Letters*, p. 21, Preiss, p. 36.

[4] Although writing as apostle, Paul does not wish to flaunt his authority over Philemon (Wickert, pp. 232f.). Cf. his reluctance to use compulsion over the Corinthians, e.g., II Cor. 13: 10 (below, pp. 242ff.), I Cor. 9: 1–27.

[5] Knox, *Philemon Among the Letters*, pp. 31f., 'The letter dealt with the release of a slave for religious service and was worthy of being read to the Church, to which the owner belonged.' Cf. Preiss, p. 34.

[6] εἰς Χριστόν, v. 6; ἐν Χριστῷ, vv. 8, 20; ἐν Χριστῷ Ἰησοῦ, v. 23; ἐν κυρίῳ, vv. 16, 20; δέσμιος Χριστοῦ, v. 9. Cf. W. J. Richardson, pp. 310ff. for the effect of the context of the Christian κοινωνία on Paul's treatment of the problem of slavery, and on the nature of his request.

in nuce Paul's usual pattern, by adapting even this small letter for a worship service in 'the church in your house' (v. 2).

As always, he follows the superscription and address with an apostolic blessing of grace and peace (v. 3). Then comes a short but deliberately composed thanksgiving period (vv. 4–7). For the subject of his thanksgiving he selects Philemon's outgoing qualities of love and faith, grounded in the Lord Jesus and expressed in his generous relationships with all his Christian brethren. He acknowledges his own personal joy and comfort at the way in which Philemon has been able to bring 'refreshment' to the believers (vv. 5, 7). Thus he prepares in a suggestive way for the acceptance of the appeal he is about to make.

Within this adroit acknowledgement of the practical Christian love of Philemon, he incorporates the usual assurance of his own continued prayers for his friend, 'always when I remember you in my prayers...that the sharing of your faith may promote the knowledge of all the good that is ours in Christ' (vv. 4, 6).

After developing his request to Philemon, he reinforces it by a confident suggestion that before long he himself may be released from prison and pay a visit to Philemon's home. This will make it all the more difficult for his appeal to go unregarded, especially as he lets it be known that he is relying on the continued interest and prayer support of his friends: 'for I am hoping through your prayers to be granted to you' (v. 22b).[1] He closes the letter with a much shortened version of his usual liturgically oriented pattern (vv. 21–5), including the indirect prayer-request (v. 22b), greetings from his companions (vv. 23f.), and a final grace blessing, 'The grace of the Lord Jesus Christ be with your spirit' (v. 25).[2]

Philemon vv. 4b and 6

The intercessory prayer-report in this letter is interwoven more closely than usual within the thanksgiving period, both through syntax and through content. By examining the thanksgiving as a whole, we may better understand the precise function of the

[1] See below, pp. 281 ff.

[2] Missing are the admonitions to prayer, a wish-prayer, a peace blessing, the mention of the holy kiss, and the stern warning.

intercessory portion and its relation to the main purpose of the letter:

(I thank my God) (v. 4a)
always when I remember you in my prayers, (v. 4b)[1]
(because I hear of your love and of the faith which you have toward the Lord Jesus and all the saints,) (v. 5)
and I pray that the sharing of your faith may promote the knowledge of all the good that is ours in Christ. (v. 6)[1]
(For I have derived much joy and comfort from all your love, my brother, because the hearts of the saints have been refreshed through you.) (v. 7) (Philem. vv. 4-7)

It is striking how the whole passage prepares the ground for the request that is to follow, as may be seen not only in its general emphasis, but also in the specific repetition of words from the thanksgiving at appropriate points in the body of the letter.[2]

The actual thanksgiving phrases are divided between verses 4a, 5 and 7.[3] At the outset Paul mentions in ceremonially poetic language suitable for the thanksgiving period those practical qualities of Christian love and faith that Philemon has demonstrated. He has heard[4] about the faith of Philemon 'toward

---

[1] The intercessory portion is given in italics.

[2] Knox, *Philemon Among the Letters*, p. 22. τῶν προσευχῶν μου (v. 4) – τῶν προσευχῶν ὑμῶν (v. 22); σου τὴν ἀγάπην (v. 5) – διὰ τὴν ἀγάπην (v. 9); ἡ κοινωνία (v. 6) – κοινωνόν (v. 17); ἀγαθοῦ τοῦ ἐν ἡμῖν (v. 6) – τὸ ἀγαθόν σου (v. 14); τὰ σπλάγχνα τῶν ἁγίων ἀναπέπαυται διὰ σοῦ (v. 7) – τὰ ἐμὰ σπλάγχνα (v. 12), ἀνάπαυσόν μου τὰ σπλάγχνα (v. 20); ἀδελφέ (v. 7) – ἀδελφέ (v. 20). Cf. Furnish, p. 94.

[3] As Schubert showed, we have here a straightforward (type 1a) thanksgiving period, in which a temporal participial construction (qualifying εὐχαριστῶ) introduces the intercessory report: I thank my God always (εὐχαριστῶ πάντοτε), whenever I make mention of you in my prayers (μνείαν σου ποιούμενος), that (asking that) the sharing of your faith may promote (ὅπως ἐνεργὴς γένηται). See above, p. 162. The line between thanksgiving and petition is here more clearly drawn than in I Thess. 1:2f., see above, pp. 176f. This is done by interrupting the construction with a participial causal phrase (qualifying εὐχαριστῶ, and citing the reasons for the thanksgiving) – ἀκούων σου τὴν ἀγάπην. Again in v. 7 the thanksgiving makes a fresh start with the words, χάραν γὰρ πολλὴν ἔσχον, where Paul now uses a 'joygiving'; Sanders, 'Transition from Opening Thanksgiving,' p. 360. Cf. the fresh starts in the extended thanksgiving in I Thess.; see above, *ibid.* However, Lohmeyer argues that v. 6 cannot be properly distinguished from the giving of thanks (*Philipper, Kolosser, Philemon*, p. 178).

[4] Probably through Epaphras, and even through Onesimus himself. See E. F. Scott, p. 103, Vincent, *Epistles to the Philippians and to Philemon*, p. 178.

(πρός) the Lord Jesus,' and the way this has been expressed in loving care extended 'toward (εἰς) all the saints' (v. 5).[1] These, then, are the two graces[2] that will form the ground of his intercessory prayer (v. 6) and of his apostolic appeal in the letter.

It may be significant that, whereas in the corresponding prayer passages in Romans and I Thessalonians Paul speaks merely of the readers' faith, in this one he is careful to point out that Philemon's faith is directed πρὸς τὸν κύριον Ἰησοῦν. For he will go on to appeal to Philemon's obedience (v. 21), based in his sharing the obligations of the new faith toward Christ.[3]

Nevertheless, faith must work through love (Gal. 5: 6), and it is even more to this warm practical good will that Paul addresses his plea:[4] 'I hear of your love... toward all the saints (v. 5), and 'Accordingly, though I am bold enough in Christ to command you to do what is required, yet for love's sake I prefer to appeal to you...' (vv. 8f.).

Having pertinently introduced the ground notes of love and faith, he interrupts the giving of thanks to describe somewhat cryptically in the prayer-report the request that forms the main content of his prayers and of the letter (v. 6).[5] Taking up the thanksgiving once again (v. 7), he pays further tribute to Philemon's love by referring to some instances of his kindness that have come to Paul's attention.[6] By continuing to employ

[1] This sentence, written in a highly condensed style, literally directs both Philemon's love and his faith, both to Jesus and to all the saints. So uncharacteristic of Paul would this be, that it is best interpreted in a chiastic manner: your love toward all the saints, and your faith toward the Lord Jesus. (E. F. Scott, p. 104, Lohmeyer, *Philipper, Kolosser, Philemon*, p. 177, Moule, *Colossians and Philemon*, p. 141, etc.) The variation of the prepositions πρός and εἰς supports such a reading (Lohmeyer, Moule) as do the parallel sentences in Col. 1: 4, and the preferred reading of Eph. 1: 15.

[2] The absence of the word 'hope' from Paul's triad of graces is unusual; the lack of explicit eschatological references in this letter suggests that it may not have been written from Paul's Roman captivity – contrast the many such references in Phil.

[3] Cf. above, p. 217. Cf. Rom. 1: 5, II Cor. 2: 9, 7: 15.

[4] Cf. the practical emphasis in the I Thess. and Phil. thanksgivings. See above, pp. 178ff. and 205.   [5] See below, pp. 221–5.

[6] Referring perhaps to a particular action of Philemon (M. Dibelius, *An Philemon, HzNT* (Tübingen, 1911), *ad loc.*), or to several, or merely to his general behavior as a well-to-do man (Lohmeyer, *Philipper, Kolosser, Philemon*, p. 180).

the elevated style appropriate to a formal opening thanksgiving, Paul lends the fullest religious significance to these benevolent actions.[1] Without a doubt his almost fulsome language is being used to suggest that they become a precedent for the decision about Onesimus:

'For I have derived much joy and comfort from your love, my brother, because the hearts of the saints have been refreshed[2] through you.' (v. 7)

'Yes, brother, I want some benefit from you in the Lord. Refresh my[3] heart in Christ. Confident of your obedience, I write to you, knowing that you will do even more than I say.' (vv. 20f.)

To what extent, then, does the prayer-report focus the purpose of the letter more sharply? It is introduced in his customary, somewhat indirect, way,[4] with an assurance that Paul is praying repeatedly for his readers:

'I thank my God always when I remember you in my prayers.' (v. 4)

Once again we are teased by the question as to how far this assurance is more than an epistolary cliché. Obviously he must have been giving much thought to brother Philemon and the church in his house. To take the responsibility for sending a runaway slave back to his master was a perplexing decision. To ask, besides, that he be released and sent back for the work of the gospel, would require still more consideration. Hence it seems certain that Paul would make this a matter of frequent and earnest prayer.

After pausing to give the reasons for his thankfulness about Philemon (v. 5), he indicates the direction of his prayers about the problem that has arisen:

and I pray that[5] *the sharing of your faith may promote the knowledge of all the good that is ours in Christ.* (v. 6)

---

[1] Lohmeyer, however, concludes from his use of such general language that Paul really knows very little about Philemon. *Ibid.*

[2] For Paul's use of a formula of mutual encouragement, see above, pp. 163, n. 3; 193, n. 2 (Rom. 1: 11f.); 204, n. 4 (Phil. 1: 6–8); and below, p. 270, n. 4 (Rom. 15: 32).

[3] Knox suggests with effect that the word 'my' should be emphasized: 'You have cheered the hearts of others; now cheer *my* heart by granting the request...' J. Knox, *The Epistle to Philemon*, IB, xi, 564.

[4] A temporal participial phrase; see above, p. 219, n. 3.

[5] ὅπως.

But so notoriously cryptic is his language, that no single inter-pretation stands out with any certainty.[1] Yet in the light of the background of the prayer, and by drawing insights from his other prayer-reports, we may attempt some tentative con-clusions as to what Paul may have intended.

The first problem concerns the many possible meanings of the phrase ἡ κοινωνία τῆς πίστεώς σου. What is it about Philemon that must promote the knowledge of the gospel? Is it 'his partaking in the faith,' or 'the sharing in his faith by his fellow believers,' or 'his generous practice of sharing, which is the natural outcome of his faith'?[2] The circumstances of the letter, the contents of the rest of the thanksgiving, and the substance of Paul's appeal, all suggest that the last meaning was at least partly intended: 'I pray that your generous practice of sharing, which is the outcome of your faith, may promote the knowledge of the gospel.'

Paul has in mind to ask Philemon for a generous loan or gift, namely Onesimus, for the mission work of the gospel. We have seen him make a similarly oblique allusion to a gift sent to him in prison by the Philippians (Phil. 1: 5). On that occasion, too, he employed the word κοινωνία, which could mean both their

[1] After a model analysis of the many options, Moule concludes with a touch of humor befitting the letter to Philemon, 'Unless and until further ἐπίγνωσις is given to Christian interpreters, the answers to these questions must remain obscure' (*Colossians and Philemon*, p. 143). Although they may not have been so obscure to the readers with their inside knowledge of the situation, we must leave room for the possibility that Paul was being inten-tionally somewhat veiled at this point.

[2] The interpretations depend partly on the nature of the genitive, τῆς πίστεως, partly on the sense assigned to κοινωνία: as a gift (sharing one's possessions with others), or fellowship, or sharing in (see above, p. 206, n. 1). The possibilities are even more varied than those suggested above (cf. Moule, *Colossians and Philemon*, p. 142): your participation in the faith (E. F. Scott, Bauer–Arndt–Gingrich); the fellowship which you have (with Christ) through your faith (Dibelius); your fellowship with other Christians created by faith (gen. of author, Lohmeyer, Wickert); the sharing in your faith by 'all the saints' (referring to the previous verse); their fellowship resulting from your faith; the active sharing of your faith with others (Vincent); the generous giving which is the outcome of your faith (see E. F. Scott, p. 104), or alternatively 'your kindly deeds of charity which spring from your faith,' J. B. Lightfoot, *St. Paul's Epistles to the Colossians and to Philemon*, 6th edn (London, 1882), *ad loc.*

partnership and their gift. Such an indirect reference would befit the formal language of a thanksgiving period[1] and may also be one more example of his hesitancy about gifts and financial aid.[2] Judging by the careful selection of terms throughout the present thanksgiving as he prepares for the details of his request, we may take κοινωνία as prefiguring the business language of verse 17,[3] 'So if you consider me your partner (κοινωνόν), receive him as you would receive me.'[4] Here, then, he is making his first allusion to the actual subject matter of the appeal – generous sharing on the part of Philemon, which will be prompted by his faith toward the Lord Jesus (v. 5),[5] and by his obedience to the new life in Christ (v. 21).[6]

Next, he prays that Philemon's sharing 'may become effective in the knowledge (ἐνεργὴς γένηται ἐν[7] ἐπιγνώσει)[8] of all the good that is ours in Christ.' But again, exactly what does this compact language mean? Is the knowledge to become effective in Philemon himself, or in his fellow believers? Here the decision seems even more doubtful, but again the circumstances and nature of Paul's request offer a clue. In asking for Onesimus, Paul is thinking mainly of the promotion of the knowledge of the gospel to others.[9] Thus he would refer not primarily to the effect of Philemon's action on his own spiritual growth, but upon his fellows, including Onesimus, others at Colossae, and those who would benefit from the future mission work of Onesimus.[10] This, then, must be the intention of the compactly stated prayer: 'I pray that the generous sharing

---

[1] See above, p. 206. [2] See above, p. 103; below, p. 237.

[3] See above, p. 216, n. 7, p. 219, n. 2.

[4] The word κοινωνός 'serves to remind the owner that he and Paul are associates in a supremely important enterprise and must share all they have with each other.' Knox, *IB*, xi, 570.

[5] For πίστις (faith) as the total Christian life of trust in God (or Christ), see above, pp. 178f. [6] See above, p. 217.

[7] Become effective in. Cf. Gal. 5: 6, πίστις δι' ἀγάπης ἐνεργουμένη (Wickert, p. 230, n. 2). [8] See above, p. 209, n. 3.

[9] Regarding the concentration of Paul's prayers on the success of the gospel mission, see e.g., above, p. 16, and n. 3. He links the destiny of the churches with his own, as one holding a unique position in the divine plan; see above, p. 49, and n. 3, etc.

[10] This is suggested also by his previous reference to Philemon's love as being directed 'to all the believers' (v. 5). That thought would carry over into the meaning of his prayer-report: Philemon must share with the

which is the outcome of your faith may serve (through your giving of Onesimus) to promote the spread of the knowledge[1] of all the good that is ours in Christ.'[2]

What knowledge does he have in view in the phrase, παντὸς ἀγαθοῦ τοῦ ἐν ἡμῖν[3] εἰς Χριστόν? Usually Paul employs the term τὸ ἀγαθόν in an active sense, as something that is done or performed according to the will of God;[4] later in the epistle he will use this active meaning when he refers to Philemon's release of Onesimus as τὸ ἀγαθόν σου (v. 14).[5] By choosing this term in the prayer-report, he must have in mind partly the obedience to God's will that he will ask of Philemon,[6] but perhaps he is thinking also in more general terms of all the blessings which flow from the life in Christ.[7]

Lastly what does he mean by the loosely attached final phrase, εἰς Χριστόν? While we may choose to translate it loosely as 'in Christ,'[8] 'the good that is ours in Christ,' others prefer the more primary meaning 'toward Christ,' e.g., 'the good that

believers, and promote the knowledge of the gospel among believers. Paul is interested, too, in Philemon as host of the house church. '[He] as well as Onesimus, was vital to the carrying out of Paul's mission,' W. J. Richardson, p. 307, referring to Filson, 'The Significance of the Early House Churches.'

[1] We may contrast his use of ἐπίγνωσις in the Phil. prayer-report (Phil. 1: 9). There, his immediate concern is for the Philippians themselves: 'that your love may abound more and more, with knowledge (ἐν ἐπιγνώσει) and all discernment' (see above, p. 209). Whereas here, his first concern is to gain a favor from the reader for the sake of disseminating the knowledge of the gospel. For the opposite view (that knowledge here, as in Phil., applied to the reader), see Dibelius, *Philemon*, p. 127.

[2] Vincent (p. 180) has a similar but more limited interpretation, 'He prays that the love and faith which so greatly aid and comfort all the saints may likewise communicate their blessings to Onesimus...'

[3] Our choice of the better attested reading ημιν for υμιν does not substantially affect the meaning of the phrase.

[4] E.g., Rom. 2: 10, 7: 13, 19, 9: 11, 12: 2, 9, 21, Gal. 6: 10, etc. See Lohmeyer, *Philipper, Kolosser, Philemon*, p. 179. [Cf. Col. 1: 9, the intercessory prayer-report, 'asking that you may be filled with the knowledge of his will.' Wickert.]

[5] Cf. above, p. 219, n. 2.   [6] Cf. Wickert, p. 234.

[7] Cf. Phil. 1: 6, 'he that began a good work (ἔργον ἀγαθόν) in you will bring it to completion.' As usual he prays here in terms of abundance, παντὸς ἀγαθοῦ.

[8] Taking εἰς as equivalent to ἐν. Blass–Debrunner–Funk, sec. 205. This is supported by Gal. 5: 6, where ἐν Χριστῷ is used.

brings us toward Christ,' or 'knowledge that brings us toward Christ,' or 'the sharing of your faith may effect (ἐνεργὴς γένηται) a union with Christ.'[1] To make a decision here seems even more problematical, and we may leave this question open without affecting the general thrust of the prayer-report, which may be stated finally as follows:

Whenever he gives thanks for Philemon's faith toward the Lord Jesus and his love toward all the saints, Paul also prays that Philemon's generous sharing which is the outcome of that faith may serve to make effective to others the knowledge of all the good that is ours in Christ and that brings us close to him. In a veiled way his prayer indicates his deep desire for the release of Onesimus to the work of the gospel, and foreshadows the difficult request that he must make of his friend and fellow Christian. Such an act of sharing in love would, he believes, be truly responsible to the faith of the gospel and to the new, corporate life in Christ.

Once again a Pauline thanksgiving has been used to prepare for the general theme and mood of the letter, while the prayer-report within it announces, however cryptically, the immediate occasion and purpose of his writing. Furthermore, the prayers point to the deeper and larger context of the new life in Christ, where apostle and believers are united in loving concern for one another before God. As the letter is read by Philemon and the church in his house, the prayers of thanksgiving and supplication will be made a part of their own worship. They will join with the apostle in praying for themselves, for Paul, for the work of the gospel, and for a right decision in their responsible treatment of the returning Onesimus, no longer a slave but a brother beloved, 'both as man and as Christian.'

[1] Cf. Bultmann, *TWNT*, I, 707, 'was...zur Verbindung mit Christus dienen muss.'

'Toward Christ' would then substitute for the usual eschatological climax, which otherwise is lacking in this thanksgiving. See above, p. 158.

A PRAYER-REPORT SURROGATE –
II CORINTHIANS 1: 7[1]

The last example[2] of an intercessory passage within the opening section of a Pauline letter is a borderline case, a declaration of hope that may be considered briefly as a surrogate for a prayer-report:

Our hope for you is unshaken; for we know that as you share in our sufferings, you will also share in our comfort. (II Cor. 1: 7)

This declaration occurs early in the first portion of II Corinthians, where (as we shall note more fully later) Paul is acknowledging with extreme relief the healing of a critical rupture between himself and the Corinthians, and writing a profoundly thankful and personal letter that will bind the readers still more closely to himself.[3] But instead of beginning with his customary thanksgiving period, where he thanks God directly for the readers – 'We give thanks to God always for you all' – he substitutes a blessing or 'praisegiving' period:[4] Εὐλογητὸς ὁ θεός ...ὁ παρακαλῶν ἡμᾶς ἐπὶ πάσῃ τῇ θλίψει ἡμῶν... (1: 3–11).[5] In this warmly personal letter he prefers to bless God, first for the comfort[6] given to himself in the midst of his own affliction,

[1] Because this declaration cannot be assumed (except by implication) to refer to intercessory prayer, it will be given only minor emphasis. Our introduction to the background, purpose, and structure of II Cor. will then follow more conveniently in the next chapter when we introduce the two important prayer-reports in the body of II Cor.

[2] The intercessory portion of the thanksgiving period in I Cor. (1: 8f.) was examined earlier as a possible wish-prayer; above, pp. 97ff.

[3] Viz., II Cor. 1–9; see below, pp. 233f.

[4] See Schubert, pp. 46ff. For the OT and Jewish background (e.g., Ps. 40: 14, LXX; Tobit 3: 11, 8: 5, 13: 1; and the synagogue liturgy), see H. Windisch, *Der zweite Korintherbrief*, 9th edn (Göttingen, 1924), p. 36. Cf. above, p. 161.

[5] Windisch (*ibid.*) sees the praisegiving period extending to v. 11. Vv. 3–7 speak in general terms of the relief and comfort which apostle and readers share; vv. 8–11 move to a more precise reference about the rescue of the apostle from deadly peril, and end with an 'inverted thanksgiving'; Sanders, 'Transition from Opening Thanksgiving,' p. 360, following Schubert. See below, p. 271, n. 4.

[6] παράκλησις, see above, p. 80, n. 6. The word, used 10 times in this short passage, expresses the mood of relief after anxiety and suffering, that will mark the letter.

and only then for what God may do through him for the readers, as they participate with him in his experience. It is within this praisegiving that our declaration passage must be interpreted.

Although Paul begins by blessing God for giving him comfort in great distress (v. 4), he goes on to emphasize that both his distress and his comfort are to enable him to bring comfort to other sufferers, and now especially to the Corinthians (vv. 4–6). Indeed that is why he shares in the sufferings of Christ and the comfort of Christ[1] (v. 5). They themselves must now be full partners with him in all his sufferings and comfort (v. 6).

By this unusual reversion from a thanksgiving to a praise-giving period,[2] which is concerned first with Paul himself and then with the readers through himself, he has clearly set the tone of the whole succeeding letter of thankful reconciliation (chaps. 1–9).[3] In all that follows he will be concerned to strengthen the close bonds between himself and the readers: to re-establish the vicarious relation of apostle to congregation, and also their mutual interdependence (e.g., 4: 11–15, 5: 13, 6: 11–13, 7: 2–16). Furthermore, the theme of suffering and comfort, shared inseparably by apostle and people, will never be far away from his thoughts, especially in his profound medi-tation on the inner nature of his apostolic ministry (2: 12 – 6: 10).[4]

[1] For Paul's sense of vicarious suffering on behalf of his churches, cf. Phil. 3: 10 [Col. 1: 24f.]. To decide exactly in what sense he regards his sharing in Christ's sufferings would open up a vast inquiry. See K. H. Schelkle, *Jüngerschaft und Apostelamt*, and the commentaries *ad loc.*

[2] Cf. Sanders, 'Transition from Opening Thanksgiving,' p. 360, n. 15, 'Paul has reverted to the *beracha* where he usually has a *hodaya* at the opening of a letter, evidently finding it a better opening for the following discourse on παράκλησις.' Cf. Schubert, p. 50. In another kind of situation, when he was writing in a mood of reprimand to the Galatians, Paul had substituted a doxology that would avoid all reference to the readers; see above, p. 125. [Praisegiving passages are found also in Eph. 1: 3–14 and I Pet. 1: 3ff.]

[3] Contrast the thanksgiving in Phil., where he may take the long-standing partnership of the readers for granted. Thus although he wishes to tell the Philippians much about his own situation, he begins with his usual thanks-giving for them. See above, pp. 203ff.

[4] E.g., 1: 8–11, 4: 7–11, 6: 4–10, 7: 4–7, 13. For the closely related theme of strength in weakness, treated in his previous letter (the 'severe letter'), see below, pp. 241f., 246.

Although this praisegiving passage contains no direct prayer-report,[1] however, it does offer the surrogate which we are studying, in the form of a declaration of hope for them (v. 7). That Paul here means hopeful prayers, may be suggested a few lines later on, when he speaks of his hope that God will deliver him: 'On him we have set our hope that he will deliver us again, You *also* must help us by prayer...' (vv. 10b, 11).[2] He uses this declaration to emphasize very succinctly the paraenetic message of his letter[3] – that in spite of all that has recently passed, he still looks forward with undiminished expectation to the growth of their renewed obedience to the gospel: 'Our hope for you is unshaken' (βεβαία).[4] He bases this hope in his conviction that as they continue their renewed partnership with him,[5] sharing with him in the sufferings of the Christian gospel, they will share also in the strengthening comfort (παράκλησις) that God will give to him and to them: 'for we know[6] that as you are partners in our sufferings, you will also be partners in our comfort.' Thus he makes clear at the outset the strength of his prayerful confidence about them[7] in a new period of intimate co-operation with himself.

By placing his prayerful hopes for their close partnership within the context of a praisegiving hymn,[8] he is preparing the

---

[1] In his previous letter he has described the main burden of his and his companions' prayers for them at the time of the recent crisis – II Cor. 13: 7, 9. See below, pp. 244ff.

[2] See Windisch, *Zweite Korintherbrief*, p. 49. As he prays, so *also* (καί), they must pray.

[3] As we have seen with nearly all the prayer-reports thus far.

[4] In the corresponding intercessory declaration in the thanksgiving of I Cor. he had used the word βεβαιώσει: 'who will sustain you (keep you unshaken) to the end...' (I Cor. 1: 8f.). This may suggest an eschatological reference also behind our present passage. His hopes for the final well-being of the Corinthians at the day of Christ are *still* unshaken by all that has transpired, for God is faithful. See above, p. 100.

[5] In his recent letter (the 'severe letter') he had challenged them to test themselves and choose again his way of power through weakness; II Cor. 13: 4–6. See below, pp. 243ff.

[6] For similar variations between hope and certainty (e.g. 'I know,' 'it is my eager expectation and hope,' Phil. 1: 19f.), see above, p. 170, n. 3.

[7] Cf. 1: 21f., 4: 1, 15–18, 5: 6f., 7: 16, 8: 24, 9: 11–13.

[8] Windisch claims that Paul's use of liturgical forms such as the blessing hymn shows that he regards his letter-writing as a cultic act; *Zweite Korintherbrief*, p. 36.

ground to ask that they too respond in their worship by supplications for him (v. 11),[1] and also by joining in the cultic
activity of the collection (chaps. 8 and 9).[2] Not only would the
collection assist his larger plans, but it would lead to a widening
of the circle of thanksgivings and intercessions (9: 11–15).[3]
Although in this blessing period Paul has changed the usual
format of his intercessory prayer passage, he would be understood clearly by the readers to have placed his message to them
within the framework of shared praises and intercessions, his
and theirs (v. 11).

In conclusion, our study of the surprisingly varied prayer-
reports in the thanksgiving periods of I Thessalonians, Romans,
Philippians, Philemon, and the borderline examples in I and
II Corinthians, has shown them to fulfil no merely conventional function. Each announces either the central message or
the precise occasion of the letter, and anticipates its main
paraenetic thrust.[4] Each illuminates in its own special way not
only Paul's mediatorial sense of the significance of his own
intercessory prayers, but also his urgent desire to remind the
churches of his prayers for them, and enlist them with himself
in the same cultic service. All believers must be drawn into the
one great underlying fellowship of loving concern 'in Christ.'

[1] See below, pp. 271ff.   [2] See below, p. 249.
[3] See below, pp. 251f.
[4] This is only very generally true in I Cor.

CHAPTER 9

FUNCTION OF THE PRAYER-REPORTS
IN THE BODY OF THE LETTERS

Having examined the prayer-reports that form an integral part
of Paul's thanksgiving periods, we must consider the functional
significance of some less formal prayer-reports – two in the body
of II Corinthians and two in Romans.[1]

TWO PRAYER-REPORTS IN THE BODY OF
II CORINTHIANS – 9: 14; 13: 7, 9b

We begin with the two that occur near the end and in the middle
of II Corinthians:

But we pray God that you may not do wrong – not that we may appear to have
met the test, but that you may do what is right, though we may seem to have
failed.... What we pray for is your improvement. (13: 7, 9b)

while they long for you and pray for you, because of the surpassing grace of
God in you.
(Thanks be to God for his inexpressible gift!) (9: 14f.)

As we try to place these prayer-reports within their original
epistolary context, we are confronted by some of the more
tangled problems in Pauline studies. By comparison with the
first letter to the Corinthians, the second is a passionately
written and uneven document, loosely organized, with breaks
of sequence and apparent contradictions of mood and sense.
Its generally fragmented structure is reflected in the scarcity
of the intercessory prayer passages and their seemingly disconnected character. Thus to understand their real significance,
we must come to some conclusions about the composition of the
letter and the circumstances behind the various segments.

The background of II Corinthians may be provisionally

[1] See Appendix III, p. 300. In addition we have already considered a
borderline intercessory prayer-report, I Cor. 5: 3, as part of a curse injunction. See above, p. 145, n. 3.

reconstructed in general outline because of the circumstantial and informative nature of the letter.[1] It is clear that a serious rebellion against Paul's authority had come to a head after the sending of I Corinthians,[2] an attempt to impugn his motives and undermine both his leadership and his doctrine. That the trouble had reached a critical level is shown by the extremity of his anxiety [1: 8ff., 2: 12f. (cf. 4: 8–16), 7: 5ff.], and the impetuosity of his reaction (chaps. 10–13).

The revolt had evidently been sparked by the arrival of a group of interlopers who found a ready following among the already discontented members of the congregation.[3] Certain outstanding members of the church must have taken a specially hurtful rôle in the rebellion (2: 1, 5, 7: 12); others were still persisting in moral laxity (12: 21, 13: 2) in spite of Paul's strong earlier warnings in I Corinthians. The blatant challenge to the apostle had suddenly grown to an extent that posed a threat to the very existence of his work.

Exactly who the intruders were (οἱ ὑπερλίαν ἀπόστολοι, 11: 5, 12: 11, and ψευδαπόστολοι, 11: 13), whether one group or two, and how related to the earlier gnosticizing opposition in the church, remains undecided.[4] But for our purpose the

[1] Yet the information is quite deceptive: many scholars hold the general view which we shall develop, others interpret the evidence in different ways. For surveys of the debate see Feine–Behm–Kümmel, pp. 206–11, and the authorities cited on p. 205; Rigaux, *Saint Paul et ses lettres*, pp. 154ff.; more recently, A. M. G. Stephenson, 'A Defence of the Integrity of 2 Corinthians,' in *The Authorship and Integrity of the New Testament*, S.P.C.K. Theological Collections, 4 (London, 1965), 82–97; J. L. Price, 'Aspects of Paul's Theology and their Bearing on Literary Problems of Second Corinthians,' in *Studies in the History and Text of the New Testament, Studies and Documents*, 29 (Salt Lake City, 1967), 95–106.

[2] Even while writing I Cor., Paul had been aware of a center of opposition among the Corinthians. See above, pp. 139f.

[3] The forthright answers given by Paul on a variety of questions in I Cor., and the severe judgment against the sexual offender, would have caused grave offense among many. See above, pp. 135ff.

[4] For the extensive debate about the identity of Paul's antagonists, see above, p. 48, n. 3; also p. 138, n. 4, regarding the earlier opponents at Corinth. No consensus has been reached about those mentioned in II Cor. as to whether they were one or more groups, whether Judaizers, Gnostics, acknowledged or unacknowledged representatives of the Jerusalem leaders, or θεῖοι ἄνδρες. For literature, see Feine–Behm–Kümmel, pp. 205, 209;

most important question is how Paul himself conceived these opponents. From his point of view they were intruders into his territory (10: 13–16), arrogantly taking advantage of the Corinthians (11: 20). They were confident in their Jewish ancestry (11: 22)[1] and in their Christian status (10: 7, 11: 23);[2] they carried letters of recommendation (3: 1) and asserted themselves as superior apostles (11: 5, 12: 11). Yet he saw them to be actually false and deceitful (11: 13), interested in financial gain (2: 17, 11: 12, 20), and in human position (5: 12), boastful in commending themselves and comparing themselves with others to their own advantage (10: 12).

The general teaching of these newcomers was evidently not the immediate point at issue. Paul's immediate concern was with their view of apostleship and their stinging attacks upon his own legitimacy as apostle.[3] Their relentless accusations are all too well documented: he is accused amongst other things of not being a properly accredited apostle (3: 1, 4: 2); bold at a distance, but humble in personal confrontation (10: 1, 10f.); weak in his attainments (4: 7ff., 12: 5–10, 13: 4) and lacking in

D. Georgi, *Die Gegner des Paulus im 2. Korintherbrief* (Neukirchen-Vluyn), 1964, pp. 7–16.

Barrett proposes that while the opponents (at least two groups) were Jews, it was 'the Corinthians [who], confronted by these rival apostolates, proceeded to compare and to judge between them on essentially hellenistic grounds.' 'Paul's Opponents in II Corinthians,' *NTS*, 17 (1970–1), 251.

Without entering into this debate, we may agree with the judicious summary of W. Marxsen, 'The apostle again finds in his opponents Gnostic ideas (the emphasis on "sufficiency") and Jewish ideas (the appeal to Moses); he no doubt saw them therefore once again as Jewish Christians with a Gnostic flavour, similar to those we have already met in Gal., Phil. and I Cor.,' *Introduction to the New Testament*, p. 83.

[1] For an emphasis on their Judaizing aspect, see D. W. Oostendorp, *Another Jesus: A Gospel of Jewish–Christian Superiority in II Corinthians* (Kampen, 1967).

[2] Not, however, that they regarded themselves as θεῖοι ἄνδρες in the strict sense argued by D. Georgi, pp. 220–34; see G. Friedrich's criticism, 'Die Gegner des Paulus im 2. Korintherbrief,' in *Abraham unser Vater, Festschrift für Otto Michel*, ed. O. Betz, M. Hengel, P. Schmidt (Leiden, 1963), p. 196.

[3] Contrast Gal., where although he hotly defends his apostleship, he devotes most of the letter to refuting his opponents' 'other gospel.' Yet at Corinth, too, the opponents' view of apostleship must have stemmed from their understanding of the gospel (II Cor. 11: 4). See Barrett, 'Paul's Opponents,' pp. 240ff.

authority (10: 8, 13: 10); vacillating in his decisions (1: 17ff.) and unclear in his pronouncements (1: 13f., 4: 3). He is one who tries cunningly and indirectly to make financial gain from the gospel (7: 2, 12: 16–18). In every way he is inferior – in speech (10: 10, 11: 6), in background (11: 22), in labors for the gospel (11: 23ff.) and in spiritual experience (12: 1–13).

By their boastful claims to superiority they compelled him eventually to answer in the same terms. By way of reply he boasts of his own achievements, but at the cost of emotional embarrassment that erupts frequently throughout the letter (1: 12, 3: 1ff., 10: 8, 13–18, 11: 1, 10–12, 16–33, 12: 1–13). Besides defending his apostolic accomplishments and his words and actions in the recent crisis, he concentrates upon a profound explanation of the inner motives of his apostleship in contradistinction to theirs (2: 14 – 6: 10). It is clear that the central issue of the letter was between two 'competing views of the apostleship'[1] and how to judge between them.

Before such a devastating attack he acted drastically and promptly. He made an emergency visit to Corinth that[2] failed miserably (2: 1–11, 12: 14, 13: 1f.). Returning to Ephesus he composed a rigorous letter,[3] written 'out of much affliction and anguish of heart and with many tears' (2: 3f., 9, 7: 8–12), and sent with his experienced companion Titus (2: 13, 7: 6). As he waited apprehensively for an answer his foreboding was almost more than he could endure (1: 8–10,[4] 2: 12f., 7: 5). At last Titus came, bringing news even better than Paul could have hoped for (7: 6–16). The situation at Corinth had been completely reversed, the Corinthians' attitude to Paul had changed from open rebellion to longing, zealous support, and repentant sorrow for all the hurt they had caused him.

It was on the receipt of this news that Paul penned a joyful message of reconciliation and thankfulness (chaps. 1–9)[5] that

[1] Ward, 'The Opponents of Paul,' p. 190.

[2] He speaks of this as the second visit (13: 2, cf. 2: 1), and says that his next visit would be the third (12: 14, 13: 1).

[3] Apparently the 'severe letter,' II Cor. 10–13; see below, pp. 234f.

[4] Assuming that 'the affliction experienced in Asia' included his fears about Corinth.

[5] Assuming for the moment that chaps. 1–9 are a separate letter; see below, pp. 234ff.

forms the first part of our present II Corinthians. His sense of relief is given lyrical expression as he blesses God for his deliverance and comfort (e.g., 1: 3–11), confirms appreciatively the changed relationship between Corinth and himself (e.g., 1: 7, 24, 7: 7ff.), acknowledges their re-acceptance of his apostolic authority (7: 7, 11, 15), and invites their concerned prayers on his behalf (1: 11). At the same time he is careful to explain some doubtful matters that might still lead to misunderstanding (1: 15ff., 2: 1–11, 7: 8–12).[1] Above all, he defends the inner nature of his apostolic ministry against the views of the intruders (2: 14 – 6: 10). Furthermore, he now feels free to take up again the delayed matter of the collection for the saints in Jerusalem (chaps. 8–9).[2] So he sends this letter back to Corinth with Titus and two companions who may prepare the way for his own coming (8: 6, 16–24).

But what, then, are we to make of the harsh concluding section of an epistle that for two thirds of its length has breathed such joy and thankful reconciliation? Can the last four chapters (10–13) be thought appropriate in the light of all that has just transpired between the apostle and the embattled, but now at last repentant, congregation? Here we arrive at the inescapable question of the integrity of the letter into which we must place our intercessory prayer passages.[3]

The present epistle breaks down roughly into three main sections: chapters 1–7, the thankful section of reconciliation; chapters 8–9, regarding the collection; and chapters 10–13, the vehement warning and counterattack against the super-apostles. Within these larger divisions occur several other breaks that suggest shorter fragments: Paul's long defense of the Christian ministry (2: 14 – 7: 4) interrupts the previous train of thought and contains within it a still shorter unrelated fragment (6: 14 – 7: 1); chapter 9 may look like an unnecessary repetition of Paul's collection appeal, already adequately stated

---

[1] These 'explanations' are better understood as the later clearing-up of misunderstandings than as similar to his vehement defence in chaps. 10–13. For a contrary view, see Price, p. 100.

[2] See below, pp. 248ff.

[3] For the principal literature, see studies cited in G. Bornkamm, 'The History of the Origin of the So-called Second Letter to the Corinthians,' pp. 258–64; see also Rigaux, *Saint Paul et ses Lettres*, p. 155, n. 5; Stephenson, Price.

in the previous chapter 8. Because of such difficulties scholarly opinion has ranged all the way from regarding II Corinthians as an editorial compilation of four or five fragments,[1] to the conviction that in spite of all appearances it was originally composed as one letter, perhaps over a period of several weeks.[2] On this latter view the sudden changes of mood and subject matter might arise from the rapidly changing circumstances of the crisis, and the intervals of time between the composing of the various sections. For our limited purpose, however, the significant breaks are that which divides chapters 1–9 from 10–13, and that between chapters 8 and 9.

First we must decide whether chapters 10–13 (containing the prayer-report, 13: 7 and 9b) represent a separate composition, perhaps a part of the intermediate 'painful letter' to which Paul refers in 2: 3f. In sum, it appears to us that the extra-ordinary change from the joy and gratitude of chapters 1–9 to the unparalleled vehemence and severity of chapters 10–13 must outweigh all other considerations. In spite of the sur-prising changes of mood in Paul's other letters, it seems im-possible that he could have allowed himself to pen such a sustained reprimand at the very time when the rift was finally on the way to complete healing, and a request was being made again for their co-operation through the collection and their prayers on his behalf. Therefore this section (which is in-dubitably Pauline) must have been written to Corinth at a time when the conflict was still raging, and was presumably a part of that earlier painful letter.[3] It is within the context of this 'severe letter,' then, that the second prayer-report (13: 7, 9b) may best be interpreted.

[1] E.g., J. Weiss, *The History of Primitive Christianity*, E.Tr. (New York, 1959), pp. 365f.; J. T. Dean, *Saint Paul and Corinth* (London, 1947), pp. 40–94; Bornkamm, 'The So-called Second Letter.'

[2] See, e.g., P. Bachmann, *Der zweite Brief des Paulus an die Korinther* (Leipzig, 1909); H. Lietzmann, *An die Korinther I – II, HzNT*, 9, 4th edn (Tübingen, 1949), p. 139; E.-B. Allo, *Saint Paul Seconde Epître aux Corinthiens*, 10th edn (Paris, 1956); J. Munck, *Paul and the Salvation of Mankind*, p. 171.

[3] In spite of Paul's custom of including a sharp warning at the latter part of his other epistles, it can hardly be thought that this extended attack fulfilled that function in his original letter. Bornkamm ('The So-called Second Letter,' pp. 261f.) thinks that it was the redactor who later chose to place the passage at the end of the letter in order to comply with this custom

Second, we are concerned to know whether the other prayer-report in the body of II Corinthians (9: 14) belongs to a separate 'collection letter' (viz., chaps. 8f., or perhaps chap. 9 alone), or to the whole preceding letter. There is no prima facie reason to think that the collection appeal should not have formed an integral part of the preceding letter of thankfulness and reconciliation. Indeed, the resumption of this interrupted project by Paul at this moment of restored relations, would serve precisely as a tangible sign of that reconciliation and mutual trust which the letter was intended to celebrate and foster.[1]

With regard to the relation between chapters 8 and 9, various theories have held the field. Some see the collection appeal in chapter 9 as an unnecessary addition to the already adequate appeal in chapter 8,[2] and part of a separate letter sent on a

(see above, p. 67, n. 3). However, Bahr, following suggestions of A. Deissmann and H. A. W. Meyer, believes that chaps. 10–13 belonged with chaps. 1–9, constituting the autograph subscription that began at 10: 1 (Αὐτὸς δὲ ἐγὼ Παῦλος); 'Subscriptions in Pauline Letters,' p. 37; see above, p. 43, n. 1. A. H. McNeile suggests that chaps. 1–9 were sent to the repentant majority, and chaps. 10–13 (as part of the same letter) were addressed to the still rebellious minority, *An Introduction to the Study of the New Testament*, 2nd rev. edn (Oxford, 1953), pp. 140f.

For a summary of the arguments opposing separation of chaps. 10–13, see Feine–Behm–Kümmel, pp. 212f., Stephenson, Price; for the arguments in favor of the partition, see Feine–Behm–Kümmel, *ibid.*, also R. H. Strachan, *The Second Epistle of Paul to the Corinthians*, MNTC (New York, 1935), pp. xvi–xxii, following J. H. Kennedy, *The Second and Third Epistles of St. Paul to the Corinthians* (London, 1900).

As to the chronological placing of this separate letter fragment, two main theories have been proposed: M. Krenkel, *Beiträge Zur Aufhellung der Geschichte und der Briefe des Apostels Paulus* (Brunswick, 1890), followed by several others, proposed it as a fifth epistle, occasioned by a recurrence of the crisis at Corinth; cf. L. P. Pherigo, 'Paul and the Corinthian Church,' *JBL*, 68 (1949), 341–50. But the apostle's plans as revealed in Rom., which was written shortly afterwards at Corinth itself, seem to preclude that possibility. Our view, proposed by A. Hausrath, *Der Vierkapitelbrief des Paulus an die Korinther* (Heidelberg, 1870), and followed by a large number of commentators (see Feine–Behm–Kümmel, p. 212), places chaps. 10–13 before chaps. 1–9. While not without difficulties, this seems to be the more likely explanation.

[1] See below, pp. 248ff.

[2] J. S. Semler in 1776 had regarded chap. 9 as a doublet of chap. 8; see Rigaux, *Saint Paul et ses Lettres*, p. 155. The two chapters are thought to display

different occasion to Achaia.[1] Others rightly point out that chapter 9 does supplement chapter 8 in a recognizable way. As Moffatt wrote, 'In 9: 1 Paul is really explaining why he needs to say no more than he has said in 8: 24. Instead of being inconsistent with what precedes, 9: 1 clinches it.'[2] That Paul continues his appeal beyond chapter 9 may stem also from the embarrassment which he constantly showed about gifts.[3] The somewhat rambling nature of his discussion[4] may demonstrate this, especially in view of the reflections that had been cast on the financial integrity of himself and Titus (12: 14–18). We shall therefore assume that chapters 8 and 9 formed Paul's original appeal and part of the letter of reconciliation (chaps. 1–9).[5] It is within that letter as a whole that the prayer-report (9: 14) must be interpreted, while, of course, its more immediate context was the collection appeal itself (chaps. 8–9).

So much for the tense and rapidly changing conflict that lay behind II Corinthians. We may now attempt to view the scattered intercessory prayer passages within the context of the two contrasting letters that arose from that situation.

inconsistencies, e.g., the first holding the Macedonians up as an example, the second praising the Corinthians. See also Dean, pp. 92–4, 'There is a note of anxiety and urgency in Chapter 9 which is absent from Chapter 8.'

[1] Cf. J. Héring, *La Seconde Épitre de Saint Paul aux Corinthiens* (Neuchâtel, 1958), pp. 12f. Bornkamm, 'The So-called Second Letter,' pp. 260f.

[2] J. Moffatt, *Introduction to the Literature of the New Testament* (New York, 1914), p. 128. All who view the whole letter as a unity make some such explanation of the relation between these two chapters.

[3] Cf. above, p. 103, n. 2. Moffatt, *ibid.*

[4] E.g., the laborious references to the three deputies in 8: 16–24, taken up again in 9: 3–5. Cf. Funk's analysis of the two passages as separate examples of the 'apostolic parousia form,' 'The apostolic "*Parousia*",' p. 254.

[5] We take chaps. 1–7 as originally undivided, with Kennedy, Strachan, Manson, *et al.* (and with those who regard II Cor. as an original whole, see above, p. 235, n. 2). Manson considers 2: 14 – 7: 4 as a long excursus 'where the profound exposition of the ministry of reconciliation is set in the framework of a detailed exposition of Paul's former plans' ('The Corinthian Correspondence,' p. 11 and n. 1).

*Survey of the intercessory prayer and related prayer
passages in II Corinthians*[1]

The severe letter – chapters 10–13

We begin with the three prayer passages in the severe letter, on
the assumption that it was written first (12: 7–9, 13: 7, 9b,
13: 14). As an incomplete fragment it lacks the usual introductory grace blessing, thanksgiving period, and assurances of
Paul's constant prayers for the readers. More significantly, it is
completely wanting in any interspersed notes of thankfulness
and praise.[2]

The first prayer passage in this letter of 'strength in weakness' is an appropriate but unusual reference to his own prayers
for himself (12: 7–9). In the course of answering his detractors
he is boasting of his own 'visions and revelations.' Then he tells
by contrast of the weakness sent to him and of his repeated
prayers that this 'thorn in the flesh' might be removed: 'Three
times I besought the Lord about this, that it should leave me;
but he said to me, "My grace is sufficient for you, for my power
is made perfect in weakness"' (12: 8f.).[3]

The second prayer passage occurs at the end of his protracted
reprimands and warnings, and within the closing liturgically
oriented section (13: 5–14). Here the concluding admonitions,
'Examine yourselves...Test yourselves...' (vv. 5f.), lead into
an intercessory prayer phrased as a prayer-report, 'But we
pray God that you may do no wrong – not that we may appear to
have met the test....What we pray for is your improvement'
(vv. 7, 9b).

The third prayer passage is the unexpectedly full trinitarian
blessing at the close of the letter (13: 14).[4] It is preceded by a

---

[1] For supplication passages, see Appendix II. See F. V. Filson, *The Second
Epistle to the Corinthians, IB*, x, 274f., for a short analysis of the prayer passages
in II Cor.

[2] Except for a conventional phrase in an oath sentence, 'he who is blessed
forever,' 11: 31.

[3] As was pointed out earlier (p. 16 and n. 3), it is noteworthy that this is
the only place where Paul gives us direct insight into his private petitions
for himself. The prayers that he reports, utters, or requests in his other
epistles, all center around the well-being of the churches and the prosecution
of his missionary work.

[4] Note also the 'peace-prayer surrogate,' 13: 11b. See above, p.107, n. 2.

rapid succession of epistolary and liturgical items (vv. 11–13), but understandably without the usual request for the prayers of the readers.[1] The surprisingly irenic spirit of these closing sentences with the full benediction raises a doubt as to whether they belonged originally to the severe letter rather than to the warm thankfulness of chapters 1–9.[2] Yet we cannot exclude the probability that Paul had prefaced the severe letter with some positive instructions and words of encouragement. In any case he would have in mind his supporters as well as his detractors in the divided congregation.[3] On balance, therefore, we may decide to include these closing verses 13: 11–14 with the severe letter and regard them as a natural attempt by Paul to end his denunciation with words of loving concern.[4]

The thankful letter – chapters 1–9

By comparison with the scarcity of prayer passages in the severe letter, there are in the thankful letter many more references to petition, praise, and especially to thanksgiving. Although most of them are brief and somewhat disconnected, they clearly reflect the overflowing joy of this epistle of reconciliation.

The letter opens with the usual benediction of grace and peace (1: 2). This is followed by a blessing hymn (1: 3–11) that enables Paul to emphasize immediately his own apostolic experience of suffering and comfort and to include the readers with himself in this experience.[5] In the middle of the blessing

---

[1] A similar lack was observed in Gal. and I Cor. Included items are the warning (13: 5f.), the summarizing prayer in the form of a prayer-report (13: 7, 9b), peace blessing (13: 11b), holy kiss (13: 12), greetings (13: 13), grace blessing (13: 14).

Missing are the admonition to prayer, the reference to a gift, the request for prayer. [2] Strachan, p. 145; cf. Dean, p. 59.

[3] Cf. McNeile's proposal of the majority and minority factions, above, p. 235, n. 3. We may compare the healing touch at the end of Gal. (above, p. 126), and I Cor. (above, p. 153, n. 4).

[4] A. Plummer argues strongly for this: *The Second Epistle of St Paul to the Corinthians*, ICC (Edinburgh, 1915), pp. xxviif. He claims it is easier to understand chaps. 1–9 (minus the ending) being added to chaps. 10–13 (minus the beginning), rather than 'the insertion of a large fragment of one letter into a break near the conclusion of another letter.' Cf. his reference to a similar joining of fragments 'in the case of other documents belonging to primitive Christian literature' (p. 385).

[5] See above, pp. 226ff., below, p. 272.

hymn he introduces a statement of hope that the readers may share in his suffering and comfort (1: 7). This sentence takes the place of the usual assurances of his prayers and focuses the main purpose of the letter. Turning to an account of his own deadly peril in Asia, he leads up to an appeal for his readers' prayers on his behalf (1: 11). At the same time he introduces his aim that thanksgivings may be multiplied from many believers and due honor may be given to God. That this was a theme of importance for Paul will be shown by his returning to it at 4: 15 and 9: 11–15.

In the body of the letter the note of praise and thanksgiving is sounded again several times. First there appears a triumphant doxology, 'That is why we utter the Amen through him, to the glory of God' (1: 20b). In these resonant words of worship Paul sums up his defense against his opponents' charges of fickleness in his travel plans (1: 15ff.). Shortly thereafter, as he moves into the extended defense of his paradoxical apostleship of life and death, he breaks out into a cry of thanksgiving for the triumph that crowns his apostolic work everywhere in spite of all his difficulties (2: 14). A little further on he refers again to his purpose that thanksgivings to God might be multiplied (4: 15).

When he takes up his plea for the collection (chaps. 8 and 9), he gives thanks that Titus shares his own concern for the Corinthians (8: 16). Finally he brings the theme of thanksgivings to a climax (9: 6–15): The generosity of the Corinthians will overflow in many thanksgivings to God (vv. 11f.). Many will glorify God because of this liberal demonstration of their obedience to the gospel (v. 13). At this point (v. 14) Paul adds to the theme of thanksgiving that of intercessory supplication:[1] the gratitude of the Jerusalem beneficiaries will be expressed in intercessory prayers as they remember the richness of God's grace to the Corinthians. So he foresees a triumphant exchange of gifts, thanksgivings, and intercessions, all to the glory of God. With this in mind, he himself gives thanks (v. 15).

To bring this thankful letter to completion, we may conjecture a liturgical passage of wish-prayers, blessings and greetings very much like 13: 11–14.[2] So the prayer passages have

[1] See above, p. 166.

[2] Nevertheless, we decided that these verses seemed to belong with the severe letter; see above, p. 239.

underlined some of the main themes of the letter: the increase of thanksgivings and honor to God, the sufferings and comfort shared by apostle and church members, his renewed hopefulness for them, and the network of intercessory concern between the apostle, his readers, and even the saints at Jerusalem.

II Corinthians 13: 7, 9b

We move on now for a closer look at the prayer-report in its place near the end of the severe letter (chaps. 10–13):[1]

But we pray God that you may not do wrong – not that we may appear to have met the test, but that you may do what is right, though we may seem to have failed. (v. 7)

(For we cannot do anything against the truth, but only for the truth. For we are glad when we are weak and you are strong.) (vv. 8 and 9a)[2]

What we pray for is your improvement. (v. 9b)   (II Cor. 13: 7 and 9b)

The location of these sentences in the liturgically oriented closing section (13: 5–14) suggests that Paul is here again focusing the main thrust of an epistle.[3] Throughout the letter he has been urging the readers to make a right decision between two competing views of apostleship – between the ψευδαπό-στολοι or ὑπερλίαν ἀπόστολοι and himself. The attacks upon his authenticity have found an all too ready welcome among the Corinthians and Paul has been compelled to answer them.[4] In particular he has argued for a different set of criteria for judging the issue. He has defended the hidden nature of his ministry – its signs of apparent impotence instead of demonstrations of triumphal power.[5] The Christian life, as he had often pointed out, must be lived in afflictions and abasement.

---

[1] Treating this before the prayer-report in II Cor. 9: 14, as having been written earlier.   [2] Context added in parentheses.

[3] Cf. the function of the similarly located wish-prayers in I Thess. 5: 23f., Rom. 15: 5, 13, Phil. 4: 19, also Gal. 6: 16 and I Cor. 16: 22.

[4] See above, p. 233.

[5] Already in I Cor. he had warned them against arrogance (see above, p. 139, n. 2), and described his own apostolic life of renunciation, chap. 9. In his letter of reconciliation he will go on to expound this aspect of his apostleship more fully (II Cor. 2: 14 – 6: 10). For important sidelights on this dual aspect of Paul's apostolic authority, see Käsemann, *Die Legitimität des Apostels*.

But its weakness is deceptive – witness not only his ceaseless labors for the gospel (11: 23–33), but also his visions and revelations (12: 1–6). Only in human weakness can the power of God be made effective (12: 7–10). Let the readers not think his lack of skill in speech has placed him beneath the 'superlative apostles' (11: 5f.), nor that his sharing in the weakness of the crucified Christ will preclude him from Christ's living power when he comes to confront them on his next visit (13: 3f.). Linked with his view of strength in weakness is his sense of the vicarious nature of his ministry. As Christ has suffered in meekness and gentleness (10: 1) to bring salvation, so his own weakness must be the occasion of the Corinthians' strength, his suffering the vehicle of their comfort (12: 15; cf. 11: 7–21).[1]

Yet power in weakness had proved as opaque a riddle to the opponents as it had to the earlier gnosticizing group at Corinth. These false apostles were themselves claiming to demonstrate overt and obvious signs of apostolic power;[2] they demanded the same from him if he were to be regarded a genuine apostle. Paul's constant reply must be that he himself stood under the judgment of Christ, not that of his opponents: 'For it is not the man who commends himself that is "accepted" (δόκιμος),[3] but the man whom the Lord commends' (10: 18, cf. 12: 19).[4]

In addition, his seemingly inconsistent method of exercising apostolic authority had been tragically misunderstood (10: 1, 10f.; cf. I Cor. 1: 17, 2: 1–5). But his reluctance to discipline them, he says, had been only for their sake. His authority (ἐξουσία) had been given for building up, not destroying (10: 8, cf. 13: 10). His delay had been neither vacillation, nor cowardice, but to encourage them to put things right themselves (10: 2, 12: 19ff., 13: 10, cf. 2: 1–4). This is why he is writing instead of coming – even at the risk of further misunderstanding (10: 10f.). He begs them not to think that by postponing his visit he is abdicating his apostolic authority at Corinth (10: 13–17).

[1] He would emphasize this further in his thankful letter, II Cor. 1: 5ff., 4: 11–15, 5: 13. See above, p. 227.

[2] As indicated by Paul's counterclaims: 11: 21b, followed by 11: 22 – 12: 13. Cf. above, p. 232.   [3] See below, p. 243, n. 6.

[4] He will bring this crucial theme to a head in the prayer-report passage (13: 3ff.) and take it up again in the thankful letter, e.g., II Cor. 1: 17–22, and 4: 1–6.

Repeatedly he reminds them that he cannot delay his third visit much longer,[1] but must come again to exercise his full judicial power, if necessary, in condemning and punishing the offenders (10: 2–6, 12: 14, 13: 1–4).[2] He would prefer to give himself to them in lowly service, not accepting support from them any more than he had before (12: 14–19), but as it is, he will give them more proof (δοκιμήν) than they want or expect of the power of the risen Christ in him (13: 3f.).[3] So he begs them to change their ways now and make unnecessary any destructive action when he arrives (10: 1–11).[4]

Finally he makes one more appeal to them to reconsider before he comes (13: 5ff.): 'Do not go on merely examining *me* and putting *me* to the test,' he says in effect. 'Examine *yourselves*. Put *yourselves*[5] to the test (ἑαυτοὺς πειράζετε...ἑαυτοὺς δοκιμάζετε).[6] See whether you are holding to your faith, or whether it is *your* mode of Christian life and practice

---

[1] For Paul's stress on visiting his churches in person, see above, p. 48, n. 2. Funk regards the whole passage 12: 14 – 13: 13 as an example of the 'apostolic *parousia* form.'

[2] Regarding Paul's claim to judicial authority in relation to the Corinthians, see above, p. 145 on I Cor. 5: 2–5.

[3] Evidently his failure on the second visit (13: 2) had exposed him to the charge that he lacked real 'power to do anything decisive.' Cf. II Cor. 10: 10. Filson, *IB*, x, 417.

[4] Cf. his desire earlier to build up rather than to destroy even the gross offender, I Cor. 5: 5b; above pp. 147ff.

[5] The reflexive pronoun ἑαυτούς is heavily stressed twice by its location; see Windisch, *Der zweite Korintherbrief*, p. 420. Cf. Barrett, 'Paul's Opponents,' pp. 248f.

[6] Here Paul takes up a characteristic theme – putting to the test (δοκιμάζειν) both their own Christian life and his apostleship. He uses the word and its cognates 17 times in I and II Cor. Cf. his earlier instruction to the Corinthians in relation to the Lord's supper: 'Let a man examine himself (δοκιμάζετω) and so eat of the bread and drink of the cup' (I Cor. 11: 28); see above, p. 147. In the present passage (II Cor. 13: 1–10) he uses δοκιμάζω or cognates 6 times.

See W. Grundmann, *TWNT*, II, 258–64: Christian existence stands between received salvation and impending judgment, I Cor. 3: 13, and so must be tested in various ways. Paul himself is putting them to the test by this letter, II Cor. 2: 9. So he is particularly concerned that his apostleship be δόκιμος, accredited by God (I Cor. 9: 27), and claims that his attestation is given by the Lord, not men, II Cor. 10: 18 (cf. I Thess. 2: 4).

Now (II Cor. 13: 5ff.) he bids the readers test themselves as well as him, in relation to Jesus Christ.

(πίστις)[1] that has become distorted' (v. 5a).[2] 'Surely you will recognize that Jesus Christ is in you – that is, unless you should fail the test (ἀδόκιμοί ἐστε)' (v. 5b). 'Then I hope you will discover that *we* have not failed the test (οὐκ ἐσμὲν ἀδόκιμοι);[3] it is our type of ministry which actually meets the test, rather than that practised by our opponents' (v. 6). 'For it is our apostleship,' he implies, 'that answers to the way of the Christ who is in you, he who "was crucified in weakness, but lives by the power of God" (v. 4). Thus you will find out for yourselves, instead of through any destructive power of mine, the proof (δοκιμήν) you seek that Christ is speaking in me' (cf. v. 3).[4] It is at this point that he moves into the prayer-report (vv. 7 and 9b). His prayers are centered around the passionate hope that they make the right decision.

The prayer-report is set forth in a brief double antithesis:[5]

But we pray God that *you* may not do wrong (κακόν)[6] –
[we do] not [pray][7] that *we* may appear to have met the test (δόκιμοι),

[1] On the use of πίστις in this general sense, see above, pp. 178f.

[2] Cf. II Cor. 11: 3f.

[3] 'If however Christ is in you, this is the result of my apostolic ministry, and I must hope therefore that you will recognize that I am not ἀδόκιμος.' Barrett, 'Paul's Opponents,' p. 249. Cf. a similar criterion of testing in I Cor. 9: 1f.

[4] In his succeeding letter (II Cor. 1: 13f., 7: 12b) Paul will look back to this hope as having been partially fulfilled.

[5] The report lacks some of the features of the prayer-reports in the thanksgiving periods: the claim that his prayers are unceasing, the mention that he prays for them all, and the eschatological climax.

[6] Several interpretations are possible: (1) the subject of ποιῆσαι is God, and there is a double object, ὑμᾶς and κακόν: 'we pray that God will not cause you harm (through my judgment on you).' (2) the subject of ποιῆσαι is Paul (we): 'we pray that we may not have to hurt you' (NEB). Here Paul prays to avoid severity when he comes, even if this deprives him of validation through the use of severe power. (3) you, ὑμᾶς, is the subject, with a single object, κακόν: 'we pray that you may not do wrong' (RSV). This would be a prayer that they make the right decision, even though this will deprive him of validation through the use of severe power.

The third interpretation is preferable because it draws the clear antithesis between the parallel expressions 'that you may not do wrong' and 'that you may do what is right.' Plummer, Lietzmann, Windisch, and many others.

[7] The ambiguity of the ἵνα constructions causes some uncertainty about the demarcation of the prayer-report. See above, p. 164. The ἵνα clauses

but that *you* may do what is right (τὸ καλόν),
though *we* may seem to have failed (ἀδόκιμοι).[1] (v. 7)

With the opening disjunction, εὐχόμεθα δέ, he implies that
he is correcting a wrong impression the letter may have
given. In spite of his concentration upon the legitimacy
of his own apostleship, sustained throughout the letter and
finally summarized in the immediately preceding verse ('I
hope you will find out that we have not failed the test'), his
real concern is for the readers:[2] but what we pray for is 'that
you may not do wrong – but that you may do what is right'
(v. 7).

Next, the very sharpness of the antithesis between κακόν and
τὸ καλόν suggests the seriousness with which he views their
decision.[3] Will they continue to be seduced by the outwardly
impressive intruders (κακόν), or face his challenge to repent
(τὸ καλόν),[4] and rediscover the true meaning of Jesus Christ

may be regarded either (doubtfully) as adding an explanation about the
purpose of his prayers that they do no wrong: viz., 'the reason that we pray
in this way is not in order that (ἵνα) we may appear to have met the test
(i.e., because of our success as apostles in guiding you aright), but in order
that you may do right, whatever the result for our reputation.' Plummer,
Second Corinthians, p. 377.

Or (preferably) they may be interpreted as continuing the content
of his prayers: viz., 'and we do not pray that (οὐχ ἵνα) we may
appear...but that (ἀλλ' ἵνα) you may do what is right....' For the
interchangeability of the inf. with ἵνα after εὔχομαι and other words for
praying, see Blass–Debrunner–Funk, 392 (1,c); cf. above, Appended
Note 1, pp. 173f. For similar ambiguities in other prayer passages, see
above, p. 61, n. 1, and below, p. 269, n. 3.

[1] Italics added.
[2] H.-D. Wendland, *Die Briefe an die Korinther*, NTD, 7, 7th edn (Göttingen, 1954), p. 174.
[3] On the surface such a wish, that they do right not wrong, appears a
mere platitude. Its true character is seen only in context. Cf. K. Prumm,
*Diakonia Pneumatos. Der zweite Korintherbrief als Zugang zur apostolischen
Botschaft*, 1 (Rome, 1967), 724.
[4] τὸ καλόν involves μετάνοια, Leitzmann, *Korinther I – II*. Paul's
own later interpretation of their submission (in II Cor. 7: 8–13) serves
to illuminate his earlier prayers for them: e.g., 'I rejoice, not because
you were grieved, but because you were grieved into repentance
(μετάνοια)...what indignation, what alarm, what longing, what zeal,
what punishment!... in order that your zeal for us might be revealed to
you in the sight of God' (vv. 9–12). Cf. Manson, 'The Corinthian
Correspondence,' pp. 9f.

within them? All his grave apprehensions about sending such a drastic letter[1] are hidden in this short petition: 'we pray God that you may make the right choice.'[2]

Closely related to his petition for them is another emphasis in his prayers – renunciation, if necessary, of the validation of his own ministry. Despite his vehement protestations in defense of his apostleship, he is ready to have his apostolic status rejected, as long as they come back to the truth of the life in Christ: 'Our prayers for you are not mainly concerned that you credit us with meeting the test for true apostleship (οὐκ ἵνα ἡμεῖς δόκιμοι φανῶμεν); but that you may do what is right, whether or not we remain unattested' (ἡμεῖς δὲ ὡς ἀδόκιμοι ὦμεν).[3] In this way he underlines another all-pervasive theme of the letter: that his apostleship must be one of weakness and loss of reputation, if only thereby they may hold to the faith.[4] Indeed the only valid reason for defending his ministry would be if the Corinthians take seriously the paradoxical meaning of Christian existence. He will gladly renounce also any display of his apostolic authority, although that is what would impress his opponents (cf. 13: 2f.).[5] His supplications, like his letter, show a directly opposite spirit to that of the 'superlative apostles,' centered in a desire for quietly upbuilding the church members, rather than lording it over them.[6]

The prayer-report is now interrupted by an explanatory sentence,[7] 'For we cannot do anything against the truth, but only for the truth' (v. 9).[8] His failure to meet the test of apostle-

---

[1] See above, p. 233. In the thankful letter he will go on to stress the terrible responsibility of his office in confronting his hearers with such a decision, II Cor. 2: 15f.

[2] Cf. his profound relief at their positive response, when he writes his letter of thankfulness.

[3] He will clarify this in the following verse.

[4] See above, pp. 241f.

[5] Throughout the letter he has shown the strength of this wish, and will mention it again in v. 10. Allo, Seconde Corinthiens, p. 184.

[6] Cf. 13: 2f. Grundmann, TWNT, II, 261.

[7] Verses 8 and 9a do not belong strictly to the prayer-report, but interrupt it with a statement (οὐ γὰρ δυνάμεθα) explaining the motivations of his prayers.

[8] Apparently a general maxim adopted by Paul for this purpose. Héring, Seconde Corinthiens, p. 103. 'Fail or succeed, I cannot work against the truth but for it,' Moffatt's translation.

ship[1] is only apparent, not real. The norm of his ministry is to keep responsible to the truth of the gospel of Christ,[2] even at the expense of apparent failure. His real accreditation, then, must depend on the judgment of Christ, not on the judgment of others. Here he focuses another central theme of his defense in this letter.[3]

Now he repeats more directly the vicarious aim behind his apostleship[4] and behind his prayers: 'For we are glad when we are weak and you are strong' (v. 9a). Not only is he willing to be deprived of the opportunity to exercise his legitimate authority, but he is actually delighted whenever his weakness becomes the occasion for their strength.

This leads him back to stress once again the heart of his supplications: 'Indeed, [our] whole prayer[5] is that all may be put right with you'[6] (v. 9b, NEB). It is around their restoration that his prayers always center, no matter what the cost to himself. For then, as he continues hopefully and for the last time, he will have no need to come to them in destructive severity (v. 10).

In conclusion, this prayer passage, located in the liturgical closing section, has sharply challenged the rebellious readers to reconsider their position.[7] By revealing the heart of his troubled supplications he prepares the letter for a more effective rôle in its reading before the fellowship. Once again he is tacitly suggesting to a divided congregation that unitedly they join in his prayers for themselves.[8] At the close of an earlier

---

[1] Suggested by his somewhat ambiguous phrase, ἡμεῖς δὲ ὡς ἀδόκιμοι ὦμεν. In Rom. 9: 3, however, he seems to go further, being willing to become actually 'anathema' and cut off from Christ for the sake of his brethren. See below, pp. 256f.

[2] ἀλήθεια, truth, probably refers here primarily to true doctrine as opposed to 'a different gospel' of the opponents (11: 4). R. Bultmann, *TWNT*, I, 244.   [3] See above, p. 242.   [4] See above, *ibid.*

[5] Note the emphasis in τοῦτο καὶ εὐχόμεθα, this indeed is what we pray. Héring, *Seconde Corinthiens*, p. 102.

[6] τὴν ὑμῶν κατάρτισιν: 'setting right what has previously gone wrong,' Plummer, Allo, *et al.* Perhaps also there is included a sense of bringing to completion, Bauer–Arndt–Gingrich. Cf. his prayer-report in I Thess. 3: 10.

[7] For the paraenetic force of this prayer, cf. Furnish, p. 95.

[8] In a situation so tense, it cannot be thought that Paul had in mind any purpose of instructing his rebellious readers in the art of prayer, as he had done in a previous letter to them. See above, p. 69, etc.

letter he had sternly enjoined them to carry out his apostolic sentence against the unworthy one in their midst (I Cor. 16: 22).[1] Now, in a less peremptory but equally decisive way he urges them to respond by prayerful and united self-examination, to make a right decision between himself and the superlative apostles.

II Corinthians 9: 14

The second prayer-report in the body of II Corinthians comes at the end of that portion of the thankful letter which has been preserved in chapters 1–9:

(Under the test of this service [they][2] will glorify God [for] your obedience in acknowledging the gospel of Christ, and [for] the generosity of your contribution for them and for all others;)[3] (v. 13)

while they long for you and pray for you, because of the surpassing grace of God in you. (v. 14)

(Thanks be to God for his inexpressible gift!)[3] (v. 15)

(II Cor. 9: 13–15)

This brief prayer-report cannot be classified exactly with the others. Unlike them it refers to intercessions made not by Paul but by other Christians; instead of describing actual prayers it anticipates future ones.[4] The Christians at Jerusalem will respond to the generosity of the readers by thanksgiving, praise, and supplication. Brief and fragmentary though this reference to supplication may be, when placed in its far-reaching context it will throw considerable light on Paul's understanding of intercessory prayer.

The 'thankful letter' to which our passage belongs breathes a sense of relief and even euphoria as the apostle acknowledges the repentance of the Corinthians and their restored relations with himself.[5] He has made his explanations about points of misunderstanding between them and about the inner nature and motivation of his apostleship. The time is ripe to mention

---

[1] See above, p. 153.
[2] See below, p. 250, n. 6.
[3] Context added in parentheses.
[4] In this regard the passage may be classified also with his requests and exhortations to prayer.
[5] See above, pp. 233f.

again his most cherished project, 'the offering for the saints' (9: 1). Their contribution will serve as a sign of renewed dedication to the gospel, loyalty to himself, and interest in the wider work of his other churches.[1] Evidently he believes that such involvement will confirm and stabilize their new decision to dissociate themselves from the enticements of the pseudo-apostles.[2] So he presses the point at considerable length (chaps. 8 and 9).[3]

Towards the end of his request for their aid Paul promises the Corinthians that their contributions will reap for them a rich harvest of many blessings, including the appreciation of the saints at Jerusalem and elsewhere; above all, a glorious increase of praises to God (9: 6-15). It is this closing part of the appeal that forms the immediate context of our 'prayer-report.' The apostle seems at first to be appealing to their material self-interest, for God blesses with abundant gifts those who give freely and cheerfully (vv. 6-9).[4] Yet, as always, he goes beyond their narrow personal gain. He points to an increased ability to give still more to others, that will be part of the harvest (vv. 7-10). In a short but typically extravagant phrase, he summarizes these general promises of blessing: 'You will be enriched in every way (ἐν παντί) so that you may be completely (εἰς πᾶσαν) generous' (v. 11a).

Now in a soaring conclusion (vv. 11b-15) he unfolds his great vision of abundant possibilities that will be opened up through the collection. He has long been planning this united effort on the part of his Gentile churches, as a crowning, sacred gesture of unity and love to the Christian Church at Jerusalem (Rom. 15: 25ff.), and as an eschatological symbol that may work even

[1] See προσαναπληροῦσα (9: 12), 'filling up in addition,' or 'helping to supply.' Paul reminds them that others are contributing too. Plummer, *Second Corinthians*, p. 265. Also he suggests that their gift will be directed towards *all* Christians (9: 13).

[2] It has been suggested that the pseudo-apostles 'showed no interest in the welfare of the needy Christians of Jerusalem.' Filson, *IB*, x, 272.

[3] See above, pp. 236f. The length and variety of his appeal underlines the great importance that he attaches to the collection at this time. For a different point of view, see Nickle, *The Collection, A Study in Pauline Strategy*, pp. 16–22.

[4] Cf. Strachan's characterization of this section, 'Giving is an Investment,' p. 142.

for the conversion of the Jews (cf. Rom. 11: 13f.).[1] The first
result he stresses is an increase of thanksgivings and glory to
God (vv. 11b–13a): because of their sacrificial offering (ἡ
διακονία τῆς λειτουργίας ταύτης)[2] not only will they bring help
to the destitute saints at Jerusalem, but God will be increasingly
thanked and honored (περισσεύουσα διὰ πολλῶν εὐχαριστιῶν
τῷ θεῷ...δοξάζοντες τὸν θεόν, vv. 12f.).[3]

But of more immediate significance than this grateful response, is what the gift will prove about their faith and about
their generosity toward Christians at Jerusalem, and indeed
toward all men:[4] 'Under the test[5] of this service, [the saints][6]
will glorify God [for] your obedience in acknowledging the

---

[1] In our present passage, however, he does not point beyond the effect on
the Jewish Christians.

For the central importance of the collection in Paul's eyes, see Rom.
15: 25–8, Gal. 2: 10, I Cor. 16: 1–4, II Cor. 8–9, cf. Acts 20: 4, 24: 17. For
its significance as a costly act of Christian charity, a decisive expression
of the unity of the Church, and an eschatological symbol of the Gentiles'
conversion that might contribute to the conversion of Israel, see Nickle,
pp. 100–43.

The strategy later proved more dangerous than he now appeared to
anticipate. Windisch, however, suggests that he is even now keeping his
doubts to himself, so as not to dampen the effect of his appeal to the
Corinthians (*Zweite Korintherbrief*, p. 283). A few months later when he
wrote to Rome, his apprehensions about the success of this service to the
mother church were given open expression; see below, pp. 269f.

[2] The phrase suggests a voluntary religious or cultic offering; for διακονία
(cf. Rom. 15: 31), see Nickle, pp. 106ff.; for λειτουργία (cf. Phil. 2: 17, 30),
see above, p. 86, n. 1.

[3] For the deep significance for Paul of thanksgivings, see above, pp.
166ff. For the importance in this letter of the multiplication of thanksgivings, see above, p. 240. At the close of his collection appeal he reiterates
it in a climactic manner: 'produce thanksgiving to God...overflow in
many thanksgivings to God...they will glorify God...Thanks be to
God...!' (vv. 11–15). For the close relation of 'glorify God' and 'give
thanks to God,' see above, pp. 170f.

[4] καὶ εἰς πάντας suggests Paul's long-standing wish that the Corinthians
become fully involved with all his churches in united responsibility for one
another. Prumm, p. 544.

[5] διὰ τῆς δοκιμῆς: Paul has referred twice already to their contribution
as a proof of the genuineness of their love, 8: 8, 24. See Nickle, pp. 127ff.

[6] The nominative δοξάζοντες (an anacoluthon) may refer to the Corinthians, but preferably to the saints at Jerusalem (Plummer, Leitzmann, etc.),
or to men in general ('many,' NEB). In any case, Paul is stressing the
increase of honor that will accrue to God.

gospel of Christ,[1] and [for] the generosity of your contribution[2] for them and for all others' (v. 13). By their liberal participation, the Corinthians will give further proof of their obedient change of heart; they will demonstrate a renewed acceptance of the gospel of Christ which they confess in this practical way.

At this point Paul comes to the intercessory prayer-report (v. 14). He has reached the center of all the benefits that will flow from the Corinthians' favorable response – in particular the effect of their significant action upon the members of the mother church. It is the praise and supplications of the saints at Jerusalem that are dominant in his thought.[3] He has described their sheer gratitude – a multitude of thanksgivings to God – for such munificence toward them (vv. 11f.). And he has gone on to say that these Jewish Christians will glorify God not primarily because their wants are supplied,[4] but because of this bountiful demonstration that the Corinthians really are loyal to the gospel (v. 13). Now he points out that as they learn to appreciate that God's grace has been given in overflowing measure even to those in Greece ('because of the surpassing[5] grace of God in you,' v. 14), they will lose their suspicions[6] and develop a new bond of friendship and even longing affection for their Gentile brethren (ἐπιποθούντων ὑμᾶς, v. 14). And because of their thankful affection[7] they will join with Paul and others in offering prayers for the readers: '*while they, too,[8] long*

---

[1] Cf. Rom. 1: 5.

[2] ἁπλότητι τῆς κοινωνίας. See Nickle, pp. 104ff.

[3] Windisch, *Zweite Korintherbrief*, p. 282.

[4] See A. Schlatter, *Paulus Der Bote Jesu*, p. 610. Yet one should not minimize Paul's sense of the material aspects of the gift; see Gal. 2: 10.

[5] ὑπερβάλλουσαν is a daring word, continuing the high key of expectation in vv. 6–11, and assuming that the readers will give with utmost generosity; cf. 8: 7, 'see that you excel in this gracious work also,' Windisch, *Zweite Korintherbrief*, p. 286.

[6] Plummer, *Second Corinthians*. Yet it should be noted that Paul allows no hint of existing ill-feeling between Jewish and Christian brethren to appear in his plea. He concentrates on the blessings in store. Schlatter, p. 611.

[7] For Paul's view of the intimate relation between thanksgiving and intercessory prayer, see above, pp. 166ff.

[8] καὶ αὐτῶν reminds the readers that in addition to those who receive gifts, others and especially Paul are thinking of them with longing and praying for them; see Filson, *IB*, x, 379. Cf. his use of καί in I Thess. 5: 25, 'Brethren, pray also for us'; see below, Appended Note 2, p. 292, sec. *f*.

for you and pray for you' (v. 14).[1] Their prayers will prove a means
of deepening their good will towards the Gentiles and also a
vehicle for expressing it.[2]

Here he brings to a conclusion not only his appeal for the
collection, but also a chain of previous allusions to intercessory
prayers: in the severe letter he had assured the Corinthians of
his own prayers for them (II Cor. 13: 7, 9), and earlier in this
letter he has mentioned his own prayerful hopes for them (1: 7).
He has requested that they, too (καί), pray for himself so that
many will give thanks on his behalf (1: 11).[3] Now he anticipates
that the saints at Jerusalem, too (καί), will join in this circle of
thanksgivings and intercessions.[4]

Because the concluding portion of the thankful letter (chaps.
1–9) is missing, we can only guess how this intercessory passage
functioned in the closing liturgical pattern.[5] Such a tantaliz-
ingly short allusion to the intercessions of the saints at Jerusalem
tells us little of what Paul hoped the content of their prayers
might be. But through its closely knit context, it does offer us a
revealing glimpse into his wide-ranging hopes for a new growth
of mutual appreciation between the divided segments of the
church, to be expressed through a united exchange of gifts,[6]
mutual affection, and unceasing prayers of praise, thanks-

---

[1] The awkward construction (καὶ αὐτῶν δεήσει ὑπὲρ ὑμῶν ἐπιποθούντων
ὑμᾶς) may best be taken as a gen. absolute, linked preferably with
δοξάζοντες in the previous verse. The participial form need not imply any
de-emphasizing of the sentence, which in reality forms a climax to the
whole section. Cf. above, p. 164.

δεήσει ὑπὲρ ὑμῶν (reading υμων for ημων with most Mss), means
'together with prayers on your behalf,' perhaps also 'expressing their
longing through prayers on your behalf,' Leitzmann, *Korinther I – II, ad loc.*
See Windisch, *Zweite Korintherbrief*, p. 285. For the meaning of δέησις, see
above, pp. 19f.

[2] Cf. the way in which Paul links his own prayers for the readers with
his longing affection for them and his desire to see them: e.g., Rom. 1: 9–11,
Phil. 1: 8, I Thess. 3: 10f.

[3] See below, pp. 271ff. As the readers' prayers for Paul would lead to
more blessing and so further thanksgivings (1: 11), now their gifts will
cause more thanksgivings resulting in further prayers.

[4] Cf. Beardslee, *Human Achievement and Divine Vocation in the Message of
Paul*, p. 108.

[5] See above, pp. 240f.

[6] Rom. 15: 26f. Cf. Nickle, pp. 119ff.

giving, and intercession on behalf of one another. His hopes embraced the whole Christian fellowship, spanning even the barrier that up till now had divided his own churches from their Judaizing brethren in Palestine.[1] So moved is he by the glorious prospect, that he bursts out at the end, 'Thanks be to God for his inexpressible gift!' (9: 15).

TWO PRAYER-REPORTS IN THE BODY OF
ROMANS — 9: 3 AND 10: 1

We come now to the second two prayer-reports in the body of a Pauline letter, those in the central section of Romans. They belong together in their passionate pleading for Israel:

(I am speaking the truth in Christ, I am not lying; my conscience bears me witness in the Holy Spirit, that I have great sorrow and unceasing anguish in my heart.)[2]
For I could wish that I myself were accursed and cut off from Christ for the sake of my brethren, my kinsmen by race.
(They are Israelites. . . .) (Rom. 9: 1–4)

Brethren, my heart's desire and prayer to God for them is that they may be saved. (Rom. 10: 1)

With these two passages belongs a third that we have already considered (Rom. 11: 1–5),[3] where Paul once again identifies himself with Israel as intercessor, now after the pattern of Elijah:

I ask, then, has God rejected his people? By no means! I myself am an Israelite, a descendant of Abraham, a member of the tribe of Benjamin. God has not rejected his people whom he foreknew. Do you not know what the scripture says of Elijah, how he pleads with God against Israel? 'Lord, they have killed thy prophets, they have demolished thy altars, and I alone am left, and they seek my life.' But what is God's reply to him? 'I have kept for myself seven thousand men who have not bowed the knee to Baal.' So too at the present time there is a remnant, chosen by grace.

What is the function of these passages within the letter as a whole? We recall that among the complex aims behind this

---

[1] For Paul's unremitting concern for the healing of the breach between Jewish and Gentile Christians, see Nickle, pp. 111–29, 'The Collection and the Unity of the Church.'
[2] Context added in parentheses.   [3] See above, pp. 14, 132f.

epistle was Paul's purpose to bring together Roman Christians of Jewish and Gentile background, to encourage each side to respect and welcome the other in Christ (15: 7).

Yet up to this point in the letter he seemed to have been writing mainly on one side of the issue – stressing the wonder of God's new work of salvation apart from works, apart from any reliance upon a Jewish heritage. In chapter eight he had reached such a mood of victory that the inconvenient questions about those who were not elect in Christ could seem to be forgotten. Once more he had laid himself open to the suspicion that he no longer cared about the fate of his 'brethren according to the flesh.' He might be interpreted as giving countenance to the very triumphalism of one party at the expense of the other, that he was trying so hard to combat.[1] Therefore he must now turn sharply around and look at the other side of the picture (chaps. 9–11). He raises the problem that had several times been referred to but always postponed – what about the Jews? Had God's plan for them finally broken down? Were they to be permanently excluded from his purpose of salvation?

He begins by declaring in the most vehement terms his own continuing involvement as intercessor for his people. *They are his kinsmen* according to the flesh and *they are Israel*, the chosen people of the covenant (9: 1–5). Again, it is only as one who intercedes for them (10: 1) that he may also intercede against them and point out their misguided zeal of the past (9: 30 – 11: 10). If he finds it necessary like Elijah (I Kings 19: 9–14) to 'plead with God against Israel' (11: 2f.),[2] he is still an Israelite, and points out that God has not rejected his people (11: 1), but still has a remnant in Israel (11: 4ff.). If the Jew may not boast or lord it over the Gentile, neither is it fitting for the Gentile as newcomer to despise the Jew (11: 13–32). As intercessor for the Jews he will witness to their secure place in God's purposes for the future: 'And so all Israel will be

---

[1] Cf. Knox, *IB*, IX, 535–8.

[2] Here Paul uses the phrase ἐντυγχάνει κατά. The word ἐντυγχάνειν is used elsewhere by him only for positive intercessory prayer. See above, p. 18. Hesse (p. 132) writes about the curses uttered by Jeremiah, 'so sind die Fluchgebete nichts anderes als eine ins 'Negative' gewendete Fürbitte....' Cf. also Johansson, *Parakletoi*, pp. 13, 17, etc., and Dahl's related comments in 'Paul as Intercessor,' pp. 175f.

saved....For the gifts and call of God are irrevocable'
(11: 26, 29).

The three intercessory passages in chapters nine and ten are
given added significance when they are seen to follow closely
upon his teaching about intercession in chapter eight – the
intercession of the Holy Spirit and the exalted Christ. As Dahl
puts it, 'In Rom. 8 the Spirit and Christ are intercessors for
the Christians, in Rom. 9f. Paul is intercessor for Israel.'[1]
Although Paul had written that nothing 'will be able to separate
us from the love of God in Christ Jesus our Lord' (8: 39),
nevertheless the intercessor must be willing to offer himself to
be separated from Christ on behalf of his brethren. Just as God
'did not spare his Son, but gave him up for us all' (8: 32), so
the Christian intercessor must not spare himself, but offer himself freely (9: 3).

By telling his readers of his own deeply felt intercessions both
against and for Israel, the apostle is appealing to them to become similarly involved in an intercessory attitude toward one
another. The 'weak in faith' must not simply pass negative
judgment on the 'strong in faith,' but neither must the strong
in faith judge or put a stumbling block in the way of his weaker
brother (Rom. 14: 1 – 15: 13).

Romans 9: 3

Turning to the first passage, we observe that again a prayer-
report is used to introduce in capsule form the main thrust of
the message that will follow:

*For I could wish that I myself were accursed and cut off from Christ for the
sake of my brethren, my kinsmen by race.*[2]

It is through this sombre cry of anguished intercessory concern
for Israel that the apostle changes the direction of his letter and
raises the dark problem of God's apparent failure with his own
chosen people.[3]

[1] 'Paul as Intercessor,' p. 175.

[2] The end of the actual prayer-report occurs formally with the words
μου κατὰ σάρκα, but the content of the prayer merges into the following
statements about Israel, introduced by the pronoun οἵτινες.

[3] See J. Munck, *Christus und Israel* (Copenhagen, 1956), p. 26.

But do we have a prayer-report, or merely a rhetorically expressed, impossible wish on the part of the deeply moved apostle? We may take it to mean a prayer,[1] in view of the corresponding passage in 10: 1, 'Brethren, my heart's desire and prayer to God for them is that they may be saved.' As to the literalness of the request, commentators have been sharply divided.[2] Could Paul have sincerely uttered such a prayer? The guarded language, ηὐχόμην, suggests that in his perplexity and concern (vv. 1f.) he did harbor such a prayer, but could hardly believe it possible of fulfilment.[3] In view of the intercessory passages in chapter eight that precede this one (especially 8: 32–4), and the examples of such prayer in the Old Testament, we may not write the prayer off as a merely rhetorical device.[4] The apostle must have had in mind the example of Moses offering himself to be blotted out of God's book for the sake of rebellious Israel (Exod. 32: 31f.).[5] Yet in making his prayer Paul must have known that for him, as for Moses, the answer lay only in God's hands: 'But the Lord said to Moses, "Whoever has sinned against me, him will I blot out of my book"' (Exod. 32: 33).

Paul offers himself to undergo a curse of annihilation (ἀνάθεμα)[6] if he may thereby save his people, and this seems to include an ultimate separation from Christ (ἀπὸ τοῦ Χριστοῦ).[7] Whatever may be the final victory of Christians in Christ, Paul himself (αὐτὸς ἐγώ) must personally be willing for a separation at judgment day. Without further explanation he maintains

[1] ηὐχόμην could mean either wish or pray. See above, p. 19.

[2] For a lengthy summary of the different interpretations, see Michel, p. 194.

[3] Moule describes the tense as a Desiderative Imperfect. 'It seems to soften a remark...as we might say "I could almost do so-and-so"...the Imperfect softening the shock of the daring statement or expressing awe at the terrible thought.' *Idiom Book*, p. 9.

[4] Cf. Michel, *Römer*, p. 194. The rabbinical expressions of this kind may have been rhetorical expressions of love; e.g., 'The children of Israel, I will be an expiation for them,' Negaim, 2: 1, or 'May I become an expiation for so and so.' Strack–Billerbeck, III, 260f.

[5] See Munck, *Christus und Israel*, pp. 27f.

[6] See above, p. 128, n. 3.

[7] Clearly more is meant than a temporary excommunication from the Christian fellowship. See above, p. 128, n. 4.

the possibility that a human intercessor may be accepted by God as an additional means of atonement on behalf of[1] another. He, Paul, apostle to the Gentiles, must offer himself on behalf of lost Israel, his kinsmen according to the flesh, the recipients of God's special covenants.

Romans 10: 1

In the second prayer-report Paul takes up again the burden of the first, but now more positively and with less vehemence:

Brethren, my heart's desire and prayer to God for them is that they may be saved. (I bear them witness that they have a zeal for God, but it is not enlightened.) (10: 1f.)

Here he pauses to introduce a new note of prayerful hope into his involved argument. Again he emphasizes his own continuing loyalty to Israel and by addressing the readers directly as 'brethren' he emphasizes the importance for them of what he has to say. In this second statement of his prayer he introduces a new ray of expectation, counteracting the darker elements of predestination in the previous chapters (9: 14ff.). His prayer is, 'that they may be saved.'[2] So he prepares the readers in advance for his disclosure of the mystery of God's future purposes for Israel (11: 25ff.).[3] Isaiah had cried out concerning Israel: '...only a remnant of them will be saved' (Rom. 9: 27), but now Paul looks forward to the salvation of all Israel (11: 26).

Once again it is as intercessor for and against Israel that he prays, testifying before God both to his gifts to them (I bear them witness that they have a zeal for God), and to their misuse of those gifts (but it is not enlightened) (10: 2).[4]

---

[1] ὑπέρ (on behalf of), rather than ἀντί (instead of, or taking the place of), Moule, *Idiom Book*, p. 64. But Windisch goes too far in suggesting that Paul must make atonement for Israel where Christ had failed. *Paulus und Christus*, p. 242.

[2] εἰς σωτηρίαν. For the nominal construction, see Moule, *Idiom Book*, p. 70.

[3] Cf. Bengel, non orasset Paulus si absolute reprobati essent. Quoted in Sanday and Headlam, p. 282.

[4] Cf. Michel, p. 222.

9   **257**   WPI

So these two prayer-reports open still another window on the scope of the apostle's far-ranging prayers. To the Corinthians he had written of the thankful prayers of Jewish Christians for their Gentile brethren. Now in his letter to the Romans he finds occasion to speak of his own deeply felt supplications for Israel. Thus he tacitly exhorts his readers to be not only accusers of Israel, but intercessors for Israel.

CHAPTER 10

REQUESTS AND EXHORTATIONS
ABOUT INTERCESSORY PRAYER

The third major functional class of intercessory prayer passages consists of those in which the apostle either exhorts the readers to practise regular prayers and intercessions; e.g.,

Rejoice always, pray constantly, give thanks in all circumstances (I Thess. 5: 16–18),

or requests them to join together in supplications on his behalf: e.g.,

You also must help us by prayer, so that many will give thanks on our behalf for the blessing granted us in answer to many prayers. (II Cor. 1: 11)

We have already remarked how he prepared for the prayer-requests in several letters, by emphasizing the urgency of his own constant thanksgivings and supplications for them, in the wish-prayers and particularly in the prayer-reports. Now we come to his pleas that the believers in return take up their own share, by offering up prayer for him in his costly work of spreading the gospel. In these passages a crucial, additional dimension will be added to our understanding of the network of intercessions that lay behind the Pauline epistles.

REQUESTS FOR PRAYER

We begin with the five direct and indirect requests for prayer,[1] and inquire first about their stylistic peculiarities in the light of any Jewish or Hellenistic usage that may be discovered.

Formal characteristics and background of the prayer-requests

When we compare the wish-prayers and the prayer-reports with the requests for prayer, we seem to encounter a more hetero-

---

[1] The requests occur in all but two of the Pauline letters and in all three of the deutero-Paulines: I Thess. 5: 25, Rom. 15: 30–2, II Cor. 1: 11, Phil. 1: 19, Philem. 22 [Eph. 6: 18–20, Col. 4: 2–4, 18b., II Thess. 3: 1–3; cf. Heb. 13: 18]. See Appendix III, p. 301.

geneous group of passages as far as their formal characteristics are concerned.[1] Three of the requests are directly expressed (Rom. 15: 30–2, II Cor. 1: 11, I Thess. 5: 25), but in the case of the other two the apostle prefers to acknowledge with approval the intercessory prayers of the readers on his behalf, thereby making a tacit appeal to them to continue praying:

For I know that through your prayers and the help of the Spirit of Jesus Christ this will turn out for my deliverance.... (Phil. 1: 19f; cf. Philem. 22)

So we cannot easily discover any single formula lying behind these appeals; the fluid syntax precludes it.[2]

Yet it may not be without significance that three out of five requests are found within the closing passages of the letter (in I Thessalonians, Romans, and Philemon)[3] and that they are similarly located in the deutero-Pauline letters (Eph. 6: 18–20, Col. 4: 18b, II Thess. 3: 1–3; cf. Heb. 13: 18). This would suggest that it was when the apostle was moving into the liturgically oriented closing pattern and adapting his letter for the eucharistic celebration, that he found it most appropriate to ask the assembled readers to engage in united supplications for him.[4]

There is little evidence to indicate that such requests for intercessions by others (especially by ordinary people) were a widely recognized part of ancient prayer style or liturgical practice.[5] But the one important parallel already noted, from the Jewish letters in Jeremiah, Baruch, and the Apocalypse of Baruch, would suggest that there were some epistolary ante-

---

[1] Little detailed systematic research has been attempted in this area. For preliminary studies see Harder, p. 205; von der Goltz, pp. 117f.; Orphal, p. 18; Greeven, *Gebet und Eschatologie im Neuen Testament*, pp. 174f.

[2] For the varied syntactical and other stylistic marks of the prayer requests, see the appended note on p. 292 below.

[3] For the early location of the prayer-request in II Cor. 1: 11, see below, p. 273, and in Phil. 1: 19f., see below, p. 278.

[4] But some papyrus letters tend to place 'requests and assurances of remembrance...in the epistolary conclusion,' Gamble, 'Textual History,' p. 170; Koskenniemi, pp. 123–6.

[5] It was, however, customary for the people in OT times to ask for the prayers of a prophet or recognized intercessor, e.g., Num. 11: 2, 21: 7, where the people ask Moses to pray for them; cf. I Sam. 12: 19, I Kings 13: 6, Job 42: 8, Isa. 37: 4, Jer. 37: 3, 42: 2, 20. Cf. Judith 8: 31, Acts 8: 24. After the destruction of the temple this custom was transferred to the rabbis. See, e.g., Ber. 34b, Yer. Ber. v. 5, etc.

cedents for this usage. The fact that the appeals for prayer are associated in a recognizable series of instructions, both in these Jewish letters and in Paul's, strengthens this suggestion.[1]

Function of the prayer-requests

In examining the various appeals of Paul to his readers for supplication on his behalf, it is our task once again to place each of them in its living context so that we may judge as to its true import. How deeply concerned was the apostle to gain the prayer support of those to whom he addressed his pleas for help?

I Thessalonians 5: 25

The first request for prayer (in the briefest of sentences) forms one of a series of instructions in the closing liturgical pattern of I Thessalonians.[2] Closely linked with the immediately preceding context (5: 16ff.), particularly the wish-prayer, it takes on deeper significance when seen in that connection:

(Rejoice always, pray constantly, give thanks in all circumstances; for this is the will of God in Christ Jesus for you (vv. 16–18)...
May the God of peace himself sanctify you wholly; and may your spirit and soul and body be kept sound and blameless at the coming of our Lord Jesus Christ (v. 23). He who calls you is faithful, and he will do it (v. 24).)
Brethren, pray [also] for us. (v. 25)   (I Thess. 5: 16–18 and 23–5)

Although commentators tend to prefer a break after v. 24, linking the request with what follows and treating vv. 25–8 as a closing unit for the epistle, yet the natural connection between the apostle's prayers for the converts, and his request to them to pray in turn for him, seems to demand that vv. 23–5 be considered together.[3]

---

[1] See above, p. 42, n. 3, and 183, n. 1.
[2] See above, pp. 51f., 70f.
[3] See C. Roetzel, 'I Thess. 5: 12–28: A Case Study,' Society of Biblical Literature, *Book of Seminar Papers*, II, ed. L. C. McGaughy (1972), pp. 367–83. However, the request for their prayers leads naturally into the injunctions that follow: the kiss of reconciliation and the corporate reading of the letter. So it functions as a transition sentence within the closing liturgical pattern.

The relationship of this prayer-request to the preceding verses depends to a considerable extent on the authenticity and significance of the word 'also' (καί). The balance of textual evidence seems to favor its retention.[1] Opinion is divided as to whether it refers as far back as to v. 17, meaning, 'Pray constantly...and when you are praying, pray also for us (as well as for yourselves and others).'[2] An easier reference would be to the wish-prayer (v. 23), so as to stress the reciprocity between the apostle's prayers and those which he seeks from the believers: 'Brothers, as we pray for you, so do you also in turn pray for us.'[3] Perhaps both links were partly intended. Paul was now continuing his earlier injunction of unceasing prayer and thanksgiving (vv. 17f.) by applying it more precisely (vv. 23–5) to the immediate situation – a mutual need for prayer in the difficulties for both apostle and converts that lie behind the letter.[4]

The address ἀδελφοί in itself suggests the concerned fellowship of love within which mutual intercessory responsibility may be fostered. It continues the motif suggested by the prayer to 'the God of peace' (v. 23), and leads to the greeting of all the brethren with the holy kiss (v. 25) and the strong injunction that the letter be read to all the brethren (v. 27).[5]

What did Paul want them to ask on his behalf? Although in such a short request no direct indication was given, must he not have meant them to ask for him the kinds of gifts he had been asking for them, namely that he in turn (καί) be strengthened in faith, love, and hope, be sanctified wholly, and kept

[1] προσεύχεσθε + καὶ p³⁰ B D* 33 81 104 326 330 436 451 1739 1877 1881 2492 itᵈ,ᵉ syrʰ,ᵖᵃˡ copˢᵃ goth arm Orig Chrys Theod Euthal. Omit καὶ ℵ A Dᶜ G K P Ψ 88 181 614 629 630 1241 1962 1984 1985 2127 2495 *Byz Lect* itᵃʳ, ᶜ, ᵈᵉᵐ, ᵈⁱᵛ, f, g, mon, x, z vg syrᵖ copᵇᵒ eth Ambr Theod John-Dam.

[2] B. Weiss, *Die Paulinische Briefe, und der Hebräerbrief*..., 2nd edn (Leipzig, 1903), Frame, *et al.*

[3] Milligan; Rigaux, *Thessaloniciens*. See above, pp. 251, n. 8, and Appended Note 2, p. 292, sec. f.

[4] [Cf. the deutero-Pauline examples where general exhortations to prayer lead immediately into specific requests for intercession for himself: Eph. 6: 18f., 'Pray at all times in the Spirit...making supplication for all the saints, and also for me... (καὶ ὑπὲρ ἐμοῦ)'; Col. 4: 2, 'Continue steadfastly in prayer...and pray for us also (προσευχόμενοι ἅμα καὶ περὶ ἡμῶν).']

[5] See above, p. 67.

sound and blameless at the parousia? More specifically, they should pray that he, like them, might 'stand fast in the Lord' amid the opposition to his preaching to the Gentiles (2: 16), the hindrances of Satan (2: 17), and the special distress and affliction of which he had told them (3: 3, 7).[1]

The short injunction, 'Brethren, pray [also] for us,' expands the wish-prayer into a compact, rounded prayer-unit within the larger liturgical section at the close of the Thessalonian letter, and thus a notable climax fulfils the intercessory theme that has continued through the epistle. At the beginning of the letter Paul has assured his readers of the unceasing prayers of thanksgiving and supplication made for them; now at the end he invites them to complete the intercessory circle of mutual responsibility. The whole letter and the crisis that lies behind it are again drawn into the network of mutual prayers, sustained by a declaration that the God who is faithful will answer their intercessions and complete the work which he had begun when he called them. In the meantime, the readers are charged to prove their mature involvement with him in supporting the wider spreading of the gospel. This they may do by joining together immediately in supplications on his behalf as they move into their further corporate worship,[2] and by taking up their own full share in the ministry of ceaseless thanksgiving and supplications (vv. 17f.).

Romans 15: 30–2

The second request for prayer goes far beyond the terse appeal that we have just been considering. In keeping with the substantial nature of the letter to the Romans, the complex concerns of the apostle,[3] and the unusually extended liturgically oriented section that brings it to a close,[4] we find an appropriately extended prayer-request:

I appeal to you, brethren, by our Lord Jesus Christ and by the love of the Spirit, to strive together with me in your prayers to God on my behalf, that I may be delivered from the unbelievers in Judea, and that my service for

---

[1] In any case the readers would understand his appeal, through having detailed oral information about his present work and needs at Corinth.

[2] See Harder, p. 83.

[3] See above, pp. 72ff.   [4] See above, pp. 95ff.

Jerusalem may be acceptable to the saints, so that by God's will I may come to you with joy and be refreshed in your company. (A closing wish-prayer or blessing is appended: The God of peace be with you all. Amen.)[1] (Rom. 15: 30–3)

Through its location in the impressive context of the closing liturgical pattern, this appeal for prayer gains emphasis as a high point of the epistle.[2] It balances the four wish-prayers and the closing benediction by eliciting the immediate co-operation of the readers, in the atmosphere of fellowship that would be symbolized by the kiss of peace. It includes the theme of the collection that we have seen to be an important item in the closing liturgical pattern.[3] It ties together the practical themes of the previous chapter with the instructions that will follow.[4]

In these closely knit verses there sounds an urgent cry for help, as the apostle finds himself dwelling upon the sombre contrast between the joy with which he anticipates his personal visit to Rome, and the dark forebodings that overhang his commission to Jerusalem.[5]

His need for their prayers had been foreshadowed in a number of ways that we have already noted throughout the letter. In the two parallel passages about his travel plans (1: 8–17 and 15: 14–29), he had revealed his extensive missionary projects and the significant part that he was hoping Rome would play in them.[6] Yet right at the outset, the note of grave uncertainty had been sounded in the hesitant tone of the opening prayer-report.[7] Later in the letter, the explanation of his design to take the collection to Jerusalem seemed to have reawakened his uneasiness (15: 25–8). In addition, his constant awareness of the hostility of his detractors, some perhaps already present at Rome, had been reflected in the very strength of his asser-

[1] See above, pp. 90f.
[2] Cf. Bjerkelund, *Parakalô-Sätze*, p. 158.
[3] See above, p. 96, n. 2.
[4] J. A. T. Robinson (citing a suggestion of E. C. Ratcliff) refers to the possibility that the passage itself may, through its internal structure, and if followed immediately by the doxology of 16: 25–7 (as in the Chester Beatty papyrus), reflect a eucharistic sequence. 'Traces of a Liturgical Sequence in I Cor. 16: 20–24,' p. 39, n. 2.
[5] Sanday and Headlam, p. 414.
[6] Above, pp. 187ff.
[7] Above, p. 191.

tions of an unfailing interest in the readers,[1] in the apologetic nature of the letter,[2] and in references to his unnamed opponents which seem to appear from time to time in the letter (3: 8, 6: 1, 6: 15, 16: 17–20).[3] His basic concern about the lack of unity at Rome had been clearly demonstrated throughout the epistle.[4] The further danger from the Jews outside the church, who constantly threatened his very life, had been indirectly shown as he wrestled with the perplexing problem of Jewish intransigence in chapters 9–11.

Because the outcome of all this lay in God's hands, he believed that he himself must constantly undergird his ministry and the well-being of his churches by intercessions for them (1: 9f.). As he had mentioned these ceaseless prayers at the opening of the letter, so towards the close he had offered two prayers which drew together and summarized the nature of his concerns for their welfare (15: 5f. and 13). Besides this, he had given them all a general exhortation to be constant in prayer, to contribute to the needs of the saints, to practise hospitality, to bless and not curse their persecutors (12: 12–14). Now at last he is ready to enlist their specific aid and prayers for his own special needs.[5]

The unusually diverse purposes behind this epistle, involving not only the needs of the church at Rome but even more the extended plans of the apostle, call for a more emphatic and a more detailed prayer-request than was needed in the other letters. Moreover, from those who are unknown to him he can assume neither their concern nor their prior knowledge of his movements and perils.[6] So the epistle has swung back and forth between the two sets of interests, his and theirs, until now he attempts to bring these together within an enduring partnership of mutual responsibility, through the medium of their intercessory prayers. Insofar as the letter has served to prepare the way for his visit, the request for their prayers will strengthen that function: the tangible fellowship with the whole community which has been solicited through the letter, will be

---

[1] Above, pp. 189ff.   [2] Above, p. 191, n. 6.

[3] Above, pp. 93f.   [4] Above, pp. 74f.

[5] Cf. P. Wendland, *Urchristlichen Literaturformen*, p. 350.

[6] By contrast, a short appeal would be sufficient in I Thess. to a group of friends already having detailed reports of his affairs, and in the other epistles to churches that knew him well.

confirmed by their answering prayers.[1] Before ever he arrives on their doorstep, he hopes that many more of them will begin to take an interest in his mission plans. Once they start praying unitedly[2] for him and with him, he will cease to be a stranger or an enigma to any of them. They will be united as a church both in 'glorifying God together with one voice' (15: 5f.),[3] and through the unifying effect of 'striving together with himself' in supplication (15: 30). They will be joined in solidarity with him against his detractors at Jerusalem and Rome, and eventually will receive him as a welcome ally. Their prayers will serve as an interim response to his letter during a period of deadly peril, and ensure that, if God wills, his visit to them will indeed be fruitful (1: 13, 15: 29, 32).

We may turn now to the details of the passage. To introduce his plea, Paul uses the emphatic παρακαλῶ opening formula: 'I appeal to you, brethren, by our Lord Jesus Christ and by the love of the Spirit, to strive together with me' (15: 30), and so recalls the impressive opening words of the paraenetic section, 'I appeal to you therefore, brethren, by the mercies of God, to present your bodies....' (12: 1). The repetition of this solemn formula shows that he is again introducing an important new note that follows from, but goes beyond, the preceding argument.[4] So the request for prayer is given the greatest possible prominence within the progression of the closing instructions.

Although the address, ἀδελφοί, belongs to this type of opening formula, it may here, as in the prayer-request in I Thessalonians, stress the note of fellowship that must be the basis of such mutual prayers.[5]

As his earlier appeal for their consecration (12: 1) had been based in the 'mercies of God,' building thereby on the foregoing chapters,[6] so now he bases his appeal for their prayers

[1] Michel, p. 335.
[2] See Harder, p. 83, and n. 2.
[3] See above, p. 82.
[4] See above, p. 81. Cf. Sanders, 'Transition from Opening Thanksgivings,' p. 350.
[5] See above, p. 262. αδελφοι is lacking in P46 B Chr, but is probably to be retained, Michel, p. 336.
[6] E.g., 11: 30–1, where the mercy of God is repeatedly stressed.

on two central emphases in the preceding letter. First, he appeals to them by 'our Lord Jesus Christ.' Through this special title he invokes 'the Lord' to whom he and all Christians jointly belong as servants of one Lord (e.g., 1: 1, 6: 23, 8: 39, 13: 14, 15: 6);[1] hence they are obligated as members one of another in the one body of Christ (12: 5), to join with Paul in the fellowship of prayer in the common service of Christ. Second, he appeals to 'the love of the Spirit,'[2] for only such a love could be an adequate basis for persevering intercessions. It is through the Spirit alone that 'God's love has been poured into our hearts' (5: 5, cf. chap. 8); and it is only through the aid and intercession of the Spirit that they may be enabled to pray (8: 16, 26f.). Thus his double invocation is rooted deep within the preceding letter, giving a firm basis for his request for their prayers.

We come now to a phrase that underscores the seriousness and strenuousness of the task to which Paul was inviting his readers: συναγωνίσασθαί[3] μοι ἐν ταῖς προσευχαῖς ὑπὲρ ἐμοῦ[4] πρὸς τὸν θεόν.

The meaning is somewhat veiled and two questions of interpretation arise: first, precisely what 'striving' of his own did the apostle have in mind for them to share with him? To be sure, it has been suggested that the word συναγωνίσασθαι conjures up the athletic imagery often used by Paul for the intense daily struggle which all Christians must undergo.[5] Yet the reference of this symbolism in Paul's letters is limited more precisely to his own costly apostolic mission, which he under-

---

[1] See above, p. 146, n. 3, referring to Kramer's discussion of the significance of the title.

[2] I.e., the love which the Spirit causes. The appeal includes a Trinitarian shape.

[3] See above, p. 20.

[4] Including υπερ εμου with the majority of Mss.

[5] For details, see Stauffer, *TWNT*, I, 134–40, and V. C. Pfitzner, *Paul and the Agon Motif*, pp. 1–75. Cf. the emphasis in Hellenistic Judaism on the imagery of the athletic arena to describe the life of the righteous in this world, and especially the heroic witness of the Jewish martyrs, e.g., IV Macc. 11: 20, 16: 16, 17: 10ff.; Sir. 4: 28. Paul is particularly fond of this symbolism, e.g., Rom. 15: 30, I Cor. 9: 24–7 (the fullest example), I Thess. 2: 2 [Col. 1: 29f., 4: 12f., I Tim. 4: 7–10, 6: 11, II Tim. 4: 7f.]. The figure of the arena merges into that of general warfare against the powers of darkness, e.g., I Thess. 5: 8 [cf. Eph. 6: 10–17].

stood as a striving ἀγών for the gospel – a continual contest against opposition in the eschatological age.[1] Thus here he is calling on the Roman readers to give prayerful aid specifically in the new phases of the apostolic conflict that he has in mind.

Second, and more important, may we assume with many commentators[2] that Paul was urging the readers to engage in an actual prayer-struggle to support him in his difficult contest – 'to join in my struggle by yourselves *struggling in your prayers* on my behalf'? Admittedly the phrase συναγωνίσασθαί μοι need not necessarily imply a prayer-struggle.[3] Yet there is no doubt that such a view of the strenuousness of intercessory prayer was shared by Paul and cannot have been far from his thoughts in this passage.[4] The wrestling of the Christian would then have to take place not only in active living, but also in-

[1] See Pfitzner, pp. 82–129. Pfitzner shows that I Cor. 9: 24–7 and similar passages in Paul do not refer to the general, traditional concept of life as a moral struggle (agon), but precisely to his difficult and costly work as an apostle, 'in the eschatological "already but not yet" tension' (p. 10). He refers to our passage Rom. 15: 30, on pp. 120ff.

[2] E.g., Sanday and Headlam.

[3] Pfitzner, pp. 121f. He cites examples from Josephus (*Bell.* 2. 139, and *Ant.* 4. 316) to show that 'in its contemporary usage the verb συναγωνίζεσθαι ...can assume the almost colourless sense, to assist or support another... This participation [through prayer] does not presuppose identity of action....The specific way in which the Roman Christians are to take part in the Apostle's contest is, because of the distance which separates them, in supplication *to* God (πρὸς τὸν θεόν), not in an Agon of prayer *with* or against God.' *Ibid.*

[4] Cf. his frequent references to the urgency of prayer, and to the need for continued, unceasing intercessions. Cf. also the central example in the NT, the struggle of Jesus at Gethsemane, as he fights to know and accept the will of God (Mk. 14: 32–4 and parallels).

For Paul, as for Jesus, however, the antagonist was not God – rather God was the powerful ally in the struggle. Cf. Sir. 4: 28, Josephus, *Ant.* XII, 285, etc. The antagonist comprised the various powers that had enslaved men, including sin, flesh, law, and death, Rom. 8: 21, I Cor. 2: 6–8, II Cor. 4: 4, Gal. 4: 3–11 [Eph. 6: 12]; Gaugler, *Römerbrief*, p. 389. Through prayer the believer wrestled in the Spirit with these powers, until there was achieved unity between his own will and the will of God (Rom. 8: 26f.). Always there was a final understanding that the outcome must be at God's disposal (Rom. 15: 32; reading δια θεληματος θεου, with the majority of Mss). Cf. the similar phrase in the opening prayer-report (1: 10). Above, p. 192.

wardly in a contest of prayer.[1] The apostle would be following a Jewish understanding of prayer, rooted in Jacob's well-known struggle with a divine being (Gen. 32: 24–32).[2]

Paul leaves them in no doubt about the particulars of the apostolic struggle for which he needs their supplication: They must intercede for his deliverance from the Jews in Judea (a ἵνα clause of purpose); then for his welcome by the Jerusalem Christians as he brings the collection to them (a parallel ἵνα clause); finally, the goal of all this is that he may be brought in triumphant joy to Rome, and be received there with mutual refreshment (ἵνα συναναπαύσωμαι ὑμῖν).[3] That Paul's anxiety about danger from the Jews in Judea[4] was well-founded, is of course borne out by the account in Acts of his ill-fated journey to Jerusalem (20: 3, 22–4, 21: 4, 11–14, 27ff.). So his request for continued prayers was not merely a tactical manoeuver to engage their sympathy, but a call for help in what he knew to be a matter of life and death.

His further question as to whether his διακονία[5] for Jerusalem would be acceptable to the saints (Rom. 15: 31b, cf. v. 26)

---

[1] Cf. the outward and inward aspects of Paul's priestly ministry, perhaps suggested at the beginning of the letter in the words, 'whom I serve with my spirit in the gospel of his Son' (Rom. 1: 9). See above, p. 190, n. 5.

The double nature of Paul's conflict for the gospel is given more explicit expression in the deutero-Pauline letters: [In Col. 1: 29 the apostle is made to refer first to his active outward struggle (ἀγωνιζόμενος). In the following verse he refers to wrestling in prayer for his readers and their associates (ἡλίκον ἀγῶνα ἔχω ὑπὲρ ὑμῶν) (2: 1). Cf. Col. 4: 12, where ἀγωνιζόμενος must mean that Epaphras wrestles in prayer on behalf of the Colossians. In Eph. 6: 10–20, after a series of instructions about the Christian's active daily life, there follows an emphasis on the inner spiritual nature of the struggle against principalities and powers (6: 10–17), culminating in a call to persevering supplication for all the saints (6: 18–20).]

[2] Cf. Ber. 53b, where the saying of grace is likened to a battle.

[3] It has been argued that, strictly speaking, Paul asks their prayers only regarding Jerusalem, with the successful arrival at Rome following as a natural result. But this final request corresponds syntactically to the 'additional benefit' of the wish-prayers and should thus be included in the prayer content. See above, pp. 29, 61, n. 1, 244, n. 7. Cf. Pfitzner, p. 121.

[4] 'The unbelievers in Judea' must refer to Jews who had not accepted Christ, and recalls such earlier references in Rom. as 2: 8f., 10: 21, 11: 30–2.

[5] For διακονια, B D* G^gr (it^{ar,d*} remuneratio) Ambros Ephr read δωροφορια.

shows that, in spite of his earlier optimism (II Cor. 9: 14),[1] he had since come to fear that things might not go so well. He now suspected such a level of hostility towards him,[2] that even his gift of good will from the Gentiles might but provoke further difficulties among Jewish Christians as well as Jews. Here, too, his suspicions were all too well-founded (Acts 21: 20ff.). But beyond the mere danger to himself, lay that deeper reconciling and eschatological significance of the collection, which we considered earlier.[3] Now he is urging the Romans to support him as he seeks to realize one of the most carefully planned and cherished hopes of his career.

The successful completion of this mission would place the coping stone on his labors in the East (15: 23, 28), assuring him that his work had been accepted by the mother church and leaving him free to move on to Rome with joy (15: 32a). He would come, relieved and thankful for past victories, 'in the fullest of the blessing of Christ' (15: 29), ready for a time of recuperation and refreshment in their company, as he looked forward to new fields of service (15: 32b).[4]

Filled with expectation of that glad day, Paul adds a brief prayer that the God of peace grant his peace to them all, and so prepares for the final messages and liturgical items that follow. He has appealed directly for their prayers, in the hope that the Roman Christians as they read will be moved to begin united prayer for him, and that by their continuing supplications they themselves may be given that responsible maturity about which he himself has been praying (15: 5f., 15: 13).

As in I Thessalonians we seem to have a deliberate climax – a completing of the intercessory circle as the letter comes to a close – drawing the total situation that lies behind the epistle, together with the immediate concerns mentioned in the epistle itself, into the orbit of the loving concern and the mutual intercessions of apostle and believers, 'the one for the many and the many for the one.'[5] Thus the ministry of writing and reading is extended and transmuted into a continuing and reciprocal ministry of prayers.

[1] But see above, p. 250, n. 1.   [2] See Nickle, n. 306.
[3] See above, pp. 249f.
[4] For the theme of 'mutual refreshment,' cf. I Cor. 16: 18, II Cor. 7: 13, Philem, 7, 20.   [5] Gaugler, p. 390.

II Corinthians 1: 11

The third prayer-request, unlike those we have been considering, comes near the beginning of an epistle – the thankful letter
of reconciliation (II Cor. 1–9), written after Paul's receipt of
the good news brought back by Titus.[1]

(He delivered us from such a deadly peril, and he will deliver us;
on him we have set our hope that he will deliver us again.) (v. 10)[2]
*You also must help us by prayer, so that many will give thanks on our behalf
for the blessing granted us in answer to many prayers.* (v. 11)

Once again we inquire as to how seriously the apostle is concerned to gain the prayer support of his readers, why does he
desire it, and for what does he want them to pray?

The answers must be sought in the circumstances surrounding
this strangely worded request. As we saw earlier, Paul is
writing at a time of intense relief and renewed hope – the crisis
at Corinth is over. Now his purpose in the letter is to do all in
his power to strengthen their ties of fellowship with himself.
Besides his words of gratitude, explanation, and encouragement
to them to share his life of power in weakness, he requests two
specific actions as tokens of their fellowship. The second of these
we have already considered – that they take part generously in
the united collection.[3] The first is that they join him in intercessions on his behalf.

The prayer-request itself, with its reference to the thanks of
many on his behalf, serves as an important conclusion for the
whole opening period (1: 3–11), both stylistically and in content: by substituting a praisegiving for his usual thanksgiving
period, he has postponed the thanksgiving statement to the
close of the period, ending with an 'inverted thanksgiving.'
Instead of beginning with thanks to God for his mercies to the
readers, and assurances of his own prayers on their behalf, he
leads up to the giving of thanks by many others for mercies to
himself, and a request for the readers' prayers on his behalf.[4]

---

[1] See above, pp. 233, 239ff.   [2] Context added in parentheses.
[3] See above, pp. 248ff.
[4] See above, p. 227. Schubert regarded the inverted thanksgiving as substituting formally for the missing thanksgiving period (pp. 46ff.). Sanders
('Transition from Opening Thanksgiving,' pp. 360f.) analyzes the praisegiving period (1: 3–11) into a theme that concludes at v. 7, followed by a

Furthermore, the praisegiving form enables him from the outset to include his readers inseparably with himself in his profound sense of relief and consolation. In the first half of the praise-giving (vv. 3–7), he sets the tone by referring generally to his own vicarious suffering and comfort on their behalf (partaking with Christ in sufferings and comfort); and then hopefully to their shared experience of suffering and comfort (v. 7).[1]

In the second half of the praisegiving period (vv. 8–11)[2] he becomes more specific. He testifies to a remarkable deliverance from a deadly peril in Asia, that, he says, had utterly and unbearably crushed him and reduced him to near desperation (vv. 8, 9a).[3] Looking back, however, he can see that he had been made to rely in prayer, 'not on [himself] but on God who raises the dead' (v. 9b).[4] And God had indeed rescued him (v. 10a). So at the beginning of the letter he had reminded the Corinthians forcibly of the extreme dangers that must accompany his eschatological ministry and of his compulsion to rely in prayer on God's power to protect and save.[5]

It is at this point that he turns their thoughts to the future,[6] so as to introduce the request for their prayers that he has been leading up to: 'He delivered us from such a deadly peril, and he will deliver us' (v. 10).[7] It is to the future that he wishes to point his readers throughout the epistle, but a future illumi-

formula of injunction in the middle (vv. 8–10), and finally an inverted thanksgiving (v. 11). In spite of the change to a praisegiving, the eschato-logical motif is included at v. 9 (God who raises the dead), and the thanks-giving motif at v. 11. Sanders rightly questions whether Paul himself was conscious of these literary devices; p. 361, n. 17.

[1] For fuller details, see above, pp. 226ff.

[2] Introduced by his characteristic emphasizing phrase, 'For we do not want you to be ignorant, brethren.'

[3] The exact nature of this deadly peril we may leave undecided. Evi-dently Paul has no need to describe the details to readers who would have heard about it. In any case, he is suggesting that his ministry will continue to be beset by many similar perils.

[4] Prayer is suggested by his use of these well-known prayer-words from the second petition of the Shemoneh Esreh. Cf. a similar reference to a severe disciplinary experience and his prayer about it, II Cor. 12: 7–10; cf. 4: 7.

[5] Cf. II Cor. 4: 8ff., 11: 23ff.; I Thess. 3: 3f. (see above, p. 49) [II Tim. 4: 17f.].   [6] Windisch, *Zweite Korintherbrief*, p. 48.

[7] Reading και ρυσεται with most commentators.

nated by God's dealings with them in the past.[1] Yet his past deliverance had come only when he had learned to rely on God in prayer. Therefore his bold declaration of future deliverance must become a more modest statement of prayerful[2] hope, based in God and conditional on the prayers of the Corinthians, in a situation that will remain difficult and dangerous. Let the fact of his rescue from recent terrible danger, then, become the impetus for their beginning a fellowship of prayer with himself: 'on him we have set our hope that he will deliver us again, *if you also help by praying for us*' (vv. 10b–11a); συνυπουργούντων καὶ ὑμῶν ὑπὲρ ἡμῶν τῇ δεήσει (v. 11a).[3]

Evidently in a letter the purpose of which is to foster close bonds between himself and his readers, Paul does not wish to delay his prayer-request until the liturgically oriented closing section.[4] Instead, he has directed their attention right at the outset to his own deadly peril so that he may appeal immediately for their support.[5]

That he counts a great deal on their intercessions is suggested by the (probably) conditional meaning of the participial phrase συνυπουργούντων κτλ.: 'he will continue to deliver us, if you will co-operate by praying for us' (NEB).[6] While his assurance

---

[1] See above, pp. 160f.

[2] 'On him we have set our hope' implies praying in hope. See below, p. 274. For similar changes from certainty to hope, see above, p. 170, n. 3, etc.

[3] Gen. Absol. As elsewhere, the participial construction in a prayer passage does not imply a mere afterthought (see above, p. 164), but here expresses the climax towards which Paul has been moving. Cf. the climax of his collection appeal in 9: 14, καὶ αὐτῶν δεήσει ὑπὲρ ὑμῶν ἐπιποθούντων ὑμᾶς, see above, pp. 251f.

For δέησις, see above, pp. 19f.   [4] See above, p. 260.

[5] Contrast the situation in Rom., where, before requesting their prayers, he had first to enlist the readers' support; or in I Thess., where the main attention was focused on the needs of the congregation rather than those of the apostle; or in Philem., where the burden of the letter was about the plight of Onesimus, so that there too the prayer-request is delayed to the end (v. 22). In Phil., however, where he is writing to a church which is deeply concerned about him, he writes in the thanksgiving and succeeding passage about his own affairs, and (as in II Cor.) moves straight into an appeal for their prayers. See below, p. 278.

[6] A conditional interpretation (if, or provided that) is suggested by the parallel prayer-request in Phil. 1: 19, where Paul's firm assurance is contingent partly on their prayers; see below, p. 279. Cf. also Philem. 22.

of final deliverance is unshakable (v. 10), interim events of the immediate future lie hidden in God's hands; therefore he depends upon the support of their prayers. Let them ask that he be rescued continually from the perils and afflictions that inevitably surround his apostleship, and thus that the gospel may be freely preached.[1]

As in other prayer-requests, so here he suggests by the word καί, 'also,' that he is already praying for them (v. 7), and for himself (v. 10b).[2] They in turn should join in praying for him,[3] thereby cementing the restored partnership of support between apostle and church, and becoming part of a wider fellowship of prayers.[4]

Although the immediate goal of their prayers is his continued deliverance, beyond that lies the honor that will redound to God through the multitude of thanksgivings that will follow. In the second half of the request (v. 11b) he broadens the purpose of their supplications and brings the whole blessing passage to a fitting culmination: 'so that many will give thanks on our behalf for the blessing granted us in answer to many prayers.'[5] Here he introduces a theme that will be prominent in his thoughts as he pens this thankful letter, and that he will use again as a culminating motif at the close of his collection appeal (9: 11–15).[6]

In this passage his language mounts to an elevated ceremonial

[1] Cf. 4: 13–15, where he seems to comment further on this desire: 'we too believe, and so we speak...for it is all for your sake, so that as grace extends to more and more people it may increase thanksgiving, to the glory of God.'

[2] See above, pp. 228, n. 2, 262, etc., below, p. 292, sec. ƒ.

[3] Taking ὑπὲρ ἡμῶν closely with τῇ δεήσει.

[4] This is underlined by the word συνυπουργούντων, working in co-operation with. Συν- must refer primarily to himself – see Rom. 15: 30, 'to strive together with me in your prayers.' See above, pp. 267ff. But it may refer also to the prayers of other churches for Paul. The Corinthians were being asked to join their prayers to those of other believers, as he would soon request them to partake with others in a united collection.

[5] See above, p. 168.

[6] II Cor. 1: 11, 4: 15, 9: 11–15. See above, pp. 240, 250, n. 3. He may have envisaged united celebrations of thankful worship; cf. Rom. 15: 6 (above, p. 82). It is not necessary (with Héring, *Seconde Épitre aux Corinthiens*, p. 23) to equate these thanksgivings with supplications. For Paul's view of the relationship between the two, see above, pp. 191ff.

level that makes the text difficult to interpret in detail,[1] and his overfull and repetitious style has tempted various copyists to try to shorten or improve it.[2] Yet the full text presents an intentional symmetry in its balanced accentuation of two moments:[3] first is the blessing granted to Paul (τὸ εἰς ἡμᾶς χάρισμα)[4] through many prayers (διὰ πολλῶν).[5] Second is the thanksgiving on his behalf (εὐχαριστηθῇ ὑπὲρ ἡμῶν), offered by many people (ἐκ πολλῶν προσώπων).[6] Thus while the details are partly ambiguous, the general intention seems clear enough. As the Corinthians read his letter, they will join in intercessions for Paul, he will be blessed through their many prayers, the gospel will be unhindered and many will be united in common thanksgivings to God[7] for his continued apostolic ministry.[8]

In sum, the prayer-request may be seen to point back to the opening words of praise, 'Blessed be the God and Father of our Lord Jesus Christ...who comforts us in all our affliction' (1: 3f.), and to be grounded specifically in the deliverance of

[1] Cf. the even more turgid language of II Cor. 9: 13f., which masses together intercession, praise, and the multiplication of thanksgivings. See above, pp. 251f.

[2] For details of the variant readings, see Plummer, *Second Corinthians*, p. 22.

[3] Windisch, *Zweite Korintherbrief*, p. 49. Although it is not certain, we take διὰ πολλῶν not with εὐχαριστηθῇ, but with τὸ εἰς ἡμᾶς χάρισμα, even though 'strict grammar requires a second article – τὸ εἰς ἡμᾶς χάρισμα τὸ διὰ πολλῶν.' Moule, *Idiom Book*, p. 108.

[4] Although the language is unclear (see Windisch, *Zweite Korintherbrief*, p. 49), the blessing refers presumably to continued rescue in the future (linking with v. 10b, 'our hope that he will deliver us again'), rather than to the past rescue (linking with v. 10a, 'he delivered us from such a deadly peril'). Paul is looking forward with hope based on past rescues.

[5] Taking πολλῶν as neuter (Windisch, Schlatter, RSV). Otherwise, if masculine, 'through the prayers of many' (Vulgate, Plummer, NEB). In either case, prayers are understood from the previous phrase, τῇ δεήσει.

[6] Either, 'from many faces uplifted in thanksgiving in a worship service' (Plummer, *et al.*), or preferably, 'from many persons' (Luther, Leitzmann, Windisch, *et al.*).

[7] The large number of participants is emphasized by the repetition of πολλῶν.

[8] The sentence ends with the words, on our behalf (ὑπὲρ ἡμῶν), thereby clinching the intercessory aspect of the whole preceding passage; Windisch, *Zweite Korintherbrief*, p. 51. Cf. ἐφ' ὑμῖν at the close of 9: 14.

the apostle from a deadly peril in Asia. As the result of the expected prayer support of the Corinthians, Paul may look forward in hope to further rescues from future dangers. Thus the gospel may be spread as apostle and people are linked together in a close partnership of mutual assistance, prayers, and thanksgivings.[1] In his appeal he anticipates the central theme of this letter of conciliation – a deepening of the bonds between them, of Christian understanding and support in the time of 'this slight momentary affliction [that] is preparing for us an eternal weight of glory beyond all comparison' (4: 17).

Philippians 1: 19f.

The fourth prayer-request is in Philippians. Like the appeal in II Corinthians, it comes near the beginning of the letter, shortly after the thanksgiving,[2] and in close association with a vivid description of the apostle's own sufferings:

(Yes, and I shall rejoice.)[3] *For I know that through your prayers and the help of the Spirit of Jesus Christ this will turn out for my deliverance, as it is my eager expectation and hope that I shall not be at all ashamed, but that with full courage now as always Christ will be honored in my body, whether by life or by death.* (vv. 19f.)

(Convinced of this, I know that I shall remain and continue with you all, for your progress and joy in the faith, so that in me you may have ample cause to glory in Christ Jesus, because of my coming to you again.) (vv. 25f.)

At the outset the indirect phrasing of the request[4] poses some problems, the first being to demarcate the limits of the intercessory passage. The opening reference to the intercessory supplications of the Philippians is clearly enough expressed in the prepositional phrase διὰ τῆς ὑμῶν δεήσεως;[5] and the substance of their prayers is suggested in the quotation from Job, 'this will turn out for my deliverance' (v. 19).[6] But it is not

[1] Cf. 4: 7–15, 6: 1–13.
[2] In II Cor. it comes at the end of the praisegiving section. Cf. above, p. 273, n. 5.
[3] The context, given in part, is placed in parentheses.
[4] Cf. below, Appended Note 2, p. 292, sec. *b*.
[5] Picking up δέησις again from v. 3. See above, p. 207.
[6] Job 13: 16, LXX. See below, Appended Note 2, p. 292, secs. *d, e*.

clear exactly where the prayer-request itself ends. We may take it that in verse 20 Paul is suggesting the kind of deliverance for which he thinks they should be praying, and that this suggestion is to be included in the prayer-request. But in verse 21 he makes a fresh start (ἐμοὶ γὰρ τὸ ӡῆν Χριστός) and moves back into a description of his own situation, taking them more deeply into his confidence, that they may the more fully intercede with and for him in his critical dilemma. Finally in verse 26 he mentions their actual prayers again, but now they are prayers of glorying or 'boasting' in Christ Jesus (ἵνα τὸ καύχημα ὑμῶν περισσεύῃ)[1] because of God's answer to their supplications. Thus the whole passage (vv. 19–26) refers to his own situation as a subject for their intercessions, with the specific prayer-request being centered in verses 19f.

This brings us to a second question – how much weight did he intend to place on this somewhat glancing reference to their intercession, in a part of the letter that concentrates mainly on the present and future affairs of the apostle himself (1: 12–26)? Although such a brief reference seems at first to be almost casual, it does imply that Paul is counting on their prayers as a necessary condition of his deliverance. It is true that he finds it inappropriate to make a direct formal request for prayers to a deeply concerned church that was already making them regularly on his behalf.[2] Yet perhaps we may catch a hint of the importance he attached to their prayer partnership, through his stress on his own prayers for them (the double use of δέησις,[3] 1: 4), followed immediately by a reference to their valued partnership in the gospel (1: 5); and then in the taking up again of the word δέησις at this point (διὰ τῆς ὑμῶν δεήσεως, 1: 19), with a reference to their partnership in prayer. May we not see a conscious cross-reference between his joyful petitions

---

[1] See above, pp. 167f.

[2] Bonnard, L'Épître de Saint Paul aux Philippiens, p. 27. The other indirect prayer-request (in Philem.) was also addressed from prison to a group whose support the apostle was apparently taking for granted. See below, p. 282.

[3] δέησις is rare in the NT, and in Paul: Rom. 10: 1, II Cor. 1: 11, 9: 14, Phil. 1: 4 (twice), 1: 19, 4: 6 [Eph. 6: 18 (twice)]. It occurs in no other Pauline prayer-report in the thanksgivings (the verb δέομαι is in Rom. 1: 10, I Thess. 3: 10), where Paul prefers to use other words and phrases; see above, pp. 19f.

for them and their petitions for him,[1] especially when we compare the similar cross-references associated with all his other prayer-requests?[2]

A related question concerns the unexpectedly early location of our passage in the structure of the epistle. It is not difficult, however, to see why in this letter, as in his letter of reconciliation (II Cor. 1–9), Paul would prefer to introduce his prayer-request early.[3] In both letters he moves immediately and naturally from the detailed description of his own extremely critical dangers to the intercessory supplications of the readers on his behalf.

What now is the burden of the petitions that the apostle has in mind when he says, 'for I know that through your prayers... this (τοῦτο) will turn out for my deliverance (σωτηρίαν)?' The word τοῦτο must have a broad reference to all that he has been describing of the recent past (τὰ κατ' ἐμέ, v. 12)[4] – especially those conditions of his imprisonment and trial that are contributing to the proclamation of Christ, and in which, he says, 'I rejoice' (v. 18b).[5] But more particularly it implies the ominous future developments, a court decision leading either to execution or release,[6] during which he will still be responsible for the honoring of Christ (v. 20). For he goes on

---

[1] This nuance would be supported by the Western text which opens this section of the letter (1: 3–26) with the words, εγω μεν ευχαριστω τω κυριω ημων, D* G it Ambst, as though the apostle were entering into the middle of a conversation with friends whom he knows for their part to be continually worrying about him and praying for him. So he says, '*I thank our common Lord*, when *I* think of *you* and pray for *you*.' K. Barth, *The Epistle to the Philippians*, p. 13. Even though this reading should be rejected, the early church understanding that must have given rise to it may be not without significance. This would strengthen our basic contention that there had existed a consciously maintained network of mutual intercessions between Paul and his churches.

[2] See below, Appended Note 2, p. 292, sec. *f.*

[3] See above, pp. 260, 273, n. 5. The sharp warning is also placed earlier in this loosely structured epistle; above, p. 203.

[4] Rather than to the immediately preceding word τουτῷ, v. 18. So Vincent, *Philippians and Philemon, ad loc.*, Lohmeyer, *Philipper, Kolosser, Philemon, ad loc., et al.*

[5] Regarding the special importance which Paul had long attached to the spreading of the gospel in the capital city of Rome, see above, pp. 188f.

[6] Barth, *Philippians*, p. 34.

to assert immediately, 'Yes, and I shall rejoice,' thus turning his attention sharply to what lies ahead.[1] It is the unknown verdict and its results that are to be the focus of their prayers, so that somehow these events may 'turn out for deliverance' to the apostle.

What kind of deliverance (σωτηρία) does Paul have in mind? Behind the awkward prepositional link (κατά) between verses 19 and 20 there lurks Paul's characteristic paradox between the certainty of God's ultimate salvation (σωτηρία) and the uncertainties of the present time of woes (θλίψεις).[2] So he can both assert, 'Yes, and I shall rejoice. For I know that through your prayers...this will turn out for my deliverance,'[3] and also speak in the more guarded terms of faith and hope, 'according to (κατά) my eager expectation and hope that I shall not be at all ashamed.' Here he echoes his earlier double statement about the readers: ultimate confidence based in God's past and present work in them, and yet concerned prayer for their immediate future (1: 5f., and 1: 9–11).[4] Now he moves from his own recent past and present (vv. 12ff., and 15ff.) to his own future and the future of the gospel (vv. 19–26). Again, his immediate assurance is dependent on their prayers in a time of uncertainty, so that in the end there may be cause for glory and praise to God (1: 11; cf. 1: 26). Thus the primary meaning of the term σωτηρία must be his ultimate vindication.

In the meantime he needs the strength of their prayers for a more immediate deliverance, especially that he be able to endure. So they must pray that he, like them, 'may be pure and without stumbling for the day of Christ' (v. 10).[5] For Paul this involves proclaiming Christ (v. 18), and thus honoring Christ 'now as always' (v. 20). Their renewed prayers will help to bring about (as he says) 'my eager expectation and hope that I shall not be

---

[1] Dibelius, *Thessalonicher, Philipper*, p. 49. The phrase ἀλλὰ καί is 'used to introduce an additional point in an emphatic way,' Blass–Debrunner–Funk, sec. 448.

[2] Cf. above, pp. 68, n. 1, 170, n. 3.

[3] (Job 13: 16). Job goes on to say, 'I know that I shall be vindicated' (13: 18). 'Paul, like Job, is confident of ultimate vindication by God, despite the hazards of his immediate situation.' Beare, *Philippians*, p. 62; Michael, *Philippians*, pp. 46ff.

[4] See above, pp. 204f.

[5] Lohmeyer, *Philipper, Kolosser, Philemon*, p. 51. See above, pp. 210f.

put to shame,[1] but that with full courage[2] now as always Christ will be honored[3] in my body,[4] whether by life or by death' (v. 20). The grace to be able to continue to the end 'in the defense and confirmation of the gospel' (v. 7) will prepare him for his ultimate salvation. He does not unequivocally assert his physical deliverance from imprisonment and death, even though he strongly expects it and even claims to know it (1: 24–6, 2: 24); for he is reconciled to life or death, as the following verses (e.g., 1: 21–3, 27) and the whole letter testify. Under the hand of God any eventuality can be turned to blessing (4: 11–13).

Hence the supplications that he asks from the Philippians are somewhat more narrowly focused than those in the other prayer-requests.[5] Where the emphasis has been on deliverance from dangers that might hinder the progress of his widespread mission, now the goal is more concentrated – that he may be enabled to further the gospel even in his ordeal of life or death.[6] This is why he adds the phrase καὶ ἐπιχορηγίας τοῦ πνεύματος Ἰησοῦ Χριστοῦ, 'and the supply of the Spirit of Jesus Christ.'[7] As it is the Spirit of Jesus who will aid especially in time of arraignment for the sake of the gospel,[8] so it is through the supply of the Spirit to Paul that the intercessions of the Philippians must be made effective now.[9]

---

[1] ἐν οὐδενὶ αἰσχυνθήσομαι, a frequent expression in the Psalms.

[2] ἐν πάσῃ παρρησίᾳ: freely, in the sense of open, public action (Bauer–Arndt–Gingrich). [Cf. Col. 2: 15.]

[3] He had already stressed the proclaiming or honoring of Christ in vv. 13, 15, 17, 18. Now he eagerly expects this to be continued and foreshadows the honoring of Jesus in the Christ-hymn (2: 9–11).

[4] I.e., 'through my bodily life,' Schlatter.

[5] The prayer-request in Philemon is also narrowly focused.

[6] Cf. Ign. Philad. 5: 1, 'But your prayers will make me perfect for God.' See Lohmeyer, *Philipper, Kolosser, Philemon*, p. 51.

[7] Taking the genitive (ἐπιχορηγίας) as appositional: 'the supply which is the Spirit,' i.e., the giving of the Spirit to Paul (cf. Gal. 3: 5), rather than the Spirit's giving of help. Lohmeyer, Michael, *et al.*

References to the Spirit are rare in Paul's intercessory passages. But see Rom. 15: 13 (p. 88 above), 15: 30 (p. 267 above) and the references in Appendix III, p. 301.

[8] Cf. Mk. 13: 11, par., 'For it is not you who speak, but the Holy Spirit'; Lk. 21: 15, 'For I (Jesus) will give you a mouth and wisdom. . . .'

[9] So Bonnard, *Philippiens*, against Dibelius and Heinzelmann. The Spirit 'is the efficient cause, and prayer the lesser aid,' Calvin. ὑμῶν should be

So this acknowledgment by the apostle of his friends' supplications has been revealed as a tactful but urgent appeal for their renewed support, guiding their prayers for him now especially at a time of intense and immediate need. His letter would strengthen in them a burning desire to uphold him with their intercessions both corporately in their assembly[1] and continually in their individual prayers. Through these prayers they would be bound even more closely to him in his ordeal, and their own fellowship would be purified, drawn together in love, and lifted beyond its present complacency.

Philemon 22b

The last prayer-request to be considered occurs in the closing section of the little letter to Philemon, after Paul has made his appeal for the release of Onesimus to the work of the gospel:[2]

(At the same time, prepare a guest room for me,)[3] (v. 22a)
for I am hoping through your prayers to be granted to you. (v. 22b)

Like the request in Philippians, it takes an indirect form,[4] but because of its simple brevity it is clearly demarcated both at the beginning and the end.[5]

Yet so short and unobtrusive is it, that taken by itself this reference to the readers' prayers would seem to be an almost cursory afterthought, mentioned only in a prepositional phrase of the briefest character: διὰ τῶν προσευχῶν ὑμῶν.[6] It is only

taken only with δεήσεως not with ἐπιχορηγίας (Vincent); i.e., it is not the Philippians who supply the Spirit, yet their prayers and the giving of the Spirit are not intended to be entirely separate modes of aid to Paul. Rather, their prayers are to be made effective through the Spirit (Michael, p. 49). Cf. I Thess. 3: 11, where 'our Lord Jesus' is the one through whom the apostle's prayers must be effected. Above, p. 55, n. 3.

A tempting, but perhaps too strained, interpretation would be 'through your prayers and the help that the Spirit of Jesus Christ gives you in praying,' referring to Rom. 8: 26f.

[1] See Harder, p. 83, and n. 2.
[2] See above, p. 216.
[3] The context is placed in parentheses.
[4] See below, Appended Note 2, p. 292.
[5] Contrast the more complex indirect request in Phil., which merges into the following part of the letter. See above, pp. 276f.
[6] Cf. the equally deceptive use of a partic. to introduce his prayer-reports. See above, p. 164.

in the light of his other prayer-requests and the references in this and other epistles to his own supplications, that we may presume to see more than an offhand allusion here. As with the indirect but deeply serious request to the Philippians, Paul prefers not to ask straight out for their prayers, but in a more tactful way to seem to take for granted that the readers are remembering him and his imprisonment constantly in prayer. Although he wants Philemon and the church in his house to pray for his release from prison, yet because the occasion of this letter is not primarily a crisis in his own situation, there is none of the paradox of certainty and uncertainty that marks the prayer-request to his friends at Philippi. Yet on this occasion, too, he is not sure of the outcome of his imprisonment: he is *hoping* to be granted to them through their prayers, but the issue is in God's hands,[1] and he is counting on their intercessions.

By soliciting their prayers at the close of the letter, he is adding one more pressure upon his friends to accede to his main appeal about Onesimus.[2] By inviting Philemon and the church at Colossae to take their place within a wider circle of active fellowship, mutual concern, and constant intercessions, he enlarges and deepens their sense of responsibility for the gospel mission beyond their own small community. To prepare a guest room for him and to pray for his release symbolize their share in the mission work to which he himself is committed, for he will come to them not only as friend, but as apostle.[3] Thus the prayers that he is expecting of them, while immediately centered upon his release from prison, must inevitably concern not only his own welfare but the all-important ministry to which he has been called and to which he is irrevocably committed.[4]

The prayer-request is made after the main purpose of the letter has been unfolded and his appeal to Philemon has been developed. It gains significance by being included in the auto-

---

[1] χαρισθήσομαι, I shall be granted to you, emphasizes that this will be 'only by the special grace of God.' E. F. Scott, *Colossians, Philemon, Ephesians,* p. 115. For the importance that Paul attached to personally visiting his churches, see above, p. 48, n. 2.

[2] See above, p. 218. This is underlined by the introductory words ἅμα δέ.

[3] See above, p. 217.   [4] Cf. above, p. 223, n. 9.

graph section (vv. 21–5),[1] where Paul adds his confirmation to all that has been written ('confident of your obedience, I write to you'), underlines his hope that the readers will take his appeal seriously ('knowing that you will do even more than I say'), and prepares his letter to be included prayerfully within the united worship of the assembled readers.[2] He has assured them of his own constant thanksgivings and prayers for them, particularly in regard to the difficult problem of Onesimus (vv. 4–7). With the words 'I am hoping,' he may be hinting at his prayers for himself.[3] Now let them add their prayers to his,[4] praying for his release from prison, for an opportunity to be given him to visit them, and (by implication) for the advancement of his work. Thus they would receive guidance about the immediate question, and would share in the larger issues of the gospel mission in an urgent eschatological age.

In summary, all the prayer-requests have been seen to contribute, each in its peculiar way,[5] a crucial dimension to Paul's relationship with his churches, as he appealed to them for understanding and support in his pressing mission. Not only does he himself constantly pray for them all, but he begs them to assume the wider responsibility of giving him prayer support as apostle in the new age. To the Thessalonians he appeals (as we conjectured) for their prayers that he, with them, be strengthened in faith, love, and hope, and that he stand fast in the Lord and be kept sound and blameless at the parousia. From the Romans he asks prayers that his central offering to the believers at Jerusalem be accepted, and that he be enabled to begin the new sweep of his mission to the Western half of the empire. The Corinthians are to confirm their renewed fellowship with him through their prayers that he continue to be rescued from deadly peril, so that the gospel may advance and

[1] See above, p. 68, n. 1, referring to Bahr, 'Subscriptions in the Pauline Letters.' Funk finds in vv. 21f. an example of the epistolary 'apostolic *parousia* form'; cf. above, p. 52, n. 3.

[2] Cf. above, p. 260.

[3] Cf. II Cor. 1: 10b, 'on him we have set our hope that he will deliver us again.' See above, p. 273, n. 2.

[4] See below, Appended Note 2, p. 292, sec. *f*.

[5] See Harder, p. 205.

many be led to give thanks. His old friends at Philippi must continue to stand by him in prayer as he faces the supreme crisis of his trial in Rome. Philemon and the church in his house are asked to face the possibility of fuller and more sacrificial responsibility for his mission work as they intercede for him in prison.

That his requests were made with the deepest seriousness and as a central aspect of his message to each church, can hardly be doubted. They are predicated upon a living fellowship of mutual love and concern in Christ. They presuppose his teaching that all believers should continually take their full share in the ministry of ceaseless thanksgivings and supplications; for, as he wrote to the Thessalonians, 'this is the will of God in Christ Jesus for you' (I Thess. 5: 16–18).

To the brief exhortations that give evidence of such teaching we shall now give our attention.

EXHORTATIONS ABOUT PRAYER

In four of his seven epistles Paul exhorts his readers to pray constantly:[1] to the Thessalonians he writes, 'Rejoice always, pray constantly, give thanks in all circumstances' (I Thess. 5: 16–18); to the Philippians, 'Rejoice in the Lord always. . . . Have no anxiety about anything, but in everything by prayer and supplication with thanksgiving let your requests be made known to God' (Phil. 4: 4–6); to the Romans he writes, 'Rejoice in your hope, be patient in tribulation, be constant in prayer,' and, 'Bless those who persecute you; bless and do not curse them' (Rom. 12: 12, 14). To the Corinthians he suggests an agreement between married couples to refrain from sexual intercourse for a time, 'that you may devote yourselves to prayer' (I Cor. 7: 5).

As is often the case in his paraenesis, three of these passages are couched in terse, loosely connected injunctions with the verb in the imperative mood or as an imperative participle:[2] e.g., ἀδιαλείπτως προσεύχεσθε, εὐλογεῖτε τοὺς διώκοντας, τῇ

---

[1] See Appendix III, p. 301. Prayer-exhortations are lacking in II Cor., Gal., Philem.

[2] See Robinson, 'Die Hodajot-Formel,' pp. 222f. See below, p. 289, n. 2.

προσευχῇ προσκαρτεροῦντες.[1] In this they reflect the pithy style of the popular ethical and religious teaching upon which Paul was dependent in his paraenetic passages.[2] A result of this stylistic terseness is that in only one of the four passages to be considered is the intercessory aspect of prayer explicitly referred to: 'Bless those who persecute you; bless and do not curse them' (Rom. 12: 14). In the other examples, it is from the context that we shall infer an intercessory sense to be included.[3]

The specific background of the exhortations to constant prayer has already been discussed, namely the Jewish and Christian practice of regular prayers[4] and the ancient epistolary assurances of constant prayer for the readers.[5] The Jewish emphasis on the duty to pray three times daily seems to have been continued in some early Christian circles,[6] so that Paul was on familiar ground in offering these admonitions. Yet the special importance that he attached to them has become clear through the frequency and variety of his references to un-ceasing and urgent prayer.[7] As far as the location of these in-junctions in the structure of his letters is concerned, two of them appear to have formed an identifiable part of the closing litur-gical pattern in I Thessalonians and Philippians, contributing to the preparation of these letters for their liturgical use.[8]

I Thessalonians 5: 17f.

The first injunction to pray forms part of a closely knit threefold exhortation:

(Rejoice always,) *pray constantly*, (give thanks in all circumstances,) *for this is the will of God in Christ Jesus for you.* (I Thess. 5: 16–18)

[1] Exceptions are the somewhat longer exhortation in Phil. and the oblique reference to prayer in I Cor. 7: 5, where the admonition forms part of a sustained passage of instructions about marriage.

[2] For a recent discussion about Paul's dependence upon and creative use of his paraenetic sources, and a summary of the lengthy debate, see Furnish, pp. 25–98, and the summary in his appendix.

[3] Cf. Furnish, p. 90. 'While Paul's concrete ethical teachings owe something in form and content to commonly accredited traditions and ideas, these materials have, within the context of the apostle's letters, a significantly different function.' [4] See above, pp. 24, 182, n. 1. [5] See above, pp. 158ff.

[6] Didache 8: 3, 'In this manner [i.e., the Lord's Prayer] pray three times a day.' [7] See above, p. 181, n. 3.

[8] The prayer-exhortations in Rom. 12: 12, 14 and I Cor. 7: 5 occur earlier in the letter.

That Paul includes an intercessory sense in his general instruction to them to pray (προσεύχεσθε),[1] becomes evident in the verses that follow. As an item in the closing liturgical section of the letter, the exhortation is linked with the wish-prayer that follows (5: 23f.), with his prayer-request (v. 25), and with his final benediction (vv. 26–8). The wish-prayer and benediction would serve to focus their prayers upon their own immediate situation, while the prayer-request would direct their prayers also towards himself.[2]

That he intended his admonition to pray 'without ceasing' (ἀδιαλείπτως) to be taken with utmost seriousness, though not in a literal sense, has already become apparent.[3]

Furthermore, we shall best understand his meaning only as we take his threefold instructions together in the integrated whole in which he has presented them – rejoicing, praying constantly, giving thanks, and thereby carrying out God's will for them. For as we argued earlier[4] the passage sums up his fundamentally paradoxical understanding of the indissoluble relation between thanksgiving and intercessory prayer amid the victories and woes of the eschatological age. It was only as the believers were joyfully and thankfully assured of God's gifts that intercessory prayer could and must be rightly offered. Only such a life of complete openness to God in prayer would be in line with his will as revealed and made possible 'in Christ Jesus.'[5]

Philippians 4: 6

The next injunction occurs in Philippians, in a dynamic and joyous passage that parallels and extends the one we have just considered:

(Rejoice in the Lord always; again I will say, Rejoice. Let all men know your forbearance. The Lord is at hand. Have no anxiety

[1] For the use of προσεύχεσθε in an intercessory sense, see above, p. 19.

[2] See above, p. 262. J. M. Robinson regards vv. 16–22 as a unit (a series of 7 admonitions belonging together stylistically), in which may be seen an early stage of the growth of church order. The further development of this may be seen in Phil. 4: 4–6, I Cor. 14: 27ff., Eph. 5: 19ff., I Tim. 2. 'Die Hodajot-Formel,' pp. 222ff. Our view of the internal prayer links in this section may perhaps complement Robinson's interpretation.

[3] See above, pp. 181f.   [4] Above, pp. 168f.

[5] We assume with most commentators that the clause 'for this is the will of God...' refers to all three moments taken together: rejoicing, thanksgiving, supplication. Cf. Furnish, pp. 189f.

about anything,) *but in everything by prayer and supplication with thanksgiving let your requests be made known to God.* (And the peace of God, which passes all understanding, will keep your hearts and your minds in Christ Jesus.) (Phil. 4: 4–7)

The question arises again as to whether it is intercessory prayer that Paul is here thinking of, and again the answer must depend on the context. In this connection we are reminded that he had already gratefully acknowledged the ongoing intercessions of the Philippians on his behalf and had tacitly encouraged their continuance (1: 19). Yet it must be recognized that at this later point in the letter the emphasis is mainly upon the pressing needs of the Philippians themselves and the way in which God would supply those needs out of his abundance (cf. vv. 7, 9b, 19). While he includes the thought of their prayers for himself as he faces the prospect of death, the main emphasis here must be upon their united thanksgivings and supplication in regard to their own anxious situation. Nevertheless, we may look briefly at the passage as illuminating Paul's view of the need for constant supplications.

The passage begins with several short admonitions cast in his usual terse paraenetic mode. But coming to the prayer-injunction, he changes his style for two less concise sentences (vv. 6f.). Lohmeyer[1] raises the intriguing question whether at this point he is not moving from exhortation into supplication. Assuming that his readers are already praying (cf. 1: 19), Paul now utters a prayerful wish that their requests may indeed be made known to God (v. 6), and then declares that God will give his abundant answer (v. 7, cf. v. 19). In the previous verse, Lohmeyer suggests, Paul had prayed that outwardly their patient moderation might be recognized (γνωσθήτω) by all.[2] Now he prays that inwardly through their prayers their needs might be made known to God: 'In everything (I pray) may your requests be made known (γνωριϡέσθω) to God by your prayer and supplication with thanksgiving.' So possibly we have another wish-prayer towards the end of the letter. On balance, however, we prefer to regard the passage as a continuation of his exhortations.[3]

---

[1] *Philipper, Kolosser, Philemon*, p. 170.   [2] Cf. Paul's own situation in 1: 20.
[3] Such a change back and forth between paraenesis and prayer is not paralleled elsewhere in Paul's letters. Also it is doubtful if the two impera-

As an integral part of the closing liturgical pattern with its pointed final instructions,[1] the exhortation takes on additional significance for the readers. In a vivid and memorable way the passage epitomizes much of the joyful mood of the whole letter. Like the exhortation in I Thessalonians, this one purposefully links rejoicing, thanksgiving, and supplication. Yet here the instructions are extended and modified so as to reflect some of the main emphases of this letter from prison:[2] rejoicing in the midst of suffering, a thoughtful reconciliation to the will of God that would lead to a humble and Christlike forbearance, the expectation of rich and abundant blessings from the divine hand, a living sense of the nearness of the parousia.[3]

Of particular interest is the fact that Paul does not support his exhortation as in Thessalonians, by appealing to the will of God. Rather in the Philippian situation prayer is urged as the antidote for anxiety. 'Have no anxiety about anything,[4] but[5]...let your requests be made known to God.' The cure for anxiety, he says, is in the constant bringing of their needs to God in such thanksgivings as will joyfully acknowledge all their blessings, and in supplications that will truthfully recognize God's power to supply. So instead of a declaration of the will of God (I Thess. 5: 18b) he concludes fittingly with a declaration of the gift of peace (Phil. 4: 7).[6] God will give them such tranquility of spirit[7] as will guard them inwardly and enable them to 'stand firm in the Lord' (4: 1). They will share the apostle's own victory: 'In any and all circumstances I have learned the secret of facing plenty and hunger, abundance and want. I can do all things in him who strengthens me' (vv. 12f.). It is evident that this prayer-exhortation is closely linked with the mood and message of the letter to the Philippians and

tive verbs γνωσθήτω and γνωριζέσθω should be interpreted as wish-prayers; elsewhere Paul always couched these in the optative. See above, pp. 32ff.

[1] See above, p. 202.

[2] See above, pp. 197ff.

[3] Taking the traditional phrase, ὁ κύριος ἐγγύς, as referring to the parousia. Cf. Bonnard, *Philippians*, p. 75.

[4] Including threats of persecution, the attacks of their opponents, concern about Paul.

[5] ἀλλά, with a disjunctive significance that opposes prayer to anxiety.

[6] The one declaration seems to substitute formally for the other.

[7] See above, p. 64, n. 4.

places thanksgivings and supplications at the center of the church situation for which Paul is writing.

Romans 12: 12c, 14

Moving to the paraenetic section of Romans, we find two related admonitions about prayer:

(Rejoice in your hope, be patient in tribulation,) *be constant in prayer.*
(Contribute to the needs of the saints, practice hospitality.)
Bless those who persecute you; bless and do not curse them. (Rom. 12: 12–14)

Once again Paul is seen to base his instructions on traditional material. Clear indications are the loosely connected style, the terseness of the sentences that compose the surrounding unit (vv. 9–21), and the use of several 'link-words' that tie the material together.[1] In addition is the surprising use of several imperative participles[2] instead of his usual hortatory imperatives. Yet as in the other passages we have considered, it is evident from the general progression of the exhortations that here too he has carefully arranged and shaped them for his own specific purposes in writing to the quarrelling Roman Christians.[3]

In turning to the first prayer-exhortation, 'Be constant in prayer,' may we assume that intercessory supplications are intended? An affirmative answer is suggested by the main theme of the context, mutual caring and concern of the believers for one another. Throughout the letter he has been seeking the unity of his readers. Now in chapters 12 and 13 he centers his total paraenesis around the practice of love as the acceptable will of God (12: 2), beginning within the Christian fellowship

---

[1] 'Love,' 'good,' 'evil'; see the commentators, in particular Michel, p. 269.

[2] E.g., ἀποστυγοῦντες, καλλώμενοι, προσηγούμενοι, etc. For the origin of these in a Hebrew code of rules of a religious community, see D. Daube, 'Participle and Imperative in I Peter,' in E. G. Selwyn, *The First Epistle of Peter* (London, 1958), pp. 467–88. For a recent survey of the debate about the Semitic origin and the significance of these participles (not found elsewhere in Paul's letters, but in Eph., Col., Heb., and I Pet.), see C. H. Talbert, 'Tradition and Redaction in Romans XII.9–21,' *NTS*, 16 (1969–70), 81–93. Talbert proposes 'a traditional unit of ethical instruction, originating probably in Semitic Christianity, into which Paul or some other person has inserted additional material,' p. 91.

[3] Cf. Furnish, pp. 100ff.

itself (12: 3–13). All the diverse spiritual gifts of the members must be used for each other's good rather than for self-concerned aggrandizement (vv. 3–8). Yet even more is required than this outer life-style – their love must be a genuine inner love (v. 9):[1] so each must warmly love and give honor to the other (v. 10), each must be joyful, hopeful, patient in tribulation, constant in prayer (v. 12). Continual intercessions for one another must be a part of their caring, together with practical contributions to those in need (v. 13). As in Paul's other letters, this exhortation to constant prayer would take on added significance in the larger context of his own ceaseless intercessions (1: 9f.), and those particular prayers for himself that he would soon be asking from them (15: 30–2).

We note in our passage that Paul once again follows a pattern made familiar in the prayer-exhortations in I Thessalonians and Philippians: the linking of supplications with rejoicing, hope, and patience. So it is from our preceding expositions that we may fill out our understanding of these bald admonitions in Romans. Their underlying significance is further revealed through his discussion earlier in this letter, where tribulation, hope, patience, and prayer have been deeply and organically connected (8: 18–27).[2]

With the second prayer-exhortation (12: 14) Paul moves beyond the narrow confines of the fellowship and introduces the question of love for those outside. How would love be expressed toward the enemies and the persecutors (vv. 14–21), how would it be shown toward the authorities of the state (13: 1–7)?[3] The answer is summarized at the outset:

Bless those who persecute you; bless and do not curse them. (12: 14)

In selecting this saying, Paul may have been influenced by several things. The pun word διώκειν (that could mean both 'practise'[4] and 'persecute') might originally have served to link it with the previous verse in a series of traditional teachings. The saying gained effect by its close echoing of the words of

---

[1] Cf. the similar progression in I Cor., from chap. 12 to chap. 13. Furnish, p. 100. [2] Leenhardt, *Romans*, p. 315.

[3] How serious their problems in relation to the state were at the time, is unknown. At any rate Paul is advising them against actions that would bring further difficulty on this score.

[4] As in 'practice hospitality' (v. 13).

Jesus.[1] But more important for Paul's immediate purpose, it expressed in a nutshell the fundamental attitude required of believers toward nonbelievers. Once again he had found it necessary to move beyond the household of faith. Here love, and the intercessions motivated by love, must include even those who persecuted them.[2]

I Corinthians 7: 5

One further prayer-exhortation need be mentioned only briefly, for it seems to add little to the apostle's teaching about intercessions. Occurring in his instructions to the Corinthians about sexual relations in marriage, it refers only incidentally to the practice or prayer, and does not necessarily imply intercessory prayer:

(Do not refuse one another except perhaps by agreement for a season,) *that you may devote yourselves to prayer;* (but then come together again, lest Satan tempt you through lack of self-control.) (I Cor. 7: 5)

Although there were ideas current among Jews and Gentiles that sexual intercourse brought cult impurity,[3] it seems unlikely that Paul himself would be greatly concerned about such ritualistic barriers to prayer. Rather he is principally concerned about the practical hindrance caused to concentration in prayer, and to the regular practice of prayer.[4] This he assumed to be important for the believers.

In summary, the exhortations to prayer, although sparse in their number and concise in their paraenetic form, may be seen as further evidence of the apostle's regular teaching to his churches: that they join together regularly in intercessory supplications with thanksgiving, for himself, for one another, and for all men.

[1] Cf. Matt. 5: 44, Lk. 6: 28. It is generally agreed that we have here an echo, though not a direct citation (Michel, p. 273, W. D. Davies, *Paul and Rabbinic Judaism*, p. 138, Talbert, p. 87, etc.).

[2] Cf. the inclusiveness in Paul's prayers for the Thessalonians, 'and may the Lord make you increase and abound in love to one another and to all men,' I Thess. 3: 12. See above, pp. 14, n. 1, 57f.

[3] See Harder, pp. 20f. for documentation; also Strack–Billerbeck, III, 372, on abstention for purposes of making a votive offering or studying the Torah. Cf. Exod. 19: 14f., Lev. 15: 18, I Sam. 21: 5.

[4] Cf. I Pet. 3: 7; Test. Patr. XII, Naph. 8: 8. Harder, *ibid.*

APPENDED NOTE 2

Syntactical and other stylistic marks of the prayer-requests

(*a*) The address to the readers is (twice) ἀδελφοί (I Thess. 5: 25, Rom. 15: 30); or alternatively a 2nd pers. pronoun, or verb in 2nd pers.

(*b*) The request for prayer is made by a verb in the imperative: I Thess. 5: 25, προσεύχεσθε [cf. Col. 4: 18, II Thess. 3: 1]; or by παρακαλῶ with the infin.: Rom. 15: 30ff.; or by a participle: II Cor. 1: 11, συνυπουργούντων (gen. absol.). [Cf. Eph. 6: 18, and Col. 4: 3, προσευχόμενοι, depending on an imperative verb.] The tacit requests use a prepositional phrase: Phil. 1: 19, διὰ τῆς ὑμῶν δεήσεως; Philem. 22, διὰ τῶν προσευχῶν ὑμῶν.

(*c*) The intercessory aspect is indicated by a prepositional phrase, περὶ ἡμῶν, ὑπὲρ ἐμοῦ, or ὑπὲρ ἡμῶν, without any appreciable difference in meaning between the phrases. [In Col. 4: 18, simply the pronoun μου.]

(*d*) In the tacit request, Phil. 1: 19, the intercessory aspect is suggested by μοι ἀποβήσεται; cf. the LXX Job 13: 16. In Philem. 22, it is expressed as ἐλπίζω...ὅτι...χαρισθήσομαι.

(*e*) The prayer content is given as follows: by a ἵνα clause with one or more subjunctive verbs: Rom. 15: 31 [Eph. 6: 18–20, Col. 4: 3f., II Thess. 3: 1f.] [In Col. 4: 18, we have simply a phrase in the gen. case, τῶν δεσμῶν.] No content is stated in I Thess. 5: 25, nor in II Cor. 1: 11.

The tacit request in Phil. 1: 19f. suggests the content by the apostle's statement οἶδα with a ὅτι clause and fut. indic. In Philem. it is suggested by Paul's hope: ἐλπίζω with a ὅτι clause and fut. indic.

(*f*) That their prayers will be in response to his own for them, is indicated by καί (also) in I Thess. 5: 25 (Mss are divided), II Cor. 1: 11 (cf. II Cor. 9: 14, καὶ αὐτῶν); suggested less directly in Phil. 1: 19 (see pp. 277f.), in Rom. 15: 30–2 (see p. 265), and probably in Philem. 22 (see p. 283).

CHAPTER II

CONCLUDING STATEMENT

At the beginning of this study we set out to examine Paul's intercessory prayer passages so as to discover not only their function within his letters, but also how important a rôle intercessory prayer played in his pastoral and priestly office and in his total apostolic strategy, and how far he relied upon a widespread practice of mutual intercessions among his churches. From time to time answers have been suggested throughout the work. Thus only a brief review is needed.

In an attempt to isolate the intercessory passages and describe their formal characteristics, we understood that within the dynamic activity of prayer there could be no hard and fast line between thanksgivings, intercessions, and representative corporate supplications. Nevertheless we argued for the significance of intercessory prayer as a recognizable type of prayer, in which the one who prays is concerned as mediator and intercessor before God, principally for the needs of others.

As our examination progressed we found a remarkable consistency in the functioning of the prayer passages in each letter. As far as the wish-prayers and prayer-reports were concerned, each in its own way epitomized the dominant message of the letter and underlined its central concerns. In Paul's hands the conventional usages of ancient letter style turned out to be weighted with new meaning and the prayers were found to give concentrated living expression to his deeply responsible love, his vital anxieties and burning hopes. Each of the prayers was evoked by and adapted to a particular context; the lines of concern flowed together through each threatening occasion, through the letter composed for that situation, and through the prayer passages that reflected it.

That the wish-prayers and prayer-reports expressed Paul's currently central interests was revealed further by their strategic location within each letter. Appearing at the beginning and the end of the letter by way of introduction and conclusion, or at important transitional points, they served to focus the letter itself by drawing attention at intervals to its underlying themes. Thus they would reinforce Paul's pastoral exhortations and rekindle the readers' aspirations. In addition we observed a liturgical purpose that must have partly shaped the prayer passages and, especially, the final section of each epistle. The prayers were related to a liturgically oriented closing pattern in such a way as to adapt the letter for use in the further corporate worship of the readers.

While immediate concerns did shape the prayers, they were grounded in and directed by the gospel of Christ. It was the salvation events of the gospel that lay behind Paul's apostolic commission and guided his ministry. So too his prayers were made possible only because of the love of God revealed in the gospel; by this their contours were guided and their range immeasurably deepened and extended. All his requests must be according to the will of God revealed in Christ. Love was the matrix in which Paul's constant intercessions were nurtured and maintained.

The vitality and weight of the prayers appeared moreover in the very extravagance of his requests, their warmth of feeling and their unbounded expectation. Paul prayed for all blessings in full measure; all his readers were included, those with him and those against him. His heightened eschatological and adventist perspective added increased urgency to his thanksgivings and intercessions. In his prayers he was always conscious of living 'before God,' already in the last days with parousia and judgment close ahead, dominated by the belief that his readers and he would stand shortly at the judgment seat of Christ. In addition we noted considerable evidence in the prayer passages that he understood himself in a special way as priestly intercessor, sharing in the intercessions of the exalted Christ and the Holy Spirit, an eschatological figure accountable for presenting his churches back to Christ at the parousia. In the light of this special commission his prayers were given a profoundly deeper import. So he prayed for nothing less than the complete sanctification of his fellow believers and agonized in supplication for his fellow Jews.

It was seen also that the wish-prayers and prayer-reports contributed directly to the practice of mutual intercession. As examples of actual prayer by the apostle, and through their emphasis on the frequency of his praying, these passages would invite the readers to view their own lives and activities prayerfully and in turn to intercede for the apostle and for one another. Thus he would encourage the readers to imitate him, composing or adapting prayers suitable for their services of worship, teaching them how to pray and what to pray for. The prayer passages, particularly those near the close of the letters, would help to lead them into their united observances of the Lord's supper after the reading of the letter.

Even the opening and closing blessings would take their place in the network of prayer. The curses, with their stringent severity, served as a drastic intercessory response to emergency situations in which Paul was forced to exercise prophetic judgment – polarizing, if necessary, the church to which he was writing.

When we came to Paul's exhortations and his requests for prayer, we noted how these underlined his hope that the believers would grow into maturity by accepting responsibility for one another across all barriers. We were reminded of a central passion of his life – to bring reconciliation and unity throughout the church. One sign of this was the unfailing corporate emphasis in all his thanksgivings and supplications, a continual effort to foster their prayerful concern for himself, for his wider mission work, and for one another. He longed for a wide-ranging network of prayers spanning the divided segments of the fragmented church, but going even beyond to include in their scope the salvation of Israel and the good of those outsiders who threatened and persecuted them.

What part did Paul's own prayers play within the actual strategy behind his intense missionary activity? It was evident that his constantly shifting tactics included several ways of aiding his scattered churches. That he much preferred to meet them face to face was shown by his unremitting journeys to visit and revisit them. In the event that this proved impossible he would send a trusted deputy, often bearing a pastoral letter from his own hand. The writing of these letters he saw as a continuation of his intercessory activity. In addition, the collection played a special rôle in bringing the churches together. But alongside of all these there was the ceaseless remembering of his churches in prayers of thanksgiving and supplication,[1] whereby he might continue to minister to them even when compelled to be absent.[2] Prayer buttressed all his mission work – in advance of his visits, during them, and after he had departed. All his plans were conceived under the constant sense of the guidance and will of God. None of his bold advances would have seemed worthwhile to him apart from continual undergirding by the prayers of the apostle and his associates. Taken together, then, the intercessory prayer passages offer impressive documentation of Paul's unfailing reliance upon the ministry of supplication, his own and that of his fellow believers.

As we examined the prayers, we noticed signs of some of the strains arising from the exercise of his complex ministry. In several prayers there was reflected the tension between his need to discipline his unruly churches and his desire to show forth the meekness of Christ, or between his apostolic relationship and his warm personal feelings for his friends. It was uncertain at times whether his prayers and benedictions should be understood as assured pronouncements or as requests for blessing upon his readers. His prophetic certainty often seemed to merge into his intercessory hopefulness, so that the apostle was constrained to express his wishes for his readers before God in prayer, while trusting all the time in the assured faithfulness of God. Linked with this ambivalence was the dialectical relation between his confident thanksgivings and his anxious supplications in the interim period of the 'already' and the 'not yet'; but invariably supplication led him back to thanksgiving as he remembered mercies already given.

Within the very center of the apostle's existence lay an inescapable intercessory element, profoundly affecting his understanding of the gospel and the exercise of his ministry. Yet in the end all of his missionary efforts were to bring increased praises and thanksgivings to God. Thus he strove for an ever-increasing circle of those who would call upon God's name in prayer. 'You also must help us by prayer, so that many will give thanks on our behalf for the blessing granted to us in answer to many prayers.'[3]

---

[1] Cf. II Cor. 11: 28, 'And apart from other things, there is the daily pressure upon me of my anxiety for all the churches.'

[2] Cf. Fisher, *Prayer in the New Testament*, p. 94.   [3] II Cor. 1: 11.

APPENDIXES

PRAYER PASSAGES IN THE PAULINE EPISTLES

(So that this list may be as complete as possible, a few borderline references are included.)

Doxology (δοξάζω): Rom. 1: 21, 23, 4: 20, 11: 33–6, 15: 6, 9, 16: 25–7; I Cor. 6: 20, 10: 31; II Cor. 1: 20, 4: 15, 9: 13; Gal. 1: 5, 24 [Eph. 3: 20f.]; Phil. 1: 11, 2: 11, 4: 20.

Praise (ἐξομολογέομαι, ἔπαινος): Rom. 14: 11, 15: 9–11 [Eph. 1: 6, 12, 14]; Phil. 1: 11, 2: 11.

Blessing (εὐλογέομαι): Rom. 1: 25, 9: 5; I Cor. 14: 16; II Cor. 1: 3ff., 11: 31 [Eph. 1: 3].

Worship (προσκυνέω): I Cor. 14: 25.

Hymns, community singing, psalms, etc. (ψάλμος, ψάλλω, ὕμνος, ᾠδή, ᾄδω): I Cor. 14: 15, 26 [Eph. 5: 19; Col. 3: 16].

Thanksgiving (εὐχαρισ-τία, -τός, -τῶ): Rom. 1: 8ff., 21, 6: 17f., 7: 25, 14: 6; I Cor. 1: 4ff., 14, 10: 30, 11: 24, 14: 16f., 18, 15: 57; II Cor. 2: 14, 4: 15, 8: 16f., 9: 11f.; Gal. none [Eph. 1: 15ff., 5: 4, 20]; Phil. 1: 3ff., 4: 6 [Col. 1: 3ff., 2: 5, 7, 3: 15b–17, 4: 2]; I Thess. 1: 2ff., 2: 13ff., 3: 9, 5: 18 [II Thess. 1: 3ff., 2: 13]; Philem. 4ff.

Boasting – in Christ or before God (καυχάομαι and cognates): Rom. 5: 2f., 11, 15: 17ff.; I Cor. 1: 29–31; II Cor. 1: 12–14, 7: 4, and frequently in chaps. 10, 11, 12; Phil. 1: 26, 2: 16, 3: 3; I Thess. 2: 19.

Petition for self (δέομαι, προσεύχομαι): Rom. 1: 10, 7: 24, 9: 3; I Cor. 14: 13; II Cor. 12: 8; I Thess. 3: 10. (Apart from II Cor. 12:8, these instances are all problematical for one reason or another.)

Intercessory prayer for others, including blessings and curses (ὑπερ-εντυγχάνω): Rom. 1: 7b, 9f., 8: 15f., 23, 26f., 34, 9: 1–3, 10: 1, 11: 2–5, 12: 12c, 14, 15: 5f., 13, 30–2, 33, 16: 20a, 20b; I Cor. 1: 3, 8, 2: 9–16, 5: 3–5, 11: 10, 15: 29, 16: 22a, 23; II Cor. 1: 2, 7, 11, 14, 13: 7, 9b, 11b, 14; Gal. 1: 3, 8f., 4: 6, 6: 16, 18 [Eph. 1: 2, 16–23, 3: 14–19, 6: 18–20, 23f.]; Phil. 1: 2, 4, 9–11, 19f., 4: 6f., 9b, 23 [Col. 1: 2b, 3b, 9–14, 29, 2: 1–3, 5, 4: 2–4, 12, 18b, 18c]; I Thess. 1: 1b, 2f., 3: 10, 11–13, 5: 17f., 23, 24b, 25, 28 [II Thess. 1: 2, 11f., 2: 16f., 3: 1–3, 5, 16, 18]; Philem. 3, 4, 6, 22b, 25.

General prayer – type not specified (προσεύχομαι, λαλέω τῷ θεῷ):
I Cor. 11: 4f., 13, 14: 14f., 28. (ἐπικαλέω): Rom. 10: 12–14;
I Cor. 1: 2; II Cor. 1: 23.

APPENDIX II

PASSAGES REFERRING TO INTERCESSORY PRAYER IN THE PAULINE EPISTLES

Rom. 1: 7b, opening blessing; 1: 9f., prayer-report; 8: 15f., 23, 26f.,
didactic references (Spirit); 8: 34, didactic reference (exalted
Christ); 9: 3, prayer-report (?); 10: 1, prayer-report; 11: 2–5,
didactic reference (Elijah); 12: 12c, 14, exhortations; 15: 5f.,
wish-prayer (optative); 15: 13, wish-prayer (optative); 15: 30–2,
prayer-request; 15: 33, peace blessing (no verb); 16: 20a,
declaration-prayer (fut. indic.); 16: 20b, closing blessing.

I Cor. 1: 3, opening blessing; 1: 8(f.), declaration-prayer (fut.
indic.); 2: 9–16, didactic reference (Spirit); 5: 3a, prayer-report
(?); 5: 3–5, injunction about a curse; 11: 10, didactic reference
(angel intercessors) (?); 15: 29, didactic reference (baptism for
the dead) (?); 16: 22a, curse; 16: 23, closing blessing.

II Cor. 1: 2, opening blessing; 1: 7, prayer-report (?); 1: 11,
prayer-request; 9: 14, prayer-report (third party); 13: 7, 9b,
prayer-report; 13: 11b, blessing (doubtful – fut. indic.); 13: 14,
closing blessing.

Gal. 1: 3, opening blessing; 1: 8f., curse; 4: 6, didactic reference
(Spirit); 6: 16, pronouncement blessing (no verb); 6: 18, closing
blessing.

Phil. 1: 2, opening blessing; 1: 4, 9–11, prayer-report; 1: 19f.,
indirect prayer-request; 4: 6, exhortation; 4: 7, peace affirmation
(fut. indic.); 4: 9b, peace affirmation (fut. indic.); 4: 19,
declaration-prayer (fut. indic.); 4: 23, closing blessing.

I Thess. 1: 1b, opening blessing; 1: 2b–3, prayer-report; 3: 10,
prayer-report; 3: 11–13, wish-prayer (optative); 5: 17f., exhortation; 5: 23, wish-prayer (optative); 5: 24b, wish-prayer (doubtful – fut. indic.); 5: 25, prayer-request; 5: 28, closing blessing.

Philem. 3, opening blessing; 4, 6, prayer-report; 22b, indirect
prayer-request; 25, closing blessing.

IN DEUTERO-PAULINE EPISTLES

Eph. 1: 2, opening blessing; 1: 16–23, prayer-report; 3: 14–19, prayer-report; 6: 18–20, exhortation and prayer-request; 6: 23f., closing blessing.

Col. 1: 2b, opening blessing; 1: 3b, 9–14, prayer-report; 1: 29 – 2: 3, prayer-report; 2: 5, prayer-report; 4: 2–4, exhortation and prayer-request; 4: 12, prayer-report (third party); 4: 18b, prayer-request; 4: 18c, closing blessing.

II Thess. 1: 2, opening blessing; 1: 11f., prayer-report; 2: 16f., wish-prayer (optative); 3: 1–3, prayer-request; 3: 5, wish-prayer (optative); 3: 16, wish-prayer (optative); 3: 18, closing blessing.

APPENDIX III

CLASSIFIED INVENTORY OF INTERCESSORY PRAYER PASSAGES IN THE PAULINE EPISTLES

CLASS I: INTERCESSORY WISH-PRAYERS

(including blessings, curses, and some passages with the verb in the future indicative instead of the optative)

Principal wish-prayers

Four clear examples with the optative:[1]
Rom. 15: 5f. (δῴη); 15: 13 (πληρῶσαι); I Thess. 3: 11–13 (κατευθύναι, πλεονάσαι, περισσεύσαι); 5: 23(f.) (ἁγιάσαι, τηρηθείη). [With these examples may be compared similar wish-prayers in II Thess. 2: 16f., 3: 5, 16; also II Tim. 1: 16, 18, 2: 25 (4: 16b); Heb. 13: 20f.]
One probable example with the optative understood:
Rom. 15: 33 ('peace' benediction).
Three questionable examples with the future indicative:[2]
Rom. 16: 20a (συντρίψει or συντρίψαι);[3] I Cor. 1: 8(f.) (βεβαιώσει); Phil. 4: 19 (πληρώσει or πληρῶσαι).[4]

---

[1] The popular phrase μὴ γένοιτο was used only as an exclamation and will be omitted from consideration. See Burton, *Syntax of New Testament Moods and Tenses*, p. 79.
[2] See above, pp. 33–6. Four other doubtful passages with the fut. indic. may be considered declarations rather than wish-prayers: II Cor. 13: 11b, Phil. 4: 7, 9b, I Thess. 5: 24b. [Cf. also II Thess. 3: 3.]
[3] See above, p. 33, n. 3.   [4] *Ibid.*

Epistolary greetings: the opening benedictions

The opening 'grace and peace' benediction remains the same in each letter, except for a shortened form in I Thess. 1: 1b:

Rom. 1: 7b, I Cor. 1: 3, II Cor. 1: 2, Gal. 1: 3, Phil. 1: 2, I Thess. 1: 1b, Philem. 3. [Cf. Eph. 1: 2, Col. 1: 2b, II Thess. 1: 2.]

Epistolary greetings: the closing benedictions

The closing 'grace' benediction varies considerably from letter to letter:

Rom. 16: 20b; I Cor. 16: 23; II Cor. 13: 13 (the 'trinitarian' form); Gal. 6: 18; Phil. 4: 23; I Thess. 5: 28; Philem. 25. [Cf. the varying benedictions in Eph. 6: 23f., Col. 4: 18c, II Thess. 3: 18.]

Curses and a 'pronouncement blessing'

I Cor. 5: 3–5 (injunction to pronounce a curse on Paul's behalf); I Cor. 16: 22 (curse); Gal. 1: 8f.(curse); 6: 16 ('pronouncement blessing').

CLASS II: INTERCESSORY PRAYER-REPORTS

In the thanksgiving periods[1]

Rom. 1: 9f.; Phil. 1: 4, 9–11; I Thess. 1: 2b–3; 3: 10; Philem. 4b, 6 (II Cor. 1: 7, a prayer-report surrogate?).[2] [With the above may be compared and contrasted the elaborate prayer-reports in Eph. 1: 16–23; Col. 1: 3b, 9–14; II Thess. 1: 11f.]

In the body of the letters

Reports of prayers by the writer(s) for the readers:
(I Cor. 5: 3, a negative prayer-report, closely associated with a curse);[3] II Cor. 13: 7, 9b. [Compare also the elaborate prayer-reports in Eph. 3: 14–19; Col. 1: 29 – 2: 3, and 2: 5.]
Reports of prayers by the writer for a third party:
Rom. 9: 3 (borderline case);[4] 10: 1.
Reports of prayers by a third party for the readers:
II Cor. 9: 14. [Compare also Col. 4: 12.]

[1] Cf. the list in Schubert's table, cols v–vii, type ia (*Form and Function*, pp. 54f.).
[2] See above, pp. 226–9.
[3] Cf. above, under curses; see also p. 145, n. 3.
[4] See above, pp. 255f.

CLASS III: PARAENETIC REFERENCES TO INTERCESSORY PRAYER

*Specific requests (direct and indirect) by writer to readers
for intercessory prayer for himself*

Rom. 15: 30–2; II Cor. 1: 11; Phil. 1: 19f. (indirect prayer-request); I Thess. 5: 25; Philem. 22 (indirect prayer-request). [Compare also Eph. 6: 18–20 (exhortation and prayer-request); Col. 4: 2–4 (exhortation and prayer-request); 4: 18b; II Thess. 3: 1–3; Heb. 13: 18.]

*General exhortations about the practice of
(intercessory?) prayer*

Rom. 12: 12c, 14; I Cor. 7: 5; Phil. 4: 6; I Thess. 5: 17f. (Except in Rom. 12: 14 the intercessory aspect is not explicit.) [Compare also Eph. 6: 18–20 (exhortation and request); Col. 4: 2–4 (exhortation and request). In both instances intercession is implied.]

CLASS IV: DIDACTIC AND SPECULATIVE REFERENCES TO INTERCESSORY PRAYER

Intercessory prayer of the Spirit:[1]
Rom. 8: 15f., 23, 26f.; Gal. 4: 6 (cf. I Cor. 2: 9–16).
Intercessory prayer of the exalted Christ:
Rom. 8: 34.
Other intercessors:
Rom. 11: 2–5 (Elijah); I Cor. 11: 10 (reference to angel intercessors?); 15: 29 (baptism on behalf of the dead).

APPENDIX IV

LITURGICALLY ORIENTED CLOSING PATTERN IN THE PAULINE EPISTLES TABULATION OF PRINCIPAL FEATURES

1. *Admonition to constant rejoicing, prayer, thanksgiving*
Rom. 12: 12–14; Phil. 4: 6; I Thess. 5: 16–18. Lacking in I Cor., II Cor., Gal., Philem. [Cf. Eph. 6: 18; Col. 4: 2.]

[1] Cf. also the following Spirit passages already listed under classes II and III: I Cor. 5: 3; Phil. 1: 19 [Eph. 6: 18; Col. 2: 5].

2. *Summarizing wish-prayer(s)*
Rom. 15: 5f., 13, 16: 20a (adapted peace blessing); II Cor. 13: 7,
9b (prayer-reports); Gal. 6: 16 (adapted peace blessing); Phil. 4: 19;
I Thess. 5: 23f. (adapted peace blessing). Lacking in I Cor. (but
see 16: 22), Philem. [Cf. II Thess. 2: 16f. (3: 3?), 3: 5; Col. substitutes a prayer-report, 4: 12.]

3. *Reference to collection or gift*
Rom. 15: 25–8; I Cor. 16: 1–9; Phil. 4: 10–18; Philem. 18–22.
Lacking in II Cor., Gal., I Thess.

4. *Request for readers' prayers*
Rom. 15: 30–2 (Gal. 6: 17, negative request); I Thess. 5: 25;
Philem. 22. Lacking in I Cor., II Cor., Phil. (anticipated at 1: 19f.).
[Cf. Eph. 6: 19f.; Col. 4: 3f., 18b; II Thess. 3: 1.]

5. *Peace blessing (related to the holy kiss)*
Rom. 15: 33, 16: 20a; II Cor. 13: 11b; Gal. 6: 16; Phil. 4: 7, 9b;
I Thess. 5: 23. Lacking in I Cor., Philem. [Cf. Eph. 6: 23; II Thess.
3: 16.] (Rom. 16: 20a, II Cor. 13: 11b, Gal. 6: 16 [II Thess. 3: 16],
are all associated with a preceding stern warning.)

6. *Greetings*
Rom. 16: 3–15, 16b, 21–3; I Cor. 16: 19f.; II Cor. 13: 13; Phil.
4: 21f.; I Thess. 5: 26 (merged with instruction for holy kiss);
Philem. 23f. Lacking in Gal. (except for addition of 'brethren' at
6: 18). [Cf. Col. 4: 10–17.]

7. *Holy kiss*
Rom. 16: 16a; I Cor. 16: 20b; II Cor. 13: 12; I Thess. 5: 26. Lacking
in Gal., Phil. (though perhaps suggested in 4: 21a), Philem.

8. *Stern warning*
Rom. 16: 17–20a; I Cor. 16: 22; II Cor. 13: 5f., 10; Gal. 6: 11–13,
17; I Thess. 5: 27. Lacking in Phil. (though anticipated at 3: 2–21),
Philem. [Cf. Col. 4: 17 (?); II Thess. 3: 14f.]

9. *Grace blessing*
Rom. 16: 20b; I Cor. 16: 23; II Cor. 13: 14; Gal. 6: 18; Phil. 4: 23;
I Thess. 5: 28; Philem. 25. [Cf. Eph. 6: 24; Col. 4: 18c; II Thess.
3: 18.]

Interspersed with the above items are assorted pastoral exhortations, instructions about messengers, and other personal items.

SELECT BIBLIOGRAPHY

Albright, W. F., and Mann, C. S. 'Two Texts in I Corinthians,' *NTS*, 16 (1969–70), 271–6.

Allo, E.-B. *Saint Paul Première Épitre aux Corinthiens*, 10th edn, Paris, 1956.

Saint Paul Seconde Épitre aux Corinthiens, 10th edn, Paris, 1956.

Althaus, P. *Der Brief an die Galater*, 5th edn, Göttingen, 1949.

Der Brief an die Römer, 6th edn, Göttingen, 1949.

Amiot, F. *Saint Paul, Épitre aux Galates, Épitres aux Thessaloniciens* (*Verbum Salutis*, vol. XIV), Paris, 1946.

Arndt, W. F., and Gingrich, F. W. *A Greek–English Lexicon of the New Testament and Other Early Christian Literature*: A translation and adaptation of Walter Bauer's Griechisch–Deutsches Wörterbuch zu den Schriften des Neuen Testaments und der übrigen urchristlichen Literatur, fourth revised and augmented edition, 1952. Chicago, 1957.

Astung, R. *Die Heiligkeit im Urchristentum*, Göttingen, 1930.

Audet, J.-P. 'Esquisse historique du genre littéraire de la "bénédiction" juive et de l'"eucharistie" Chrétienne,' *Revue Biblique*, 65 (1958), 371–99.

Bachmann, P. *Der zweite Brief des Paulus an die Korinther*, Leipzig, 1909.

Baelz, P. R. *Prayer and Providence*, New York, 1968.

Bahr, G. J. 'The Use of the Lord's Prayer in the Primitive Church,' *JBL*, 84 (1965), 153–9.

'The Subscriptions in the Pauline Letters,' *JBL*, 87 (1968), 27–41.

Bain, J. A. *The Prayers of the Apostle Paul*, London, n.d. (1937?).

Barrett, C. K. *A Commentary on the First Epistle to the Corinthians*, New York, 1968.

The Epistle to the Romans (HNTC), New York, 1957.

'Paul's Opponents in II Corinthians,' *NTS*, 17 (1970–1), 233–54.

Barth, K. *The Epistle to the Philippians* (E.Tr.), London, 1962.

The Resurrection of the Dead (E.Tr.), New York, 1933.

Bartsch, H.-W. 'The Concept of Faith in Paul's Letter to the Romans,' *Biblical Research*, 13 (1968), 41–53.

Bauer, W. *Der Wortgottesdienst der Ältesten Christen*, Tübingen, 1930.

Beardslee, W. A. *Human Achievement and Divine Vocation in the Message of Paul* (*SBT*, 31), London, 1961.

Beare, F. W. *The Epistle to the Colossians*, IB, vol. XI.

The Epistle to the Philippians (HNTC), New York, 1959.

Behm, J. 'ἀνάθεμα,' *TWNT*, I, 356f.
'παράκλητος,' *TWNT*, V, 798–812.
Berger, K. 'Zu Den Sogennanten Sätzen Heiligen Rechts,' *NTS*, 17 (1970–1), 10–40.
Best, E. 'Spiritual Sacrifice. General Priesthood in the New Testament,' *Interpretation*, 14 (1960), 273–99.
Betz, O. *Der Paraklet: Fürsprecher im häretischen Spätjudentum im Johannes-Evangelium und in neu gefundenen gnostischen Schriften* (Arbeiten zur Geschichte des Spätjudentums und Urchristentums II), Leiden, 1963.
Betz, O., Hengel, M., and Schmidt, P. (eds.). *Abraham unser Vater, Festschrift für Otto Michel*, Leiden, 1963.
Beyer, H. W. 'κανών,' *TWNT*, III, 600–6.
Bicknell, E. J. *The First and Second Epistles to the Thessalonians* (Westminster Commentaries), London, 1932.
Bieder, W. 'Gebetswirklichkeit und Gebetsmöglichkeit bei Paulus. Das Beten des Geistes und das Beten im Geiste,' *TZ*, IV (1948), 22–40.
Bjerkelund, C. J. *Parakalô: Form, Funktion und Sinn der parakalô-Sätze in der paulinischen Briefen*, Oslo, 1967.
'Stilen i de paulinske formaningssetninger' (The Style of the Pauline Exhortation-Clauses), *Norsk Teologisk Tidsskrift*, 61 (1960), 193–217.
Blass, F., and Debrunner, A. *A Greek Grammar of the New Testament and Other Early Christian Literature*. Translated and revised from the ninth–tenth German edition incorporating supplementary notes of A. Debrunner, by Robert W. Funk. Chicago, 1961.
Boer, P. A. H. de. *De Vorbede in het Oude Testament* (*Oudtestamentische Studiën*, III), Leiden, 1943.
Boer, W. P. De. *The Imitation of Paul; an Exegetical Study*, Kampen, 1962.
Bonnard, P. *L'Épître de Saint Paul aux Galates*, Neuchâtel, 1953.
L'Épître de Saint Paul aux Philippiens, Neuchâtel, 1950.
Bornemann, W. *Die Thessalonicherbriefe* (Meyer's Kommentar), 6th edn, Göttingen, 1894.
Bornkamm, G. 'Das Anathema in der urchristlichen Abendmahlsliturgie,' *TLZ* (1950), 227–30.
'The History of the Origin of the So-called Second Letter to the Corinthians,' *NTS*, 8 (1961–2), 258–64.
'Der Philipperbrief als Paulinische Briefsammlung,' *Neotestamentica et Patristica, Freundesgabe O. Cullmann* (*Nov. Test.* Suppl. 6), 1962, 192–202.

Brichto, H. C. *The Problem of Curse in the Hebrew Bible*, Philadelphia, 1963.

Büchsel, F. 'εἰλικρινής,' *TWNT*, II, 396.

Buck, C., and Taylor, G. *Saint Paul: a Study of the Development of his Thought*, New York, 1969.

Bultmann, R. *Exegetische Probleme des zweiten Korintherbriefes*, Uppsala, 1947.

The History of the Synoptic Tradition (E.Tr.), New York, 1963.

Der Stil der Paulinischen Predigt und die Kynischstoische Diatribe, Göttingen, 1910.

Theology of the New Testament (E.Tr.), 2 vols, New York, 1951–5.

'ἀλήθεια,' *TWNT*, I, 233–48.

'γινώσκω, ἐπίγνωσις,' *TWNT*, I, 688–715.

'ἔλεος,' *TWNT*, II, 474–82.

'καυχάομαι,' *TWNT*, III, 646–54.

Bultmann, R., and Rengstorf, K. H. 'ἐλπίς, ἐλπίζω,' *TWNT*, II, 515–30.

Bultmann, R., and Weiser, A. 'πιστεύω, κτλ.,' *TWNT*, VI, 174–230.

Burton, E. DeW. *Syntax of New Testament Moods and Tenses*, 3rd edn, Chicago, 1898.

Cambier, J. 'La Chair et l'Esprit en I Cor. v. 5,' *NTS*, 15 (1968–9), 221–32.

Campbell, J. Y. 'ΚΟΙΝ∩ΝΙΑ and its cognates in the New Testament,' *JBL*, 51 (1932), 378ff.

Campenhausen, H. Frhr. von. *Die Begrundung kirchlicher Entscheidungen beim Apostel Paulus. Zur Grundlegung des Kirchenrechts*, Heidelberg, 1957.

Kirchliches Amt und Geistliche Vollmacht..., Tübingen, 1953.

'Der urchristeliche Apostelbegriff,' *Studia Theologica*, 1 (1947), 96–130.

Champion, L. G. *Benedictions and Doxologies in the Epistles of Paul*, Oxford, 1934.

Charles, R. H. *The Apocrypha and Pseudepigrapha of the Old Testament*, 2 vols, Oxford, 1913.

Chase, F. H. *The Lord's Prayer in the Early Church*, Cambridge, 1891.

Conzelmann, H. *Der erste Brief an die Korinther* (Meyer's Kommentar), Göttingen, 1969.

Cooper, R. M. 'Leitourgos Christou Iesou. Toward a Theology of Christian Prayer,' *ATR*, 47 (1965), 263–75.

Coutts, J. 'Ephesians I.3–14 and I Peter I.3–12.' *NTS*, 3 (1956–7), 115–27.

Craig, C. T. *The First Epistle to the Corinthians*, IB, vol. x.

Cranfield, C. E. B. 'Hebrews 13.20–21,' *Scot. Journ. Theol.*, 20 (1967), 437–41.

Cullmann, O. *Christ and Time: The Primitive Christian Conception of Time and History* (E.Tr.), rev. edn, Philadelphia, 1964.

Early Christian Worship (E.Tr.) (*SBT*, 10), London, 1953.

'Le caractère eschatologique du dévoir missionaire et de la consciènce apostolique de S. Paul. Étude sur le κατέχον (-ων) de II Thess. 2, 6–7,' *Revue d'Histoire et de Philosophie Religieuses*, 16 (1936), 210–45.

Dahl, N. A. *Das Volk Gottes*, Oslo, 1941.

'Paul and the Church in Corinth in I Cor. 1: 10 – 4: 21,' *Christian History and Interpretation: Studies presented to John Knox*, ed. W. R. Farmer *et al.*, Cambridge, 1967, pp. 313–35.

'Paulus som Föresprakere,' *Svensk Theologisk Kvartalskrift*, 18 (1942), 173–82.

'Zur Auslegung von Gal. 6: 16,' *Jud.* 6 (1950), 161–70.

Dalman, G. H. *Die Worte Jesu*, Leipzig, 1898.

Daube, D. 'Participle and Imperative in I Peter,' in Selwyn, E. G., *The First Epistle of Peter*, London, 1958, pp. 467–88.

Davies, W. D. *Paul and Rabbinic Judaism*, London, 1948.

Dean, J. T. *Saint Paul and Corinth*, London, 1947.

Deichgräber, R. *Gotteshymnus und Christushymnus in der frühen Christenheit*, Göttingen, 1967.

Deissmann, A. *Light from the Ancient East; the New Testament illustrated by recently discovered texts of the Graeco-Roman world* (E.Tr.), London, 1910.

Paul (E.Tr.), London, 1911.

Delling, G. *Worship in the New Testament* (E.Tr.), Philadelphia, 1962.

'Das Abendmahlsgeschehen nach Paulus,' *Kerygma und Dogma*, 10 (1964), 61–77.

'αἴσθησις,' *TWNT*, I, 186–8.

'παραλαμβάνω,' *TWNT*, IV, 11–15.

'πληρόω,' *TWNT*, VI, 289–96.

'στοιχέω,' *TWNT*, VII, 666–9.

Denis, A.-M. 'L'Apôtre Paul, Prophète "Messianique" des Gentils,' *EphTL*, 33 (1957), 245–318.

Dhorme, P. 'L'emploi metaphorique des noms de parties du corps en Hébreu et en Akkadien, VI. – Les parties internes,' *Revue Biblique*, 31 (1922), 489–517.

Dibelius, M. *A Fresh Approach to the New Testament and Early Christian Literature* (E.Tr.), New York, 1936.

An Die Thessalonicher I II. An Die Philipper (*HzNT*), Tübingen, 1937.

An Philemon (*HzNT*), Tübingen, 1911.

Dieterich, A. *Eine Mithrasliturgie*, Berlin, 1923.

Dinkler, E. 'Zum Problem der Ethik bei Paulus. Rechtsnahme und Rechtsverzicht (I Kor. 6: 1–11),' *ZThK*, 49 (1952), 167–200.

Dobschütz, E. von. *Christian Life in the Primitive Church* (E.Tr.), London, 1904.

Die Thessalonicher-Briefe (Meyer's Kommentar), 7th edn, Göttingen, 1909.

'Zum Wortschatz und Stil des Römerbriefs,' *ZNW*, 33 (1934), 51–66.

Dodd, C. H. *The Epistle of Paul to the Romans* (MNTC), New York, 1932.

'The Mind of Paul: I,' *New Testament Studies*, Manchester, 1953.

Donfried, K. P. 'A Short Note on Romans 16,' *JBL*, 89 (1970), 441–9.

Doskocil, W. *Der Bann in der Urkirche; eine rechtsgeschichtliche Untersuchung*, Münchener theologische Studien, 3, 11 (Munich, 1958).

Doty, W. G. 'The Classification of Epistolary Literature,' *Catholic Biblical Quarterly*, 31 (1969), 183–99.

Dugmore, C. W. *The Influence of the Synagogue upon the Divine Office*, Oxford, 1944.

Eadie, J. *A Commentary on the Greek Text of the Epistles to the Thessalonians*. London, 1877.

Eichrodt, W. *Theology of the Old Testament* (E.Tr.), 2 vols, Philadelphia, 1961–7.

Elbogen, I. 'Bemerkungen zur alten jüdischen Liturgie,' *Studies in Jewish Literature issued in Honour of Professor Kaufmann Köhler*, Berlin, 1913, pp. 74–81.

Der jüdische Gottesdienst in seiner geschichtlichen Entwicklung, 3rd edn, Frankfurt am Main, 1931.

Die messianische Idee in den alten jüdischen Gebeten, Berlin, 1912.

Elderen, B. Van. 'The Verb in the Epistolary Invocation,' *Calvin Theological Journal*, 2 (1967), 46–8.

Ellicott, C. J. *A Critical and Grammatical Commentary on St. Paul's Epistles to the Thessalonians*, Andover, 1864.

Enslin, M. S. *The Ethics of Paul*, Nashville, 1957.

Exler, F. X. J. 'The Form of the Ancient Greek Letter; a Study in Greek Epistolography,' Diss., Catholic University of America, 1923.

Fahy, T. 'St. Paul's Romans were Jewish Converts,' *The Irish Catholic Quarterly*, 26 (1959), 182–91.

Feine, P., Behm, J., and Kümmel, W. G. *Introduction to the New Testament* (E.Tr.), 14th rev. edn, Nashville, 1965.

Festugière, A.-J. ''Ὑπομονή dans la tradition greque,' *Recherches de Science Religieuse*, 21 (1931), 477–86.

Filson, F. V. *The Second Epistle to the Corinthians, IB*, vol. x.

'*Yesterday.*' *A Study of Hebrews in the Light of Chapter 13* (*SBT*, Second Series, 4), London, 1967.

'The Significance of the Early House Churches,' *JBL*, 58 (1939), 105–12.

Findlay, G. C. *The Epistles to the Thessalonians* (Cambridge Bible for Schools and Colleges), Cambridge, 1894.

Fisher, F. L. *Prayer in the New Testament*, Philadelphia, 1964.

Foerster, W. 'εἰρήνη im N.T.,' *TWNT*, ii, 409–16.

'κτίζω,' *TWNT*, iii, 1032–4.

'σατανᾶς,' *TWNT*, vii, 161f.

Frame, J. E. *The Epistles of St. Paul to the Thessalonians* (ICC), Edinburgh, 1912.

Fridrichsen, A. J. *The Apostle and his Message* (E.Tr.), Uppsala, 1947.

Friedrich, G. 'Die Gegner des Paulus im 2. Korintherbrief,' in *Abraham unser Vater, Festschrift für Otto Michel*, ed. O. Betz, M. Hengel, and P. Schmidt, Leiden, 1963.

'Lohmeyers These über "Das paulinische Briefpräscript" kritisch beleuchtet,' *ZNW*, 46 (1955), 272–4.

'Propheten und Prophezien im Neuen Testament,' *TWNT*, vi, 849–58.

Funk, R. W. *Language, Hermeneutics, and Word of God*, New York, 1966.

'The apostolic "*Parousia*": Form and Significance,' in *Christian History and Interpretation: Studies presented to John Knox*, ed. W. R. Farmer *et al.*, Cambridge, 1967, pp. 249–68.

'Saying and Seeing: Phenomenology of Language and the New Testament,' *JBR*, 34 (1966), espec. 209–13.

Furnish, V. P. *Theology and Ethics in Paul*, Nashville, 1968.

Gamble, H. Y. 'The Textual History of the Letter to the Romans,' Diss., Yale University, 1970.

Gaster, T. H. 'Satan,' *IDB*, iv, 224–8.

Gaugler, E. *Der Römerbrief*, 2 vols (Zürcher Bibelkommentare), Zurich, 1945–50.

Georgi, D. *Die Gegner des Paulus im 2. Korintherbrief*, Neukirchen-Vluyn, 1964.

Gevirtz, S. 'Curse,' *IDB*, i, 749f.

Goltz, E. F. von der. *Das Gebet in der Ältesten Christenheit: Eine Geschichtliche Untersuchung*, Leipzig, 1901.

Goodenough, E. R. 'Paul and Onesimus,' *HTR*, 22 (1929), 181–3.

Greeven, H. *Gebet und Eschatologie im Neuen Testament* (Neutestamentliche Forschungen), Gütersloh, 1931.

'δέομαι, δέησις,' *TWNT*, ΙΙ, 39–41.

'προσεύχομαι, προσευχή,' *TWNT*, ΙΙ, 806–8.

Grundmann, W. 'ἀνέγκλητος,' *TWNT*, Ι, 358f.

'δόκιμος,' *TWNT*, ΙΙ, 258–64.

'δύναμαι,' *TWNT*, ΙΙ, 311–14.

Gunkel, H. *Die Psalmen, übersetzst und erklärt* (Göttinger Handkommentar zum Alten Testament), 4th edn, Göttingen, 1926.

Einleitung in die Psalmen: die Gattungen der religiösen Lyrik Israels, Zu Ende geführt von J. Begrich (Göttinger Handkommentar zum Alten Testament), Göttingen, 1933.

Guy, H. *New Testament Prophecy, Its Origin and Significance*, London, 1947.

Gyllenberg, R., 'De inledende hälsningsformlerna i de paulininska breven,' *Svensk Exegetisch Arsbok*, 16 (1951–2), 21–31.

Haenchen, E. *Die Apostelgeschichte, neu übersetzst und erklärt* (Meyer's Kommentar), 13th rev. edn, Göttingen, 1961.

Hamman, A. *La Prière I. Le Nouveau Testament*, Tournai, 1959.

Harder, G. *Paulus und das Gebet* (Neutestamentliche Forschungen), Gütersloh, 1936.

Harnack, A. 'Das Problem des Zweiten Thessalonicherbriefs,' *Sitzungsberichte der Königlich Preussischen Akademie der Wissenschaften*, 31 (1910), 560–78.

Harner, P. B. 'Exodus, Sinai, and Hittite Prologues,' *JBL*, 85 (1966), 233–6.

Harrelson, W. J. 'Blessings and Cursings,' *IDB*, Ι, 446–8.

Harrison, P. N. 'Onesimus and Philemon,' *ATR*, 32 (1950), 268–94.

Hauck, F. 'καρπός,' *TWNT*, ΙΙΙ, 617f.

'κοινωνός,' *TWNT*, ΙΙΙ, 798–810.

'κόπος,' *TWNT*, ΙΙΙ, 827–9.

'πλοῦτος,' *TWNT*, VI, 326–8.

Hausrath, A. *Der Vierkapitelbrief des Paulus an die Korinther*, Heidelberg, 1870.

Heinemann, J. *Prayer in the Period of the Tanna'im and the Amora'im: Its Nature and its Patterns*, Jerusalem, 1964.

Heinzelmann, G. *Der Brief an die Philipper*, Göttingen, 1949.

Héring, J. *The First Epistle of St. Paul to the Corinthians* (E.Tr.), London, 1964.

La Seconde Épitre de Saint Paul aux Corinthiens, Neuchâtel, 1958.

Hesse, F. *Die Fürbitte im Alten Testament*, Inaugural-Dissertation..., Friedrich-Alexander-Universität, Erlangen, 1949.

Hillers, D. R. *Treaty-Curses and the Old Testament Prophets*, Rome, 1964.

Hofmann, J. Ch. K. von. *Die Heilige Schrift Neuen Testaments zusammenhängend untersucht....* vol. 1: *Die Briefe Pauli an die Thessalonicher*. Nördlingen, 1862.

Hofmann, K. M. *Philema Hagion*, Gütersloh, 1938.

Hunter, A. M. *Paul and His Predecessors*, Philadelphia, 1961.

Hurd, J. C., Jr, *The Origin of I Corinthians*, New York, 1965.

Jastrow, M. *Die Religion Babyloniens und Assyriens*, vol. II, Giessen, 1912.

Jeremias, J. *The Eucharistic Words of Jesus* (E.Tr.), London, 1966.
The Parables of Jesus (E.Tr.), New York, 1962.
The Prayers of Jesus (E.Tr.) (*SBT*, Second Series, 6), London, 1967.

Jewett, R. 'The Agitators and the Galatian Congregation,' *NTS*, 17 (1970–1), 198–212.
'The Epistolary Thanksgiving and the Integrity of Philippians,' *Nov. Test.*, 12 (1970), 40–53.
'The Form and Function of the Homiletic Benediction,' *ATR*, 51 (1969), 18–34.

Johansson, N. *Parakletoi; Vorstellungen von Fürsprechern für die Menschen vor Gott in der alttestamentlichen Religion, im Spätjudentum und Urchristentum*, Lund, 1940.

Johnston, G. *The Spirit-Paraclete in the Gospel of John* (SNTSM, 12), Cambridge, 1970.

Joüon, P. 'Reconnaissance et action de grace dans le Nouveau Testament,' *RSR*, 29 (1939), 112–14.

Jowett, B. *The Epistles of St. Paul to the Thessalonians, Galatians, Romans*, vol. 1, 2nd edn, London, 1859.

Juncker, A. *Das Gebet bei Paulus*, Berlin, 1905.

Kadushin, M. *Worship and Ethics, A Study in Rabbinic Judaism*, Northwestern University Press, 1963.

Käsemann, E. *Die Legitimität des Apostels; Eine Untersuchung zu II Korinther 10–13*, Darmstadt, 1956.
'Sentences of Holy Law in the New Testament,' *New Testament Questions of Today* (E.Tr.), London, 1969.

Kennedy, J. H. *The Second and Third Epistles of St. Paul to the Corinthians*, London, 1900.

Kerkhoff, R. *Das Unablässige Gebet. Beiträge zur Lehre von immerwährende Beten im Neuen Testament*, München, 1954.

Kittel, G. 'δόξα,' *TWNT*, II, 250–5.

Klein, G. *Die Zwölf Apostel*, Göttingen, 1961.

Klijn, A. F. J. 'Paul's opponents in Philippians iii,' *Nov. Test.* 7 (1965), 278–84.

Knox, J. *The Epistle to the Romans*, IB, vol. IX.
The Epistle to Philemon, IB, vol. XI.

Philemon Among the Letters of Paul, rev. 3rd edn, Nashville, 1959.

'Romans 15: 14–33 and Paul's conception of His Apostolic Mission,' *JBL*, 83 (1964), 1–11.

Koester, H. 'The Purpose of the Polemic of a Pauline Fragment (Philippians III),' *NTS*, 8 (1961–2), 317–32.

Koskenniemi, H. 'Studien zur Idee und Phraseologie des griechischen Briefes bis 400 n. Chr.,' *Annales Academiae Scientiarum Fennicae*, B, 102, Helsinki, 1956.

Kramer, W. *Christ, Lord, Son of God* (E.Tr.) (*SBT*, 50), London, 1966.

Kredel, E. M. 'Der Apostelbegriff in der neueren Exegese,' *Zeitschrift für Katholische Theologie*, 78 (1956), 169–93, 257–305.

Krenkel, M. *Beiträge zur Aufhellung der Geschichte und der Briefe des Apostels Paulus*, Brunswick, 1890.

Kuhn, K. G. 'Der Epheserbrief im Lichte der Qumrantexte,' *NTS*, 7 (1960–1), 334–45.

'μαραναθά,' *TWNT*, IV, 270–5.

Kümmel, W. G. 'Das Literarische und Geschichtliche Problem des Ersten Thessalonicherbriefes,' *Neotestamentica et Patristica, Freundesgabe O. Cullmann* (*Nov. Test.* Suppl. 6), 1962, 213–27.

Kuss, O. *Der Römerbrief*, vol. I, Regensburg, 1957.

Lagrange, M.-J. *Saint Paul, Épître aux Galates*, Paris, 1950.

Saint Paul, Épître aux Romains, Paris, 1950.

Lake, K. *The Earlier Epistles of St. Paul; their Motive and Origin*, 2nd edn, London, 1914.

Leenhardt, F.-J. *The Epistle to the Romans* (E.Tr.), 3rd edn, London, 1964.

Liddell, H. G., and Scott, R. *A Greek–English Lexicon*, rev. edn, Oxford, 1951.

Lietzmann, H. *An die Korinther I – II* (*HzNT*, 9), 4th edn, Tübingen, 1949.

An die Römer (*HzNT*, 8), 3rd edn, Tübingen, 1928.

Mass and Lord's Supper (E.Tr.), Leiden, 1953–.

Lightfoot, J. B. *St. Paul's Epistles to the Colossians and to Philemon*, 6th edn, London, 1882.

St. Paul's Epistle to the Galatians, 7th edn, London, 1881.

Lindblom, J. *Prophecy in Ancient Israel*, Philadelphia, 1962.

Lohmeyer, E. *Die Briefe an die Philipper, an die Kolosser und an Philemon* (Meyer's Kommentar), 10th edn, Göttingen, 1954.

Die Offenbarung des Johannes (*HzNT*), enlarged 2nd edn, Tübingen, 1953.

'*Our Father*' (E.Tr.), New York, 1965.

'Probleme paulinischer Theologie. I. Briefliche Grussüberschriften,' *ZNW*, 26 (1927), 158–73.

Lünemann, G. *Kritisch exegetisches Handbuch über die Briefe an die Thessalonicher...*, 3rd edn, Göttingen, 1867.

Lütgert, W. *Freiheitspredigt und Schwarmgeister in Korinth*, Gütersloh, 1908.

Lütgert, W. *Der Römerbrief als historisches Problem*, Gütersloh, 1913.

McDonald, J. I. H. 'Was Romans XVI a Separate Letter?,' *NTS*, 16 (1969–70), 369–72.

Mackay, B. S. 'Further Thoughts on Philippians,' *NTS*, 7 (1960–1), 161–70.

McNeile, A. H. *An Introduction to the Study of the New Testament*, 2nd rev. edn, Oxford, 1953.

Manson, T. W. 'St. Paul in Ephesus: (3) the Corinthian Correspondence,' *BJRL*, 26 (1941–2), 101ff.

'St Paul's Letter to the Romans – and Others,' *BJRL*, 31 (1948), 3–19.

Marxsen, W. *Introduction to the New Testament* (E.Tr.), Philadelphia, 1968.

Masson, C. *Les Deux Épitres De Saint Paul Aux Thessaloniciens* (Commentaire Du Nouveau Testament, XIa), Neuchâtel, 1957.

'Sur I Thessaloniciens, v, 23. Note d'anthropologie paulinienne,' *Revue de Theologie et de Philosophie*, 135 (1945), 97–102.

Meyer, W. *Der erste Brief an die Korinther*, 1, Zurich, 1947.

Meynenveld, F. H. van. *Het Hart (Leb. Lebab) in het oude Testament*, Leiden, 1950.

Michael, J. H. *The Epistle of Paul to the Philippians* (MNTC), New York, 1927.

Michaelis, W. 'Teilungshypothesen bei Paulusbriefen,' *TZ*, 14 (1958), 321–6.

Michel, O. *Der Brief an die Römer* (Meyer's Kommentar), Göttingen, 1955.

Milligan, G. *St. Paul's Epistle to the Thessalonians; The Greek text with Introduction and Notes*, London, 1908.

Minear, P. S. *Christian Hope and the Second Coming*, Philadelphia, 1954.

The Obedience of Faith: The Purposes of Paul in the Epistle to the Romans (*SBT*, Second Series, 19), London, 1971.

'Paul's Missionary Dynamic,' *Andover-Newton Theological School Bulletin*, 36 (1944), 1–11.

Moffatt, J. *The First Epistle of Paul to the Corinthians* (MNTC), London, 1938.

Introduction to the Literature of the New Testament, New York, 1914.

Moltmann, J. *Theology of Hope* (E.Tr.), New York, 1967.

Morris, L. *The First and Second Epistles to the Thessalonians* (New International Commentary on the N.T.), Grand Rapids, 1959.

Moule, C. F. D. *The Birth of the New Testament* (HNTC), New York, 1962.

The Epistle of Paul the Apostle to Colossians and Philemon (CGTC), Cambridge, 1962.

An Idiom Book of New Testament Greek, 2nd edn, Cambridge, 1960.

Worship in the New Testament (*Ecumenical Studies in Worship*, 9), Richmond, 1961.

'A Reconsideration of the Context of *Maranatha*,' *NTS*, 6 (1959–60), 307–10.

Moulton, J. H. *A Grammar of New Testament Greek*, vol. I, Edinburgh, 1906.

Müller-Bardoff, J. 'Zur Frage der literarischen Einheit des Philipperbriefes,' *Wissenschaftl. Zeitschrift*, Jena, 7 (1957–8), 591ff.

Mullins, T. Y. 'Greeting as a New Testament Form,' *JBL*, 87 (1968), 418–26.

'Petition as a Literary Form,' *Nov. Test.* 5 (1964), 46–54.

Munck, J. *Christus und Israel*, Copenhagen, 1956.

Paul and the Salvation of Mankind (E.Tr.), London, 1959.

'I Thess. 1.9–10 and the Missionary Preaching of Paul,' *NTS*, 9 (1962–3), 95–110.

Neil, W. *The Epistle of Paul to the Thessalonians* (MNTC), New York, 1950.

Nickle, K. F. *The Collection, A Study in Pauline Strategy* (*SBT*, 48), London, 1966.

Noack, B. *Satanás und Soterı́a*, Copenhagen, 1948.

Nygren, A. *Agape and Eros* (E.Tr.), London, 1953.

Oepke, A. *Der Brief des Paulus an die Galater*, 3rd edn, Berlin, 1964.

Oesterley, W. O. E. *The Jewish Background of the Christian Liturgy*, Oxford, 1925.

Oesterley, W. O. E., and Box, G. H. *The Religion and Worship of the Synagogue; An Introduction to the Study of Judaism from the New Testament Period*, London, 1907.

Oostendorp, D. W. *Another Jesus: A Gospel of Jewish–Christian Superiority in II Corinthians*, Kampen, 1967.

Orphal, E. *Das Paulusgebet; psychologisch-exegetische untersuchung des Paulus-gebetslebens auf grund seiner selbstzeugnisse*, Gotha, 1933.

Perrin, N. *The Kingdom of God in the Teaching of Jesus*, Philadelphia, 1963.

Rediscovering the Teaching of Jesus, New York, 1967.

Pfitzner, V. C. *Paul and the Agon Motif*, Leiden, 1967.

Pherigo, L. P. 'Paul and the Corinthian Church,' *JBL*, 68 (1949), 341–50.

Plummer, A. *The Second Epistle of St. Paul to the Corinthians* (ICC), Edinburgh, 1915.

Pollard, T. E. 'The Integrity of Philippians,' *NTS*, 13 (1966–7), 57–66.

Preisendanz, K. (ed.). *Papyri Graecae magicae*, 1, Leipzig, 1928.

Preiss, T. 'Life in Christ and Social Ethics in the Epistle to Philemon,' in *Life in Christ* (E.Tr.) (*SBT*, 13), London, 1954, 32–42.

Price, J. L. 'Aspects of Paul's Theology and their Bearing on Literary Problems of Second Corinthians,' in *Studies in the History and Text of the New Testament, Studies and Documents*, 29, Salt Lake City, 1967, 95–106.

Proksch, O. 'ἁγιωσύνη,' *TWNT*, 1, 116.

Prumm, K. *Diakonia Pneumatos. Der zweite Korintherbrief als Zugang zur apostolischen Botschaft*, 1, Rome, 1967.

Pujol, A. 'De salutatione Apostolorum "Gratia vobis et pax,"' *Verbum Domini*, 12 (1932), 38–42, 76–82.

Quell, G., and Stauffer, E. 'ἀγαπάω,' *TWNT*, 1, 20–55.

Rahtjen, B. D. 'The Three Letters of Paul to the Philippians,' *NTS*, 6 (1959–60), 167–73.

Ramsey, A. M. *The Gospel and the Catholic Church*, 2nd edn, London, 1956.

Rengstorf, K. H. 'Die klassische Ausprägung des Apostolats in der Person des Paulus,' *TWNT*, 1, 438–44.

'Paulus und die römische Christenheit,' *Studia Evangelica*, 2 (1964), 447–64.

Richardson, P. *Israel in the Apostolic Church* (SNTSM, 10), Cambridge, 1969.

Richardson, W. J. 'Principle and Context in the Ethics of the Epistle to Philemon,' *Interpretation*, 22 (1968), 301–16.

Rigaux, B. *Saint Paul et ses lettres, Studia Neotestamentica*; Subsidia II, 1962.

Saint Paul. Les Épitres aux Thessaloniciens. (Etudes Bibliques), Paris, 1956.

Robertson, A., and Plummer, A. *First Epistle of St. Paul to the Corinthians* (ICC), Edinburgh, 1911.

Robertson, A. T. *A Grammar of the Greek New Testament in the light of Historical Research*, 5th edn, New York, 1931.

Robinson, H. W. *The Christian Doctrine of Man*, Edinburgh, 1952.

Robinson, J. Armitage. *St. Paul's Epistle to the Ephesians*, 2nd edn, London, 1914.

Robinson, J. A. T. *Jesus and His Coming*, London, 1957.

'Traces of a Liturgical Sequence in I Cor. xvi. 20–24,' *JTS*, New Series, 4 (1953), 38–41.

Robinson, J. M. 'Basic Shifts in German Theology,' *Interpretation*, 16 (1962), 76–97.

'Die Hodajot-Formel in Gebet und Hymnus des Frühchristentums,' *Apophoreta. Festschrift für Ernst Haenschen*, ed. W. Eltester, Berlin, 1964, pp. 194–235.

'The Historicality of Biblical Language,' in *The Old Testament and Christian Faith: A Theological Discussion*, ed. B. W. Anderson, New York, 1963, pp. 124–58.

Roetzel, C. 'The Judgment Form in Paul's Letters,' *JBL*, 88 (1969), 305–12.

'I Thess. 5: 12–28: A Case Study,' Society of Biblical Literature, *Book of Seminar Papers*, II, ed. L. C. McGaughy, 1972, pp. 367–83.

Roller, O. *Das Formular der paulinischen Briefe; ein beitrag zur lehre vom antiken briefe*, Stuttgart, 1933.

Roosen, A. 'Le genre littéraire de l'Epître aux Romains,' *Studia Evangelica*, 2 (1964), 465–71.

Sanday, W., and Headlam, A. C. *The Epistle to the Romans* (ICC), Edinburgh, 1896.

Sanders, J. T. 'Paul's "Autobiographical" Statements in Galatians 1 – 2,' *JBL*, 85 (1966), 335–43.

'The Transition from Opening Epistolary Thanksgiving to Body in the Letters of the Pauline Corpus,' *JBL*, 81 (1962), 348–62.

Sass, G. *Apostelamt und Kirche; eine theologisch-exegetische untersuchung des paulinischen apostelbegriffs*, München, 1939.

Schelkle, K. H. *Jüngerschaft und Apostelamt: Eine historische Untersuchung*, Freiburg, 1957.

Schlatter, A. *Paulus, der Bote Jesu*, Stuttgart, 1934.

Schlier, H. *Der Brief an die Galater* (Meyer's Kommentar), 12th edn, Göttingen, 1962.

'ἀμήν,' *TWNT*, I, 339–42.

'θλίβω,' *TWNT*, III, 139–48.

Schmidt, K. L. 'ἐπικαλέω,' *TWNT*, III, 498–501.

Schmiedel, P. W. *Die Briefe an die Thessalonicher* (*HzNT*, II, 1), Freiburg, 1891.

Schmithals, W. *Die Gnosis in Korinth: Eine Untersuchung zu den Korintherbriefen*, 2nd edn, Göttingen, 1965.

The Office of Apostle in the Early Church (E.Tr.), Nashville, 1969.

'Die Irrlehrer des Philipperbriefes,' *ZThK*, 54 (1957), 297–341.

'Die Thessalonicherbriefe als Briefkompositionen,' *Zeit und Geschichte. Dankesgabe an Rudolf Bultmann zum 80. Geburtstag*, ed. E. Dinkler, Tübingen, 1964, pp. 294–315.

'Sur Abfassung und ältesten Sammlung des paulinischen Haupt-briefe,' *ZNW*, 51 (1960), 225–45.

Schmitz, O. *Die Opferanschauung des späteren Judentums; und die Opferaussagen des Neuen Testaments*, Tübingen, 1910.
'παρακαλέω,' *TWNT*, v, 790–8.

Schoeps, H. J. *Paul* (E.Tr.), Philadelphia, 1961.

Schrenk, G. 'Was bedeutet "Israel Gottes"?' *Jud.*, 5 (1949), 81–94.
'Der Segenswunsch nach der Kampfepistel,' *Jud.*, 6 (1950), 170–90.

Schubert, P. *Form and Function of the Pauline Thanksgivings*, Berlin, 1939.

Schweizer, E. 'πνεῦμα,' *TWNT*, vi, 433–5.

Scott, E. F. *The Epistles of Paul to the Colossians, to Philemon, and to the Ephesians* (MNTC), New York, 1930.

Scott, W. (ed.). *Hermetica*, i, Oxford, 1924.

Seeberg, R. *Aus Religion und Geschichte*, 1906.

Seesemann, H. *Der Begriff* Κοινωνία *im Neuen Testament*, Giessen, 1933.

Spicq, C. ''Υπομονή, Patientia,' *RSPT*, 19 (1930), 95–105.

Stacey, W. D. *The Pauline View of Man*, London, 1956.

Stählin, G. 'ἀπρόσκοπον εἶναι als eschatologisches Ziel (Phil. 1 : 10),' *TWNT*, vi, 757.

Stamm, R. T. *The Epistle to the Galatians*, IB, vol. x.

Stauffer, E. *New Testament Theology* (E.Tr.), New York, 1955.
'ἀγών,' *TWNT*, i, 134–40.

Stempvoort, P. A. van. 'Eine Stilistische Lösing einer Alten Schwie-rigkeit in I. Thess. v.23,' *NTS*, 7 (1960–1), 262–5.

Stephenson, A. M. G. 'A Defence of the Integrity of 2 Corinthians,' in *The Authorship and Integrity of the New Testament* (S.P.C.K. Theological Collections, 4), London, 1965, pp. 82–97.

Strachan, R. H. *The Second Epistle of Paul to the Corinthians* (MNTC), New York, 1935.

Strack, H. L., and Billerbeck, P. *Kommentar zum Neuen Testament aus Talmud und Midrash*, 4 vols, München, 1922–8.

Strathmann, H. 'λατρεύω,' *TWNT*, iv, 58–66.
'λειτουργός,' *TWNT*, iv, 236–8.

Sukenik, E. L. *Ancient Synagogues in Palestine and Greece*, London, 1934.

Talbert, C. H. 'Tradition and Redaction in Romans XII. 9–21,' *NTS*, 16 (1969–70), 81–93.

Towner, W. S. '"Blessed Be YHWH" and "Blessed Art Thou, YHWH": The Modulation of a Biblical Formula,' *Catholic Biblical Quarterly*, 30 (1968), 386f.

Trocmé, E. 'L'Épître aux Romains et la Méthode Missionaire de l'Apôtre Paul,' *NTS*, 7 (1960-1), 148-53.

Unnik, W. C. van. 'Dominus Vobiscum,' *New Testament Essays; in mem. T. W. Manson*, ed. A. J. B. Higgins, Manchester, 1959, pp. 270-305.

'Reisepläne und Amensagen...,' in *Studia Paulina* (in hon. J. de Zwaan), eds. J. N. Sevenster, and W. C. van Unnik, Haarlem, 1953, pp. 215-34.

Vincent, M. R. *The Epistles to the Philippians and to Philemon* (ICC), Edinburgh, 1902.

Ward, R. B. 'The Opponents of Paul,' *Restoration Quarterly*, 10 (1967), 185-95.

Warneck, D. J. *Paulus im Lichte der heutigen Heidenmission*, Berlin, 1913.

Webber, R. 'The Concept of Rejoicing in the Letters of Paul,' Diss., Yale University, 1970.

Weiss, B. *Die Paulinische Briefe, und der Hebräerbrief...*, 2nd edn, Leipzig, 1903.

Weiss, J. *The History of Primitive Christianity* (E.Tr.), New York, 1959.

Weiss, K. 'Paulus – Priester der christl. Kultgemeinde,' *TLZ*, 79 (1954), 355-63.

Welles, C. B. *Royal Correspondence in the Hellenistic Period*, New Haven, 1934.

Wendland, H.-D. *Die Briefe an die Korinther* (NTD, 7), 7th edn, Göttingen, 1954.

Wendland, P. *Die Urchristlichen Literaturformen* (*HzNT*), Tübingen, 1912.

White, J. L. 'Introductory Formulae in the Body of the Pauline Letter,' *JBL*, 90 (1971), 91-7.

Whiteley, D. E. H. *The Theology of St. Paul*, Philadelphia, 1964.

Wickert, U. 'Der Philemonbrief – Privatbrief oder apostolisches Schreiben?' *ZNW*, 52 (1961), 230-8.

Wilckens, U. *Weisheit und Torheit*, Tübingen, 1959.

Windisch, H. *Der zweite Korintherbrief*, 9th edn, Göttingen, 1924.

Paulus und Christus: Ein biblisch-religionsgeschichtlicher Vergleich, Leipzig, 1934.

'βάρβαρος,' *TWNT*, 1, 549f.

Witkowski, S. (ed.). *Epistolae privatae graecae*, Leipzig, 1906.

Wohlenberg, J. *Der erste und zweite Thessalonicherbrief* (Zahn's Kommentar), Leipzig, 1903.

Ziemann, F. *De epistolarum graecorum formulis solemnibus questiones selectae*, Halle, 1911.

Zunz, L. *Die gottesdienstlichen Vorträge der Juden. Historisch entwickelt*, 2nd edn, Frankfurt am Main, 1892.

INDEX OF PASSAGES CITED

A. THE OLD TESTAMENT

B. THE NEW TESTAMENT

333

C. DEAD SEA SCROLLS

D. APOCRYPHA AND PSEUDEPIGRAPHA
OF THE OLD TESTAMENT

E. RABBINICAL LITERATURE

F. WRITINGS OF THE EARLY CHURCH

G. HELLENISTIC AUTHORS

H. GREEK PAPYRI

INDEX OF AUTHORS

338

INDEX OF SUBJECTS